Hellenic Studies 67

# PLATO'S FOUR MUSES

# Recent Titles in the Hellenic Studies Series

*Divine Yet Human Epics*
*Reflections of Poetic Rulers from Ancient Greece and India*

*The Web of Athenaeus*

*Eusebius of Caesarea*
*Tradition and Innovations*

*The Theology of Arithmetic*
*Number Symbolism in Platonism and Early Christianity*

*Homeric Durability*
*Telling Time in the Iliad*

*Paideia and Cult*
*Christian Initiation in Theodore of Mopsuestia*

*Imperial Geographies in Byzantine and Ottoman Space*

*Loving Humanity, Learning, and Being Honored*
*The Foundations of Leadership in Xenophon's Education of Cyrus*

*The Theory and Practice of Life*
*Isocrates and the Philosophers*

*From Listeners to Viewers*
*Space in the Iliad*

*Aspects of History and Epic in Ancient Iran*
*From Gaumāta to Wahnām*

*Homer's Versicolored Fabric*
*The Evocative Power of Ancient Greek Epic Word-Making*

*Christianity and Hellenism in the Fifth-Century Greek East*
*Theodoret's Apologetics against the Greeks in Context*

*The Master of Signs*
*Signs and the Interpretation of Signs in Herodotus' Histories*

*Eve of the Festival*
*Making Myth in Odyssey 19*

*Kleos in a Minor Key*
*The Homeric Education of a Little Prince*

*Plato's Counterfeit Sophists*

*http://chs.harvard.edu/chs/publications*

# PLATO'S FOUR MUSES

## THE *PHAEDRUS* AND THE POETICS OF PHILOSOPHY

### *ANDREA CAPRA*

CENTER FOR HELLENIC STUDIES
Trustees for Harvard University
Washington, DC
Distributed by Harvard University Press
Cambridge, Massachusetts, and London, England
2014

*Plato's Four Muses*
by Andrea Capra
Copyright © 2014 Center for Hellenic Studies, Trustees for Harvard University
All Rights Reserved.
Published by Center for Hellenic Studies, Trustees for Harvard University, Washington, DC
Distributed by Harvard University Press, Cambridge, Massachusetts, and London, England
Production: Ivy Livingston
Cover design: Joni Godlove
Printed by Edwards Brothers, Inc., Ann Arbor, MI and Lillington, NC

ISBN: 9780674417229
Library of Congress Control Number: 2014953138

# Contents

## Contents

# Abbreviations

IN THE SPIRIT OF THE SERIES, I have kept abbreviations to a minimum, so as to make the book as reader-friendly as possible. Some of them, however, are very frequent or very convenient, and although most readers are likely to recognize them at first glance, others may find it useful to have them explained. Accordingly, here is a list of the very few abbreviations that are found in the present book:

AB    Austin, C. and G. Bastianini, eds., *Posidippi Pellaei quae supersunt Omnia*. Milano, 2002.

CIG    *Corpus Inscriptionum Graecarum*.

CLE    *Carmina Latina Epigraphica*.

FGrH    *Die Fragmente der Griechischen Historiker*, ed. F. Jacoby. Berlin 1923–1930. Leiden, 1940–1998.

GP    Gow, A. S. and D. L., Page, eds., *The Greek Anthology: Hellenic Epigrams*. 2 vols. Cambridge, 1965.

IG    *Inscriptiones Graecae*.

P.Herc.    *Herculaneum Papyri*.

PMG    *Poetae Melici Graeci*, ed. D. L. Page. Oxford, 1962.

PMGF    *Poetarum Melicorum Graecorum Fragmenta,* Vol. I: *Alcman, Stesichorus, Ibycus*, ed. M. Davies. Oxford, 1991.

P.Oxy.    *Oxyrinchus Papyri*.

SEG    *Supplementum Epigraphicum Graecum*.

SSR    *Socratis et Socraticorum Reliquiae*, ed. G. Giannantoni. 4 vols. Naples, 1991.

W    West, M. L., ed., *Iambi et Elegi Graeci ante Alexandrum cantati*. 2 vols. Oxford, 1971–1972.

W[2]    West, M. L., ed., *Iambi et Elegi Graeci ante Alexandrum cantati*. 2 vols. 2nd ed. Oxford, 1989.

# Preface

*The Giants drag down everything from heaven and the invisible to earth, grasping rocks and trees with their hands ... and if anyone says that anything else, which has no body, exists, they despise him utterly, and will not listen to any other theory ... Therefore the Gods who contend against them strike cautiously from above, and they use noetic weapons from an invisible world, maintaining forcibly that real existence consists of certain ideas which are only conceived by the mind and have no body.*

Sophist 246a–b, trans. Goold (modified)

## Orientation

LIKE SO MANY OTHERS, I sometimes indulge in idle fantasies about my published work. I envisage a mythological creature called the "General Reader," who will sip it like champagne, or devour it in one sitting as if it were a tasty novel. At other times, I imagine another prodigious figure, the "Platophagus," an insatiable beast that chases me back and forth throughout the book, chews on my lengthy footnotes, repeatedly bites into all sorts of Platonic minutiae, and still clamors for more ... This is pathetic, I know. Nevertheless, I have tried my best to write not just a painstaking book but an enjoyable one too. In so doing, I have aimed at catering for different kinds of readers, including even such fantastic animals as the GR and the Platophagus, or at least their less implausible fellow creatures.

Even the latter, however, are likely to be rather thin on the ground, because—let's face it—we simply do not live in that kind of world. The tide of scholarly work is always on the rise, making reading time increasingly frantic and desultory. Some readers might want to find out something about a single dialogue, a passage, or even a textual reading. Others might just be looking for references, and so on. In short, I cannot rule out any possibility. What I *can* do, however, is provide directions so as to help my readers save precious time. Before they decide how or, indeed, whether to read the book at all, I ask them to read at least these pages.

This might sound like the prologue to some grand hermeneutical declaration, which would not be altogether inappropriate: debate is always raging in Platonic scholarship, and it is surely important to be clear about one's assumptions. Theory *does* matter. However, I hope that my assumptions, which have not significantly changed over time, will be sufficiently apparent without the need for too much explicit theorizing. I do provide some indications of them, especially in the Introduction, but I shall desist from entering into yet another lengthy theoretical discussion (I attempted one in my 2001 book on Plato's *Protagoras*).

In the next three paragraphs, I intend to make just a few brief remarks. Firstly, I comment on some specific problems related to Platonic studies in an attempt to forewarn the reader and help him or her decide *whether* or not to read the book. Then I explain the book's structure and general features, so that different readers may decide *how best* to use it according to their specific needs. Finally, I draw an outline of its contents, so that whoever reads it may know *what* to look for, and—with the help of the relevant indexes—*where* to locate it.

## Should I Read This Book? Plato and Hellenic Studies

Besides Platonists, the book is targeted at readers interested in lyric poetry (especially in Stesichorus and Sappho) and its classical reception, in the history of Greek poetics and in the cult of the hero (notably the poet-hero) from the Archaic to the Hellenistic age. It also takes into account Gorgias and Isocrates, while the intersections between philosophy and rhetoric are central to the book throughout. Other subjects include nympholepsy, the arboreal cult of Helen, different models of memory, the performance of poetry in classical Athens, the lives of the poets, Socratic iconography, the early history of Plato's Academy, and early Greek notions of authorship. In the spirit of the CHS series, this book is meant to be a contribution to Hellenic studies. Every specific subject should be seen as part of a multidisciplinary Greek whole, which I have tried to approach by reading and learning as much as possible, often with the generous help of people who know much more than I do. It is from this "holistic" perspective that I address my primary audience, namely Platonists. This accounts for my lengthy footnotes and bibliography, which draw on a number of cultural and linguistic areas, and sometimes privilege works that have been ignored or forgotten by mainstream scholarship.

My reason for stressing this point is the often lamented insularity and oblivion of Platonic scholarship: different languages, traditions, and approaches are becoming increasingly self-referential. The epigraph describes the battle of the gods and the giants. Plato's giants and gods are of course materialistic and idealistic thinkers respectively, but in terms of contemporary Platonic scholarship, the battle might be equally fitting as a caricature of the divide between opposed factions of Platonists. The giants want to feel the text, better still grasp the codex or the papyrus in their hands: any more general or abstract interpretation is likely to prompt a patronizing smirk on their faces, as if they were listening to some lunatic fantasizing about tragelaphs and unicorns. An equally dismissive grin is often seen on the faces of the gods whenever they encounter people who read the text with a painstakingly philological eye: surely these banausic accountants, who waste their time counting the instances of a given word in the Platonic corpus, or assessing the merits of two rival *lectiones*, are unable to contribute anything serious to our understanding of the father of western thought. Historically, the deepest divide is of course that between different species of philosophers and philologists, often resulting in an uneasy cohabitation. The two were soon divorced (indeed, as early as ancient times), and ever since they have lived apart under one, albeit ample, Platonic roof, even if, they now live in many countries in semi-detached, self-catering departments. In the meanwhile, further schisms have arisen.

This growing compartmentalization is alarming and, I believe, sadly un-Platonic. My ideal reader, on the other hand, whatever disciplinary perspective he or she may adopt, will resist the common temptation to construe Plato's complexity as if he suffered from some kind of dissociative identity disorder and will be intent, instead, on understanding and appreciating Plato's world as fully as possible. This, in my view, demands an interest in history, and a curiosity in a universe that is at once both mysterious and familiar. In some ways Plato is both the *father* of our philosophy and, curiously, the *child* of a civilization very different from our own, where *philologos* and *philosophos* (Socrates uses both words in the *Phaedrus*) could easily be one and the same non-schizophrenic person. Another crucial requirement is a willingness to entertain the idea that the ultimate goal of Plato's dialogues is to influence, persuade, and convert people to the life of philosophy. Accordingly, the poetic or rhetorical quality of Plato's works, together with his own theories about the role of poetry and philosophical discourse in society, are not embellishments or quirks of fancy, but lie at the very heart of Plato's *philosophia*. To read the dialogues solely, or even primarily, as an exposition of a set of doctrines may result, I believe, in a fatal misunderstanding.

At this point, the reader may either dislike my approach and decide to close the book right away or, in a fantastic scenario, may feel like reading it from cover to cover. The two following paragraphs, however, are particularly relevant for all those other potential readers who may be either interested in parts of the book or else have not as yet made up their minds.

## How to Use This Book: Structure and Features

My attempt to combine different perspectives and approaches will possibly require some patience on the part of the reader. For *my* part, I have opted for a particular structure, designed to make things easier. The book's four chapters are devoted to the *Phaedrus*, whereas the Introduction and the Conclusion, taken together, expand the scope of the book beyond the *Phaedrus*, to include the entire Platonic corpus. Each chapter has a cover page providing both textual and iconographic material, partly in the form of a handout, so as to avoid overloading the main exposition, and partly as an eye-catcher designed to set the tone of the chapter. The cover page is typically followed by a brief introduction, in which my own interpretation is developed against the background of other approaches, in an attempt either to break new ground or to provide new evidence for the solution of crucial interpretative problems. Each chapter, moreover, presents its own set of conclusions (as opposed to the book's general Conclusion), complete with an endnote called "Facts." Whereas the conclusions focus on general implications, the note highlights more detailed results of my work in a way that should be palatable to the giants, in that it briefly lists the literary and philological discoveries relevant to any given chapter.

Needless to say, the distinction between facts and interpretation is to a large extent artificial, and it does not require any particularly sophisticated hermeneutics to recognize that the very notion of "fact" can be a slippery one. Still, I hope it will prove useful. At the risk of sounding naively positivist, my emphasis is on *new* "facts." All too often, we tend to believe that factual advance in Platonic scholarship is no longer possible, as if all the relevant data, historical, textual, literary etc., were already available once and for all, much like over-microwaved leftovers. By contrast, my aim is to provide new evidence and fresh ingredients, set firmly within Plato's historical framework. No-nonsense "giants" can check my lists of "facts" for themselves. I hope they will also be interested enough to trace some of my arguments in the relevant chapters and see the larger interpretative implications of the new evidence. The "gods," in turn, can have a look at my general Introduction and my Conclusion to see what position the book occupies in the field of Platonic studies. Once again, I hope to stir their curiosity and persuade them to go through some of the details of the central chapters and the philological data on which my interpretations are built. Ultimately, dialectics is the art of matching the general with the particular, and Plato is both the "astronomying" philosopher who falls into the well *and* the whimsical maid from Thrace who has a hearty laugh at his expense.

## What and Where? Summary of the Book

The aim of the book is to reconstruct Plato's self-portrait as an author through a fresh reading of the *Phaedrus*, with an Introduction and Conclusion that contextualize the construction more broadly. The *Phaedrus* is Plato's most self-referential dialogue, as I argue on the basis of largely neglected data, both internal and external. I take my cue from Plato's reference to four Muses in *Phaedrus* 259c–d (Terpsichore, Erato, and the couple Ourania and Calliope), which I read as a hint at the "ingredients" of philosophical discourse. Plato's dialogues—and this is the book's main contribution to the field of Hellenic Studies—turn out to be, among other things, a form of provocatively old-fashioned *mousikê*.

My Introduction steers clear of the usual question "why did Plato write (dialogues)?" More radically, I ask *"what is* a Platonic dialogue?" My starting point is Plato's "self-disclosures," that is, those passages where he implicitly refers to his dialogues as poetry and music. Such "self-disclosures" have been partially studied by Konrad Gaiser, Stephen Halliwell, and others. The Introduction, together with the Appendix, aims to provide the most complete discussion of this aspect so far and to pave the way for my reading of the *Phaedrus*, where I detect a new set of powerful "self-disclosures." In order to introduce the reader to the *Phaedrus*, I also provide some general background for its interpretation and new evidence on its self-referential character.

Chapter 1, "Terpsichore," argues that the first half of the *Phaedrus* is also a consistent reenacting of Stesichorus' Helen poem and, more specifically, of its performance, as I demonstrate by discussing unexplored linguistic, philological, and metrical data. By appropriating Stesichorus, who was highly valued by Plato's Pythagorean friends, Plato builds on the opposition between Stesichorus and Homer, and thus conceptualizes philosophy as a topical or flexible discourse as opposed to "rhapsodic," or crystallized, rhetoric. In this formulation, philosophical discourse is unique in its capacity to adjust itself "musically" to the needs of different listeners.

Chapter 2, "Erato," focuses on Helen. I argue that, in his great speech, Socrates reproduces the quadripartite structure of Gorgias' *Encomium* and also toys with Isocrates' Helen. Both works allude to Sappho 16 Voigt, and so does Plato, who makes Helen's presence felt through the Phaedrus' plane-tree, which refers to the arboreal cult of Helen. The as-yet-unnoticed reworking of 16 Voigt is integral to Plato's definition of philosophy as eroticized rhetoric. Plato inherits from Sappho a notion of erotic oblivion: lyric *eros* proves crucial for severing the ties that bind us to the sensible world, and for sparking the process of recollection. Plato's recollection, however, differs markedly from Sappho's in that it uncovers the general as opposed to the particular.

Chapter 3, "Ourania and Calliope," takes its cue from Ion's magnet simile. My argument in this case is that the image applies equally well to philosophy, which the *Phaedrus* specifically assigns to the two Muses. *Sokratikoi logoi* take the form of an oral chain of accounts, whereby the human "rings" experience precisely the same symptoms as Ion and his audience. This, once again, points to philosophy as inspired *mousikê* as opposed to uninspired rhetoric. Philosophy, however, distances itself from epic rhapsodies in that the rings are vigilant and active. Similarly, the story of the cicadas is Plato's reenacting of a common myth, that is, the poet's initiation as a result of the Muses' epiphany in the country (cf. Hesiod, Archilochus, Epimenides). Again, deviations from the pattern are the code Plato uses to highlight the special status of his own production, which is, among other things, rationally vigilant and intrinsically dialogic (hence *two* Muses).

Chapter 4, "The Muses and the Tree," begins with a new interpretation of Socrates' prayer to Pan in the light of poetic initiations: in fact, Socrates invokes a poetic license and hints at the possibility of heroization. Comparison with similar stories of heroism *in fieri* (especially Posidippus) and with the relevant honors (I compare Socrates' statue in the Academy's *mouseion* with that of other poet-heroes) allows one to interpret the passage in the light of the cult of Socrates, as developed in the Academy from the fourth century onwards. The setting of the *Phaedrus*, I argue, prefigures both the cult of Socrates in the Academy, where he was worshipped as a *logos*-inspirer (i.e. a quasi-poet), and that of Plato, the writer (and quasi-poet) who constantly disavowed authorship. In other words, the *Phaedrus* provides an *aition* for the foundation of Plato's Academy.

In my Conclusion, I argue that Plato's return to *mousikê*, a recurring theme in a number of dialogues, amounts to a self-conscious paradox, which I construe to be the hallmark of Plato as author. I conclude with Socrates' conversion to "demotic," as opposed to metaphorical, music in the *Phaedo*, which, I maintain, closely parallels the *Phaedrus* and is apologetic in character, since Socrates was held responsible for dismissing traditional *mousikê*. This parallelism reveals three surprising features that define Plato's works: firstly, a measure of anti-intellectualism (Plato "musicalizes" philosophy so as to counter the rationalistic excesses of other forms of discourse, thus distinguishing it from prose as well as from poetry); secondly, a new beginning for philosophy (Plato conceptualizes the birth of Socratic dialogue in, and against, the Pythagorean tradition of the birth of philosophy, with an emphasis on the new role of writing); thirdly, a self-consciously ambivalent attitude with respect to the social function of the dialogues, which are conceived both as a kind of "resistance literature" and as a preliminary move towards the new poetry to be performed in the Kallipolis.

# Acknowledgments

THIS BOOK WAS WRITTEN almost entirely at the Center of Hellenic Studies: I owe to the Center much more than I can put down in words. I loved the place and I adored the people. In the *Phaedrus*, Socrates says that trees, unlike people, have nothing to teach him, but the dialogue belies him. I suspect I cannot thank places, but I remember them with gratitude and affection—the shady creek of the nearby wild park made me think of Plato's Ilissos, and the two landscapes merge in my head with poignant nostalgia. The city, too, helped me a lot with its cheerful variety and, of course, its great libraries: Dumbarton Oaks, Georgetown University, the Library of Congress ... Who could ask for more? I felt like Tityrus seeing Rome for the first time.

The library of the CHS is unmatched, not least because of the great people who work there. Most of the time, I count myself lucky when I meet librarians who are *either* kind *or* competent. But Erika Bainbridge, Sophie Boisseau, Lanah Koelle, and Temple Wright, besides forming an amazing combination of diverse characters, stand out for both kindness and knowledge: their smiling competence was a treasure. I cannot begin to mention all of the other nice people who work at the CHS, but I have sweet memories of each of them. However, I owe a special mention to Zoie Lafis. I heard people say that "she has the magic," and it's true: she helped me well beyond the duration of my fellowship. Ivy Livingston, Valerie Quercia, and Jill Robbins provided invaluable help when it came to revising the book for publication. I warmly thank the editorial team: everybody was friendly, encouraging, and professional. Greg Nagy suggested the "Four Muses" of the title, so I thank him here. But of course Greg meant much more, not only as the CHS director and as an inspiring scholar but also in his everyday epiphanies: in my memory, his iconic figure—jogger, smiling host, cheerful white-shirt tablemate—is part of the CHS landscape.

How could I ever thank enough my "fellow fellows," as we used to call each other? The shortest of notes for the sweetest of memories: they have been a second family for almost a year and will be in my heart forever. In an attempt not to (further) surrender to sentimentalism, let me say something scholarly:

they attended my CHS research talk and/or my paper at the 2012 CHS symposium, and their multi-faceted and interdisciplinary suggestions and criticisms greatly contributed to my understanding and enthusiasm. The help and affection I got from Alex, Cristina, and Madeleine is far beyond words, but at least I can jokingly switch to other languages: ευχαριστώ, *grazie*, 고마워 (hope this one is right).

I owe a very special thank to two friends who made it all possible for me: with uncommon generosity, Stefano Martinelli Tempesta and Giuseppe Zanetto volunteered to teach "my" course in Milan while I was on leave. After being my wedding witness, Luana Rinaldo visited me at the Center under the fantastic title of my "best woman," just because I was silly enough to call her that on a CHS form. This did not affect her generosity: she provided the beautiful drawings for the cover pages of my four chapters: *grazie Lu*!

A few people have been so kind as to read (parts of) the manuscript at various stages. Rudolf Carpanini and Aglae come first, and by far. I have sweet memories of Rudolf, a dearest family friend from my childhood. He reappeared in my life a few months ago, and he read and improved the book with stylistic competence and immense care. Aglae, too, read it again and again. Generic conventions, at least in my country, would suggest something like "with unfailing patience, my wife supported and tolerated me during the long and painstaking process of writing and revising the book" etc. Happily, this would be totally off the mark. It was hard work, but writing a book was definitely not prescribed to me: I did it because I liked it, and if I look back I see great moments, including a few wonderful months together in DC. Granted, reading the same book over and over again must be boring, but, whatever the reason, I'm very happy that she seems to like Plato better than she did a few years ago.

My other readers include Antonio Aloni, Matteo Cadario, Daniela Colomo, Lucia Floridi, Luigi Lehnus, Stefano Martinelli Tempesta, Cecilia Nobili, Alexandra Pappas, Alice Patrioli, Mario Regali, Alessandro Sgobbi, the anonymous CHS reader and, last but not least, my parents. They all helped me immensely, and I thank them all from deep in my heart. I have delivered and discussed parts of my research at various sites and institutions: Bryn Mawr College, University of Virginia, University of Durham, University of Pennsylvania, Universidade Federal de Minas Gerais, Universidade de São Paulo. I was lucky enough to find very perceptive audiences, who helped me with all sorts of suggestions and constructive criticism. Among the many nice people I had the privilege to meet, let me thank at least those who invited and/or hosted me: Radcliffe Edmonds, Georgia Sermamoglou-Soulmaidi, Phillip Horky, Johannes Haubold, Barbara Graziosi, Jeremy McInerney, Christian Werner, Daniel Rossi Nunes Lopes, Marco Zambrano.

This book is dedicated to Ermenegilda Bianchi Favara, my unforgettable high school teacher of Greek and Latin. She introduced me and my classmates to the amazing complexity of the *Phaedrus*—we read it together in Greek when I was 17—and I couldn't imagine my lifelong engagement with Plato without her example: she just opened my eyes.

# Introduction

# Plato's Self-Disclosing Strategies

WHY DIALOGUES? Readers of Plato have asked this question again and again over the centuries, and there is no sign of them relenting.[1] Scholars in particular struggle to understand why Plato wrote dialogues as opposed to philosophical treatises, as if he had deviated from the natural course of things in some way.[2] A related question is why did he write at all, given that his master is reported to have written nothing.[3] Yet the question is not so much "why?" as the more radical (and more Socratic) "what?"[4]

## What is a Platonic Dialogue? Poetry and Knowledge

There is a growing consensus that Plato's ambition was not only to put forward his ideas, but also to provoke and persuade.[5] This viewpoint has important implications that have rarely been explored. If the ultimate goal is to persuade

[1]  As a result, skeptical readings have appeared, arguing that the problem allows for no single solution (cf. Long 2008).

[2]  For a good introduction to the problem, see e.g. Michelini 2003 and Ford 2008. A learned and very informative discussion of the origins of Socratic dialogue can be found in Charalabopoulos 2012:32–43.

[3]  In the ambitious *Why Plato Wrote*, D. Allen argues that Plato was "the western world's first think tank activist and its first message man" (Allen 2010:4), and that writing, as opposed to Socrates' oral philosophy, was part of his political mission. The book is clever and interesting, but there is, of course, nothing particularly original about its professedly revolutionary thesis. The very same general idea is found, say, as early as in Dicaearchus as quoted by Philodemus of Gadara (see below) and fully corresponds to Friedrich Nietzsche's interpretation of Plato, who in 1871 described Plato "als agitatorischen Politiker, der die ganze Welt aus den Angeln heben will und *unter anderem* auch zu diesem Zweck Schriftsteller ist ... er schreibt, um seine akademischen Gefährten zu bestäerken im Kampfe" (Nietzsche 1995:9). Gaiser 1984 and 2004 (see below), as well as Cerri 1991 (and 2008, an updated version with a different title), and Hadot 2005 make a similar case for Plato's "sociological" approach.

[4]  Narcy 2007 rightly notes that scholars hardly ever ask the question "Che cosa è un dialogo socratico?"

[5]  E.g. Moors 1978, Trabattoni 1994, Rowe 2007, Werner 2012 (which is a penetrating study of the *Phaedrus*). Predictably, the growing tide of studies on emotions is affecting this aspect of Platonic scholarship as well: see Henderson Collins II on dialogues as "prompts for participation" (2012,

or convert people, it follows that a literary/rhetorical dimension must be crucial to Plato's dialogues, the study of which cannot be reduced to a subordinate activity—to be pursued only insofar as it allows us to extract or reconstruct Plato's doctrines.[6] Secondly, the very question of "why Plato wrote dialogues" is somehow misplaced, and should be preceded by a bolder one: "what is a Platonic dialogue?"

Surprisingly few ancient writers discussed dialogue as a genre.[7] Yet in his short second-century CE introduction to Plato, Albinus formulated the problem clearly (τί ποτ' ἔστιν ὁ διάλογος), and provided a straightforward answer to what he sees as the very first question any Platonist should ask.[8] For Albinus, Plato's dialogues were a form of philosophical drama, which could be described by way of an analogy with, and difference from, comedy and tragedy.[9] Characterization and style are key features of his definition, which, by modern standards, clearly privileges form over content. But can we be satisfied with such a definition? Some modern readers will be irritated by the parallel with tragedy and poetry, but our perspective is very remote from that of the ancient Greeks. We tend to assume that poetry and knowledge are two different, even opposite, phenomena. The Greeks, however, thought otherwise.

Plato's efforts to deny or qualify the poets' claims to knowledge countered the general view of his time. That is to say that poetry was, in fact, a form of knowledge whereby the poets, to quote from Simonides' Plataea elegy written in the aftermath of the Persian wars, gained access to "the whole truth."[10] The poets' hegemony was, of course, declining by the time Plato began to write. Simonides himself, who composed his Plataea elegy a century or so before, contrasts Homer's omniscience with his own craft, of which he seems to have a much more mundane view. In the course of time, sophistic and rhetorical discourse largely displaced poetry. Many authors, such as Hecataeus, Herodotus, and Thucydides, for example, had long been writing prose works in which they

---

with further bibliography). Educating people can also be seen as part of Plato's agenda: see Scott 2000.

[6] For such a position, see e.g. Bowen 1988. "Platonism," i.e. the effort to extract a Platonic "system" from the dialogues, is to a great extent the result of two momentous events: the discontinuation of the Academy after Sulla's sack of Athens and the movement to oppose the skeptical interpretation of Plato. See Ferrari 2012.

[7] See Segoloni 2012.

[8] For a painstaking discussion of Albinus' text against the background of other ancient treatments of dialogue as a genre, see Nuesser 1991. As Ford 2008 suggests, Albinus "was a well-trained and orthodox Platonist, and so some of the elements of the definition he proposes may date from earlier times and illuminate practices of the fourth century BCE" (34).

[9] Section 1 in Hermann's 1853 edition of Plato puts the question, "what is dialogue?" Section 2 explores the analogy with the theater.

[10] Fr. 11.17 W².

fiercely attacked poetic myth,[11] and the fourth century is by and large dominated by prose writing. So why did not Plato do the same? Why choose a form of writing that incorporates poetic genres, abounds in myths, indulges in seemingly ironic invocations to the Muses and even, at times, plays *muthos* against *logos*?[12]

My answer rests on a simple, if somewhat neglected, distinction. Even though their relationship with the inspiring Muses changed over time, the poets did not cease to present themselves as teachers of the *polis*. This seems to be integral to the defining status of their art, which continued to be seen as a form of *mousikê*, an "art of the Muses," an inspired and inspiring educational agency. On the other hand, and herein lies my distinction, questioning the role of poetry was a relatively easy task for the "non-musical" genres such as logography, historiography, rhetoric, and medical prose, which dispense with divine knowledge and, broadly speaking, emphasize human agency. The subjects of these genres or discourses are not heroic or divine realities discernible only to inspired poets: human things and natural phenomena can be observed directly, and it does not take a Muse to reveal them.[13] Strictly speaking, such genres are not a form of *mousikê*.[14]

These "human" genres rival and attack poetry and song, and their agonistic stance takes the form of a human discourse that deliberately does without the Muses. Interestingly enough, the Muses are never mentioned in classical Greek literature by either orators or historians, as if Muse were a kind of taboo word. By contrast, several philosophers—if I may oversimplify a little—share the

[11]  See e.g. Saïd 2007.
[12]  Examples of all these features are well known. Some of them are discussed in the next chapters. Recent scholarly trends pay much attention to *muthos* against *logos*: cf. e.g. Lincoln 1997 and Fowler 2011 (with interesting observations on Plato's ambivalent position). As for the *Phaedrus* in particular, I refer the reader to the important book by D. Werner (2012, cf. in particular 19–42 for the redemption of myth as against *logos*). Werner provides a penetrating discussion of myth in the *Phaedrus*, with far-reaching implications for the whole corpus.
[13]  Sophists, too, are surely part of the picture. According to Corradi 2011, Protagoras' ἄνθρωπος-μέτρον tenet directly challenges the traditional notion of the Muses bestowing on poets their gifts, resulting in Solon's ἱμερτῆς σοφίης μέτρον (1.51–52 W²).
[14]  To the surprise of us moderns, the same is true of the figurative arts, which in archaic and classical Greece were not associated with the Muses. After all, painters and sculptors based their work on visible models, and they had no need for divine inspiration when they had to reproduce a beautiful body or to render in visual form the myths of the gods and the heroes. As Herodotus famously says, "Homer and Hesiod shaped the Greek pantheon (θεογονίας): they gave the gods their epithets, they allotted them their several offices and occupations, and described their forms" (2.53). Even when, in Hellenistic times, the Muses were given individual and specific functions as well as a codified iconography (cf. Cohon 1991–1992), each of them came to preside over specific *literary* genres, not visual arts.

poets' claim to enjoy access to a superior knowledge veiled from the naked eye.[15] One thinks of Pythagoras, for example, who is traditionally considered to be the inventor of the word "philosopher":[16] the very birth of Pythagorean philosophy is closely connected with the worship of the Muses.[17] This possibly influenced Empedocles, who seems to summon Calliope as the Muse of philosophical *logos*.[18] Similarly, it is no coincidence that Parmenides claimed to have received his knowledge from a deity and, accordingly, expressed his thought in epic hexameters. The same is true of Xenophanes, who seems to have been a wandering rhapsode, ready to attack Homer and Hesiod with typically visceral hatred. In criticizing the immoral, anthropomorphic gods of poetry, Xenophanes is no doubt advocating a new *Weltanschauung*, though he would seem to be equally intent on discrediting epic rhapsodes, his immediate rivals and colleagues.[19] All in all, we can confidently say that rhetoric, history, and scientific prose are not "arts of the Muses" (*mousikê*), but that this was not necessarily the case with philosophy.[20] So what about Plato, then? Plato's *Sophist* refers to pre-Socratic philosophy as undiluted *muthos*, while Heraclitus and Empedocles, together with their followers, are referred to as "Ionian and Sicilian Muses."[21] Yet is Albinus justified in construing Plato as a quasi-poet?

An exhaustive answer to such a question would require a very long discussion and would have to take into account a large body of disparate evidence. And it would have to consider, as a minimum requirement, the following points:

1. Plato's Academy was sacred to Apollo and the Muses, the latter having their own altar (e.g. Pausanias 1.30.2). The tradition was further promoted by Plato's immediate successors.[22]

---

[15] Cf. Barfield 2011:32. In fact, the relationship between pre-Socratic philosophy and Muse-inspired poetry is a multifaceted phenomenon, giving rise to multiple and conflicting tendencies. See Sassi 2009, particularly chapter 5. As for Plato's prose, Butti de Lima rightly observes that it may be difficult to pin down its musical nature, "ma se la filosofia si rappresenta come tale, nella sua armonia, è perché deve distinguersi dalla *prosa della città*" (de Lima 2012:42).

[16] Heraclides Ponticus 87–88 Wehrli. Scholars hotly debate whether this testimony can be trusted. For two opposing views, see e.g. Burkert 1960 and Joly 1970.

[17] See Boyancé 1937:233–247.

[18] See Hardie 2013.

[19] For a lucid account, cf. Sassi 2009:144–150.

[20] Cf. Nonvel Pieri 2002:78–80.

[21] 242c–d. As Adomenas 2006 points out: "The repeated reference to the mythical mode of communication shows that it applies not only to the pluralists, but likewise to the Eleatics and Heraclitus with Empedocles. Therefore, the mythical, or mythically-poetical way of communication is imputed to all 'schools' of the pre-Socratic philosophy" (332).

[22] This point is nicely summarized by Büttner 2000, who presents the evidence on the Academy's cult of the Muses and concludes that "Platon wende sich gegen eine sophistische Position, die den Menschen für … autark gegenüber den Göttern hält" (268). For an abridged English version of Büttner's arguments, see Büttner 2011. The most recent papyrological and archaeological

2.  Not only does Aristotle include Plato's dialogues in the *Poetics*, where he defines them in terms of *mimêsis* and poetry (1447b), but many others, including Platonic philosophers, regarded Plato as a poet, even a new Homer (e.g. Proclus on Plato's *Republic* 1.196.9–13 Kroll).[23]

3.  Time and again, Plato's dialogues refer to philosophy as the highest form of *mousikê* (e.g. in the *Phaedo* 60e–61a). Needless to say, the dialogues abound in myths and even invocations to the Muses (e.g. in the *Phaedrus* 237a, and in the *Republic* 545d).[24]

4.  Plato's dialogues were sometimes recited during *symposia* along with excerpts from comedy (cf. e.g. Plutarch *Table Talks* 711b–c).[25]

5.  The anecdotal tradition reports that Plato, a former tragic poet (e.g. Dicaearchus fr. 40 Wehrli), was strongly influenced by the mimes of Sophron as well as by the comedies of Epicharmus and Aristophanes.[26]

6.  Plato himself, or at least the characters of his dialogues, seem to allude to his output as if it were a kind of song or drama.

Each of these points would require specific discussion, which is of course beyond the scope of the present study.[27] Suffice it to say that, though they raise very different problems, they also share a close affinity in that they all invoke the notion of poetry. It would seem that Plato's philosophy, or at least his dialogues, are indeed a form of *mousikê*, and that modern scholars are simply not in a position to minimize or explain away these facts.

In what follows, I shall limit myself to point 6, which cannot be dismissed as a later superimposition. By Plato's time, as I have already mentioned, poetry's claims had long been questioned. Nevertheless, the idea that poetry was a form of knowledge, albeit refashioned, was an established belief, and even Aristotle

---

data regarding the Academy's cult of the Muses are usefully collected and discussed in Caruso 2013:38–42. In the light of the new data, it must be concluded that the skepticism expressed by John Lynch (1972), who famously entered in polemic with Wilamowitz (1881) by arguing that the Academy was a wholly secular institution, was ultimately unfounded. "La centralità delle Muse sembra un dato di fatto" (Caruso 2013:41).

[23] Intriguingly, in late antiquity the allegorical interpretation of Plato ended up overlapping with that of Homer. See Lamberton 1992 and Heath 2013 (Chapter 5, "The Marriage of Homer and Plato").

[24] I shall often return to this point in the course of the current book, and especially in the Conclusion.

[25] This tradition is thoroughly explored by Charalabopoulos 2012, ch. 4.

[26] The relevant anecdotes are collected by Riginos 1976.

[27] Perhaps other points may be equally relevant, such as the recent much discussed thesis of Kennedy 2011, who thinks that Plato's dialogues were written according to a musical structure founded on Pythagorean doctrines. I am not in a position to assess the merits of Kennedy's ambitious theory.

thought that poetry was more philosophical than history and that it could function as a repository of *endoxa*.[28] To illustrate this point, I draw a comparison between two passages in which the role of poetry is discussed against the background of the crisis of the *polis*. The first is the famous assessment of poetry in Aristophanes' *Frogs*, written on the eve of the fall of Athens in the Peloponnesian war (404 BCE):

> Αι.   ... ἀπόκριναί μοι, τίνος οὕνεκα χρὴ θαυμάζειν ἄνδρα ποιητήν;
> Ευ.   δεξιότητος καὶ νουθεσίας, ὅτι βελτίους γε ποιοῦμεν
> τοὺς ἀνθρώπους ἐν ταῖς πόλεσιν

> Aeschylus   ... Come, tell me: why should we admire a noble poet?
> Euripides   For his ready wit and his good counsels
> and because we make men better in our cities.

Aristophanes *Frogs* 1008–1010

Needless to say, this passage has its own function within the comedy, and yet, in all probability, it represented widely accepted ideas.[29] The Athenians voted to allow the *Frogs* to be produced again by anyone who wished to do so, and thus it became the first comic classic in history.[30] In the same comedy, moreover, we hear that the degradation of Euripides' poetry is tantamount to its losing the status of *mousikê*, which only confirms the relevance of the distinction I make above between "musical" and "non-musical" arts.[31]

The second passage is found in Lycurgus' *Against Leocrates*, a postwar reflection written after the battle of Chaeronea (338 BCE), which, for most modern readers at least, marks the end of the classical era. After quoting a lengthy passage from the *Erectheus* in order to remind his fellow Athenians that Euripides "used to educate" their fathers,[32] Lycurgus goes on to say:

---

[28]   On this second and less obvious point see e.g. Sassi 2009:54–60, and the introduction in Guastini 2010. Poetry is seen as a vivid digest of *endoxa*, and as such it plays a crucially dialectical role in any practical argument. As a consequence, most of the issues discussed in Aristotle's ethical, rhetorical, and political works can hardly be conceived of outside the frame of poetry. As Halliwell 2000 puts it: "even Aristotle, who keeps aloof from the assumption that philosophical contentions stand in need of poetic support, cites and quotes poetry regularly in his own writings in ways which indicate the influence on him of a prevailing mentality that regarded poets and philosophers as pursuers, up to a point at least, of a common wisdom" (94).

[29]   For a balanced judgment, complete with the relevant parallels and further literature, cf. Halliwell 2011b:122–132.

[30]   The evidence for this exceptional honor is discussed by Dover 1993:73–75.

[31]   *Frogs* 1491–1495. The loss of music is famously put down to Socrates' influence, which probably prompted Plato's emphasis on the "musical" quality of philosophical discourse. Cf. my Conclusion to this volume.

[32]   Lycurgus *Against Leocrates* 101 (Ταῦτα ὦ ἄνδρες τοὺς πατέρας ὑμῶν ἐπαίδευε).

Βούλομαι δ᾽ ὑμῖν καὶ τῶν Ὁμήρου παρασχέσθαι ἐπῶν. οὕτω γὰρ
ὑπέλαβον ὑμῶν οἱ πατέρες σπουδαῖον εἶναι ποιητήν, ὥστε νόμον
ἔθεντο καθ᾽ ἑκάστην πεντετηρίδα τῶν Παναθηναίων μόνου τῶν
ἄλλων ποιητῶν ῥαψῳδεῖσθαι τὰ ἔπη, ἐπίδειξιν ποιούμενοι πρὸς τοὺς
Ἕλληνας, ὅτι τὰ κάλλιστα τῶν ἔργων προῃροῦντο. εἰκότως· οἱ μὲν
γὰρ νόμοι διὰ τὴν συντομίαν οὐ διδάσκουσιν, ἀλλ᾽ ἐπιτάττουσιν ἃ δεῖ
ποιεῖν, οἱ δὲ ποιηταὶ μιμούμενοι τὸν ἀνθρώπινον βίον, τὰ κάλλιστα
τῶν ἔργων ἐκλεξάμενοι, μετὰ λόγου καὶ ἀποδείξεως τοὺς ἀνθρώπους
συμπείθουσιν.

I want also to recommend Homer to you. In your fathers' eyes he was a
poet of such worth that they passed a law that every four years at the
Panathenaea he alone of all the poets should have his works recited;
and thus they showed the Greeks their admiration for the noblest
deeds. They were right to do so. Laws are too brief to give instruction:
they merely state the things that must be done; but poets, depicting
life itself, select the noblest actions and so through argument and
demonstration convert men's hearts.

Lycurgus *Against Leocrates* 102, trans. Burtt

Interestingly, Lycurgus credits the poets with quintessentially philosophical
procedures such as "argument" (λόγος) and "demonstration" (ἀπόδειξις).

The two passages frame the adult life of Plato, whose own work would
confirm the crucial role of the poets. The tragedians figure importantly among
the supposedly wise people questioned by Socrates in the *Apology*, and in the
*Laws* Plato goes so far as to define Athens as a "theatrocracy."[33] One may add that
the sophists were ready to present themselves as the direct heirs of the archaic
poets in educating the citizens,[34] and it is interesting to note that the *Republic*'s
full-scale attack on poetry takes place in the house of Cephalus, a man whose
vision of life, and of the afterlife in particular, is clearly shaped by traditional
poetry. Perhaps unsurprisingly, then, poetry is duly superseded by the eschatological *myth* at the end of the dialogue.[35]

---

[33] *Apology* 22a–c and *Laws* 701a. In fact, in the latter passage the Athenian refers to "theatrocracy"
with regard to music, but its implications, as is clear from what follows, affect the whole *polis* and
its values.

[34] Cf. *Protagoras* 316d–e and Allen 2010:34–35. For sophists as part of a larger wisdom tradition, see
in general Tell 2011.

[35] Undoubtedly, the myth of Er "displaces the conceptualization of the afterlife that Cephalus had
first offered" and "adheres to the principles of poetic composition articulated in Books 3 and 4."
(Allen 2010:35). Even more importantly, I should add that the myth is clearly conceptualized as a
morally acceptable alternative to Homer's *Nekyia*, which is fiercely criticized in the first part of

These and other facts can be used to argue that, as Danielle Allen puts it, "Plato wrote ... all his dialogues to displace the poets."[36] In my view, this is far too radical. At the risk of stating the obvious, it must be added that Plato was not satisfied with either rhetoric or sophistry, the very forms of thought and expression that had partly displaced/replaced the poets, and which were so prominent in the fourth century BCE.[37] Plato surely felt "the need for a shibboleth separating Socratic from dubious sophistic *logoi*," as Andrew Ford puts it.[38] And this, I believe, is precisely where poetry comes in. As we shall see in the course of this book, the *Phaedrus* can be read as a partial defense of poetry against the attacks of rhetorical and eristic discourse; it is as if Plato were looking for an appropriate compromise—which squares well with Plato's own choices as an author and (potential) legislator. For not only did he opt for a form of prose that has much in common with poetry, but he clearly envisages an ideal city, both in the *Republic* and in the *Laws*, where a (reformed) *mousikê* will continue to be the predominant medium in the education of the citizenry, even if literacy and speech are also given their fair share.[39] As Myles Burnyeat so aptly puts it: "the cave is not abolished in the ideal city, only purified."[40]

In emphasizing the poetic quality of Plato's dialogues, Albinus was simply following in the footsteps of Aristotle. In discussing the *Republic* and, surprisingly, the *Laws*, Aristotle claims in the *Politics* that "all the discourses of Socrates possess brilliance, cleverness, originality, and keenness of inquiry."[41] Even more famously, in the *Poetics* he associates Socratic *logoi* with the mimes of Xenarchus and Sophron.[42] The latter were probably a mixture of prose and verse, which complements another statement by Aristotle, to the effect that Plato's dialogues stand somewhere between (μεταξύ) poetry and prose.[43] Aristotle's view that *Plato's dialogues are meant as a kind of poetry* provides us with a useful working hypothesis, and it neatly rounds off my argument that the function of poetry, as discussed in Plato's *Republic* and *Laws*, is to influence people and shape their

---

the *Republic*. For this and other "poetic" strategies in the *Republic* and *Timaeus-Critias*, see Nagy 2002 and Capra 2010a, with further bibliography.

[36] Allen 2010:77.

[37] See e.g. Nehamas 1990.

[38] Ford 2008:42. Ford singles out *ethopoiia* as the hallmark of dialogue as opposed to rhetoric (a solution which is not incompatible with my own).

[39] In many ways, Plato aims at restoring traditional music (see e.g. Rocconi 2012), and the musical education he puts forth in the *Laws* is based on very traditional reality, with a preference for Crete and Sparta (Calame 1997:222–223).

[40] Burnyeat 1999:245. Burnyeat argues that poetry and *mimêsis* are meant to be pervasive in Plato's ideal city.

[41] 1265a12–14.

[42] *Poetics* 1447a28–1447b14.

[43] In Diogenes Laertius 3.37.

beliefs. It follows logically that Plato's dialogues themselves should be read as poetry, which gives us a provisional definition of the dialogues. And yet, how sufficient and warranted a definition is this? What would Plato himself have said if, in mockingly Socratic style, we had knocked at his door and asked, "For the dog's sake, Plato: what is a Platonic dialogue? Is your pupil Aristotle right when he says that your own writings are some kind of fancy poetic stuff?" It is a pity we cannot ask him directly; yet we can probe his dialogues for clues. What I shall be looking for in particular is a *Platonic* answer to this question.

## Towards a Self-Definition of Platonic Dialogue

Plato's dialogues never mention Plato's dialogues, and with good reason: they are all set in a relatively distant past (second half of the fifth century), and their characters, Socrates and others, are in no position to comment on a set of works that were yet to be born.[44] From this point of view, Plato's dialogues resemble tragedies. No overt reference to the tragic genre can be found in a tragedy, for the simple reason that tragedies are set in a pre-theatrical past. However, one might expect references to the dialogues in the *Letters*, where, exceptionally, Plato speaks in his own voice.[45] Yet what we find is a notorious and astonishingly negative statement. In the *Seventh Letter*, Plato famously declares that philosophy is a lifelong process involving a number of stages, none of which takes a written form, and it is for this reason that he, Plato, has not confided his philosophy to writing.[46] This is indirect confirmation that Plato's dialogues are not primarily an exposition of doctrine and that they must have had a different aim. So once more we find ourselves asking, what are Plato's dialogues?

Clearly, the answer cannot simply be that they are (a new kind of) tragedy or drama.[47] The parallel I have put forward is only valid insofar as Plato's

---

[44]  Of recent, interesting attempts have been made at reading Plato's dialogues in the light of their dramatic dates, that is, in sequence. Zuckert 2009 has come up with a comprehensive interpretation along these lines. Stella 2006 also construes (some of) Plato's dialogues as chapters of a philosophical novel.

[45]  I am in accord with the vast majority of critics in accepting the authenticity of *Letters* 6, 7, and 8. See e.g. the unsurpassed monograph by Giorgio Pasquali (1938) and, more recently, Isnardi Parente 2002.

[46]  *Letter* 7.341a–e. (It is, of course, the introduction of the so-called philosophical digression.)

[47]  To be sure, some scholars do read Plato's dialogues purely as drama: Arieti 1992 is an extreme and well-known example. However, it should be kept in mind that tragedies deal with the words and deeds of heroes, whereas the dialogues have a self-referential quality that is lacking in drama: they consist, in fact, of people engaged in dialogue, that is, philosophical works involving philosophical characters. On the contrary, only occasionally, and then only in comedies, do playwrights include playwrights among their characters. Blondell 2002 makes much of this interesting distinction in her Chapter 2. More recent discussion includes Rossetti 2008 and Vassallo 2012, who emphasize, to different degrees, the discontinuity between the dialogue and drama.

characters, like tragic heroes, "predate" the genre they belong to. Just as Medea, for example, cannot possibly mention Euripides' tragedies or discuss what's on at the Dionysus theatre, so Socrates cannot possibly name or discuss Plato's dialogues.[48] In both cases, direct comment is not possible, but allusive references most certainly are. We know very well that the tragedians had ways of discussing their own work (and their colleagues') through allusion. Euripides's *Electra*, for example, famously "criticizes" Aeschylus for his implausible handling of the relevant recognition scene, and a similar attitude can be found in the *Phoenician Women*, where Euripides implicitly compares his own version to Aeschylus'.[49] The same can be expected of Plato, who could rely on a shared code that he only needed to adapt to his own purposes. Thus, far from being an overly subtle or anachronistic exercise, searching for such allusions is a perfectly plausible agenda: the technique was already well known as early as the fifth century BCE. But how does it work in the case of Plato? A quotation from a recent article by Stephen Halliwell makes the point clearer:

> There is, to put it concisely, the seemingly Platonic attitude (and, consequently, the Platonism) which criticizes, censors and even "banishes" poets, and which speaks in terms of unmasking the false pretensions and the damaging influences of poetry. But there is also the Platonic stance which never ceases to allow the voices of poetry to be heard in Plato's own writing, which presupposes not only extensive knowledge but also "love" of poetry on the part of Plato's readers, and which at certain key junctures claims for *itself* nothing less than the status of a new kind of philosophical poetry and art: the status, indeed, of the "greatest music" and even of "the finest and best tragedy" ... The notion of Platonic writing as itself a kind of poetry has roots ... in explicit moments of self-consciousness in the dialogues as well as in their multiple literary qualities.[50]

---

[48] Needless to say, other aspects of Plato's dialogues point to tragedy. As Clay 2000 remarks, "Socrates is a tragic figure in the two senses of the word now familiar: Socrates offered Plato a serious and noble object of representation, a human who contains within his satyr's exterior 'images of divinity'; and, as Plato came to adopt the irony of the tragic poet, Socrates emerged as a character whose full career was well known to Plato's audience. Because Plato invested his dialogues in historical settings and because he composed his dialogues after the death of Socrates, the dialogues also resemble Attic tragedies" (143).

[49] Cf. Euripides *Electra* 524–537 and *Phoenician Women* 734–753. Some scholars do not agree with this interpretation (e.g. Ieranò 2006 agrees that the latter passage rests on Aeschylus' subtext, but favors a Homeric subtext in the case of the former). However, the general principle seems to be a long-established and widely accepted one.

[50] Halliwell 2011a:241–242. The references to "the greatest music" and "the finest and best tragedy" are to *Phaedo* 61a, *Phaedrus* 248d and 259d, and *Laws* 817b.

Halliwell emphasizes the relative novelty of such an approach, especially as regards scholarship in English, and he shows how effective it can be by very successfully highlighting the subtle (and no doubt self-conscious) ambiguity of Plato's attitude towards poetry in the *Republic*. In fact, Halliwell's "explicit moments of self-consciousness" had long been studied by one of the most important Platonists of the 20th century, namely Konrad Gaiser.

Gaiser has devoted an entire book (and an impressive array of profound scholarship) to this fascinating subject:[51] I am referring to his *Platone come scrittore filosofico*, which in turn builds upon his previous work *Protreptik und Paränese bei Platon*.[52] Unfortunately, Gaiser, as an exponent of the so-called "Tübingen school," is commonly associated with the declining *querelle* that revolves around Plato's "unwritten doctrines"[53] (largely a "continental" affair[54]), even though the book's main arguments *are not* committed to the "unwritten doctrines" hypothesis (which, incidentally, I wholly disagree with).[55] One can only conclude that its virtual absence from the landscape of scholarship in English is yet another example of what Francisco Gonzalez refers to as "a growing insularity in Platonic studies, especially among English-speaking scholars: extremely helpful

---

[51]  This does not detract from the overall originality of Halliwell's analysis, which focuses on the *Republic* and thus covers an area that Gaiser merely hints at.

[52]  Gaiser 1984 and 1959, respectively. A German version of Gaiser 1984 is integrated into Gaiser 2004 (*Platon als philosophischer Schrifsteller*, pp. 3–72).

[53]  The book received a number of substantial reviews by distinguished Platonists such as Joachim Dalfen, Michael Erler, and Gabriele Giannantoni (Dalfen 1987, Erler 1987b, Giannantoni 1985) but, alarmingly, its English reception was limited to a very brief and ultimately uninformative notice by Julia Annas. Though not unsympathetic, her notice is seriously misleading, as she claims that the book "restate[s] in a clear and unencumbered way G's basic approach to the Plato of the dialogues" (Annas 1985:401). This is simply not true: compared to previous scholarship (including Gaiser's own earlier work), the book contains important new insights, and it is a pity that Annas fails to mention, let alone discuss them. Gaiser 1959, likewise, received no reviews in English, which clearly hindered its worldwide reception. Finally, no English review of Gaiser 2004 discusses Gaiser's work on "self-consciousness," i.e. *Platon als philosophischer Schrifsteller*, 3–72.

[54]  Nikulin 2012 is a recent attempt to bring "the other Plato" to the fore of Anglo-American scholarship.

[55]  This is not to say, of course, that Gaiser did not endorse it (after all, he tried hard to reconstruct it, cf. Gaiser 1968). At least to a certain extent, the same is true for the work of Thomas Szlezák, who is in many ways Gaiser's heir and was the editor of Gaiser's collected works (Gaiser 2004). Both Szlezák 1985 (an unmatched examination of Plato's *Aussparungstellen* in the early and middle dialogues) and Szlezák 1991 (an excellent introduction to the interpretation of Plato's writings) endorse and promote the unwritten doctrines hypothesis. But Szlezák's fresh and penetrating examination of the dialogues is of extreme interest to the "unaffiliated" as well, and is largely compatible with the alternative idea that philosophy, in the eyes of Plato, is first and foremost a "dialogical" affair (cf. Trabattoni 1994, who takes advantage of both Gaiser's and Szlezák's readings only to argue argue that the superiority of oral dialogue over fixed speech—whether written or spoken—has nothing to do with the allegedly secret doctrines advocated by the "Tübingen school").

and worthy work is ignored simply because it is not in the right language or school."[56] What follows is a summary of Gaiser's conclusions, which, at the same time, are integrated with new insights within a broader perspective.

Gaiser's starting point derives from reception theory: what was the intended readership of Plato's dialogues? By piecing together the little specific evidence we have,[57] he reminds us that, contrary to the assumptions of most modern readers, Plato's dialogues were written for the general public and had a protreptic and/or "hypomnematic" function,[58] whereas "real" philosophy was a personal affair, taking place in Plato's Academy for the benefit of both pupils and "casual hearers."[59] Gaiser made a crucial breakthrough when he analyzed, and definitively clarified, an important passage from Philodemus' *Index Academicorum*.[60] It is worthwhile quoting it in full:

> ... τῶν πάντων [ἀνθρώ]|πων οὗτος εὔξεσε[ν φ]ιλο|σοφίαν καὶ κατέλυσ[ε] προ|[ετ]ρέψατο μὲγ γὰρ ἀπε[ίρ]ου[ς]|ὡς εἰπεῖν ἐπ' αὐτὴν διὰ|τῆς ἀναγραφῆς τῶν λ[ό|γω]ν. ἐπιπολ[α]ίως δὲ καί|[τινας] ἐπο[ίησ]ε φιλοσοφεῖν|φαγερὰν ἐκτρέ[πων ...

> ... [Plato] both promoted and damaged philosophy more than anyone else. By composing his dialogues, Plato, as it were, led to philosophy (προετρέψατο) countless people; on the other hand, he caused some people to philosophize superficially, and he misled them ...

> Philodemus *Index Academicorum*, col. I 9–17, ed. Dorandi

---

[56] Gonzalez 1998:ix.

[57] Notably Themistius *Speech* 23.395c–d and Xenophon *Memorabilia* 1.4.1. Cf. Plato *Cleitophon* 408c–409a (Gaiser 1984:41–42). Another interesting piece of information is a fragment of the middle comedy playwright Ophelion, where reference is made to a βιβλίον Πλάτωνος in what seems to be an everyday context (3 PCG), possibly poking fun at the ψυχρότης of Plato's writings (as Gaiser 1974 convincingly suggests). Surprisingly, H. Thesleff, in a paper devoted to "Plato and his Public," resorts to this fragment in an argument designed to argue that Plato "was very much in favor of 'narrowcasting' instead of broadcasting" (Thesleff 2009:549).

[58] See Chapter 2 in this volume.

[59] Watts 2007:108 (on Epicrates fr. 5 PCG). Once again, this does not require that we endorse the "unwritten doctrines" hypothesis. Rather, the sources Gaiser discusses, together with the many problems that arise from a reading of the dialogues, "convey the belief that contact with the author of these dialogues in the Academy would supply whatever was found wanting in his written dialogues" (Clay 2000:xi).

[60] It is through Gaiser's own "genial conjectures and supplements," as Jonathan Barnes puts it, that the text is now, to a great extent, "luminously clear and intelligible" (Barnes 1989:142). For Gaiser's contribution, see Gaiser 1983 and 1988. By and large, Dorandi's edition (1991) espouses Gaiser's reconstructions, though he differs on a number of points that are irrelevant to my present discussion. Very recently, Del Mastro 2012 has published a hitherto unidentified fragment of Philodemus' work, from the same papyrus and also from the life of Plato. Among other things, Plato is described as a man of peace.

A few lines later, we learn that Philodemus is quoting Dicaearchus, who goes on to declare that the misleading aspect of Plato's philosophy lies in his emphasis on *eros*. We also learn important details of the Academy's way of life, to which Dicaearchus devotes much attention, possibly to conclude that Plato's dialogues motivated many other people who did not directly attend. The importance of such an early authoritative source as Dicaearchus cannot be overstated:[61] Plato's dialogues, it would seem, aimed at stimulating and possibly encouraging people.[62]

If the dialogues were indeed meant for the general public, then it follows that Plato did not assume any systematic reading of his works on the part of his readers and would have allowed for the possibility that they would have only a limited knowledge of them;[63] as Diskin Clay remarks, "disconcertingly, in the Platonic dialogues, 'the sun is new every day.'"[64] This raises crucial hermeneutic issues. We may, for example, presume to reconstruct Platonic doctrine(s) by means of a thorough, comparative reading of all his dialogues, and there is no doubt that the history of philosophy, by evolving as a "series of footnotes to Plato," has benefited from such efforts.[65] Nevertheless, such a bookish enterprise was not what Plato would have expected from his original public, and it is no coincidence that his exoteric dialogues, unlike Aristotle's esoteric writings, do not contain cross-references.[66]

---

[61]  As Gaiser 1983 notes, Dicaearchus is a reliable source. He had access to firsthand information and had no reason to distort the facts.

[62]  According to Barnes 1989: "The construe is surely wrong. First, Dicaearchus is not talking about Plato's *intentions* at all: he is talking about the *effects* of the dialogues. He may have thought that Plato intended his dialogues to have a protreptic force; but he does not say so. Secondly, and more importantly, Dicaearchus does not state or imply that Plato's *sole* intention in writing the dialogues was protreptic" (147). Barnes's objections are, in my view, of limited relevance. First, Dicaearchus uses a *middle* form (προετρέψατο) in a sentence of which Plato (and not the dialogues) is the subject: this is sound evidence that Dicaearchus is clearly highlighting Plato's *intentions*. This also affects Barnes's otherwise convincing second point. For even if Dicaearchus' Plato had other goals, the emphasis is clearly on "protreptic force." This is all the more evident in the light of what follows, as Dicaearchus quickly moves on to *life* at the Academy: the implication seems to be that those who were exposed to the protreptic force of the dialogues opted for philosophy as a way of life and attended the Academy (note that this is precisely what Themistius *Speech* 23.395c–d maintains).

[63]  This is not to deny the existence of "many intertextual connections, both linguistic and intellectual, that link the dialogues into a loosely built but mutually supportive network" (Michelini 2003:4).

[64]  Clay 2000:x.

[65]  This celebrated quotation, which in full reads "The safest general characterization of the European philosophical tradition is that it consists of a series of footnotes to Plato," is taken from Whitehead 1929 (Part II, Chapter 1, Section 1).

[66]  The few exceptions are either elusive (the *Timaeus* does not evoke the *Republic* proper, but a number of points that have a very loose and even contradictory relation with the *Republic* as we

A related point is the effect of philosophical discourse as described in the dialogues. Gaiser reminds us, as a number of other scholars have also noted, that Plato often compares such discourse to a kind of therapy produced through *katharsis* (purification) and *epôidê* (incantation), i.e. two fundamental aspects of ancient medicine.[67] These two aspects were meant to counterbalance the spell of other forms of "magic" discourse such as the poetic, the rhetorical, and the sophistic. As Elizabeth Belfiore observes, they corresponded to two distinct stages (or "weapons") in the philosophical process: namely, "one that purifies the rational element, driving out false belief (the *elenchos* or a process similar to it that will 'turn around' reason to its proper objects, as the *Republic* 518e describes it) and another procedure that will actively train and strengthen the emotions so that they will be in harmony with reason (the *epôidê*, the myth, musical education)."[68]

These two phases represent the "critical"/"dialectical" and the "constructive"/"dogmatic" modes of Plato's philosophy respectively, and are most famously contrasted in Gregory Vlastos's theory of the two distinct (and opposed) Socrateses within Plato's dialogues.[69] The antinomy *katharsis/epôidê* can be (and has been) interpreted in many different ways,[70] and one can always engage in a favorite exercise of Platonists—that is, project the distinction on to the tripartite division of the soul as outlined in the *Republic* and elsewhere.[71] However, such qualifications, along with their possible evolution over time, are of limited relevance to my present argument, which is based on a rather simple

---

know it) or apparent, in that they create a link between two dialogues that are in fact one and the same work built in the form of a diptych (*Timaeus-Critias*; *Sophist-Politicus*). Cf. e.g. Haslam 1976.

[67] As for the former (cf. e.g. *Charmides* 175a–176b; *Menexenus* 80a–b; *Phaedo* 77e–78a; *Theaetetus* 149c–d and 157c; *Crito* 54d; *Symposium* 215c–e; *Republic* 608a), Gaiser builds on the work of Marignac 1951 and Belfiore 1980. His argument is further developed, with the *Charmides* as their particular focus, by Erler 1987a:332–340 and Tulli 1996. The latter aptly points out the nuances, both literary and medical, of the term *epôidê* in this dialogue. On this point, Gaiser, like most scholars, interprets *Sophist* 230b–e as a description of the *katharsis* induced by Socratic elenchus.

[68] Belfiore 1980:135.

[69] Vlastos 1991:45–81 (Chapter 2, "Socrates *contra* Socrates in Plato"). Vlastos's book continues to fuel discussion, often resulting in opposite, and equally radical reconstructions (cf. e.g. the strongly unitarian interpretation provided by Peterson 2011).

[70] For instance, one could object that the boundaries are much more blurred than Vlastos would have them: sometimes the two Socrateses appear in one and the same dialogue, and the method of one can be seen to be complementary to, rather than incompatible with, the other. One thinks of the *Symposium* for example in which Socrates both refutes (i.e. purifies) and instructs (i.e. enchants) Agathon and Alcibiades.

[71] As Belfiore notes, elenchus is also an emotional procedure, which one could argue is related to both *thumos* and reason (Belfiore 1980:132). Among other passages, *Sophist* 229b–230e is discussed in connection with *Republic* 440b and *Laws* 646e–650b.

premise: Plato's philosophical discourse can be described as a form of purification followed, either logically or chronologically, by a form of incantation.[72]

The twofold "therapeutic" characterization discussed by Gaiser and Belfiore squares well with an aspect of Plato's writings that no reader can fail to notice: the dialogues abound in myths, metaphors, similes, ethopoeias, and so on; i.e. quintessentially poetic devices aimed, one might say, at influencing people's minds and emotions.[73] Against this general background, Gaiser explores a number of passages that can be construed as "moments of self-consciousness," which I prefer to call "self-disclosures."[74] It would be long to discuss them here, so I refer the reader to the Appendix. Suffice it to say that a reappraisal of Plato's self-disclosures as discussed by Gaiser results in a rich (and ultimately consistent) picture. Philosophical discourse has a twofold nature: "comic" purification and "serious" enchantment. The first may take the form of comedy (*Symposium*), playfulness (*Phaedrus*), or popular tale (*Phaedo*), while the latter is called hymn (*Phaedo*) or tragedy (*Symposium* and *Laws*).

However broad, Gaiser's discussion by no means exhausts the number of Plato's self-disclosures. There is Halliwell's discussion of *Republic* 10 for example, where Socrates seems reluctant to banish poetry and advocates a form of "counter-enchantment," plausibly interpreted as a reference to the dialogues themselves.[75] The *Gorgias*, where Plato appropriates structurally the subtext provided by Euripides' *Antiope*, is also part of the picture. As Andrea Nightingale has argued, Plato "invites his readers to juxtapose his dialogue to its tragic model, and he reinforces this message by persistently probing at the nature of the tragic and the comic. At the heart of Plato's critique of tragic

---

[72] With "followed by," I mean that "purification" is a preliminary stage to "incantation." From another point of view, however, "incantation" came first, since Plato was fully aware that "purification," in the Socratic sense, was a recent invention, as opposed to more traditional forms of *paideia* that are largely based on incantation.

[73] In her 2010 discussion of Plato's *Republic*, Allen rightly observes that "There are, on the one hand, shadows or *eidôla*, which are what poets produce. Socrates repudiates these. But there are also useful and valuable images, which he endorses. Socrates refers to the latter with terms like: theoretical models (*paradeigma logôi*, 472c), paradigms (*paradeigmata*, 361b, 472c), types (*tupos*, 443c), images (*eikones*, 487e, 488a, 588a, 588b–c), paintings (*zôigraphiai*, 472d, 488a, 501a–b), sculptures (*andriantopoioi*, 540c, also 420c–d), patterns after the divine pattern (*paradeigmata en ouranôi*, 592b), and diagrams (*diagrammata* 529d–e)" (Allen 2010:29; cf. also Appendix 1, 148–153). Allen's well-argued thesis is that "Socrates offers a defense of the kinds of images or word-pictures he himself makes ... this distinction between epistemologically worthy and epistemologically unworthy symbols (and particularly images), combined with his account of their social and psychological importance, provides the basis for an explanation of why philosophers may and should write" (Allen 2010:30).

[74] Gaiser himself calls them "autotestimonianze." Sharp 2008 expresses a similar idea through the phrase "inside views," although his main focus is Socrates rather than Plato.

[75] Halliwell 2011b:184–207. On Socrates' reluctance to abandon poetry (607e–608b), cf. Brancacci 2012.

wisdom, finally, is a detailed and complex portrait of its newly invented adversary: philosophy."[76] The lyre of Amphion-Socrates, too, can be construed as the symbol of philosophy's musical nature, as Mauro Tulli has suggested.[77] The epic story of the *Critias*, embedded as it is in rhapsodic language while at the same time incorporating other poetic genres,[78] can be shown to be in line with Plato's criticism of poetry as expressed in the *Republic*, of which the *Timaeus-Critias* is a sequel.[79] Finally, in the *Lysis*, a young sophist attacks old-fashioned poetry, but Socrates ends up comparing philosophical discourse to a form of old-fashioned poetry designed to correct the excesses of eristics.[80] Yet the most "disclosing" dialogue is certainly the *Phaedrus*, which in the current book's four chapters will reveal a new set of powerful "self-disclosures." It is about time to say a few introductory words on the *Phaedrus* itself.

## Prologue to the *Phaedrus*

The core of this book is devoted to the *Phaedrus* and its fascinating cultural background, with particular regard for archaic poetry in its performative and biographical dimensions. These are important and surprisingly neglected issues, which, if correctly understood, can shed fresh light on how Plato positioned himself in the context of Athenian society, both as writer and thinker. Yet this is not the place to anticipate the more general import of my arguments. Rather, my immediate concern is to provide some general background for the interpretation of this dialogue. There are two things, in particular, to be borne in mind: firstly, that in the *Phaedrus* Plato is arguably at his most self-referential;

---

[76] Nightingale 1995:73. The *Gorgias* also voices Socrates' criticism of tragedy as flattery (502b–503b). But, as Trivigno 2011 has argued, this should be understood in relative terms, since the *Antiope* might have been introduced as an example of good tragedy.

[77] "Dunque Callicle, nobile, convinto erede di Zeto, nel mettere fra le mani di Socrate la lira di Anfione, offre una conferma del rapporto fra filosofia e poesia, centrale nelle opere di Platone già nella prima fase. La vita speculativa che respinge non è che la forma nuova di una vita nel segno della poesia" (Tulli 2007b:76). A previous article (Tulli 1996) reads the *Charmides* along similar lines.

[78] See Nagy 2002 and Regali 2012:12–43.

[79] See Capra 2010a and Regali 2012:71–78.

[80] *Lysis* 221d. The way the previous discussion is referred to (ὕθλος τις ἦν, ὥσπερ ποίημα κρόνιον, according to the text established by Martinelli Tempesta 2003a) is designed to sound like a reply to Ctesippus' scathing criticism of poetry (cf. 205c κρονικώτερα). Cf. Capra 2004. The case of the *Lysis* is especially significant in that it shows how the pattern is discernible in purely elenchic and "early" dialogues too, thus countering a possible objection that Gaiser himself preemptively raises. A weaker version of Gaiser's own argument suggests that Plato's construing of the dialogues as a form of poetry might have been a later development and is, therefore, relevant only for the mature/non-elenchic dialogues. Dalfen 1974 has espoused this weaker version (cf. also Clay 2000:147, on the *Laws*: "Plato is less guarded here than he had been earlier in his career. He characterizes his dialogues as a new form of tragedy").

and, secondly, that the dialogue is unique in presenting a sustained case for a positive form of inspiration. Both aspects are connected with another remarkable feature: the unparalleled importance of the natural landscape.

The landscape of the *Phaedrus* is not so much a gentle, out-of-town glade as a jungle of symbols, often deeply ambiguous, and designed to trigger all kinds of associations in the minds of Plato's contemporaries.[81] Take the chaste-tree, for example (230b). Scholars have patiently prized out its meaning, which conveys the idea of both chastity and lust,[82] thus playing subtly with the erotic potential of the scene: Socrates and a young man are lying alone in a very sensual ambient at a time of the day (noon in midsummer) that the Greeks associated with Pan's sexual exuberance.[83] The importance of the landscape can hardly be overestimated, and it is important to note that ancient readers, much more so than ourselves, would have felt its spell throughout the dialogue. Not only were there innumerable imitations of it, to the point that Plutarch felt the need to distance himself from the "commonplaces" of its imitators,[84] but it seemed to acquire a kind of metonymic status.[85]

In a letter addressed to the *Imperator*, Themistius argues for the philosophical character of the kingdom, and he does so by pointing to Plato's "famous *Republic*, divine *Laws*, and the whole discussion by the thick and tall plane-tree."[86] It is fascinating, therefore, to find the plane-tree used as a title almost. Even more interesting is the following passage from Timon of Phlius:

> τῶν πάντων δ' ἡγεῖτο πλατίστακος, ἀλλ' ἀγορητὴς
> ἡδυεπής, τέττιξιν ἰσογράφος, οἵ θ' Ἑκαδήμου
> δένδρει ἐφεζόμενοι ὄπα λειριόεσσαν ἱεῖσιν.

> And a plate-fish was leading them all, though it was a speaking one, and sweet-voiced at that! In his writings, he matches the cicadas, pouring out their lily song from the tree of Academus.

> Timon of Phlius fr. 30 Di Marco

---

[81] For a detailed, up-to-date reconstruction of the landscape (including the banks of the Ilissus and its relevant cults), see Greco 2011:476–494, whose new multi-volume topography of Athens is finally superseding Travlos 1971.

[82] Motte 1963:470.

[83] Gottfried 1993.

[84] Plutarch *Dialogue on Love* 749a.

[85] The *Phaedrus* and its landscape take center stage in R. Hunter's perceptive study of the literary reception of Plato's dialogues in ancient times (Hunter 2012). Needless to say, there are innumerable discussions of Plato's influential *locus amoenus* and its literary precedents. For a good introduction, see e.g. Thesleff 1981. On the actual topography, which seems to be accurate as well as meaningful, see e.g. Nelson 2000.

[86] πᾶσα ἡ περὶ τὴν πλάτανον διατριβὴ τὴν ἀμφιλαφῆ τε καὶ ὑψηλήν (Themistius *To Constantine the Emperor* 32b–c).

Despite some textual complications,[87] these lines, as elsewhere in Timon's verse, make a pun out of Plato's name, given that the word *platista(k/t)tos* calls to mind the name Plato.[88] The pun, moreover, is extended well into the third line. The mention of the cicadas is no doubt an allusion to the *Phaedrus* (and to *Iliad* 3.150–152).[89] At a key point in the dialogue, the cicadas singing from the plane-tree become the very subject of Plato's myth, which equates their beautiful song with the voice of philosophy.[90] At the same time, Plato's Academy was famous for its trees, and planes were a celebrated feature of its landscape.[91] We have, therefore, an implicit joke revolving around the word *platanos*, plane-tree, with its pun on Platon and *platista(k/t)tos*. Thus, the plane-tree stands for the *Phaedrus* and, more generally, for Plato's writings. This is confirmed beyond all reasonable doubt by other authors, such as Philitas, Cicero, Petronius, and Aristaenetus, who unhesitatingly associate Plato with the plane-tree of the *Phaedrus*.[92]

Was Plato himself punning on his own name? This is certainly possible, since "Plato" was soon interpreted as a nickname related to the adjective *platys*, from which the word *platanos*, plane-tree, was also derived.[93] Some scholars have put forward convincing arguments to this effect, not only in relation to the *Phaedrus*, but also to other dialogues.[94] Whatever the case may be, if this had been the perception of ancient readers, many of whom were persuaded that the *Phaedrus* was Plato's "first" dialogue, it would have been fully justified by a number of details.[95] This is not the place for a full discussion of this

---

[87] See Clayman 2009:108, with further bibliography.

[88] Cf. fr. 19 and 20 Di Marco. A similar pun on a "Platonic" fish is found in Lucian *Fisherman* 49. Lucian probably had Timon in mind (cf. Clayman 2009:107).

[89] Cf. Di Marco 1989 *ad loc.*

[90] See Chapter 3 in the current volume.

[91] See Pliny *Natural History* 12.9 and cf. Aristophanes *Clouds* 1005–1008, as well as Plutarch *Life of Cimon* 13.7, with Arrigoni 1969–1970:359. (Arrigoni discusses comparative evidence and concludes that the trees planted by Cimon in the Academy were most certainly planes.) Athena's olive-trees (μορίαι), too, were integral to the Academy's landscape from an earlier time. Besides *Clouds* 1005–1008, cf. Pausanias 1.30.2 and Anaxandrides fr. 20 PCG (which, however, simply suggests that Plato was fond of olives, cf. Diogenes Laertius 6.25). A famous mosaic from Torre Annunziata (Museo Archeologico Nazionale di Napoli, Inv. Nr. 124545), which possibly represents Platon and his followers in the Academy, includes a tree which is more likely to be an olive-tree than a plane-tree, although the latter interpretation has also been put forward. Cf. Gaiser 1980:65, who opts for an olive-tree on iconographic and chromatic grounds.

[92] See e.g. Görler 1988, Hardie 1997, Repath 2010, González Rendón 2010, and Capra 2013.

[93] For the nickname Platon, which is said to have replaced his real name, Aristocles, cf. Diogenes Laertius 3.4 with Swift Riginos 1976:35–38.

[94] Zaslavsky 1981 argues that the mention of the plane-tree in the *Phaedrus* is meant to be a pun on Plato's (nick)name. Similar puns, especially in the *Republic*, are the subject of de Boo 2001.

[95] On the *Phaedrus* as Plato's earliest dialogue, cf. Diogenes Laertius 3.38. Schleiermacher famously shared this view and construed the *Phaedrus* as a kind of introduction to the dialogues (cf. Lafrance 1992).

fascinating subject, which would have to take into account possible references to other dialogues.[96] It should at least be noted, however, that the Socrates of the *Phaedrus* is invested, quite unusually, with a kind of "authorial aura," as if he were Plato himself. At least six points are worth mentioning: first, Socrates compares himself to Plato's rival Isocrates;[97] second, he worships a *mouseion*, which calls to mind Plato's Academy and its *mouseion*;[98] third, he criticizes writing, as Plato does in his own voice in the *Seventh Letter*;[99] fourth, he apparently alludes to Plato's friend and beloved Dion;[100] fifth, he compares the philosopher to a caged bird, which closely recalls an image Plato used of himself;[101] sixth, and possibly

[96] Kahn 1996 provides a rich list and concludes as follows: "I doubt whether there is any other dialogue that shows a comparable density of self-referential reminiscences" (374).

[97] Born in 436 BCE, Isocrates was Plato's principal rival on the Athenian educational scene. The reference to him in the *Phaedrus* (278e) is the only time he is explicitly mentioned in the entire Platonic corpus, and for Plato's original readers it probably amounted to a quasi-anachronism, one that "removes" them "from the dramatic frame of the dialogue (the fifth century [BCE]) and repositions them back in the actual context of the day (the fourth century [BCE])" (Werner 2012:227). The *Phaedrus* certainly evokes Isocrates' fourth-century works. Thus, Plato's Athens, and the rivalry between the Academy and Isocrates' school, make their presence felt in some way in the fifth-century setting of the dialogue (ca. 416–410 BCE). As Michelini 2003 notes: "Isocrates is, aside from a few Socratics who appear as characters in the dialogues, the only contemporary mentioned by name in any Platonic dialogue" (5).

[98] Cf. 278b. On the Academy's *mouseion*, cf. Chapter 4 in the current volume.

[99] The *Phaedrus* is the only dialogue in the entire corpus where we find clear and sustained criticism of writing. Fixed discourse is inadequate to expressing the full potential of philosophy, and writings always risk ending up in the wrong hands. Even though the terms of the relationship are debatable (and debated: cf. e.g. Gill 1992), no other dialogue resonates so closely with what Plato states in his own voice in *Letter 7*: philosophy as such cannot be written, and Plato expresses his disappointment that allegedly "Platonic" writings might have been circulated beyond his control (cf. 341b–e and 344a–e).

[100] At 250b, Socrates recalls the moment "when with a happy company they saw a blessed sight before them—*ourselves* (ἡμεῖς) following with Zeus, others with different gods—and were celebrated." Ancient and modern commentators have taken this striking, emphatic switch to the first person plural as a self-reference on Plato's part (cf. e.g. Hermias p. 186.3–4 Lucarini-Moreschini and de Vries 1969 *ad loc.*). This impression is reinforced by the way Socrates, a few pages later, expands the point (252e): "And so those who belong to Zeus seek that the one they love should be someone like Zeus" (Διὸς δῖόν τινα εἶναι ζητοῦσι). Wilamowitz 1920:537 suggested that this must be a kind of *señal*, pointing to Plato's beloved Dion. The point is further developed by Nussbaum 1986:229, who notes that Dion's name resonates with Phaedrus', since "both mean 'brilliant' or 'sparkling.'" At first this may seem very speculative, but there is another important passage to be taken into account. At *Timaeus* 41a Plato borrows a very similar pun on Zeus' name from Hesiod (*Works and Days* 2), as Regali 2010 has shown. It may be worth mentioning that the famous epigram to Dion (*Palatine Anthology* 7.99), quite possibly the only authentic one among those ascribed to Plato (see Bowra 1938 and Ludwig 1963), refers to Plato's madness as a result of his longing for Dion.

[101] Cf. *Phaedrus* 249e, προθυμούμενος <u>ἀναπτέσθαι</u> ... <u>ὄρνιθος δίκην βλέπων</u> ἄνω). An extraordinarily close parallel is provided by a passage from *Letter 7*, in which Plato describes his captivity in Syracuse in an unusually emotional tone (cf. Brisson 1993:45): he is like a caged bird, gazing out and yearning to fly away (348a, ἐγὼ μὲν <u>βλέπων</u> ἔξω; <u>καθάπερ ὄρνις</u> ποθῶν ποθὲν <u>ἀναπτέσθαι</u>).

most important, he describes philosophy as both an oral and a *written* enterprise, a description that fits Plato, but is totally inappropriate for someone like Socrates, who never wrote anything.[102] These points, all together, would have given Plato's readers the impression that Plato was coming very close to breaking the dramatic illusion and revealing his authorial identity.

So much for the *Phaedrus'* self-referential quality. I shall now deal with the theme of inspiration, which, given that Plato is after all the author of the *Phaedrus*, is wholly consistent with its "authorial aura." In the *Phaedrus*, Plato has Socrates deliver his famous palinode, whereby he seems to rehabilitate divine madness over and against mere *tekhnê*. Madness can take various forms: divination, purification, poetry, love.[103] Although his primary focus is *eros*, Socrates rehabilitates them all. It should also be noted that the boundaries between the four forms are rather blurred. After all, Socrates' palinode is an offer to Eros, even though it takes the form of a "hymn" or "myth" ostensibly divining supernatural realities and purifying Socrates of his sins against the Gods.[104] These four instances of madness, moreover, are well conveyed by Socrates' suggestion that the "divine landscape" (*theion topon*) is making him equally "divine" (*theion*) and prone to "nympholepsy," an idea that is rendered through a strange and rare word (*nympholêptos*), but which is later expressed in plainer language. Socrates now feels "enthusiastic," completely at the mercy of the nymphs, and the dialogue concludes with Socrates' celebrated prayer to "Pan and all you gods of this place."[105]

The earliest instance we have of someone described as *nympholêptos* is from a late fifth-century graffito from a cave sacred to Pan and the nymphs on the slopes of mount Hymettos.[106] The present study does not allow for a full discussion of the question, but nympholepsy, in the light of some recent studies, may be seen as both a literal experience (being snatched by the nymphs) and, more frequently, as a particular form of divine possession resulting in a "heightened fluency and awareness, a concentration of faculties, an elevation of expression, and ultimately the reorganization of personality into a new identity and a new

---

Remarkably, in the *Phaedo* Socrates compares himself, as a servant of Apollo, to the god's dying swans (84e–85b), and the association between Plato and Apollo's birds was later to become proverbial (cf. Swift Riginos 1976:9–32).

[102] Cf. 278b–e. I develop this point in Chapter 4 and in the Conclusion.

[103] Cf. 244a–245c, where Socrates discusses *mantikê*, *telestikê*, and *poiêsis* and hints at love, the fourth kind of madness that is amply discussed in the following pages. *Telestikê* is described only briefly and is not mentioned specifically until much later in the dialogue (249d).

[104] Cf. e.g. 247c, 257a–b, 262d.

[105] 279b. For nympholepsy, cf. 238c–d with 241e. Also cf. Carter 1967, who argues that "Plato paints a portrait of Socrates as possessing in himself all four types of divine madness" (118).

[106] See Schörner and Rupprecht Goette 2004 for a full discussion of the relevant material and Chapter 2 of Pache 2011 for a more concise presentation.

social role."[107] As such, it is explicitly linked with practices of divination and purification, as expressed through the medium of lofty poetry or as in erotically charged contexts. This takes us back to the *Phaedrus'* four kinds of madness.

Socrates' palinode is, then, a multifaceted, multilayered text that reflects the complexity of its cultural background. Unsurprisingly, it is nigh impossible to pin down its topic by way of a straightforward definition, and the same is true of the entire dialogue. More than any other Platonic work, the *Phaedrus* defies definition,[108] which is why Derrida was so fond of it, since it provided him with such fertile ground for his deconstructive exercises.[109] Crucial questions remain open: What is the *Phaedrus* about? Is it about love, or rhetoric? Or maybe both? But then what is the relationship between the two? Ever since the scathing remarks of Norden, who found the *Phaedrus* wholly deficient in clarity and force,[110] the unity of the dialogue has been the subject of endless interest and discussion. This, in turn, has led scholars to compare modern and ancient notions of unity.[111] Here is not the place to resume the debate.[112] Suffice it to say that, once more, the problem would benefit more from a circular than a linear approach. By the end of the dialogue we learn that true love inspires true rhetoric, and that true rhetoric is achieved only when addressed to a beloved soul. Thus, true rhetoric is erotic and true *eros* is rhetorical, in what would seem to be a full circle. Apparently, the *Phaedrus* is carefully constructed so as to stimulate lateral thinking by means of an extraordinarily *dense* textuality, as if its intention were to defy the inevitable linearity of writing and thus provide an internal antidote to Socrates' devastating critique of written speech within the *Phaedrus* itself. Few would doubt that such density is the result of a quintessentially poetic technique, which results in hardly any meaning being simple or univocal.

---

[107] Connor 1988:58. On nympholepsy, see also Pache 2011. Calasso 2005 provides an illuminating, if idiosyncratic, discussion of the literary sources, and Caillois 1987 provides fascinating comparisons with modern lore. Görgemanns 1993 rightly points to a number of passages in which the *Phaedrus* presupposes nympholepsy.

[108] Cf. e.g. Ebert 1993.

[109] Derrida 1972. In a similar fashion, the *Phaedrus* has also encouraged the kind of self-contained scholarship one finds in a well-known and pleasant book such as Ferrari 1987, in which the author avoids straightforward argumentation, philological engagement with the text, and historical contextualization in an attempt to "live for a while within the environment of a single dialogue" and "to sit on the grass and breathe its special atmosphere" (Ferrari 1987:ix).

[110] Norden 1923:112.

[111] I am referring to the lively exchange between C. Rowe and M. Heath that took place in the 1980s. See Rowe 1986 and 1989, and Heath 1989.

[112] For a recent account, cf. e.g. Giannopoulou 2010 and Werner 2007. I expressed my own views on the unity problem in Capra 2000. Among works specifically devoted to this problem, the most recent one I am aware of argues that the *Phaedrus'* "two parts consider two methods of soul-leading, love and rhetoric, and the dialogue as a whole asks how either or both can be successful in directing the soul towards truth and the good life" (Moss 2012:3).

Poetic density, then, is a crucial factor in the dialogue. But to what extent is Plato engaging with poetry? Here is a crucial question that can tell us much about how Plato perceived his own work and, ultimately, about his deepest concerns as a writer and philosopher eager to reform society. According to Andrea Nightingale, the *Phaedrus* is quite exceptional among Plato's dialogues in that "it abandons the notion that traditional genres of poetry and rhetoric are inherently 'unphilosophical.'"[113] On the one hand, Plato "actively" attacks Lysias:[114] he "imposes his will upon an alien genre," so that he "is the active party," the alien text being "the passive victim."[115] Thus, Lysias' speech is delivered in full by Phaedrus only to be dismantled by Socrates.[116] On the other hand, however, Nightingale argues that elsewhere in the *Phaedrus* Plato "assumes a more passive stance, thus allowing the alien genre to play an active and relatively autonomous role in his text."[117] Nightingale refers to such an attitude as a sort of "alliance" or "conspiracy," and focuses on two important instances: the tragic story of Palamedes which provides the background to Socrates' narration of the invention of writing, and lyric poetry as a crucial, positive element in Socrates' palinode. As for the latter, Socrates is quite literally dealing with sources, since his whole speech is inspired by both the divine landscape and by the "streams" (*namata*) provided by earlier poets, who, as he says, fill his breast "like a vessel."[118] Socrates mentions Sappho, Anacreon, Stesichorus, and Ibycus, and quotes them often, more or less explicitly, besides other sources.[119]

Except for the occasional hint of irony, Plato "respects and preserves" the voice of lyric poetry: "it is precisely by leaving the genre of love poetry—with its discourse of madness, invasion, and the destruction of the boundaries of the psyche—more or less intact that Plato is able to create one of the most extraordinary paradoxes in his entire corpus: the notion that reason and madness, at a certain level, converge."[120] The result is a kind of philosophical discourse, which Nightingale labels as "authentic" since it is both inspired and erotic: it is inspired, though the inspiration is not divorced from rational thought; and it is

---

[113] Nightingale 1995:133.

[114] And possibly Isocrates, as Nightingale argues. The mention of Isocrates at the end of the *Phaedrus* (278e), however, can be interpreted in a more favorable light. See e.g. Tulli 1990 and Fermani 2000.

[115] Nightingale 1995:149.

[116] In Bakhtin's terms, as adopted by Nightingale, this amounts to quite a lot of "active double-voiced discourse" (Nightingale 1995:148).

[117] Nightingale 1995:149.

[118] 235d. Both as a physical presence and as a symbol, water takes center stage throughout the *Phaedrus*.

[119] Heitsch 1993:248–253, provides a useful, if not exhaustive, list of such sources. See now Cairns 2013:240n13.

[120] Nightingale 1995:161.

erotic, but only insofar as it lovingly addresses one particular soul (in this case Phaedrus') with the aim of triggering *from within* the recollection of the Forms and the creation of new speeches.[121] This is of course the background for Plato's celebrated image of "writing in the soul":[122] authentic *logoi* "enter into another person's soul *as seeds*; the philosopher does not hand over knowledge that is ready-made … since knowledge can only be achieved if the student rears up the seeds himself."[123] Ultimately, however, Nightingale concludes that "Plato does not offer a definition or even a description of philosophic discourse,"[124] so that the best we can do is single out its ingredients (both "active" and "passive") and focus on the philosopher instead.

Apart from her skeptical conclusion, I fully endorse Nightingale's view. Moreover, similar conclusions with regard to Plato's ultimate endorsement of (some) poetry have been drawn recently by scholars with very different approaches and agendas, ranging from the most theoretical to the most philological.[125] This is an encouraging indication that they are probably right, and my own interpretation will, therefore, take these conclusions as its premise. Some of the issues Nightingale raises will occasionally make their appearance in the four chapters that follow. For the most part, however, we shall be traversing uncharted territory. I shall argue that the *Phaedrus*, when interpreted against its cultural background, yields precisely what Nightingale found to be lacking in the dialogue: a description of philosophical discourse and its role in society, conveyed through a number of metaliterary hints and undertones that were probably as obvious to Plato's original public as they are hard to pin down for modern readers. Adjusting our eyes and ears to such tenuous clues will, needless to say, require some walking on the banks of the Ilissus.

---

[121] Cf. Chapter 2.

[122] 276e–277a. Interestingly, the image is also found in Antisthenes fr. 188 Decleva Caizzi (ἐν τῇ ψυχῇ αὐτὰ καὶ μὴ ἐν τοῖς χαρτίοις καταγράφειν). Cf. also Chrysippus fr. 83.3–5 Arnim. Mesturini 2001 points out that "il verbo γράφειν nel *Fedro* copre, dunque, una nozione positiva solo quando sia usato metaforicamente, nella locuzione 'scrivere nell'anima,' dove lo 'scrivere' paradossalmente è chiamato in realtà a indicare il suo esatto contrario, il 'non scrivere,' ossia un insegnamento condotto dal filosofo per mezzo dell'arte dialettica e basato essenzialmente sull'oralità" (117).

[123] Nightingale 1995:167.

[124] Nightingale 1995:166.

[125] Cf. e.g. Giuliano 2005 and Gonzalez 2011.

# 1

# TERPSICHORE

*To Terpsichore, the cicadas report those who have honored her in the choral
dance (τοὺς ἐν τοῖς χοροῖς τετιμηκότας), and make them dearer to her*

*Phaedrus* 259c–d

From the third frieze of the François vase, ca. 570 BC. The frieze depicts the procession of the gods to the wedding of Peleus and Thetis, including nine Muses,
all duly labelled by this graphomaniac painter.

- On the third frieze of the François vase, the names of the Muses closely match Hesiod's
  nine Muses in the *Theogony*, with one major exception: as is clear from the above image,
  one STÊSICHORÊ has "replaced" TERPSICHORÊ. This has prompted the suggestion that
  a Stesichorean performance might have influenced the depiction of the processing
  gods (see e.g. Stewart 1983 and, contra, Haslam 1991).

- Perhaps the very name STÊSICHOROS was itself a *sprechender Name* ("chorus setter"),
  the real name of the poet being TEISIAS. Such is the information provided by the lexicon Suda, s.v. "Stesichoros (IV p.433 Adler)."

- In the *Phaedrus*, Plato openly puns on Stesichorus' name: his own speech is modelled
  after STESICHORUS of HIMERA son of EUPHÊMUS: Socrates will discuss HIMEROS
  (desire) in a respectful way (EUPHÊMÔS), and he will describe the celestial CHORUSES
  and of the gods and the blessed, celestial CHOREUTÊS (cf. 247a, 250b, 252d).

# 1

# Terpsichore

## Socrates' Palinode in the *Phaedrus*

"THIS IS NOT A GENUINE *LOGOS*": here is the famous beginning of Socrates' palinode in the *Phaedrus*.[1] The false *logos* is of course Socrates' own previous speech, in which he puts forward the idea that love, and by implication a number of related phenomena, such as madness and poetry, are intrinsically bad. Socrates' words, however, are thought to reflect a more general issue—one that goes well beyond the limits of the *Phaedrus* and refers back, instead, to Plato's own philosophical development. Martha Nussbaum, for example, has adopted the phrase "This Story Isn't True" (a slightly different version of the Greek) as part of the chapter title of her lucid and influential account of the *Phaedrus* in her 1986 book.[2] In the view of Nussbaum and many others, the "false *logos*" is taken to be Plato's philosophical past, and, for these scholars, Phaedrus' and Socrates' first speech neatly encapsulates a number of features and tenets that Plato had elaborated in previous dialogues. Their argument continues with the claim that Socrates' palinode is in fact Plato's, and the *Phaedrus* itself a turning point in Plato's philosophical career: that is, he has finally found a way to accommodate the irrational element in his otherwise "Apollonean" world. Thus, the *Phaedrus* is said to stage Plato's own "recantation," since "he admits that he has been blind to something," and has set about "revising the world of the *Symposium*."[3]

Such interpretations, however brilliantly argued, fail to recognize one obvious fact: well before it became the *incipit* of Socrates' (or Plato's) recantation, "this is not a genuine *logos*" was a verse in a famous song by the melic poet Stesichorus, and, as we shall see, it is very likely that the song included both the

---

[1] Socrates utters the phrase twice, in the form of a quotation (Οὐκ ἔστ' ἔτυμος λόγος οὗτος, 243a) and as a statement of in his own (Οὐκ ἔστ' ἔτυμος λόγος ὃς ἂν ... φῇ ..., 244a).

[2] Nussbaum 1986:200–239. The full title of the chapter runs as follows: "'This Story Isn't True': Madness, Reason, and Recantation in the *Phaedrus*."

[3] Nussbaum 1986:203, 212. Another influential and lucid account of the *Phaedrus* as a transitional dialogue is that of Kahn 1996:371–392. Even Lysias' speech arguably features "Platonic" elements (cf. Trabattoni 2011, who is not a developmentalist).

*ode* and the *palinode*. Socrates, I maintain, reenacts Stesichorus' performance closely and subtly, and his two speeches are really the two halves of a uniformly inspired and performative *sunolon*. This, together with other important aspects of the Greek cultural tradition that need to be taken into consideration, suggest a rather different interpretation than that provided by evolutionary accounts such as Nussbaum's.

## Plato's Stesichorus

The core of this chapter will be a close analysis of Stesichorus' multifaceted presence *within* the Platonic text. Before embarking on it, however, I would like, very briefly, to provide some *external* evidence that may account for Plato's engagement with Stesichorus and set the background for the actual examination of the internal data.[4]

I shall begin with the most basic question, which concerns the circulation of Stesichorus' poems: was he popular and well-known during Socrates' and Plato's lifetimes? Very much so, it seems. Stesichorus was a major influence on both tragedy and comedy, which is tantamount to saying that, potentially, he was known to every Athenian.[5] His poems were widely adapted for sympotic performance, and Plato's three-line quote from Stesichorus' palinode was a favorite in Athenian symposia during the classical age.[6] It is also important to note that a number of linguistic features found in Stesichorus' poems, such as certain Dorisms from the dialect of Syracuse, suggest the existence of a Sicilian "edition" of his works.[7] In all likelihood, the edition was made possible by the patronage of Dionysius I, the tyrant of Syracuse. In the light of Plato's unfortunate visit(s) to Syracuse, this has an immediate relevance to the *Phaedrus*.

Plato, however, had even more personal (and surely more inspiring) reasons to be familiar with Stesichorus' poetry. Plato was a close friend, and possibly a pupil, of the Pythagorean Archytas of Taras, who played an important role in Plato's escape from Syracuse. By Plato's time, the Pythagoreans had developed a peculiar way of reviving epic myths, which consisted largely

---

[4]  For these general points, which are hardly ever mentioned in Platonic scholarship, I owe much to Marco Ercoles's recent, outstanding monograph: it contains a full edition and commentary of the testimonies concerning the life and works of Stesichorus (Ercoles 2013). The book, which I had the opportunity to consult before its publication, has an excellent command of the relevant literature and provides extensive references.

[5]  For Stesichorus' influence on tragedy, see Ercoles and Fiorentini 2011. For comedy, see the current chapter, below.

[6]  See Ercoles 2013:30–32.

[7]  Cf. Pavese 1972:100–101 and Cassio 1999:202–203, 207–220. Ercoles 2013:576–578 provides a learned survey, with added bibliography.

in "clearing" Homer's bloody heroes, in an attempt to turn them into morally acceptable paradigms of behavior.[8] Stesichorus, the poet who had spectacularly cleared Helen's name, suited their needs perfectly, which is why, in different stages, they manipulated the poet's biography so as to make him a protegé of the heroine.[9] The same cultural ambient was also responsible for developing Stesichorus' reputation as a fearless opponent of tyrants,[10] something that could not have failed to impress Plato after his experiences in Sicily.[11] Finally, and even more importantly, the *Phaedrus* calls the palinode "an ancient form of purification" (*katharmos arkhaios*, 243a): such vocabulary clearly calls to mind Pythagoreanism.

Plato had every reason to sympathize with Stesichorus' poetry from a musical point of view as well. To the surprise of modern readers, Plato's *Republic* and *Laws* repeatedly trace the corruption and decadence of society to the innovations of modern music, in which modes are mixed and melody eventually takes the upper hand over text. This, of course, is not an idiosyncrasy of Plato's, for the theme is well attested by a number of authors, from Aristophanes to Aristoxenus (and others).[12] Apparently, Stesichorus was a follower of the Phrygian mode,[13] which Plato approved of, and Stesichorus quickly acquired a steady reputation for his sober and austere melodies, in which the melody was firmly subordinated to the words. In this context, the following two quotations from Eupolis (ca. 446–411 BCE) are pertinent:

> Τὰ Στησιχόρου τε καὶ Ἀλκμᾶνος Σιμωνίδου τε
> ἀρχαῖον ἀείδειν, ὁ δὲ Γνήσιππος ἔστ' ἀκούειν.

> Stesichorus, and Alcman, and Simonides:
> it is outmoded to sing them, we should go for Gnesippus.

> Eupolis fr. 148 PCG, 1–2

---

8 Cf. Delatte 1915, Chapter 3 ("L'exégèse pythagoricienne des poèmes homériques"). Special attention was given to Achilles and Helen. For the latter, cf. following note. For the former, cf. e.g. the *scholium* for Homer's *Iliad* 1.66c (I p. 30 Erbse), *Iliad* 16.225 (IV p. 217 Erbse), and Detienne 1962.

9 Cf. Eustathius *Commentary on Odyssey* 4.122 (I p. 154.30–36 Stallbaum), with Detienne 1957 and Jesi 1961.

10 See Aristotle *Rhetoric* 1393b8–1394a1 (Stesichorus vs. Phalarides) and Conon FGrH 26 F 1 42 (Stesichorus vs. Gelon). Cf. Sgobbi 2003:26–37.

11 Plato's *Letter* 3 to Dionysius, which, if not genuine, is at least very close to being contemporary with Plato, ends with a quote from Stesichorus' *Palinode*, in an attempt to persuade the tyrant to abandon falsehood and embrace truth (3.319e). On this letter, cf. Isnardi Parente 2002:xxiii–xxiv.

12 Cf. e.g. Lasserre 1967, and, more recently, Pelosi 2010:29–67 ("The theory of ethos and musical mimesis"). However, the idea of a purely aesthetic evaluation of music is not completely absent from Plato's dialogues: see Rocconi 2012.

13 Cf. e.g. PMG 212, with the commentary of Ercoles 2013:596–597. For Plato's appraisal of the Phrygian mode, see *Republic* 399a–c, with Gostoli 1995 and Pagliara 2000.

δεξάμενος δὲ Σωκράτης τὴν ἐπιδέξι' ⟨ᾄδων⟩
Στησιχόρου πρὸς τὴν λύραν οἰνοχόην ἔκλεψεν.

And Socrates, receiving the song[14] from the right in relay
while singing Stesichorus to the lyre, stole the wine vessel.

Eupolis fr. 395 PCG

Given that Gnesippus was regarded as a morbid poet, it is clear that in this context Stesichorus stands for sober and austere music. We do not know why Eupolis decided to have Socrates sing a poem by Stesichorus, nor can we determine how this relates to the anecdote reported by Ammianus Marcellinus, whereby Socrates, before he died in prison, wanted to learn one of Stesichorus' poems.[15] Yet in the light of Socrates' "performance" in the *Phaedrus*—as we shall see, he reenacts Stesichorus' palinode in some way—this is surely an interesting detail.

## The Divine Turn

As I mentioned in the Introduction, inspiration is undoubtedly one of the main themes of the *Phaedrus*. At 242d–243e, Socrates suddenly feels very uneasy about the speech he delivered (to match Lysias' speech), in which he argued, as Lysias had done, that a young boy should give his favors to a "non-lover." Phaedrus thinks the speech was brilliant, but Socrates now says that it was a "dreadful, dreadful *logos*," one that foolishly went "parading itself" (the personification is noteworthy) for its capacity to deceive "a couple of homunculi" (242e). The speech was also impious, in that it offended the gods, namely Eros, in an attempt to curry favor with mortals. Socrates is ready to get up, cross the river, and walk back to the city, but his "divine voice," so he claims, prevents him from doing so. He must now purify himself with a new speech "of unsalted water" (243d). It is precisely at this point that Stesichorus comes in, as we shall see shortly. So far, Socrates has already referred to a number of inspirational sources he deems responsible for his unusual fluency. And more soon follow. Here they are, in their order of appearance:[16]

---

[14] Or possibly a cup, or some other symposiastic implement (cf. Olson 2007:235, who favors cup). This is not an important difference anyway, given the frequent metaphorical overlapping between wine and song in symposia.

[15] 28.15.

[16] Some of the items, along with other factors such as Phaedrus' role in eliciting Socrates' speeches, can be seen as "frequent disclaimers of authorial responsibility" on Socrates' part (Giannopoulou 2010:155).

1. Sappho, Anacreon, and prose writers (Socrates' bosom is "full" of them, 235c).

2. Muses (Socrates summons the Μοῦσαι ... λίγειαι to contribute to his μῦθος, 237a).

3. Landscape (it makes Socrates νυμφόληπτος, 238d).[17]

4. Nymphs (they "enthuse" Socrates ὑπὸ τῶν Νυμφῶν ... ἐνθουσιάσω, 241d).

5. Ibycus and Stesichorus (implicitly: Socrates follows their lead, 242d–243b).

6. Muses (they arouse tender souls to a Bacchic frenzy, 245a).

7. The cicadas (they can bestow upon humans the gift of the Muses, 258e–259d).

8. Local gods and Muses' prophets (i.e. the cicadas, inspiring Socrates, 262c–d).

9. Pan and Nymphs (they are superior to Lysias, 263d; cf. 278b, Νυμφῶν νᾶμά τε καὶ μουσεῖον).

Socrates' sources fall into two clear categories:[18] on the one hand, he is inspired by a number of local *numina*; on the other, by the Muses and certain poets—Socrates mentions Sappho, Anacreon, Ibycus and Stesichorus. It is important to note that two of these sources are mentioned *before* Socrates delivers his first, non-erotic speech (1, 2), one in a pause of speech shortly afterwards (3) two between the first and the second speech (4, 5), one within the second speech (6) and three after the end of both speeches (7, 8, 9). It would seem, therefore, that both speeches must be taken to be inspired, though the first, by extolling human prudence, is soon criticized as impious and non-divine. This is indeed a crucial problem, which I will discuss it in due course.

One may wonder what is the common ground, if any, between landscape and poetry. A promising starting point is the role of gardens as a favorite setting for erotic scenes.[19] This is a common feature of archaic lyric, and all four poets

---

[17] And it may result in divine inspiration, ἐπιόν. However, the meaning of ἐπιόν is disputed and is construed as either "inspiration" (e.g. Hermias p. 59.29–31 Lucarini-Moreschini and Velardi 2006 *ad loc.*) or as "incumbent danger" (e.g. de Vries 1969 *ad loc.*, Ryan 2012 *ad loc.*).

[18] Of course, the supernatural landscape also includes its own "sign" (242b–c).

[19] Motte 1973. Philip notes that the *locus amoenus* of the *Phaedrus* closely recalls the haunts of Eros as described by Agathon in the *Symposium* (Philip 1981:469). Aristophanes, too, takes for granted that "les amours naturels sont liés à la campagne" (Thiercy 1986:330), and satyr-plays, often replete with scenes of sex and rapes, are of course set in the countryside (cf. *Laws* 815c–d; along with, for example, Paganelli 1989:242).

provide striking examples of it. It would seem that Stesichorus even went so far as to recount the story of a nymph who abducted Daphnis![20] As Aelian remarks,[21] he thus initiated the bucolic genre, with a striking example of literal nympholepsy. Nympholepsy is, of course, another crucial point of intersection between inspiration and landscape: "the term *numpholêptos* ... has several possible meanings, but in this case it describes an access of poetic inspiration brought on by Socrates' surroundings."[22]

The influence of Anacreon and Sappho on Socrates' second speech is the subject of a number of studies and has been amply demonstrated: in the words of Liz Pender "Plato draws directly on the poetic language of the lyric poets, but he sets against them a need for self-control to redirect the soul's energy from physical beauty to the Forms."[23] In so doing, I may add, Plato was merely conforming to a peculiarly Athenian way of appropriating the lives of certain poets. As Paul Zanker has convincingly argued, the mid-fifth-century statue of Anacreon that stood on the Acropolis beside Pericles' father expressed the quintessentially Athenian love of beauty epitomized in Pericles' celebrated epitaph.[24] The external appearance of Anacreon, who had spent some years in Athens and was often portrayed as an Ionian debauchee,[25] was remodeled

---

[20] Cf. e.g. Ibycus 286 PMG, Sappho 2 Voigt, Anacreon 417 PMG, Stesichorus 279 PMG. The poem *Daphnis* (279 PMG) shared with the *Kalyke* and *Rhadine* (277 and 278, respectively) a romantic subject, which has been construed as a Hellenistic feature. Consequently, some scholars have rejected its attribution to Stesichorus (Page himself includes 277–279 PMG among the *spuria*). But, as Lehnus 1975 has argued, the poems also share an "esigenza religioso-etiologica" (193), and this squares well with Stesichorus' extant poetry. Even the romantic subject is far from being unparalleled in archaic melic poetry: Lehnus cites Pindar (frr. 72 and 252) and Myrtis (716 PMG).

[21] Cf. Aelian *Historical Miscellanies* 10.18 and *On the Nature of Animals* 17.37, with De Martino 1984:124–127.

[22] Larson 2001:10.

[23] Pender 2007:54; Pender 2011 is an abbreviated version. As Cornford 1950:68–80 famously pointed out, the idea that the soul is equipped with "fluxes" that can be variously channeled is typical of Plato's philosophy of *eros* as found in the *Symposium*, which can be fruitfully compared with "flux" passages such as *Republic* 328d, 485d, 588e–589a. Building on Cornford's findings, Sassi 2007 has convincingly shown that similar examples can be found in a number of dialogues, including the *Gorgias* (493a–b), the *Timaeus* (42d and *passim*), and in particular the *Phaedrus* (245c–246a), where the very vocabulary points to Empedocles and to the Hippocratic corpus (at p. 287 Sassi quotes, *exempli gratia*, *On the Sacred Disease* 7.1, *On Aliment* 1.27.2–3 and 1.35.3). Thus, Plato's flux theory in the *Phaedrus* features an interesting (and quintessentially Platonic) blend of lyric and Hippocratic motives.

[24] Zanker 1995:22–31. (By contrast, Ridgway 1998 argues against a classical date for the original statue.) In Corso's words "Athenian imperial policy clearly aimed at creating an Athenian culture which epitomized and appropriated the best of earlier Greek poetry" (Corso 2008:270, on the Athenian statues of Anacreon and Pindar).

[25] "Besides the *barbiton*, there is a variety of other features that mark the Anacreontic singer in Anacreontic vase paintings. They include (1) a long *khitôn* with a cloak or *himation* worn over it, (2) boots, (3) earrings, (4) a parasol, (5) a turban; significantly, all of these features, including (6),

to reflect the image of a noble symposiast and, as is further argued by Alan Shapiro in the light of illuminating parallels with fragments of Greek painting, of a moderate *paiderastês.*[26] By Plato's time, the Athenians had fully appropriated Anacreon,[27] both as an idealized singer and virtuous lover. This explains why Plato's Anacreon is called "the wise one" and inspires Socrates' erotic speech, and why Sappho becomes "Sappho the beautiful."[28]

It seems, therefore, that a moral concern was integral to Plato's choice of these poets, and I have already pointed out that Stesichorus had the best credentials from this point of view.[29] Both he and Ibycus are mentioned to the effect that they somehow sensed the danger of offending the gods by placing human recognition before divine favor, which is Socrates' explicit concern in the *Phaedrus.* Ibycus was probably alluded to very early in the dialogue, when Phaedrus invokes the myth of Boreas: one of his most famous poems contrasts the delightful charm of a garden with the erotic mania induced by Boreas.[30] Be that as it may, Socrates' first pang of guilt for his impious speech is expressed through the verse of Ibycus. The intervention of Socrates' *daimonion,* and the failed attempt to cross the river and return to Athens, signal a remarkable turning point (242b–d):[31] from this moment onwards, values and perspectives would be reversed, with divine concerns replacing human preoccupations. Ibycus' verse, as quoted and partly rephrased in the expression of Socrates' fear that "for offences against the gods, I win renown from all my fellow men" illustrates the point perfectly.[32] Various other authors also quote these same lines, and the relevant contexts suggest that

---

the *barbiton,* were linked with Asiatic Ionia" (Nagy 2007:240). These six features "are not only Ionian and Asiatic in theme: they are also orientalizing, even feminizing" (Nagy 2007:242).

[26] Cf. Shapiro 2012.

[27] In earlier days, "Hipparchos made the powerful gesture of sending a warship to Samos to fetch Anacreon and bring him to Athens (Pl[ato] *Hipparch[us]* 228c). This way, the Ionian lyric tradition as represented by Anacreon was relocated from its older imperial venue in Samos to a newer imperial venue in Athens. Likewise relocated was the Aeolian lyric tradition as represented by Sappho—and also by Alcaeus" (Nagy 2007:226).

[28] 235c. Note the adjective *kalos* chosen by Plato/Socrates, indicating a "serious" reception of Sappho as opposed to her presence as a character on the comic stage. On Sappho as a Muse in vase painting, see Chapter 2 in this volume.

[29] In a moment of jocund festivity due to his recovery after some episode of "academic violence" (cf. Penella 2007:69), Himerius (*Speech* 69.5–6) explicitly associates Anacreon with Ibycus and Stesichorus (and no one else), on the grounds that they too, were involved in some kind of "incident" from which they successfully recovered. As Lazzeri 2002 has shown, Himerius' passage is clearly meant to evoke Stesichorus' palinode. A similar incident was possibly part of Sappho's biographical tradition as well. (On Sappho and the rock of Leukas, see Compton 2006:102–105.)

[30] PMG 286.

[31] For the symbolism associated with the crossing of the river, and for the relevant topography in the *Phaedrus,* see Treu 2003.

[32] 242d: καί πως ἐδυσωπούμην κατ' Ἴβυκον, μή τι παρὰ θεοῖς "ἀμβλακὼν τιμὰν πρὸς ἀνθρώπων ἀμείψω" (cf. PMG 310).

biographical tradition connected them with Ibycus' proverbial renunciation of political power (a most Socratic—and Platonic—motif indeed).[33]

The quotation from Stesichorus follows immediately in a kind of crescendo:

ΣΩ. Δεινόν, ὦ Φαῖδρε, δεινὸν λόγον αὐτός τε ἐκόμισας ἐμέ τε ἠνάγκασας εἰπεῖν. ΦΑΙ. Πῶς δή; ΣΩ. Εὐήθη καὶ ὑπό τι ἀσεβῆ· οὗ τίς ἂν εἴη δεινότερος; ΦΑΙ. Οὐδείς, εἴ γε σὺ ἀληθῆ λέγεις. ΣΩ. Τί οὖν; τὸν Ἔρωτα οὐκ Ἀφροδίτης καὶ θεόν τινα ἡγῇ; ΦΑΙ. Λέγεταί γε δή. ΣΩ. Οὔ τι ὑπό γε Λυσίου, οὐδὲ ὑπὸ τοῦ σοῦ λόγου, ὃς διὰ τοῦ ἐμοῦ στόματος καταφαρμακευθέντος ὑπὸ σοῦ ἐλέχθη. εἰ δ' ἔστιν, ὥσπερ οὖν ἔστι, θεὸς ἤ τι θεῖον ὁ Ἔρως, οὐδὲν ἂν κακὸν εἴη, τὼ δὲ λόγω τὼ νυνδὴ περὶ αὐτοῦ εἰπέτην ὡς τοιούτου ὄντος· ταύτῃ τε οὖν ἡμαρτανέτην περὶ τὸν Ἔρωτα, ἔτι τε ἡ εὐήθεια αὐτοῖν πάνυ ἀστεία, τὸ μηδὲν ὑγιὲς λέγοντε μηδὲ ἀληθὲς σεμνύνεσθαι ὡς τὶ ὄντε, εἰ ἄρα ἀνθρωπίσκους τινὰς ἐξαπατήσαντε εὐδοκιμήσετον ἐν αὐτοῖς. ἐμοὶ μὲν οὖν, ὦ φίλε, καθήρασθαι ἀνάγκη· ἔστιν δὲ τοῖς ἁμαρτάνουσι περὶ μυθολογίαν καθαρμὸς ἀρχαῖος, ὃν Ὅμηρος μὲν οὐκ ᾔσθετο, Στησίχορος δέ. τῶν γὰρ ὀμμάτων στερηθεὶς διὰ τὴν Ἑλένης κακηγορίαν οὐκ ἠγνόησεν ὥσπερ Ὅμηρος, ἀλλ' ἅτε μουσικὸς ὢν <u>ἔγνω τὴν αἰτίαν, καὶ ποιεῖ εὐθύς</u>—Οὐκ ἔστ' ἔτυμος λόγος οὗτος / οὐδ' ἔβας ἐν νηυσὶν εὐσέλμοις, / οὐδ' ἵκεο Πέργαμα Τροίας· καὶ ποιήσας δὴ πᾶσαν τὴν καλουμένην Παλινῳδίαν <u>παραχρῆμα ἀνέβλεψεν.</u>

S.: A dreadful speech it was, Phaedrus, dreadful, both the one you brought with you, and the one you compelled me to make P.: How so? S.: It was foolish and somewhat impious; what speech could be more dreadful than that? P.: None, if you're right in what you say. S.: What? Don't you think Love to be the son of Aphrodite, and a god? P.: So it is said. S.: Not I think by Lysias, at any rate, nor by your speech, which came from my mouth, bewitched as it was by you. But if Love is, as indeed he is, a god, or something divine, he could not be anything evil; whereas the two recent speeches spoke of him as if he were like that. So this was their offence in relation to Love, and besides their foolishness was really quite refined—parading themselves as if they were worth something, while actually saying nothing healthy or true, in case they would deceive some poor specimens of humanity and win praise from them. So I, my friend, must purify myself, and for those who offend in the telling of stories there is an ancient method of purification, which Homer did not understand, but Stesichorus did. For when he was

---

[33]    De Martino and Vox 1996:292, 333.

deprived of his sight because of his slander against Helen, he did not fail to understand, like Homer; because he was a true follower of the Muses, *he knew the cause, and immediately composed the verses*: "This is not a genuine *logos*, / you made no journey in the well-decked ships / Nor voyaged to the citadel of Troy." And after composing the whole of the so-called Palinode *he at once regained his sight*.

Plato *Phaedrus* 242d–243b, trans. Rowe (modified)

This is a remarkable passage for many reasons. Phaedrus is still unconvinced.[34] As for Socrates, he is here adopting an anti-intellectualistic stance: his first, impious speech is emphatically labeled as *deinos*, which, given the rhetorical context, should mean something like "clever" or "terrific." This is probably how Phaedrus himself is inclined to understand it, given that he uses the very same word to describe Lysias' unmatched ability as a speech writer at the beginning of the dialogue.[35] However, as I argue more thoroughly in my Conclusion, Socrates ends up re-denoting the significance of this famously ambiguous word by emphasizing its purely pejorative meaning of "terrible."[36] Then there is also Stesichorus, whose quoted lines and purification story are equally interesting for the history of lyric poetry *per se*.

## The Palinode: Socrates' Re-Vision

Many scholars have shown interest in the lines quoted (or perhaps we should say sung) by Socrates, but only to the extent they might reveal clues to an understanding of Stesichorus. Along with Isocrates' *Encomium on Helen*, Plato's *Phaedrus* is the only classical source to inform us about this poem, or, as many believe, "poems" in the plural. Socrates' words can in fact be construed in such a way as to imply that Stesichorus wrote an earlier poem denigrating Helen of Troy (the *Helen*), and a later one designed to rehabilitate her (the *Palinode*).

In his *Encomium*, Isocrates dwells at some length on Helen's capacity to compensate Menelaus, whom she made a god forever: as Spartan traditions attest, the Spartans made sacrifice to the immortal couple as gods rather than heroes (61–63). This is where Stesichorus comes in:

---

[34] Phaedrus' remark "so it is said" echoes the very same words he had used to express his skepticism towards the myth of Boreas. Compare 242e λέγεταί γε δή and 229b λέγεταί γάρ. Few commentators have shown awareness of the sinister overtones of Phaedrus' skepticism. As Bonazzi 2011 points out, Boreas was an Athenian war hero (Herodotus 7.189, Pausanias 1.19.5), and Phaedrus' rationalism "ben si attaglia a un personaggio noto per aver profanato i misteri di Eleusi e per aver partecipato alla distruzione delle statue di Hermes" (15n20).

[35] 228a, δεινότατος ... τῶν νῦν γράφειν.

[36] The *locus classicus* for the ambiguity of δεινός is, of course, Sophocles *Antigone* 332–333.

Ἐνεδείξατο δὲ καὶ Στησιχόρῳ τῷ ποιητῇ τὴν αὑτῆς δύναμιν· ὅτε μὲν γὰρ ἀρχόμενος τῆς ᾠδῆς ἐβλασφήμησέν τι περὶ αὐτῆς, ἀνέστη τῶν ὀφθαλμῶν ἐστερημένος, ἐπειδὴ δὲ γνοὺς τὴν αἰτίαν τῆς συμφορᾶς τὴν καλουμένην παλινῳδίαν ἐποίησεν, πάλιν αὐτὸν εἰς τὴν αὐτὴν φύσιν κατέστησεν. Λέγουσιν δέ τινες καὶ τῶν Ὁμηριδῶν ὡς ἐπιστᾶσα τῆς νυκτὸς Ὁμήρῳ προσέταξεν ποιεῖν περὶ τῶν στρατευσαμένων ἐπὶ Τροίαν, βουλομένη τὸν ἐκείνων θάνατον ζηλωτότερον ἢ τὸν βίον τὸν τῶν ἄλλων καταστῆσαι· καὶ μέρος μέν τι καὶ διὰ τὴν Ὁμήρου τέχνην, μάλιστα δὲ διὰ ταύτην οὕτως ἐπαφρόδιτον καὶ παρὰ πᾶσιν ὀνομαστὴν αὐτοῦ γενέσθαι τὴν ποίησιν.

And she [Helen] displayed her own power to the poet Stesichorus also; for when, at the beginning of his ode, he spoke in disparagement of her, he arose deprived of his sight; but when he knew the cause of his misfortune and composed the Palinode, as it is called, she restored to him his normal sight. And some of the Homeridae also relate that Helen appeared to Homer by night and commanded him to make a poem on those who went on the expedition to Troy, since she wished to make their death more to be envied than the life of the rest of mankind; and they say that it is partly because of Homer's art, yet it is chiefly through her that his poem has such charm and has become so famous among all men.

Isocrates *Encomium on Helen* 64–65, trans.
Goold (modified)

It is obvious that Isocrates, like Plato, is referring here to both Homer and Stesichorus,[37] and he might equally be taken to imply that the latter composed *two* odes. The problem has been greatly complicated by the fact that a papyrus published in 1963 has the Peripatetic Chamaeleon referring to as many as two *Palinodiai*, complete with different beginnings.[38]

As far as we know, Hesiod's *Catalogue* was the first poem to mention the *eidôlon* of Helen.[39] This implies that the poet knew of a story according to which Helen never reached Troy, where the Achaeans fight for what is actually a

---

[37] As well as to the Homeridae, the performers of Homer that were supposedly Homer's biological offspring. The *Phaedrus* attributes them with two verses, though Plato may have written them himself. For opposite views, see Huxley 1960 and Labarbe 1994, and cf. below, page 46.

[38] P. Oxy. 2506 fr. 26 col. i. See below.

[39] The fragment features as number 358 M-W, i.e. among *Dubia*. However, scholars are increasingly inclined to accept it as genuine. See Brillante 2001–2002:n1. It is worth remembering that the story of Helen's *eidôlon* has clear Indian equivalents, both in its names and contents, so it cannot be considered Hesiod's (or Stesichorus') invention. See Pisani 1928, and, more recently,

phantom crafted for their ruin by the gods. So, according to one interpretation, Stesichorus assimilated and criticized both traditions: not only was Helen not in Troy (versus Homer), but she did not even leave Sparta (versus Hesiod).[40] Herodotus knew the story of the phantom, and he considered it to be true, for he believed that the Trojans would surely have returned Helen, if she had been in their hands.[41] Herodotus attributes the story to Egyptian priests, and claims that Homer knew it too, though he preferred to have Helen reach Troy so as to build a "more epic" narrative.[42] Later sources often refer either to the *Helen* or to the *Palinodia*, but, on the whole, they do not quote them together, so that one is left with the impression that the *Helen* and the *Palinodia(i)* might have been be one and the same poem divided into different sections after all.[43]

Even from my simplified account it is obvious that this is a thorny problem, the sources being "both confused and confusing."[44] It is no wonder, then, that classicists have been hotly debating it for decades, with an impressive array of arguments and fine scholarship. Were there one, two, or three poems? And was it a Spartan or otherwise Doric audience, with its own particular performative and political mindset, that persuaded Stesichorus to rehabilitate Helen?[45] The

---

Skutsch 1987. Helen and her *eidôlon* can be construed as the feminine counterpart of Helen's twin brothers (cf. Bettini and Brillante 2002:74–75).

[40] Bowie construes Stesichorus' twofold invocation to the Muses as criticism of Homer and Hesiod "for being misled by false utterances of the Muses" (Bowie 1993:25). Cf. also Brillante 2001–2002:23.

[41] Herodotus 2.112–120.

[42] Herodotus 2.116. This is part of a broader strategy, designed to provide a paradigm polemically at variance with the epic tradition (cf. Nicolai 2012).

[43] "Yet it is noticeable that neither of the two later sources who refer to the *Helen* by name (Athenaios and the author of the *argumentum* to Theokritos 18) ever cite the *Palinode*, and the same is true *mutatis mutandis* of the very much larger group of authors who cite the *Palinode* but not the *Helen*" (Kelly 2007:13).

[44] Blondell 2013:119.

[45] Cf. Massimilla 1990 for a very lucid *status quaestionis*. More abundant material is found in Constantinidou 2004, which provides an unparalleled amount of information about Herodotus, and in Vasilescu 2004, who, interestingly, sees the palinode as a reaction to the story of the Doric invasion of the Peloponnese. Many scholars have argued that either Locri or Croton commissioned Stesichorus to write the palinode, on the grounds that the best known version of the story of Stesichorus' healed blindness is associated with that of Leonymus (cf. e.g. Pausanias 3.19.11–13; Conon FGrH 26 F 1 18), the general from Croton who was allegedly wounded in the battle of Sagra and then healed by Ajax and Achilles on the island of Leuke (where he *also* met Helen, who asked him to inform Stesichorus of the real reasons for his blinding). However, Sgobbi has provided conclusive evidence that the legend of Leonymus took shape under the influence of Pythagoras, that is to say, in the first half of the sixth century BCE, and ended up including Stesichorus only on the eve of the battle of Himera (Sgobbi 2003:480), when Croton and Himera formed an alliance against the Doric league. The palinode certainly fits in very well with the Pythagoric reinterpretation of the Homeric heroes, so that it is easy to see how Stesichorus' story was connected to Leonymus' story. Consequently, "il fatto che il collegamento di Stesicoro con la saga di Leonimo sia secondario e non possa risalire ad una 'fase originaria' di essa, fa

evidence has proven inconclusive, and a clear consensus has yet to be reached. However, in 1989 David Sider suggested a different approach.[46] In his view, both Plato and Isocrates evoke a highly *performative* context: this consists of Stesichorus (or another performer adopting his persona) rising up at the end of a song that heaped slander upon Helen, as if deprived of sight; then, after addressing and rehabilitating Helen with a revised song, the performer would, very theatrically, pretend to recover his sight, his palinode thus becoming quite literally a form of "re-vision."[47] This interpretation is consistent with a detail that is very hard to explain otherwise: according to Socrates, Stesichorus composed his palinode "immediately" and recovered his sight "at once" after composing "the whole of the palinode," that is, possibly, at the end of it. The "immediate" creation of the quoted lines would seem to indicate a performance, as does Isocrates' hint that Stesichorus "went blind at the beginning of the ode" and then "arose."[48]

Of course, no interpretation of this kind can possibly settle the number of Stesichorus' poems conclusively. As some scholars have suggested, what was once a single song might later have circulated in the form of two, or even three, distinct poems.[49] A reverse scenario is also possible: Stesichorus might have composed two or three separate songs, which at some point he (or some other performer) stitched together in a highly spectacular performance, possibly for the benefit of a Doric audience. Nor should one exclude intermediate solutions such as that put forward by Adrian Kelly, whose main argument is that a single composition by Stesichorus, possibly divided into "two hymnodic 'segments'"

---

cadere tutta una serie di ipotesi che legavano la composizione della *Palinodia* ai fatti accaduti lungo le rive della Sagra ed il contenuto di essa alle leggende sorte intorno a quegli avvenimenti" (Sgobbi 2003:17, with bibliography).

[46] Sider 1989.

[47] I owe the pun to Bassi 2000:18. On the (pre-)theatrical nature of Stesichorus' compositions, see Ercoles 2012.

[48] To this I might add that Isocrates' reference to Stesichorus' "standing up" suggests a typical rhapsodic gesture, one which could be reconstructed in the light of two passages from Lucian (*Encomium on Demosthenes* 17.4–14) and Synesius (*Letter* 5 p. 18.1–6 Garzya). Moreover, the staging of the blinding probably influenced the production of Sophocles' *Thamyras*: according to Pollux (4.141), Thamyris' mask had one sightless and one functioning eye, which suggests that the Muses struck him blind on stage (see e.g. Meriani 2007; of course, one also thinks of Oedipus, although in Sophocles' play the blinding takes place offstage). This may well have contributed to a revival of Stesichorus' performance.

[49] According to Arrighetti 1994, it is highly unlikely that Stesichorus got to know the Spartan version of Helen's myth at some point in his life, i.e. when he had already composed the *Helen* along traditional lines. According to Plato the poet proceeds to the Palinode "right away" (εὐθύς), which implies that he knew this very famous story (especially for the Dorians) from the very beginning. Arrighetti endorses Sider's interpretation, and thinks the poem eventually circulated in two books (*Helen* and *Palinode*, as it were).

in the rhapsodic manner,[50] was devoted to Helen's epiphany, prompting Stesichorus' poetic persona to rehabilitate her (note the "apostrophizing" character of the quoted lines).[51]

Stesichorus' poem would, then, have followed a common pattern, according to which "each composition is driven by an encounter in which the poet-narrator appears as a character referring to a (generally) past episode, but one contained *entirely* within the current poem."[52] As so often happened, this, in turn, would have given rise to the biographical tradition of an alleged exchange between Stesichorus and Helen, and at the same time would have provided material for the likes of Chamaeleon, who "may well have been the first critic to separate the hymnody for biographical reasons, but was not necessarily right to do so."[53] Whatever the number of poems, Sider's and Kelly's "performative" interpretations are more than plausible: their explanations are convincing, and a performance involving spectacular gestures (Sider) and Helen's epiphany (Kelly) constitutes a very attractive argument.[54] As we shall see, a close examination of the *Phaedrus* cannot but confirm their hypothesis, and this kind of reconstructed performance on the part of Stesichorus would shed light on a number of otherwise inexplicable details in Plato's dialogue.

As already mentioned above, a debate has been raging among classicists, many of whom are primarily interested in Stesichorus, and who, therefore, tend to read Plato and Isocrates only insofar as they provide clues for a reconstruction of the *Realien* of Stesichorus' poetry. So what about Platonists then? The almost esoteric tone of many philological discussions has not helped them and, to make matters worse, Platonists seem to have no interest whatsoever in Stesichorus' role in the *Phaedrus*.[55] The result of this mutual incommunicability

---

50   Kelly 2007:1.

51   According to Costantinidou, the "'apostrophizing' character of the *Palinode* ... does not function for creating emotional effect or highlighting its theme, as most apostrophes do in Homer according to modern critics, but by addressing Helen Stesichoros seems to validate and justify his poetry through her" (Costantinidou 2004:174).

52   Kelly 2007:6. Another attractive viewpoint is that put forward by Bowie, who claims that "what Chamaeleon said ... was not that Stesichorus composed two Palinodes, but that the Palinode had two beginnings (*archai*), or, as Aristides 33.2 puts it, a second prelude (*prooimion*)" (Bowie 1993:24).

53   Kelly 2007:18.

54   And certainly one that squares well with what we know about Helen cults in Sparta. As Constantinidou notes: "Herodotos' story [6.61.2–5, cf. Pausanias 3.7.7] according to which in the sixth century [BCE], and most probably in his time, Helen was worshipped in Therapne for the possession of powers of attributing beauty to ugly human beings, especially to young girls, nearly coincides with the period when tradition said that with similar powers she inflicted Stesichoros with blindness because he had accused her for running away to Troy" (Constantinidou 2004:187).

55   Some of them have discussed the relationship between the *Phaedrus* and Isocrates' *Encomium* (see e.g. Burger 1980:118), whereas the study of Stesichorus as quoted in the *Phaedrus* has had only

is that scholars tend to see Plato's quotation from Stesichorus as a mere embellishment, with the tacit assumption that it has no bearing on the interpretation of the *Phaedrus*.[56]

## Socrates' Performance

It is important to interpret Socrates' strange gestures from a performative point of view, and in the light of Stesichorus' song, for he covers his head in a veil, ostensibly out of shame,[57] before delivering his first "impious" speech:

> ἐγκαλυψάμενος ἐρῶ, ἵν' ὅτι τάχιστα διαδράμω τὸν λόγον καὶ μὴ βλέπων πρὸς σὲ ὑπ' αἰσχύνης διαπορῶμαι ... "ἄγετε δή, ὦ Μοῦσαι, εἴτε δι' ᾠδῆς εἶδος λίγειαι, εἴτε διὰ γένος μουσικὸν τὸ Λιγύων ταύτην ἔσχετ' ἐπωνυμίαν, 'ξύμ μοι λάβεσθε' τοῦ μύθου, ὅν με ἀναγκάζει ὁ βέλτιστος οὑτοσὶ λέγειν, ἵν' ὁ ἑταῖρος αὐτοῦ, καὶ πρότερον δοκῶν τούτῳ σοφὸς εἶναι, νῦν ἔτι μᾶλλον δόξῃ."

> I shall speak with my head covered, so that I can rush through my speech as quickly as I can and not lose my way through shame, from looking at you ... "Come then, you Muses, clear-voiced (*ligeiai*), whether you are called that from the nature of your song, or whether you acquired this name because of the musical race of the Ligurians, 'take part with me' in the myth which this excellent fellow here forces me to tell, so that his friend, who seemed to him to be wise even before, may seem even more so now."

> Plato *Phaedrus* 237a–b, trans. Rowe (modified)

---

limited appeal for scholars interested in literature as opposed to philosophy. See e.g. D'Alfonso 1994 and Demos 1999, discussed below.

[56] Of course, a large number of Plato's citations from the poets do amount to mere embellishments, as opposed to others that may be labeled "integral." (see Tarrant 1951, who offers a very useful survey). According to Halliwell 2000, "we need to consider Plato's specific citations in relation to a double model of meaning as, on the one hand, grounded in internal context, and, on the other, modified by a further interpretative act of application or appropriation" (Halliwell 2000:101). Both authors stress how blurred the boundaries between these modes often are. For my purposes, it is important to remember that some quotations, like that from Euripides' *Antiope* in the *Gorgias* (484e–486d), can be fundamental for the argument of a given dialogue. See Nightingale 1995:67–92. Capra 2007a makes the further point that the *Gorgias* also presupposes Eubulus' parody of the *Antiope*. See also Tarrant, who argues that "a particular kind of anti-intellectual argument, or anti-intellectual rhetoric ... did have a place in public debate in the Athens of the late 420s, and for very good reasons" (Tarrant 2008:20).

[57] Douglas Cairns has explored the cultural meanings of the gesture of veiling in ancient Greek culture (see most recently Cairns 2009, with added bibliography).

Thus, the beginning of the "impious" speech features, among other things, Socrates covering his head, and his no less curious invocation to the Muses.

On the subject of this curious head covering, Marian Demos makes the important point that "the legend that Stesichorus lost his sight because of his defamation of Helen is analogous to Socrates' lack of vision during the speech he delivers with his head covered ... Immediately before delivering his palinode, which is intended as an apotropaic gesture, Socrates uncovers his head. When in reality he regains his vision (at 243b6–7), he simultaneously regains his figurative sight into the true nature of love."[58] This makes perfect sense provided we replace "legend" with "performance." Socrates' delivery of his two speeches is clearly analogous to Stesichorus' performance, and Socrates, it may be added, goes so far as to ask Phaedrus for directions, as if he were a blind man ("where is my boy, the one I was talking to?").[59]

It is also significant that Socrates, just before launching into his palinode, draws attention to his *daimonion*, which has prevented him from leaving the scene before "making expiation" (ἀφοσιώσωμαι) towards the god.[60] As we know from "Plutarch" (*On Music*), singers of hymns "make expiations (ἀφοσιωσάμενοι) to the gods as they wish" and then "move immediately (εὐθύς)" to the poetry of Homer and other poets.[61] This corresponds perfectly to the "performance" of Socrates, who makes expiation and then, at the beginning of the palinode proper, adopts the persona of Stesichorus, who, says Socrates, "being *mousikos* immediately (εὐθύς) composed the verses" of the palinode. Socrates is precise enough even to specify the details where his own performance departs from Stesichorus'. This is what he says immediately after quoting the poet's lines:

ἐγὼ οὖν σοφώτερος ἐκείνων γενήσομαι κατ' αὐτό γε τοῦτο· πρὶν γάρ τι
παθεῖν διὰ τὴν τοῦ Ἔρωτος κακηγορίαν πειράσομαι αὐτῷ ἀποδοῦναι
τὴν παλινῳδίαν, γυμνῇ τῇ κεφαλῇ καὶ οὐχ ὥσπερ τότε ὑπ' αἰσχύνης

---

[58] Demos 1999:70.

[59] 243e. I owe this observation to Pieper 2000 (originally published in 1962): "'Where is that boy?' Socrates asks, like a blind man calling for his companion. At the same time, however, he means the boy he addressed earlier. Moreover, he is speaking not as himself, Socrates, but as another; a perfidious deceiver. 'Where is that boy I was talking to? He must listen to me once more, and not rush off to yield to his non-lover.' Strictly speaking, neither the boy who guides the blind man, nor the one to whom the previous blasphemous speech was directed, is meant; the one actually meant, but not mentioned by name, is Phaedrus! And Phaedrus, at once understanding, plays along: 'Here he is, quite close beside you, whenever you want him'" (Pieper 2000:44).

[60] Plato has Socrates use this verb only here and in the *Phaedo* (60e–61a). This is a highly significant fact, as I argue in my Conclusion.

[61] *On Music* 1133b–c τὰ γὰρ πρὸς τοὺς θεοὺς ὡς βούλονται ἀφοσιωσάμενοι, ἐξέβαινον εὐθὺς ἐπί τε τὴν Ὁμήρου καὶ τῶν ἄλλων ποίησιν. δῆλον δὲ τοῦτ' ἐστὶ διὰ τῶν Τερπάνδρου προοιμίων. Cf. Power 2010:187.

ἐγκεκαλυμμένος ... Καὶ γάρ, ὦγαθὲ Φαῖδρε, ἐννοεῖς ὡς ἀναιδῶς εἴρησθον τὼ λόγω, οὗτός τε καὶ ὁ ἐκ τοῦ βιβλίου ῥηθείς.

So I shall follow a wiser course than Stesichorus and Homer in just this respect: I shall try to render my palinode to Love before anything happens to me because of my slander against him, with my head bare, and not covered as it was before for shame ... for you see how shameless the speeches were, this second one and the one which was read from the book.

Plato *Phaedrus* 243b–c, trans. Rowe (modified)

After this, Socrates elaborates briefly on the shamelessness of both speeches, which, he explains, would be suitable for a gathering of vulgar salesmen. Consequently, he now needs to "wash out their salty taste," and to this effect he pretends to address the same beautiful boy as before in the flesh, preparing to utter the speech that belongs not to Phaedrus, but "to Stesichorus son of Euphemus, of Himera, and it must go like this, 'this is not a genuine *logos*'" (243e–244b).

It is worth noting the very strong emphasis on Stesichorus' role, which makes Socrates' remarks all the more meaningful. He actually informs us that he is introducing a variant in Stesichorus' performance by regaining his sight even *before* delivering his palinode. As no commentator has failed to notice, Socrates makes a pun on, or partly makes up, the poet's name: Stesichorus, namely the "chorus setter," son of "Euphemus," that is "speaking respectfully," and born in "Himera," which sounds like Passionville,[62] thus prefiguring the crucial role of passion (*himeros*) in the palinode. This brings to mind a suggestion put forward by Francesca D'Alfonso, who claims that Stesichorus' "musical" nature, unlike Homer's lack of it, points to the capacity of oral, "topical" discourse to adapt itself and address the expectations of the audience, as opposed to the fixed forms of speech (written or not) exemplified by what can be described as the monumentalization of Homer's poems.[63] This idea is consistent with what Alexander

---

[62] As Nussbaum 1986 concisely renders it (211). It is no coincidence that Socrates, at 251c, etymologizes the word *himeros*, and later, at 265b, claims to have sung Eros "respectfully" (*euphemôs*). Note, moreover, that according to Suda, "Stesischorus" was also a nickname (s.v. ... ἐκλήθη δὲ Στησίχορος, ὅτι πρῶτος κιθαρῳδίᾳ χορὸν ἔστησεν· ἐπεί τοι πρότερον Τισίας ἐκαλεῖτο), and that Plato's punning might be even more extended, involving the—real—name of Phaedrus too (cf. Nussbaum 1986:472n23). Cf. Ercoles 2013:282–282 for a detailed discussion.

[63] D'Alfonso 1994:172. Needless to say, I have no intention of entering into the hotly debated question of Homer's text in the late archaic and classical age: whether, and to what extent, it was written or oral. For my purposes, it is sufficient to refer to it as a fixed text. See e.g. Cassio 2002, with further bibliography, who allows for the possibility that both oral and written phenomena were responsible for the fixation of the text that "was regarded as sacrosanct" (132).

Beecroft refers to as Stesichorus' "revenge of the epichoric." As summarized by Beecroft himself, this means that an examination of the vocabulary found in the lines quoted by Socrates "shows that the language ... is carefully chosen to situate Stesichorus' work in opposition to epic and Panhellenic versions of the story of Helen."[64]

I believe that the foregoing arguments, put forward by Demos, D'Alfonso, and Beecroft, all together constitute more than sufficient grounds to doubt whether Plato ever meant his quotations to be embellishments. On the contrary, Stesichorus, whether his poems were originally choral or cytharodic,[65] fully resonates with three essential elements of the *Phaedrus*: namely, Socrates' strangely "theatrical" behavior, the opposition of oral versus fixed or written, and an unparalleled emphasis on local setting and related myths.[66] I would venture to say that, besides "resonating," they help us to understand a number of facts, and, in particular, Socrates' otherwise puzzling behavior. The second and third points are more complex, but I should like to point out in passing that the opposition between Stesichorus' local flexible song and Homer's fixed Panhellenic poetry is a neat summation of what scholars have being arguing about on more theoretical grounds. Namely, that what is at stake in the *Phaedrus* is not an opposition between oral and written speech as such, but one between the erotic, "local," flexible discourse of philosophy, capable of adapting itself and taking into account the true nature of the addressee by sowing "seeds" in his soul, and the fixed anonymous discourse of traditional rhetoric, incapable of a true relationship with the soul of the addressee and passively absorbed by way of memorization.[67]

## Socrates vis-à-vis Stesichorus: Verse and Muses

In what follows, I shall try to unravel a number of hitherto unrecognized threads that tie Socrates' performance—allow me to call it that now—even more closely

---

[64] Beecroft 2006:47.

[65] Plato emphasizes Stesichorus' "choral" name, but this is not the place to revive once again this debated issue (is Stesichorus' poetry choral or cytharodic? Power 2010:234-243, from a "choralist" perspective, provides a recent and informed discussion). For my purposes, it is sufficient to admit, as a minimal requirement, that a chorus must have been involved in performances of Stesichorus' poems at least as a *dancing* chorus, as is the case with Demodocus' performance in the *Odyssey* (see D'Alfonso 1996, part 2, for a survey of the relevant scholarly positions and cf. the sensible point made by Ercoles 2012:5, namely that "nel caso dei coreuti che accompagnavano Stesicoro è verosimile pensare ad una maggiore integrazione tra canto e danza").

[66] In other words, Stesichorus has a *structural* impact on the *Phaedrus*. Interestingly, the same is true for Euripides, whose *Phoenician Women* are structurally influenced by Stesichorus' so called *Thebaid* (cf. Ercoles and Fiorentini 2011).

[67] Cf. e.g. Trabattoni 1994:48-99 and Nightingale 1995:166-168.

to Stesichorus'. And, as is only fitting, I shall start with the Muses. Thanks to the two-palinode papyrus, we now know the beginnings of what were probably two hymnodic sections of the poem:

[μέμ-/φεται τὸν Ὅμηρο[ν ὅτι Ἑ-/λέ]νην ἐποίηcεν ἐν Τ[ροίαι/καὶ οὐ τὸ εἴδωλον αὐτῆ[c, ἔν/τε τ[ῆι] ἑτέραι τὸν Ἡcίοδ[ον/μέμ[φετ]αι· διτταὶ γάρ εἰcι πα-/λινωιδ⟨ίαι δια⟩λλάττουcαι, καὶ ἔ-/cτιν ⟨τ⟩ῆ⟨c⟩μὲν ἀρχή· δεῦρ' αὖ /τε θεὰ φιλόμολπε, τῆc δέ·/χρυcόπτερε παρθένε, ὡc/ἀνέγραψε Χαμαιλέων· αὐ-/τὸ[c δ]έ φηc[ιν ὁ] Cτηcίχορο[c/τὸ μὲν ε[ἴδωλο]ν ἐλθεῖ[ν ἐc/Τροίαν τὴν δ' Ἑλένην π[αρὰ/τῶι Πρωτεῖ καταμεῖν[αι·

(in one Palinode) he blames Homer because he put Helen in Troy, not her phantom; and in the other he blames Hesiod: for there are two different Palinodes, and the beginning of one is "Hither again, goddess, lover of song and dance" and of the other "Golden-winged maiden," as Chamaeleon wrote. Stesichorus himself says that the phantom went to Troy while Helen remained with Proteus

P. Oxy. 2506 fr. 26 col. I, trans. Campbell =<br>PMGF = PMG 193.2–16

Predictably, both beginnings feature an invocation, although the second one is probably directed to a Siren rather than to a Muse.[68] Now, let us have a second look at the beginning of Socrates' speech:

<u>ἄγετε δή, ὦ Μοῦcαι</u> ... "<u>ξύμ μοι</u> λάβεcθε" τοῦ μύθου

*Come then, you Muses*, clear-voiced (*ligeiai*) ... "take part *with me*" in the myth

Plato *Phaedrus* 237a, trans. Rowe (modified)

A number of details should be noted here. To begin with, the mere fact that Socrates is summoning the Muses, though not unique,[69] sounds surprising to modern, as well as to ancient, ears: one has only to recall the amusing commentary provided by Dionysius of Halicarnassus, who depicts himself quietly reading the *Phaedrus*, lulled by the serene rhythm of the prose, until Socrates' lofty invocation strikes him as a bolt from the blue, making him jump out of his

---

[68]  As Cerri 1984–1985 has argued, on the grounds that golden wings were appropriate for a siren, but not for the Muses.

[69]  E.g. *Euthydemus* 275c–d, *Republic* 545d–e, cf. *Timaeus* 27c. The meaning and import of these more or less jocular invocations is not always easy to pin down.

skin.[70] Remarkably, Socrates does not ask for a full revelation, but limits himself to a request for cooperation: he expects the Muses to help him along with his performance ("with me"). Now, *this* is surely unparalleled in Plato, and, indeed, very rare elsewhere.[71] On the other hand, Stesichorus' *Oresteia* also began with precisely the same request for cooperation:

Μοῖσα σὺ μὲν πολέμους ἀπωσαμένα μετ' ἐμοῦ

*Muse*, leaving aside wars and *with me* ...

Stesichorus 210.1 PMG

Stesichorus' request is striking, and it is no surprise that it was remembered: Aristophanes echoes it in the *Peace* (774–779), a sure indication that it was widely known to Athenian audiences.

The epithet *ligeiai* is another remarkable feature: this is the only place in extant classical prose to feature the adjective *ligus*, and Socrates emphatically provides a twofold etymology of this word. The form *ligeia* is rare even in poetry, except in epic, where it modifies mainly the lyre in the archaic period. Very occasionally *ligeia* modifies the Muse(s),[72] but no pre-Hellenistic poet, including epic and tragic, uses it more than once in this way. No one, that is, except Stesichorus,[73] in whose scanty fragments it appears *twice* with reference to the Muses.[74] At this point, a pattern starts to emerge, because Socrates' strange invocation is beginning to look more and more like a curious concoction of Stesichorean mannerisms. That Plato's intention was to create a kind of Stesichorean pastiche is confirmed, I believe, by the conclusion of Socrates' first speech, the manuscript text of which, as printed by Burnet, is as follows:

ταῦτά τε οὖν χρή, ὦ παῖ, συννοεῖν, καὶ εἰδέναι τὴν ἐραστοῦ φιλίαν ὅτι οὐ μετ' εὐνοίας γίγνεται, ἀλλὰ σιτίου τρόπον, χάριν πλησμονῆς, ὡς λύκοι ἄρνας ἀγαπῶσιν, ὡς παῖδα φιλοῦσιν ἐρασταί.

---

[70] *On the Style of Demosthenes* 7.9–19. Cf. Aristotle *Rhetoric* 1408b12–20, referring to irony as the hallmark of poetic style in the *Phaedrus*.

[71] In fact, it is paralleled, only partially and much later than Stesichorus, in the verse of two very innovative poets: Timotheus (in the *Persians* 202–205) and the Simonides (in the late *Elegy for Plataea* fr. 11.21 W²) Note that both were in fact describing historical, rather than mythical, facts, and so it was of course much easier for them to dispense with a full revelation.

[72] E.g. Homer *Odyssey* 24.62.

[73] And the *Homeric Hymns*, if one considers them to be the work of one and the same poet. *Ligeia* modifies a Muse in four minor Hymns, thus providing some evidence for Kelly's suggestion that Stesichorus' poetry might be hymnodic in character (Kelly 2007).

[74] PMG 240 and 278.1.

So these, my boy, are the things you must bear in mind, and you must understand that the attentions of a lover are not a matter of goodwill, but of appetite which he wishes to satisfy: *just as wolves love lambs, so is lovers' affection for a boy.*

Plato *Phaedrus* 241c–d, trans. Rowe (modified)

The very last words of Socrates, as reported by the manuscripts (ὡς λύκοι κτλ.) feature a quasi-hexameter, though Socrates actually claims he is now uttering *epê*, epic verses.[75] Accordingly, recent editors, with some support from indirect tradition,[76] tend to prefer a slightly different text, which results in a complete hexameter:[77]

ὡς λύκοι ἄρν' ἀγαπῶσ', ὡς παῖ<u>δα</u> φιλοῦσιν ἐρασταί

just as wolves love the lamb, so is lovers' affection for a boy

This hexameter line is irregular in that the word παῖδα breaks the rhythm in an unusual position (violation of Hermann's bridge).[78] Interestingly, Socrates will later quote two lines allegedly taken from the repertoire of the Homeridae, one of which features precisely the same violation.[79] Somewhat paradoxically, then, the very irregularity of the hexameter has been construed as yet one more reason for preferring the indirect tradition to the non-hexametric text of the manuscripts, as if the crafting of slightly irregular hexameters were some kind of jocular "signature" on the part of Plato.[80]

In my view, none of these arguments—indirect tradition, Socrates' uttering of *epê*, self-conscious violation of Hermann's bridge—is even remotely persuasive. Firstly, the indirect tradition is clearly inconsistent. This seems to

---

[75]  241e. Socrates says he is now uttering epic verses (*epê*) rather than dithyrambs.

[76]  "ἄρν' ἀγαπῶ' Hermias 61,26 Bekker ἄρνα φιλοῦσιν Hermias 61,7 Stephan. ἄρνα φιλεῦσ' Hermog." (Apparatus from the 1985 Belles Lettres edition by C. Moreschini.)

[77]  For example, Yunis 2011, the author of the recent yellow-and-green Cambridge commentary, claims that "it is certain ... that Plato composed a hexameter verse for this spot" (*ad loc.*). Cf. also e.g. Hackforth 1952 *ad loc.* and de Vries 1969 *ad loc.*, with further bibliography.

[78]  The violation is in fact extremely rare. By the count of Cantilena (1995:39–40), there are only sixty-six instances in Homer (= 0.24%), and it is a well-known fact that post-Homeric examples are even less frequent.

[79]  See *Phaedrus* 252b–c.

[80]  For this argument, see Labarbe who duly notes that the hexameter "est mal ficelé. Il comport, en effet, une grave irrégularité du coupe. Au 4e pied d'un hexamètre grec, s'il est un dactyle, les brèves ne peuvent être partagées entre deux mots différents" (Labarbe 1994:229). This feature is shared by the first hexameter—probably of Plato's own making—quoted at 252c (τὸν δ' ἤτοι θνητοὶ μὲν ἔρωτα καλοῦσι ποτηνόν). According to Labarbe, this is a subtle indication of parody. On the contrary, Cantilena 2007 argues that Plato would have hardly noticed what we moderns refer to as a "violation."

reflect independent attempts to create a full hexameter line in order to confirm Socrates' claim to epic inspiration.[81] The reverse scenario—a full hexameter corrupted by tradition—is very unlikely: as a general rule, the meter tends to "protect" the older wording.[82] Secondly, *epê* does not have to imply hexameters: as some authors attest, *epê* can refer equally well to the verse of Stesichorus,[83] and in Plato's *Protagoras* the word is even used to introduce a melic poem.[84] Thirdly, the parallel with the lines from the Homeridae simply backfires: by assigning them to the Homeridae, Socrates is clearly discrediting these two lines, and he even registers the shameless irregularity of one of them (252c).

In short, there is nothing wrong with the manuscripts. What are we left with, then? In my view, Socrates' closing words *do* form a complete verse anyway (ὡς παῖδα φιλοῦσιν ἐρασταί). This is precisely the kind of verse we find in Stesichorus' palinode as quoted by Socrates to introduce his second speech. Moreover, we know from Chamaeleon that this same verse marked the very beginning of Stesichorus' twofold palinode. Thus, the overall picture is as follows:

- ὡς παῖδα φιλοῦσιν ἐρασταί (last words of Socrates' first speech)

- Οὐκ ἔστ' ἔτυμος λόγος οὗτος (PMG 192.1, i.e. line 1 of palinode)

- οὐδ' ἵκεο Πέργαμα Τροίας (PMG 192.3, i.e. line 3 of palinode)

- Δεῦρ' αὖτε θεὰ φιλόμολπε (PMG 193.9–10, i.e. *incipit* 1 of palinode)

- Χρυσόπτερε πάρθενε ⟨Μοῖσα⟩[85] (PMG 193.11, i.e. *incipit* 2 of palinode)

---

[81]  Both Hermogenes and Hermias explicitly connect Socrates' claim to epic (ἔπη φθέγγομαι) with the crafting of the hexameter. The same is true for a further passage that has found no place in the editors' critical apparatus. I refer to Syrianus *Commentary on Hermogenes' Book on Types of Style*, 41–42 Rabe, reporting the hexametrical form ὡς λύκοι ἄρν' ἀγαπῶσ' κτλ. Note, moreover, that in the following passage, Aristaenetus seems to side with the manuscripts: ὡς γὰρ λύκοι <u>τοὺς ἄρνας</u> <u>ἀγαπῶσιν</u>, οὕτω τὰ γύναια ποθοῦσιν οἱ νέοι, καὶ λυκοφιλία τούτων ὁ πόθος (2.20.26–28).

[82]  This would receive further confirmation if some relationship were proved to exist between Socrates' words and a proverb that, according to the relevant Homeric scholia, underlies *Iliad* 22.263, a passage that Socrates allegedly parodies when uttering his own hexameter. A few scholia (263b) give the proverb in metrical form as follows: ἄρνα φιλοῦσι λύκοι, νέον ὡς φιλέουσιν ἐρασταί. Further material is collected in the *Corpus Paroemiographorum Graecorum* (I 268).

[83]  Cf. Heraclides Ponticus 157 Wehrli (†ἀλλὰ καθάπερ <u>Στησιχόρου</u> τε καὶ τῶν ἀρχαίων μελοποιῶν οἳ ποιοῦντες <u>ἔπη</u> †τούτοις μέλη περιέθεσαν. Cf. Power 2010:231–234) and Pausanias 9.11.2 (ἐπιδεικνύουσι δὲ Ἡρακλέους τῶν παίδων τῶν ἐκ Μεγάρας μνῆμα, οὐδέν τι ἀλλοίως τὰ ἐς τὸν θάνατον λέγοντες ἢ <u>Στησίχορος</u> ὁ Ἱμεραῖος καὶ Πανύασσις <u>ἐν τοῖς ἔπεσιν</u> ἐποίησαν). A similar misunderstanding of the term ἔπη has long prevented a correct interpretation of an epigram of Theocritus' (*Palatine Anthology* 7.664 = Gow 21 = Gow-Page 14), which I discuss in Chapter 4. For a correct understanding of ἔπη in this epigram, cf. Aloni 1984:2.

[84]  338e.

[85]  West's Supplement (cf. PMGF 193). Quite possibly, a Siren should be supplied instead of Μοῖσα: cf. Cerri 1984–1985.

These lines all share the same metrical pattern (which scans --∪∪-∪∪-x). To the ears of Plato's original audiences, then, Socrates' final words in the first speech *announced the characteristic rhythm of the palinode*, which is why Socrates calls them *epê*. Note also that the first line of the quotation (οὐκ ἔστ' ἔτυμος λόγος οὗτος) is uttered a second time by Socrates, who introduces his second speech by punning on Stesichorus' name (as we have seen) and by saying that "this is not a genuine *logos*, if it says that when a lover is there for the having one should rather grant favors to the man who is not" (244c). As such, this line stitches the two speeches together and is given a very special emphasis. Thus, a powerful Stesichorean network is at work here, insofar as the first speech ends on the very same "note" struck by the beginning of the second.

## Stesichorus' Shadow

Stesichorus' poem undoubtedly takes on board the story of Helen's phantom or *eidôlon*, according to which Helen never reached Troy, and the war was fought over a false image, "out of ignorance of the truth"—as Plato remarks in the *Republic* when he explicitly mentions Stesichorus.[86] The phantom theme is already to be found in Hesiod and is integral to Herodotus' and Euripides' accounts,[87] though Stesichorus seems to have given it a unique slant. In his version, Proteus is said to have provided Paris with a Helen-like *eidôlon* in a tablet so that, by contemplating it, he could "soothe his *eros*" after losing his (real) beloved (ἵνα ὁρῶν παραμυθοῖτο τὸν αὐτοῦ ἔρωτα).[88] If authentic, this arresting detail would be a perfect example of objectified feeling, the tablet somehow standing for Helen's haunting image. It would also account for a very strange detail in Socrates' second speech:

ἐρᾷ μὲν οὖν, ὅτου δὲ ἀπορεῖ· καὶ οὔθ' ὅτι πέπονθεν οἶδεν οὐδ' ἔχει φράσαι, ἀλλ' οἷον ἀπ' ἄλλου ὀφθαλμίας ἀπολελαυκὼς πρόφασιν εἰπεῖν οὐκ ἔχει, ὥσπερ δὲ ἐν κατόπτρῳ ἐν τῷ ἐρῶντι ἑαυτὸν ὁρῶν λέληθεν. καὶ ὅταν μὲν ἐκεῖνος παρῇ, λήγει κατὰ ταὐτὰ ἐκείνῳ τῆς ὀδύνης, ὅταν

---

[86] 586b–c.

[87] For a general discussion, see Austin 1994.

[88] *Scholium* on Aelius Aristides' *Speech* 13.131 (I p. 212 Dindorf). Cf. Brillante: "Non conosciamo altri elementi di questo racconto singolare. Anche l'attribuzione a Stesicoro resta dubbia (Page non include questo testo tra i frammenti del poeta). Apparentemente questa storia presuppone l'instaurarsi di uno scambio, in qualche modo concordato, tra Paride e Proteo, che consente al primo di rifarsi parzialmente della perdita subita con la sottrazione della donna. Non possiamo tuttavia escludere che l'autore di questa versione fraintendesse il ruolo svolto dall'immagine nell'opera stesicorea cui forse non aveva accesso e, attribuendo al termine *eidôlon* il significato di 'pittura, disegno,' immaginasse che Proteo avesse donato a Paride un'immagine di Elena a titolo di indennizzo" (Brillante 2001–2002:26–27).

δὲ ἀπῇ, κατὰ ταὐτὰ αὖ ποθεῖ καὶ ποθεῖται, <u>εἴδωλον ἔρωτος ἀντέρωτα</u>
<u>ἔχων</u>· καλεῖ δὲ αὐτὸν καὶ οἴεται οὐκ ἔρωτα ἀλλὰ φιλίαν εἶναι.

So he is in love, but with what, he does not know; and he neither knows
what has happened to him, nor can he even say what it is, but like a man
who has caught an eye-disease from someone he can give no account of
it, and is unaware that he is seeing himself in his lover as if in a mirror.
And when his lover is with him, like him he ceases from his anguish;
when he is absent, again like him he longs and is longed for, because *he
has an eidôlon as a counter-love for love*. So he calls his name and thinks he
is experiencing friendly affection rather than love.

Plato *Phaedrus* 255d–e, trans. Rowe (modified)

The whole expression "he has an *eidôlon* as a counter-love for love" (εἴδωλον
ἔρωτος ἀντέρωτα ἔχων) is rather obscure, and—what is more—the word
"counter-love" (ἀντέρως) has no real parallel: all of its very few later instances
depend on the *Phaedrus*.[89] Plato's creation, I suggest, is best explained as a
reworking of Stesichorus' *eidôlon*, that is, of an image designed to provide a
weird kind of ersatz love (note, also, the strange mention of the eye-disease,
possibly one more reference to Stesichorus).

The last point I wish to discuss extends the scope of Stesichorus' influence
beyond the boundaries of Socrates' two speeches. On the way to the plane-
tree, Phaedrus questions the credibility of the myth of Oreithyia, who was
supposedly abducted by Boreas on the banks of the Ilissus (229b–c). Socrates
famously replies that he has no time for the rationalization of myth, and that
in such matters he prefers to stick to tradition (*nomizomenon*). With characteristic pompousness,[90] Phaedrus refers to the story of Oreithyia as a "piece of
mythology" (*mythologêma*), another very rare word probably drawn from some
kind of rationalistic jargon:[91]

---

[89] Cf. de Vries 1969, on 255d8–e1: "ἀντέρως in the sense of counter-love is found only in Plato and
in his imitators; but the cognate ἀντερᾶν is found elsewhere (including Aeschylus *Agamemnon*
544). Pausanias VI 23,3 reports on altars for Eros and Anteros in Elis." However, the instances of
ἀντερᾶν that imply reciprocal love are of little or no use in determining the meaning of Plato's
strange expression.

[90] Phaedrus is subtly presented as an opinionated *maître à penser* throughout the dialogue: cf. e.g.
Griswold 1986:37.

[91] Once again, Plato's choice of words is striking: there are only two instances of the word
*mutologêma* in BCE literature (Plato *Laws* 663e and Philochorus FGrH 328 F 109 17 = Plutarch *Life of
Theseus* 14.2, in addition to the passage under discussion) and in all three cases the context is one
in which the credibility of a story is put to the test. Accordingly, it is likely to be a technical word
related to the rationalization of myths, and thus a very appropriate one for a character such as
Phaedrus. Cf. Brisson, who examines the two Platonic instances and suggests that "*mutologêma*

ἀλλ' εἰπὲ πρὸς Διός, ὦ Σώκρατες, σὺ τοῦτο τὸ <u>μυθολόγημα</u> πείθῃ <u>ἀληθὲς</u> εἶναι;

But by Zeus, Socrates: do you believe this *piece of mythology* to be *true?*

Plato *Phaedrus* 229c

Is this story true? Local myths command respect. Is that other *logos* true, i.e. the one provided by wily rhetoric? Definitely not; that is not a genuine *logos*. As scholars have often pointed out, Plato's beginnings often contain his agenda in a nutshell.[92] By triggering off the Stesichorean subtext, which will prove to be so important and far-reaching, Phaedrus' question and Socrates' reply function in precisely this way. Stesichorus casts his shadow over the whole of the first part of the dialogue, i.e. until Socrates completes his palinode to mighty Eros.

The first part of the *Phaedrus* is consistently projected on to Stesichorus' Helen poem in the form song and anti-song (palinode).[93] The resulting "song" is, in a certain sense, dialectical: Socrates' ode and palinode amount to an argument *in utramque partem*, thus providing a dialectical assessment of the treated topic, namely *eros*. Plato's "song" is also dialectical or dialogic in its being "topical," and insofar as it takes into account the nature and needs of the listener-interlocutor. Thus, the discourse of philosophy is conceptualized as a form of dialectical music. Perhaps this explains why Stesichorus too is given a strange philosophical aura. As Socrates says, "because he was a true follower of the Muses," "he knew the cause, and immediately composed the verses (ἔγνω τὴν αἰτίαν, καὶ ποιεῖ εὐθὺς): 'This is not a genuine *logos*,' [etc.] (243a). Stesichorus' ability to "know the cause" is, on the whole, a philosophical quality: thus, philosophy is "musical," and music, conversely, is philosophical.

By adopting the persona of Stesichorus, Socrates can compare unfavorably the fixed impersonal discourse of a Homer with the flexible personal speech of the lyric poet, who can "know the cause" and adapt his song accordingly. This implicit tension between "lyric" and "rhapsodic" forms of discourse becomes quite explicit towards the end of the dialogue, when Socrates makes a strange comparison in order to describe his ideal writer:

---

indicates more than the result of the action designated by the verb *muthologeô*. In Plato, this word also means that the myth in question has been subject to a labor of elaboration and/or interpretation" (Brisson 1998a:152).

[92] See e.g. Clay 1992 and Burnyeat 1997, who, however, refer to the very first words of a given dialogue. Although he does not mention *muthologêma*, Lebeck has some good points to make about the links connecting the prologue of the *Phaedrus* to the rest of the dialogue (Lebeck 1972:280–284). Nesselrath 2006 surveys Plato's use of the stem *mutholog-*.

[93] Or *psykhagôgia*, the word that Socrates will use, retrospectively, to qualify his own "performance." Cf. 261b; 271c–d and Chapter 2 in the current volume.

Ὁ δέ γε ἐν μὲν τῷ γεγραμμένῳ λόγῳ περὶ ἑκάστου παιδιάν τε ἡγούμενος πολλὴν ἀναγκαῖον εἶναι, καὶ οὐδένα πώποτε λόγον ἐν μέτρῳ οὐδ' ἄνευ μέτρου μεγάλης ἄξιον σπουδῆς γραφῆναι οὐδὲ λεχθῆναι, <u>ὡς οἱ ῥαψῳδούμενοι ἄνευ ἀνακρίσεως καὶ διδαχῆς πειθοῦς ἕνεκα ἐλέχθησαν</u>, ἀλλὰ τῷ ὄντι αὐτῶν τοὺς βελτίστους εἰδότων ὑπόμνησιν γεγονέναι ... οὗτος δὲ ὁ τοιοῦτος ἀνὴρ κινδυνεύει, ὦ Φαῖδρε, εἶναι οἷον ἐγώ τε καὶ σὺ εὐξαίμεθ' ἂν σέ τε καὶ ἐμὲ γενέσθαι.

But the man who thinks that there is necessarily much that is merely for amusement in a written speech on any subject, and that none has ever yet been written, whether in verse or in prose, which is worth much serious attention—or indeed spoken, *in the way the rhapsodes speak theirs, to produce conviction without questioning or teaching*, but that the best of them have really been a way of reminding people who know ... this is likely to be the sort of man, Phaedrus, that you and I would pray that we both might come to be.

Plato Phaedrus 277e–278b, trans. Rowe

This ideal writer, who does not take writing too seriously and who prefers "genuine *logoi*" (*gnêsious*) is of course the philosopher, as Socrates promptly remarks (278d). Thus, everything comes full circle: the "genuine" discourse of lyric-philosophy is contrasted with the "spurious" (*ouk etumos*) discourse of rhapsody-rhetoric.[94]

A second and related point is that Plato's "song" highlights a tension between current rhetoric and philosophy (or philosophical rhetoric) in such a way as to suggest a distinction between "musical" and "non-musical" arts. As I have mentioned in my Introduction, rhetoric, along with historiography and other forms of "human" (as opposed to divine) discourse, defined itself as non-musical, whereas philosophy, from the archaic period up until Plato, seems to occupy an ambiguous position as regards the divide between "musical" and "non-musical" arts. From this point of view, Socrates' "divine turn," i.e. his siding with the poets against the "cleverness" (δεινότης) of the likes of Lysias, can hardly be coincidental. Socrates identifies fixed discourse, i.e. current rhetoric, with static Homeric rhapsodies, and in so doing he adopts the persona of "musical" Stesichorus as opposed to that of "non-musical" Homer, i.e. to the fixed text of Homer as monumentalized and recited by rhapsodes. This is highly

---

94  Incidentally, by contrasting Homer to such diverse poets as Sappho, Anacreon, Ibycus, and Stesichorus, Plato comes close to "inventing" the very notion of lyric poetry, which is otherwise considered to be a modern category, unknown to the ancient writer (especially so after the seminal work of Genette 1979. *Republic* 379a is a possible exception: cf. Stanzel 2012).

significant from a cultural point of view in that it builds on the historical opposition "Rhapsodes versus Stesichorus," indeed the title of a seminal article by
Walter Burkert.[95] In the sixth century BCE, the rivalry revolved around, or even
resulted in, highly musical performances of Stesichorus' songs as opposed to the
rhapsodes' abandoning of "the element of *music* and the element of improvisa-
tion in favor of a fixed text." Thus, the rhapsodes were "ousted from the field of
music," and reacted by sticking to a fixed text to be recited, thus promoting the
first ever "separation of performer and author."[96]

Nor was Socrates' siding with "musical" Stesichorus any mere "archaeological" exercise designed to revive a long-gone rivalry. On the contrary, it had
a very contemporary relevance, as a proverb preserved in a number of sources
suggests. Here is Zenobius' version:

> <u>οὐδὲ τὰ τρία τῶν Στησιχόρου γιγνώσκεις</u>· ἐπὶ τῶν ἀπαιδεύτων καὶ
> <u>ἀμούσων</u> εἴρηται ἡ παροιμία

> "You don't even know the three by Stesichorus." The proverb is said
> about uneducated non-musical people

> Zenobius Athous I 23 Miller 351.23

Unlike other sources, which provide no context, Zenobius understands
"the three" to be a reference to the triadic structure of Stesichorus' verse. It has
been argued convincingly, however, that "the three" originally referred to three
verses sung in symposia, as other sources clearly attest.[97] The proverb may be
traced back to some Attic comedy, in which an uneducated character was ridi-
culed *precisely for his inability to sing the three lines Socrates quotes in the Phaedrus
and to take active part in the symposium.*[98]

---

[95]  Burkert 1987. Further discussion in Sbardella 2012:223–244.
[96]  Burkert 1987:53;55. Cassio 2012 argues that Stesichorus reworked Homer's text, one that—he
      claims—was already relatively fixed.
[97]  Cf. Hesychius τ 1343 (= Tb9(c) in Ercoles 2013): τρία Στησιχόρου· ἔθος ἦν παρὰ πότον ᾄδεσθαι, ὡς
      καὶ τὰ Ὁμήρου.
[98]  Here is how Ercoles reconstructs the story of the proverb: "Nell'antichità (probabilmente già a
      partire dal IV sec. a.C.) doveva essere piuttosto diffusa l'espressione proverbiale 'non conosci
      nemmeno i tre di Stesicoro?' come documentano le numerose attestazioni presso le raccolte
      paremiografiche. Il riferimento originario del detto era, con tutta probabilità, ai tre versi della
      *Palinodia* citati da Platone nel *Fedro* (243a = PMGF 192) ... una chiara prova di questa valenza origi-
      naria è fornita dalla testimonianza di Esichio ... ove si attesta che vi era un tempo l'abitudine di
      cantare durante il simposio 'i tre di Stesicoro' ὡς τὰ Ὁμήρου: è evidente che il termine da sottin-
      tendersi è ἔπη, non μέρη. La notizia, d'altronde, concorda perfettamente con quanto sappiamo
      da altre fonti ... riguardo all'uso di cantare brani delle opere del melico ... in occasioni simposiali.
      In séguito, tuttavia, venne perdendosi il vero significato dell'espressione, e la si intese riferita ai
      τρία μέρη della struttura triadica del canto (strofe, antistrofe, ed epodo), della quale Stesicoro

# Conclusions

Throughout the first half of the *Phaedrus*, Socrates identifies with pious Stesichorus and reenacts his ode-cum-palinode. A close examination of the numerous points of contact helps to shed light on both Stesichorus and the *Phaedrus*. Among other things, it adds corroborative evidence to the performative interpretation of Stesichorus' Helen poem, illuminates Socrates' theatrical behavior in the *Phaedrus*, and demonstrates the complementarity of his two speeches. A more general point also emerges: both speeches are ostensibly "inspired" and must be seen as forming a whole. The palinode should not, therefore, be read as a statement of Plato's alleged evolution from the (equally alleged) intellectualism of his early career to a more mature philosophical outlook. Rather, by reviving the opposition between Stesichorus' poetry and epic rhapsodies, Socrates is in fact exalting the virtues of philosophical discourse against the shortcomings of rhetoric. As becomes clear towards the end of the *Phaedrus*, philosophical discourse includes philosophical writing, and, given that Socrates was no writer, this can only objectify the opposition between Platonic writing and, primarily, fourth-century rhetoric.[99] Above all, in the light of what I have already argued in the Introduction, we are confronted with yet another instance of Platonic "self-disclosure." Philosophical discourse, moreover, is once again construed as a form of poetry, at least insofar as it takes the form of long speeches, as is the case in the first half of the *Phaedrus*.[100]

---

era ritenuto il πρῶτος εὑρετής. Questa è la spiegazione che si può ritrovare in Zenobio (Tb9(a)) e nella tradizione paremiografica (vd. *ad* Tb9(a)), nella tradizione S (Fozio e *Suda*: cf. Tb9(b)) e nel *Lexicon Coislinianum* ... Tale *interpretamentum* ... si sarà verosimilmente affermato nel momento in cui il detto οὐδὲ τὰ τρία τῶν Στησιχόρου γιγνώσκεις è stato incluso in un lessico ordinate alfabeticamente ed è stato lemmatizzato. Nel corso di questo processo, l'espressione τὰ τρία τῶν Στησιχόρου, conservata nella *recensio Athoa* di Zenobio, ha subito la decurtazione dell'articolo τὰ; davanti a τρία (o la sua posposizione, per es. in *Suda* t 943,3 A. = Tb9(b),4) e del τῶν pronominale davanti a Στησιχόρου (fondamentale per la comprensione del senso originario), riducendosi a τρία Στησιχόρου, il cui referente—perdutosi ormai quello originario—è stato individuato in un tratto macroscopico della produzione stesicorea, la sua articolazione strofica triadica. Questa spiegazione si è ampiamente affermata ed è stata ripresa anche nella *recensio Athoa* di Zenobio, ove pure la disposizione non alfabetica del materiale paremiografico ha fatto sì che si conservasse la forma originaria del proverbio, quella che ha permesso di risalire al suo reale significato" (Ercoles 2013:533–534). As for the comic origin, at n728 Ercoles endorses Crusius's opinion "che si tratti di una citazione estrapolata da una commedia del V sec. a.C. e divenuta espressione proverbiale. Nella commedia antica, infatti, erano frequenti i riferimenti all'ignoranza dei contemporanei in fatto di poesia arcaica" (Ercoles 2013:533n908).

99  I develop this point in the last paragraph of Chapter 4.

100  Since it culminates in a mythic hymn not devoid of a jocular element, this new moment of self-disclosure is wholly consistent with the seriocomic nature of Plato's dialogues. Presented as the charming purification of an earlier song, the palinode combines the two modes of Plato's philosophy, "purification" and "incantation," perfectly. Cf. the Introduction to the current volume.

It must be concluded, therefore, that Socrates' ode and palinode further enrich Plato's implicit description of philosophical discourse. Philosophy is clearly looked upon as a form of *mousikê*, albeit of a proto-philosophical kind: unlike Homer, Stesichorus "knows the cause" and adjusts his song accordingly. Plato, on the other hand, was perfectly aware of "the three of Stesichorus'" which were seen as the hallmark of the "musical" man.[101] Thus, *mousikê* is integral to philosophical rhetoric, which ventures to explore, much as poetry does, the invisible realms of the soul and the divine. It is also the saving grace of philosophical writing, since it makes it flexible and capable of "seeing" the needs of any given interlocutor and of adjusting itself accordingly. In Plato's dialogues, speeches are addressed primarily to specific *persons*, and only secondarily to Plato's audience. In so doing, they constantly emphasize their personal, provisional, and ultimately protreptic nature. By contrast, ordinary rhetoric, just like Homer, is notionally "blind": it results in fixed and self-contained texts, either written or oral, consumed by undifferentiated and passive audiences. Phaedrus' endeavour to memorize Lysias' speech slavishly, and his failure to question it and "know the cause," can be seen as a living embodiment of "unmusical" writing and passive consumption.

## Endnote: New "Facts"

- A complete survey of the inspirational sources mentioned in the *Phaedrus* shows that Socrates is consistently portrayed as an inspired "poet" throughout the dialogue. The palinode is no exception.

- Among his "sources," Socrates mentions four poets. According to biographical tradition, three of them, namely Anacreon, Ibycus, and Stesichorus, recovered after being involved in some kind of "incident," and a similar story was probably circulated about Sappho. As is confirmed by later

---

[101] Stesichorus, the figure who opens this chapter on the cover page, is surely an appropriate name for this Plato-Socratic Muse. The name *Stêsichorê* is unlikely to be an extemporaneous invention of Kleitias, the painter of the François vase. Regarding the names of the Muses on the vase, it has been suggested that "the observation that the variants which occur on our vase also fit the meter, practically rules out the possibility that they are just careless mistakes on the part of the vase painter. A second argument against this view is the Ionic form ... which clearly shows that this list is a faithful citation from a literary text, as was pointed out by W. Schulze ... moreover it seems more likely that such small differences between the two hexametrical lists of Muses we are dealing with, one in Hesiod and one reflected in our vase-painting, came about in a context of oral poetry rather than of copying a fixed text within the first century of its existence. If this is correct, it might even tell us something about the much discussed question of whether Hesiod invented the names of the nine Muses or not. Personally, I do not think he did, but in view of the lack of contemporary hexametrical lists ... we have no means of proving that this list reflected a tradition that was alive already before Hesiod" (Wachter 1991:108).

sources, the simultaneous mention of these poets is not coincidental, and there is evidence that Athens had incorporated the traditional biographies of some of them into the fabric of its own ideology.

- Scholars have long debated the number of poems Stesichorus devoted to Helen, given that the sources are random and contradictory. According to a recent interpretation, there was just one poem, which was delivered in the form of a theatrical performance divided into different parts (or acts) that later came to be known as distinct poems. This interpretation is consistent with a fresh and thorough reading of the *Phaedrus*:

  1. Points of vocabulary suggest that the invocation Socrates addresses to the Muses prior to his impious discourse is a Stesichorean pastiche.

  2. The final words of Socrates' first speech are in the same meter as the first of Stesichorus' palinode, as quoted by Socrates before he launches into his second (pious) speech (as such, they may hint at an unknown Stesichorean fragment).

  3. As Marian Demos has suggested, Socrates' removal of his veil before delivering his second discourse corresponds to Stesichorus' regaining of his sight in the performance of his Helen poem. At some point, Socrates even pretends to be blind and "makes expiation," which may have been the cue for the singers to start their song. Taken together, these facts suggest that Socrates is reenacting Stesichorus' performance.

  4. The whole conversation between Socrates and Phaedrus is actuated by the latter's questioning of the myth of Boreas and Oreithyia: is the "mythostory" (*mythologêma*) true? *Mythologêma* is an intellectual catchword used specifically in a context where a rationalization of myth is attempted. At the same time, it prepares us for Stesichorus' palinode, which is famously introduced by the words: "This story is not true."

# 2

# ERATO

*To Erato, the cicadas report those who have honored her in the affairs of love*

*Phaedrus* 259d

"Athens, N.M. 1260. RF hydria. From Vari. Group of Polygnotos. 440–430 (Beazley). Third quarter fifth. SUBJECT: in the center, a seated woman reading from a book roll; on the left, a companion holds out a wreath; on the right, another holds out a lyre; a third. INSCRIPTIONS: companion on the left: Νικοπολις; companion with lyre: Καλλις; the third companion is not inscribed. The reader: Σαπτως = Σαππους. On the roll, vertical on the rolled up parts: επεα and πτεροε⟨ν⟩τα. On the sheet: θεοι. ηερι|ων vac. |επε|ων v. |αρχ|ομ|αι Α|ΙΝ?ΛΎ|Ν?Τ|ΤΙ|Ν. The last word miswritten for αειδειν" (Attic Vase Inscriptions Database).

- Plato is alleged to have recognized the tenth Muse in Sappho, and composed a couplet in which he addresses Sappho as the "Tenth Muse" (*Palatine Anthology* 9.506).

- As one critic puts it, "The chelys lyre in the Polygnotan scene brings Sappho into the realm of the Muses, a compliment to her talent akin to Plato's sobriquet 'the tenth Muse'" (Bundrick 2005:101).

- Famously, the great statesman Solon, a contemporary of Sappho and an ancestor of Plato, is said to have heard a boy singing one of her songs and to have asked him to teach it to him so that he might learn it and die.

- According to Maximus of Tyre, Sappho should be regarded as the "mother" of Socrates' speech in the *Symposium*: "What else could one call the art of love of the Lesbian woman other than the Socratic art of love? For they seem to me to have practiced love after their own fashion, she the love of women, he of men. For they said they loved many, and were captivated by all things beautiful" (*Dissertations* 18.9).

# 2

# Erato

## Erotic Rhetoric: Sappho's Helen and the Plane-Tree

IN THE PREVIOUS CHAPTER, I explored the wealth of connections between the *Phaedrus* and Stesichorus' Helen poem. Another major influence was, of course, Isocrates, who is mentioned explicitly only once in the Platonic dialogues, at the end of the *Phaedrus*.[1] I shall begin this chapter, therefore, by examining the relationship between the *Phaedrus* and two prose works devoted to Helen: Isocrates' *Encomium on Helen*, and the *Helen* of Isocrates' master, Gorgias. Scholars have noticed for some time that both works are reminiscent of Sappho's Helen poem, and Plato's references to both texts seem to highlight their Sapphic overtones. These combine to create a full-fledged network of allusions pointing to Helen. This is somewhat surprising: after all, the heroine is named only once in the *Phaedrus*. However, I will argue that Helen is present in the very landscape of the *Phaedrus*, given that Plato's celebrated plane-tree seems to be designed deliberately to evoke the arboreal cult of Helen *dendritis*. It is no surprise, therefore, to find that the *Phaedrus* interacts with a number of works devoted to Helen. Of these, Sappho's Helen poem, which I believe to be integral to Socrates' palinode, has a crucial (if overlooked) role to play. It is through Sappho that the theme of memory and oblivion is put into sharper focus, with the result that Sappho's Helen becomes a part of Plato's philosophical argument. And it is through Sappho's Helen again that Plato sketches his theory of poetic inspiration, which I shall examine in more detail in Chapter 3. Helen, therefore, proves to be a key figure (a "stone guest") through which Plato merges rhetorical and lyric discourse.

---

[1] 278e–279b. The only other (passing) mention is in *Letter* 13.360c, probably a spurious work. On the other hand, there is a general consensus that the unknown character dialoguing with Crito at the end of the *Euthydemus* should be identified as Isocrates. For a persuasive attempt to reconstruct the political background of Plato's references to Isocrates in the *Euthydemus*, see Dušanić 1999.

# Gorgias' and Isocrates' Helen

It is generally agreed that the *Phaedrus* registers Plato's reaction to a number of attacks he had suffered at the hands of Isocrates: scholars have tried to reconstruct these exchanges and critiques in a number of works.[2] In addition to *Against the Sophists*,[3] scholars point to Isocrates' *Encomium on Helen* as a likely intertext for the *Phaedrus*, given that both works, with almost the same words, cite Stesichorus' *Palinode* along with Homer; both direct and reverse analogies can be adduced, moreover, as proof of some kind of relationship between the two texts.[4] When first declaring himself to be inspired (235c), Socrates also mentions "a number of prose writers" besides Sappho and Anacreon. This might point to Isocrates, and to Isocrates' master, Gorgias, whose *Helen* is the explicit model for the *Encomium on Helen*.

Gorgias' *Helen* is not really about Helen. At a certain point, Gorgias breaks off the account of her life abruptly, because, so he claims, "to tell those who know ... does not provide pleasure."[5] In fact, by Gorgias' time, Helen had already been the subject of endless discussion and countless poetic accounts,[6] and it is very clear that her myth was only the starting point for the presentation of a theory and an example of the power of *logos*. Between the striking lines of his poetic prose, we see Gorgias evoking poetic tradition: when he lingers on the beauty of war as a foil for Helen, for example, he is alluding to Sappho's celebrated juxtaposition between military and erotic beauty,[7] though he generalizes and sometimes reverses Sappho's viewpoint.[8]

Acknowledging the limits of human understanding, Gorgias starts from the premise that man is carried away by irrational forces that captivate and enslave his mind, and of these the principal one is *logos*, namely rhetoric. The *Phaedrus* shares the view that rhetoric is a force capable of captivating and enchanting a man's mind, and it seems to me that Plato goes so far as to reproduce the quadripartite argument that forms the core of Gorgias' *Helen*. Four are the irrational forms that lead Gorgias' Helen astray, and four are the divine types of madness that Plato rehabilitates in the *Phaedrus*. In fact, Plato devises a specific word

---

[2] See e.g. Asmis 1986 and Brancacci 2011, with bibliography. Cf. also Rossetti 1992: many of the shorter contributions collected in the second part of the volume address the question.

[3] See e.g. McAdon 2004 and Roscalla 1998.

[4] For a new persuasive argument pointing to *Phaedrus* 279a–b as a reply to the beginning of the *Encomium on Helen*, see Brancacci 2011:32. Heitsch 1993:257–262 makes a very strong case for "Isokrates im *Phaedrus*."

[5] Gorgias *Helen* 5.

[6] Blondell 2013, a recent and clear discussion of the relevant literary traditions, discusses Isocrates as "the last classical author to make Helen the focus of a major work" (222).

[7] Gorgias *Helen* 15–16. Cf. Pelliccia 1992:70–71.

[8] Cf. Race 1989–1990 and Pelliccia 1992.

for enchanting rhetoric, *psykhagôgia*, which comes very close to Gorgias' idea of rhetoric.[9]

Textual echoes highlight the connection between the *Phaedrus* and the *Helen*,[10] but it should also be noted that Plato's *psykhagôgia* is fundamentally related to truth, whereas Gorgias' rhetoric develops a wholly "doxastic" perspective, and, apparently, ends up denying the very possibility of truth.[11] Gorgias' *Helen* ends with the shocking remark that the whole speech is only a "game," whereas Plato's Socrates refers to his palinode retrospectively as a quadripartite game in the form of a playful hymn *not devoid of truth*. Later on, he also reminds Phaedrus of Gorgias' claim "that probabilities (τὰ εἰκότα) were to be given preference over truths" (267a), which sounds very much like a reply to the sophist.[12]

The notion of *psykhagôgia* provides us with a convenient introduction to Isocrates. Elizabeth Asmis points out that Isocrates resorts to this term when describing either poetry or Gorgias' poetic rhetoric, which he deems to be

---

[9] See 261a–b, which may reflect or reproduce Gorgias' words (cf. Buchheim 1989:148, with further references), and 271c–d. For a comparison of Gorgias' and Plato's theories of rhetoric, see Leszl 1985, who makes a strong case for their similarity, except of course for the relationship between truth and *eikos*. Cf. also Asmis 1986:156 and Tulli 2007a (on the *Menexenus*). As far as I know, however, no scholar has identified the important ways in which Gorgias' *Helen* is echoed in the *Phaedrus* (only a hint is found in Laplace 2011). Among the most recent works on Plato's *psykhagôgia*, see Peixoto 2011, who sees it as an unifying element of the dialogue, whose parts can all be "esaminate e raggruppate sotto il segno della psicagogia" (205), and Perine 2011, who advocates a sharp distinction between *psykhagôgia* and *didaskalia*, to the detriment of the former.

[10] In paragraphs 20–21, Gorgias *explicitly* summarizes the four irrational causes that led Helen astray and reveal the author's jocular attitude: 1. love (ἐρασθεῖσα); 2. speech (λόγωι πεισθεῖσα); 3. violence (βίαι ἁρπασθεῖσα); 4. divine intervention (ὑπὸ θείας ἀνάγκης ἀναγκασθεῖσα). He concludes that the encomium is jocular in character (Ἑλένης μὲν ἐγκώμιον, ἐμὸν δὲ παίγνιον). Note that in this summary the order is reversed, whereas in the actual speech (15) *eros* was mentioned as the *fourth* element (τὴν δὲ τετάρτην αἰτίαν); and note that persuasion is radically divorced from truth at 11 (πείθουσι δὲ ψευδῆ λόγον πλάσαντες) and 13 (οὐκ ἀληθείαι λεχθείς). In like manner, at *Phaedrus* 265b–c Socrates summarizes the four types of mania. The list culminates with the mention of *eros*, and Gorgias' direct influence is suggested by Socrates' combined mention of persuasion, truth, and a jocular element. (The idea of the *logos* as a game is conveyed by the verb προσεπαίσαμεν, which resurfaces at 265b–c.)

[11] For this paradox, see Halliwell 2011b:266–284. Valiavitcharska 2006 offers a different interpretation, whereby Gorgias is in fact committed to *orthos logos* rather than to deceptive *doxa*.

[12] Such a reference would hardly be surprising: scholars have argued persuasively that Plato's *Apology* closely follows the blueprint of Gorgias' *Apology of Palamedes*. Cf. Calogero 1957 (featuring no fewer than nine important parallels), Coulter 1964 (who interprets Plato's imitation as polemical), Barrett 2001 (more nuanced—Plato evokes the "traditional" Palamedes as well as that of Gorgias). For Gorgias' *Palamedes* as a subtext for Plato's *Phaedrus*, see Nightingale 1995:149–154. Finally, it should be noted that the opposition between "philosophical" truth and sophistic "probabilities" (εἰκός) is possibly a malicious distortion on the part of Plato, who may be deliberately misinterpreting the original meaning of εἰκός. See Kraus 2006.

cheap.[13] On the other hand, his own *Encomium* is no more informative about Helen, who is apparently "almost incidental to Isocrates' program."[14] Paragraphs 1–15 serve as a self-congratulatory introduction, whereby Isocrates criticizes the writings and methods of other authors or thinkers, including his master Gorgias.[15] Paragraphs 16–38 are devoted to Theseus, who eventually gives way to Helen's other suitors, and to Paris in particular. There is also some brief mention of the Trojan War, seen as the archetypal divide between East and West, Greeks and barbarians (39–53).[16] Paragraphs 54–60 are concerned with beauty. Not until the last paragraphs does Helen take center stage (61–69), when Isocrates, like Plato, cites Stesichorus' *Palinode*. Unlike Plato, however, Isocrates glosses over Stesichorus' criticism of the epic tradition: Homer is cited immediately after Stesichorus, and, astonishingly, receives honorable mention as a poet inspired by Helen herself.

Two things should be noted about Isocrates' treatment of Helen. Firstly, as is clear from the paragraphs devoted to beauty, Helen is by and large a symbol: she stands for the ultimate goal of all human striving. Secondly, her presence is probably stronger than it seems, since Isocrates, like Gorgias, echoes the time-honored tradition of praise and blame that had pursued Helen down the ages. This background is taken for granted and only occasionally alluded to. The *Encomium* begins by criticizing those who "have grown old" asserting a number of implausible things, and Plato is unmistakably included among these "old" men. They are described as follows:

Εἰσί τινες οἳ μέγα φρονοῦσιν, ἢν ὑπόθεσιν ἄτοπον καὶ παράδοξον ποιησάμενοι περὶ ταύτης ἀνεκτῶς εἰπεῖν δυνηθῶσι· καὶ καταγεγηρά-κασιν οἱ μὲν οὐ φάσκοντες οἷόν τ' εἶναι ψευδῆ λέγειν οὐδ' ἀντιλέγειν

---

[13] "Plato uses the noun, *psykhagôgia*, only in the *Phaedrus*; but the verbal form occurs in two other dialogues. In the *Laws* (909b), he plays on the basic sense of 'conjuring' souls of the dead to add to it the notion of 'beguiling' the living; and in the *Timaeus* (71a) he uses the verb to refer to the beguilement of the desiring part of the soul by means of images. His contemporary and rival, Isocrates, uses the verb to describe the effect of poetic devices on the listener. In *Evagoras* (10), he points out that poets can 'charm' their listeners with beautiful rhythms and harmonies even though their diction and thoughts may be poor; and in *To Nicocles* (49), he remarks that rhetoricians who wish to 'allure' their listeners must use the crowd-pleasing device of myth, just like the poets. Gorgias did not use the term, as far as we know. But it is well suited to convey his notion that speech has the power to effect 'most divine' deeds, as attested by poetry and magical incantation" (Asmis 1986:156; cf. Pizzone 2009).

[14] Edmunds 2011:22. Yet Gorgias' Helen possibly stands for Rhetoric, which would make her integral to Isocrates' work.

[15] Cf. Papillon 1995–1996.

[16] Unsurprisingly, Aristotle criticized the unity of Isocrates' *Encomium* (*Rhetoric* 1414b24–28), which can be described as an attempt "to praise Helen via an *encomium* of Theseus, or even on the basis of Theseus' opinion on her" (Constantinidou 2008:105).

οὐδὲ δύω λόγω περὶ τῶν αὐτῶν πραγμάτων ἀντειπεῖν, <u>οἱ δὲ</u> διεξιόντες ὡς ἀνδρία καὶ σοφία καὶ δικαιοσύνη ταὐτόν ἐστιν καὶ φύσει μὲν οὐδὲν αὐτῶν ἔχομεν, μία δ' ἐπιστήμη καθ' ἁπάντων ἐστίν, <u>ἄλλοι δὲ</u> περὶ τὰς ἔριδας διατρίβοντες τὰς οὐδὲν μὲν ὠφελούσας, πράγματα δὲ παρέχειν τοῖς πλησιάζουσιν δυναμένας. Ἐγὼ δὲ ...

Some say that it is impossible to say, or to gainsay, what is false, or to speak on both sides of the same questions; *others* that courage and wisdom and justice are identical, and that we possess none of these as natural qualities, but that there is only one sort of knowledge concerned with them all; and *still others* waste their time in captious disputations that are not only entirely useless, but are sure to make trouble for their disciples. *But as for me, I* ...

Isocrates Helen 1–2, trans. Norlin

It has been rightly suggested that this incipit, with its very emphatic *Priamel*, is meant to recall one of the most celebrated beginnings in Greek literature.[17] Once again, I am referring to Sappho's Helen poem which presents the same structure: "Some say (*hoi men ... phais*) ... (*hoi de*) on foot ... still others (*hoi de*) borne but I say (*ego de*)," etc. As no reader of Isocrates can fail to remember, the ensuing stanzas focus on Helen as a living proof of Sappho's tenet. Similarly, Isocrates postpones the mention of Helen, who is ostensibly the subject of his speech.

It is well known that literary beginnings tend to display what Gian Biagio Conte refers to as a "rhetoric of imitation,"[18] and are thus densely intertextual, both as echoing texts (they allude to other works, particularly to their beginnings) and as echoed subtexts (they are likely to be remembered and alluded to by other authors). When Isocrates attacks those who "have grown old" thinking that "courage and wisdom and justice are identical," he is no doubt referring to Plato's Socrates and to his famous "unity of the virtues" thesis.[19] It is not surprising that Plato's only mention of Isocrates in the *Phaedrus*, and indeed in his whole *corpus*, also includes a precise reference to the beginning of the *Encomium on Helen* and its somewhat rude attack on those who "have grown old":

<u>νέος ἔτι</u>, ὦ Φαῖδρε, Ἰσοκράτης· ὃ μέντοι μαντεύομαι κατ' αὐτοῦ, λέγειν ἐθέλω ... οὐδὲν ἂν γένοιτο θαυμαστὸν <u>προϊούσης τῆς ἡλικίας</u> εἰ περὶ

---

[17]  See Tulli 2008b:93. According to Pelliccia 1992, Herodotus and Gorgias also interacted with Sappho's *Priamel*. Later imitations include Plato *Lysis* 211d–e, Synesius *Hymn* 9.20–24, *Anacreontea* 26. Cf. Yatromanolakis 2007:256n392.

[18]  Conte 1986.

[19]  And to the *Protagoras* in particular. See e.g. Tulli 2008b and Brancacci 2011.

αὐτούς τε τοὺς λόγους, οἷς νῦν ἐπιχειρεῖ, πλέον ἢ παίδων διενέγκοι τῶν πώποτε ἀψαμένων λόγων, ἔτι τε εἰ αὐτῷ μὴ ἀποχρήσαι ταῦτα, ἐπὶ μείζω δέ τις αὐτὸν ἄγοι ὁρμὴ θειοτέρα· φύσει γάρ, ὦ φίλε, ἔνεστί τις φιλοσοφία τῇ τοῦ ἀνδρὸς διανοίᾳ.

Isocrates is *still young*, Phaedrus, but I'd like to say what I prophesy for him ... there would be no surprise, *as he grows older*, if in the very speeches that he works at now the difference between him and those who have so far undertaken speech-writing were greater than that between man and boys ... for there is innately *a philosophy of sorts* in the man's mind.

Plato *Phaedrus* 278e–279a, trans. Rowe (modified)

The point about Isocrates' age is an amusing and telling one. By the time the *Phaedrus* was in circulation, Isocrates, who completed his last, and almost longest, speech in his late nineties, was in all likelihood known as a persistent coffin dodger, still busy reshuffling his self-congratulatory writings in an attempt to please new patrons.[20] From another point of view, however, the remark on Isocrates' "youth" sounds like a pointed reply to the orator's attack in the *Encomium on Helen*.

It would appear, then, that the two most obvious parallels between the *Phaedrus* and the *Encomium* are both closely associated with Helen and poetry.[21] Not only does Plato echo Isocrates when he cites Stesichorus' palinode to Helen, but he also alludes to the beginning of the *Encomium*, where Isocrates interacts with Sappho's Helen poem. Moreover, Plato's seemingly marginal mention of Stesichorus, as we have seen in the first chapter, amounts to a full-fledged appropriation of Stesichorus' Helen poem(s).[22] Something similar happens with Sappho, but before I try to assess her far-reaching presence in the *Phaedrus*, I

---

[20] This is precisely the allegation we find in the *Letter to Philip* by Plato's nephew Speusippus, who succeeded his uncle as head of the Academy. In his attack on the *Philippus*, which Isocrates composed in his early nineties, he ridicules Isocrates' self-congratulatory statements about his lucidity in old age and harshly criticizes him for dedicating basically the same speech, with minor adjustments, to Agesilaus, Dionysius of Syracuse, Alexander the Thessalian, and, finally, to Philip himself. *Panathenaicus* 1–38 is, by and large, a self-serving (and unusually lengthy) introduction designed to discredit Isocrates' opponents. Astonishingly, Isocrates claims he will resume his argument in a *future* speech (*Panathenaicus* 34).

[21] Cf. also *Phaedrus* 261b, with the commentary of Heitsch 1993:260.

[22] This is all the more important because—as Belfiore 2011 has shown for the *Symposium*—the ability to quote contextually and critically, as opposed to the use of quotation as mere embellishment, is the very hallmark of Socrates, who, in this as in other respects, triumphs over any other speaker. Belfiore argues that Plato emphasizes Socrates' superiority over his table companions "by means of each speaker's use of literary quotations and allusions." (166). Cf. Most 1994. The opposite, anti-contextualist approach was of course the rule, especially for Homer: cf. Ford

would like to dwell further on the role of Helen. As in the case of Stesichorus, Plato mentions the heroine only once in the *Phaedrus* (243a), though a network of allusions makes her presence very much felt. Not only does Helen "haunt Socrates' second speech," as Nicole Loraux has perceptively noted,[23] she is somehow *physically* present in the *Phaedrus* too, as I shall try to demonstrate.

## Helen's Tree

As I mentioned in the previous chapter, Isocrates reminds his reader that Helen was the object of special devotion in Sparta:[24]

Καὶ τούτοις ἔχω τὴν πόλιν τὴν Σπαρτιατῶν τὴν μάλιστα τὰ παλαιὰ διασῴζουσαν ἔργῳ παρασχέσθαι μαρτυροῦσαν· ἔτι γὰρ καὶ νῦν ἐν Θεράπναις τῆς Λακωνικῆς θυσίας αὐτοῖς ἁγίας καὶ πατρίας ἀποτελοῦσιν οὐχ ὡς ἥρωσιν ἀλλ᾽ ὡς θεοῖς ἀμφοτέροις οὖσιν.

And I can produce the city of the Spartans, which preserves with especial care its ancient traditions, as witness for the fact; for even to the present day at Therapne in Laconia the *people offer holy and traditional sacrifices to both Menelaus and Helen, not as to heroes, but as to gods.*

Isocrates *Helen* 63, trans. Norlin

Isocrates goes on to mention Stesichorus' blindness, the palinode, and Helen's dream-epiphany, whereby, according to some of the Homeridae, she commanded Homer to celebrate the heroes of Troy "to make their death more to be envied than the life of the rest of mankind" (64–65).[25]

---

1997. Socrates' superiority also prevails in relation to other competing genres, as Sider 1980 has demonstrated brilliantly.

[23] "Helen haunts Socrates' second speech: 248c2 (allusion to Adrasteia, epithet for her mother, Nemesis); 251a (the beautiful face of the young boy is, like that of Helen, of divine aspect and, like her face, makes one shudder); 252a (leave everything for the beautiful object, as Helen in Sappho fr. 16 Campbell); 252d (make the beloved into an *agalma*), etc." (Loraux 1995:314n3).

[24] Scholars, especially after Martin West's study devoted to "Immortal Helen" (1975), tend to assume that Helen was the object of a divine rather than heroic cult, a view that has recently been questioned by Edmunds, with regards to the passage from Isocrates (Edmunds 2011) and in other respects (Edmunds 2006–2007). Cf. Nagy 2008, who points out that "in the wording of Herodotos (9.120.3) concerning the hero cult of Protesilaos and in the wording of Pausanias (9.39.12) concerning the hero cult of Trophonios, there are references to the cult hero as a *theos* 'god' in the context of imagining him in an afterlife" (Nagy 2008:259).

[25] Isocrates recalls Helen's divine power again at 66, where he goes on to pan-Hellenize Helen's divine status by including wealthy and cultivated "philosophers" in the cult (i.e. the likes of Isocrates himself, presumably).

Plato seems to have no time for Helen's cultic status as described by Isocrates. One striking detail, however, does prompt second thoughts. The plane-tree of the *Phaedrus* is somehow personified, as Phaedrus' words make clear in the following passage:

οὔκ, ἀλλὰ καὶ δὴ λέγω· ὁ δέ μοι λόγος ὅρκος ἔσται. ὄμνυμι γάρ σοι <u>τίνα</u> <u>μέντοι, τίνα θεῶν</u>; ἢ βούλει τὴν πλάτανον ταυτηνί; ἦ μήν, ἐάν μοι μὴ εἴπῃς τὸν λόγον ἐναντίον αὐτῆς ταύτης, μηδέποτέ σοι ἕτερον λόγον μηδένα μηδενὸς μήτε ἐπιδείξειν μήτε ἐξαγγελεῖν.

No I shall [say it]; and it'll be an oath. I swear to you—but *by whom, by whom among the gods?* What about this plane-tree here?—I swear that if you don't make your speech in her very presence I shan't display or report to you any speech of anyone's ever again

Plato *Phaedrus* 236d–e, trans. Rowe (modified)

The plane-tree is referred to, surprisingly, as a divinity.[26]

In Greek terms, the quasi-personification of the plane-tree can only be read as an instance of the very common idea that trees (always feminine in Greek) stand for, or are the embodiment of, divine creatures.[27] On the island of Lesbos, an inscription mentions a nymph called Plataneis,[28] but even more interesting is the fact that *platanê* seems to have been a Spartan word for nymph.[29] Now, the first example of the word "nymph" in Greek literature appears in *Iliad* III, where it is used to summon Helen herself.[30] Similarly, in what is clearly an echo from *Odyssey* 15.171–178, Stesichorus refers to Helen as a *nympha*.[31] Nor is this all. Pausanias informs us of another Doric tradition in Rhodes, where, after being

---

[26] This oath was bound to become famous, even notorious, and although it is actually uttered by Phaedrus, was used over and over again as evidence of Socrates' alleged (im)piety. References can be roughly divided among accusatory or otherwise aggressive (e.g. Lucian *Sale of Creeds* 16.2), apologetic (e.g. Philostratus *Life of Apollonius* 6.196), and neutral (e.g. Lucian *Icaromenippus* 9.3).

[27] This is also reflected in literary sources: cf. e.g. Callimachus *Hymn* 6.38, Apollonius Rhodius 4.1312. Of course, such associations are typical of many cultures: cf. e.g. Schröder 1953–1954, who provides ample, though disparate, material on trees and cults in different cultures and at different times. Despite its title, *Die Platane am Ilissos*, the book has hardly anything to say about the *Phaedrus*. The most informative work on the Greek cult of trees is still the impressive, and almost forgotten, *Baumcultus der Hellenen* by K. Bötticher (1856).

[28] IG XII 2,129. For the connection of the inscription with the Trojan War (see below), cf. the learned and lucid study by Curbera and Galaz 1995:154–155, with further bibliography.

[29] *Scholium* on Lycophron's *Alexandra* 1294 (πλᾶτιν καὶ πλατανας, πλατῖδας καὶ λῖνας δαγῖλας τὰς νύμφας καλοῦσι Λάκωνες, Κύπριοι καὶ ἕτεροι). This and other data on plane-trees are largely taken from an analysis of all the instances of plane-trees in Greek literature as given by TLG.

[30] Homer *Iliad* 3.130. Needless to say, the word *nympha* can mean very different things in different contexts. Cf. e.g. Andò 1996 and Larson 2001 (Chapter 1, "What Is a Nymph?").

[31] See PMG 209.1 (νύμφα ... Ἑλένα), with Frame 2009:610–611.

hung on a tree, Helen was worshipped as δενδρῖτις, or the goddess of the tree.[32] As for Sparta, Helen was worshipped in two places: Therapne, and, more importantly for my argument, *Platanistas*, a self-explanatory toponym.

It is interesting to note that the only plane-tree found in Homer is in the setting of the famous sacrifice in Aulis that resulted in the prodigy of the dragon.[33] The plane-tree is thus ominously associated with the Achaean expedition launched to win back Helen, and Troy itself was at a certain point associated with the Platanae, a race of nymphs haunting the destroyed city and its plane-trees.[34] Pausanias also mentions that Menelaus was said to have planted a plane-tree (an example of ersatz love?)[35] while gathering the heroes for the Trojan war.[36] Finally, Helen's iconography provides us with further evidence: a red-figure *lekythos* depicting the heroine crouching naked under a tree may represent the traditional story of her bathing,[37] while, more importantly still, a coin from Gythion seems to represent her as a tree rising between her twin brothers, the Dioscuri.[38]

What I have discussed above is surely enough to suggest that the goddess "hidden" in Plato's plane-tree could indeed be Helen. In actual fact, I regard it as no more than added confirmation of yet another crucial piece of evidence. This is a passage from Theocritus' *Epithalamion to Helen*, a poem that, according to a *scholium*, is indebted to Stesichorus' *Helen*.[39] A chorus of maidens sings the

---

[32] 3.19.11. See Wide 1893:343–345.

[33] Homer *Iliad* 2.307. As certain details (such as the religious setting, the fresh water spring, and the mystic atmosphere) suggest, the passage was probably an important model for Plato's *Phaedrus*.

[34] Cf. Murr 1969: "Am Grabe des Protesilaos, welcher zuerst unter den Griechen vor Troia gefallen war, liessen die Nymphen Platanen wachsen, welche, wo oft sie eine solche Höhe erreicht hatten, dass von ihnen aus Troia gesehen werden konnte, tertrocknet, dann aber immer wieder von neuem emporgesprossen sein sollten (Plinius *Natural History* 16.44.89; Antiphilus in *Palatine Anthology*. 7.141). Ebenso, befanden sich zu des Plinius Zeit am Grabe des Ilos neben der Stadt Troia Platanen, welche schon damals gepflantzt worden sein sollten, als die Stadt den Namen Ilion erhielt" (Murr 1969:12).

[35] On the connection, cf. e.g. Wide 1983, who mentions Menelaus' plane-tree and maintains that "Die Vergleichung mit der spartanischen Helenaplatane liegt auf der Hand" (345). Borghini 1996 connects this story with Herodotus' account of an unusual episode (Xerxes "courts" a plane-tree, 7.31). It is worth recalling that Statius, too, recounts a story in which a plane-tree stands for the loss of a beloved *nympha*, the disillusioned lover being Pan (*Silvae* 2.3).

[36] Pausanias 8.23.4.

[37] See Shapiro 2005:55–56.

[38] Chapouthier 1935:90, 149. The identification is questioned by Edmunds 2006–2007, whose laconic comment is that "despite his [i.e. Chapouthier's] assertion, it is far from certain that the object between the Dioscuri is a tree" (12n42). I am unable to confirm the identification in any way, though it seems strange that the scholars who catalogued the relevant coin, and who had no agenda other than that of cataloguing it, had no such doubts: see Mionnet 1829:233n75, and cf. Imhoof-Blumer and Gardner 1886:66n7.

[39] *Scholia on Theocritus* (*argumentum*, p. 331 Wendel). Moreover, Luccioni 1997 argues that a number of similarities between lines 29–31 of Theocritus' poem and Gorgias' Helen are best explained if one posits Stesichorus as a common source.

praises of Helen and make offers to her under a shady plane-tree (ὑπὸ σκιερὰν πλατάνιστον) near Sparta. As a crowning touch, they inscribe the plane with an appropriate name:

> γράμματα δ᾽ ἐν φλοιῷ γεγράψεται, ὡς παριών τις
> ἀννείμῃ Δωριστί· "σέβευ μ᾽· Ἑλένας φυτόν εἰμι."

> And a Doric rede be writ i᾽ the bark for him that passeth by to mark,
> "I am Helen's tree; worship me."

Theocritus 18.47–48, trans. Edmonds (modified)

Whether Helen is considered a goddess, a heroine, a pre-Greek arboreal divinity, or something else again,[40] it is quite clear that plane-trees could stand for Helen;[41] or even, as Carl Bötticher bluntly put it, the name of Helen and that of the plane-tree could be interchangeable.[42]

Isocrates' very choice to celebrate Helen in an Athenian context testifies to Helen's popularity in classical Athens. In fact, in the last decades of the fifth century the cult of Helen became wide-spread in Attica, where—according to the Athenian tradition—she was conceived by Nemesis.[43] Some time later she was certainly the object of direct worship, since "a sacrificial calendar of the fourth century BCE, carved on stone ... includes sacrifices to her together with her brothers."[44] The specifically Athenian connection with Nemesis possibly points to Helen's power to punish and reward, and it may be no coincidence that the *Phaedrus* explicitly mentions Nemesis.[45] Besides Plato's well-known philolaconism,[46] it is worth mentioning that Plato's Academy, which was famous

---

[40] I am not concerned with the thorny problem of Helen's divine status, which is of great interest, of course, for the history of religion. The debate is vast: see the very informative accounts by Bettini and Brillante 2002:43–65 and by Edmunds 2006–2007. For a concise and balanced study, with further insights and bibliography, see Frame 2009:75, 95–97.

[41] It is also interesting to note that Theocritus' poem has clear similarities with Alcman 1 PMG, which can be construed as an early testimony of Helen's cult. See e.g. Brillante 2003:185.

[42] "So lebte Helena im Baume fort, der Baum nahm das Wesen der Helena in sich auf, wie der Mandelbaum an welchen sich Phyllis erhing und wie es überhaupt für jeden Baum der Fall ist in welchen eine menschliche Persönlichkeit verwandelt oder aufgenommen wird. Hiervon bekam er den Namen der Helena und umgekehrt" (Bötticher 1856:51).

[43] On Helen's popularity in Attica, see Bettini and Brillante 2002:70–71; Edmunds 2006–2007; Shapiro 2009.

[44] Shapiro 2009:52.

[45] Under the alternative name of Adrasteia (248c).

[46] Plato's philolaconism, which can be easily inferred from the many Spartan characteristics of his *Kallipolis* as well as from the Academy's famously frugal *sussitia* (Athenaeus 4.186b) and from the principle of *homoiotês* (cf. Cherniss 1945:73–74), has recently found spectacular confirmation. A Hellenistic replica of a ca. 370–365 BCE portrait of Plato, previously believed to be a modern forgery, has been (re-)discovered, and we now know that Plato, during his lifetime, was

for its plane-trees, owed its name to Hecademus,[47] who is only known to us as the rescuer of Helen after Theseus abducted her. (As Richard Hunter has argued, the episode was most certainly included in Stesichorus' Helen poem, on which Socrates projects his palinode.[48]) In short, I believe that the plane-tree in the *Phaedrus* is a powerful symbol for Helen. As Plato's poetic (and political?) entanglements suggest, the heroine is integral to the *Phaedrus*, and with good reason. For not only is she the quintessential manifestation of beauty and *eros*, but "her association with *logos* is implicit from the beginning" of her literary career.[49] Thus, she embodies perfectly the two main themes of the *Phaedrus*.

## Plato's Sappho

As we have seen, Helen is almost physically present in the *Phaedrus*. But what about Sappho? The network of "rhetorical" connections pointing to Helen ultimately calls to mind the poetess, and Sappho is one of Socrates' explicit sources of inspiration. In what follows, I shall explore Plato's involvement with Sappho's poetry, and, more specifically, with Sappho's Helen.

Phaedrus has just finished reading aloud a clever speech by Lysias, which maintains that a beloved boy, an *erômenos*, should grant his favors to a non-lover rather than to a lover. A fan of Lysias, Phaedrus is confident that such a paradox will not fail to impress Socrates. Yet the latter has reservations and does not share Phaedrus' statement that Lysias' speech is a matchless achievement:

> {ΣΩ.} Τοῦτο ἐγώ σοι οὐκέτι οἷός τ' ἔσομαι πιθέσθαι· παλαιοὶ γὰρ καὶ σοφοὶ ἄνδρες τε καὶ γυναῖκες περὶ αὐτῶν εἰρηκότες καὶ γεγραφότες ἐξελέγξουσί με, ἐάν σοι χαριζόμενος συγχωρῶ. {ΦΑΙ.} Τίνες οὗτοι; καὶ ποῦ σὺ βελτίω τούτων ἀκήκοας; {ΣΩ.} Νῦν μὲν οὕτως οὐκ ἔχω εἰπεῖν· δῆλον δὲ ὅτι τινῶν ἀκήκοα, ἤ που <u>Σαπφοῦς τῆς καλῆς ἢ Ἀνακρέοντος τοῦ σοφοῦ</u> ἢ καὶ συγγραφέων τινῶν. πόθεν δὴ τεκμαιρόμενος λέγω; <u>πλῆρές πως</u>, ὦ δαιμόνιε, <u>τὸ στῆθος ἔχων</u> αἰσθάνομαι παρὰ ταῦτα ἂν ἔχειν εἰπεῖν ἕτερα μὴ χείρω. ὅτι μὲν οὖν παρά γε ἐμαυτοῦ οὐδὲν αὐτῶν ἐννενόηκα, εὖ οἶδα, συνειδὼς ἐμαυτῷ ἀμαθίαν· λείπεται δὴ οἶμαι

---

represented in such a way as to suggest the philolaconian practice of wrestling (see Miller 2009). Of course, this is not to deny that the dialogues, to quote the title of Monoson 2000, feature a number of "democratic entanglements" such as the philosopher's *parrhêsia*.

[47] Cf. the Introduction and Chapter 4 in the current volume.

[48] Hunter 1996:150 (and cf. PMG 190 and 191). P. Oxy. 2735, whose fragments contain the remnant of a "Spartan" poem, may be relevant here. The poem mentions the Dioscuri and the athletic contests on the Eurotas, and M. West assigned it to Stesichorus: "it must have been one of the Helen poems" (West 1969:148).

[49] Wardy 1996:25.

ἐξ ἀλλοτρίων ποθὲν ναμάτων διὰ τῆς ἀκοῆς πεπληρῶσθαί με δίκην ἀγγείου. ὑπὸ δὲ νωθείας αὖ καὶ αὐτὸ τοῦτο <u>ἐπιλέλησμαι</u>, ὅπως τε καὶ ὧντινων ἤκουσα.

SOCRATES There I cannot go along with you. Ancient sages, men and women, who have spoken and written of these things, would rise up in judgment against me, if out of complaisance I assented to you. PHAEDRUS Who are they, and where did you hear anything better than this? SOC. I am sure that I must have heard; but at this moment I do not remember from whom; perhaps from *Sappho the fair, or Anacreon the wise*; or, possibly, from a prose writer. Why do I say so? Why, because I perceive that *my bosom is full*, and that I could make another speech as good as that of Lysias, and different. Now I am certain that this is not an invention of my own, who am well aware that I know nothing, and therefore I can only infer that *I have been filled through the ears*, like a pitcher, *from the waters of another*, though *I have actually forgotten* in my stupidity who was my informant.

Plato *Phaedrus* 235b–d, trans. Jowett[50]

With its mention of Sappho and Anacreon, the passage provides an interesting litmus test for Platonic scholarship. In the past, such references to poetry as these under discussion would have either been ignored or quickly dismissed as light-hearted embellishments. Plato, it would have been argued, notorious censor of poetry as he was, must not be taken too seriously when referring to poetic authorities. But that was some time ago.

The first article specifically devoted to our passage dates back to 1966, when a distinguished scholar made the novel suggestion that "the purpose for naming these poets is to anticipate poetic reminiscences."[51] Nowadays, most readers would find such a statement amusingly unsophisticated, since a lively debate is currently being waged regarding "Plato's Sappho."[52] To mention but a few, the key issues under discussion include the following: how did the philosopher view the poetess? To what extent do Sappho's poems inform Socrates' speeches? What is the precise relationship, if any, between Platonic

---

[50]  C. Rowe construes this passage as wholly ironic (see note 54), and his translation seems to reflect his interpretation. This is why I opt for Jowett's version in this case.

[51]  Fortenbaugh 1966:108.

[52]  Along with Pender 2007 (cf. Pender 2011) and Fortenbaugh 1966, see Burnett 1979, Dubois 1985 and 1995, and Foley 1998. A similar, if much less extensive, debate revolves around Anacreon (see especially Pender 2007). A discussion of the echoes of Anacreon and other poets and writers is beyond the scope of this work. For a very useful list of Plato's possible sources, see Cairns 2013:240n13.

and Sapphic love—whatever these notions may mean? And is Plato's notion of memory indebted to Sappho's?

I shall return to this debate later. For the time being, suffice it to say that at least four poems seem to be echoed in the *Phaedrus*,[53] and that *both* of Socrates' speeches feature lyric reminiscences.[54] Ode 31 Voigt, Sappho's so-called "Poem of Jealousy," is a crucial source for Socrates' list of love symptoms (251a–b); Sappho 2, the "Ostrakon Ode," is an important precedent for the setting of the *Phaedrus*, and Sappho's *locus amoenus* has much in common with Plato's; Sappho 1, the "Ode to Aphrodite," is possibly echoed in Socrates' first speech, when he describes the lover's flip-flop (241a–b), and is again discernible in the second speech's recurrent image of the charioteer; Sappho 96, the poem expressing a girl's poignant nostalgia for Sappho's pupil Atthis, may have been the inspiration for Plato's images of natural growth in Socrates' second speech, when he describes how the lover grows wings (251b).

The question is not just one of specific echoes from specific poems. Scholars have become increasingly interested in the thematic and even philosophical links between Plato and Sappho, given also the longstanding tradition that has looked upon Sappho as a proto-philosopher, "concerned," to quote Bruno Snell's grand formulation, "to grasp a piece of genuine reality: to find Being instead of Appearance."[55] Besides love, Plato's Sapphic entanglements include the feeling for nature, the emphasis on sight, together with what may be called a visual aesthetics, and, last but not least, memory and the notion of time. All in all, the relationship between Plato and Sappho seems to be firmly established, though many points, including Plato's overall attitude towards the poetess, are hotly debated. In what follows, I shall integrate a new poem and a new subject into this debate: namely Sappho's Helen poems and oblivion as a necessary counterpart to memory.

---

[53] For a full survey, see Pender 2007 and 2011.

[54] This is not a trivial point, given that Socrates names Sappho and Anacreon before delivering his *first* speech. Thus, Rowe 1988 finds it "impossible to accept Robin's suggestion that he is already looking forward to his *second* speech" and argues that Socrates' praise of the two poets is ironic and points exclusively to the first speech, alleging that the subject of Sappho's and Anacreon's poetry is "ordinary, non-philosopical love" (151). Yet Socrates' two speeches are conceptualized as a uniformly inspired speech-act (cf. Chapter 1 in the current volume), and the evidence for lyric echoes in the second speech is overwhelming. Arguably, the poets provide both good and bad examples of love.

[55] Snell 1953:50. Philosophical interpretations of Sappho, though not as idealistic, are now common in the Anglo-Saxon world too. See e.g. Baxter 2007, who builds on the testimony of Maximus of Tyrus (18.9), and Green-Skinner 2009 on the "new Sappho" and its philosophical issues. Sappho's poems have been rightly described as "both intensely passionate and resolutely abstract" (Most 1996:34). For other references, see below. (Given the vast bibliography on the subject, my references to Sappho as a proto-philosopher are limited to the poem directly under discussion, namely Sappho 16 Voigt).

# Plato's Hymn to Memory

Socrates' palinode opens with the famous distinction between two opposed forms of madness; one good and divine, one bad and human. Here is a major innovation, which has remarkable consequences, for Socrates' vocabulary too. For example, the lover is described as astonished and overwhelmed, the Greek word being *ekplêttô*.[56] Along with its cognate *ekplêxis*, which LSJ renders as "mental disturbance," this verb is a favorite of Plato's; it conveys the basic idea that passions overwhelm and blot out human rationality. As one would expect, therefore, its Platonic usage bears very negative connotations.[57] Only in Socrates' speech and in Aristophanes' myth in the *Symposium* does the verb bear positive connotations.[58] In both cases, Plato, through the persona of an inspired speaker, deals with the subject of divinely mad love provoking a reversal of values. Aristophanes' and Socrates' lovers are similar inasmuch as their love is an exclusive, overpowering passion that obliterates all other concerns. Although there are important differences between Socrates' speech and Aristophanes' myth, divine love is apparently a "poetic" characteristic that finds its way into the fabric of Plato's philosophical discourse.

Memory is another key factor in divine madness, in that *ekplêxis* strikes the lover's mind leaving it blank, while at the same time rekindling the recollection of the Forms, which the chariot of the soul can glimpse in its journey through the hyperuranion world. On spotting a youth bearing the marks of beauty, the lover is shocked and overwhelmed. This, in turn, triggers the growth of wings and "a recollection (*anamnêsis*) of those things which our soul once saw when it travelled in company with a god" (249c). But this divine reaction is, of course, the privilege of a philosophical soul only: "for so far as it can it is close, through memory (*mnêmê*), to those things his closeness to which gives god his divinity." Other souls are struck by oblivion (*lêthê*) and are unable to recapture eternal beauty. Few souls are capable of recollection (*anamimnêskô*: twice in 249e–250a) or memory (*mnêmê* 250a). Only those who *are* capable are struck by beauty (*ekplêttontai* 250e) as by lightning (cf. 254a *opsin astraptousan*), which leaves them completely beside themselves. The lightning strikes and sparks off glimpses of their divine past, when they followed their gods dancing through the skies and visited "the plain of *alêtheia*" (truth or, perhaps, "non-oblivion").[59] Has this anything to do with Sappho?

---

[56] 250a, 255b, cf. 259b. The "Platonic" definition of *ekplêxis* is "fear caused by the expectation of something bad" (*Definitions* 415e Ἔκπληξις φόβος ἐπὶ προσδοκίᾳ κακοῦ).

[57] Pace 2008 discusses the meaning of the word in pre-Platonic texts.

[58] 192b, echoed in some way at 211d. There are about forty instances of the verb in the Platonic corpus. See Capra 2000.

[59] 248b (τὸ ἀληθείας ἰδεῖν πεδίον οὗ ἐστιν, "to see the plain of Truth where it lies").

Before attempting an answer, I would like to emphasize the concluding remarks of the passage I have been examining. With yet another reference to memory, Socrates proceeds to deal with a new topic, beauty:

Ταῦτα μὲν οὖν <u>μνήμῃ κεχαρίσθω</u>, δι᾽ ἣν πόθῳ τῶν τότε νῦν μακρότερα εἴρηται· περὶ δὲ κάλλους ...

Let this be our *token of gratitude/farewell* to memory, which has made me speak now at some length out of longing for what was before; but on the subject of beauty ...

Plato Phaedrus 250c, trans. Rowe (modified)

The very unusual expression μνήμῃ κεχαρίσθω is usually translated more or less as "thanks be given to memory."[60] The notion of gratitude, of course, is not entirely irrelevant, but the verb *khairô*, used as a device to change the subject, recalls its hymnodic usage. In the Homeric hymns, the verb is regularly used to take leave of a god and to introduce a new hymnal theme, and such usage surfaces in other genres as well.[61] One should also bear in mind that Socrates' speech is guaranteed by divine inspiration, and at a certain point it is referred to with the verb *humneô*, an explicit reference to poetry (247c). As such, the speech was considered by Menander the Rhetor as an early example of prose hymn.[62] In short, our passage can be construed as a prose hymn to Mnêmê, with a capital "M," as a goddess of Memory.

Once it has been established that Memory is being introduced as a godlike faculty, the question arises as to whether this prose hymn is consistent with Plato's overall conception of memory? Although no systematic theory of memory is discernible in the dialogues, we know that Plato carries out interesting analyses of this faculty, both as an intentional process (in the *Theaetetus*) and as a process complete with propositional content (in the *Philebus*).[63] This is understandable, because memory is a vital component of human behavior and regarded by Plato, in particular, as an important quality of the philosophical soul. Plato makes it quite clear, however, that no *tekhnê* based on empirical memory can qualify as authentic knowledge, and he is very quick to debunk any so-called knowledge

---

[60] Overall, the TLG counts six more instances of κεχαρίσθω in the whole of Greek literature. Three of them are direct quotations from the *Phaedrus* (Hermias p. 87.3 and 10 Lucarini-Moreschini; Proclus *Commentary on Plato's Republic* 1.205.22 Kroll), and the other three are quite obviously direct imitations (Ammonius *Commentary on Aristotle's De Interpretatione* p. 186.9 Busse; Simplicius *Commentary on Aristotle's Physics* IX p. 90.2 Diels; *Commentary on Epictetus' Enchiridion* p. 89.26 Dübner). The form, then, is virtually a *hapax legomenon*, although no commentary, to my knowledge, makes that point.

[61] Cf. Hesiod *Theogony* 963–965, Pindar *Isthmian Odes* 1.33; Simonides 11.19 W².

[62] See Velardi 1991.

[63] See Cambiano 2007.

based on experience.[64] Thus, memory is a characteristic quality of the cave's inhabitants, who remember the patterns and movements of the cave's shadows, and are thus pathetically lulled into thinking they are wise.[65] Consequently, memory can be good only insofar as it remembers good things, which rules out memory as an empirical tool in such areas as rhetoric or current affairs.

Good memory presupposes a good choice of what to remember and what to forget. An unqualified hymn to Memory, therefore, may seem out of place in Plato's world, but the necessary qualifications are implicit, inasmuch as Socrates' memory is based on the recollection of the highest and most desirable entities. As such, recollection is tantamount to dialectics, as is clear from Socrates' first mention of recollection:

> δεῖ γὰρ ἄνθρωπον συνιέναι κατ᾽ εἶδος λεγόμενον, ἐκ πολλῶν ἰὸν αἰσθήσεων εἰς ἓν λογισμῷ συναιρούμενον· τοῦτο δ᾽ ἐστὶν ἀνάμνησις ἐκείνων ἅ ποτ᾽ εἶδεν ἡμῶν ἡ ψυχὴ συμπορευθεῖσα θεῷ καὶ ὑπεριδοῦσα ἃ νῦν εἶναί φαμεν, καὶ ἀνακύψασα εἰς τὸ ὂν ὄντως.

> A man must comprehend what is said universally, arising from many sensations and being collected together into one through reasoning; and this is a recollection of those things which our soul once saw when it travelled in company with a god and treated with contempt the things we now say are, and when it rose up into what really is.

> Plato *Phaedrus* 249b–c, trans. Rowe

The process of arising and *collecting* things together is an unmistakable reference to dialectics, and such a process is said to be equivalent to *recollection*.[66]

---

[64] *Gorgias* 463a–d is the *locus classicus*.

[65] *Republic* 516c–d. Similarly, memory, as discussed in the *Theaetetus*, seems to be a form of empiricist "memorism," as Frede 1990 puts it.

[66] This is no mere pun (see e.g. Carter 1967:115–116). As Trabattoni points out, "this connection may seem bizarre to contemporary scholars only, who maintain there is a fundamental incompatibility between the doctrine of recollection and dialectics: it is commonly held that at first Plato based his epistemology on the mythical theory of *anamnêsis*, but later abandoned this naive and fanciful doctrine in favor of a far more scientific process, represented by dialectics. In this perspective, a diachronic history charting the development of Platonic thought would set forth before us the makeover from muddled philosopher—mainly devoting himself to telling legendary tales and framing metaphysical theories as far-fetched as they are childish—to contemporary analytical philosopher who is both mature and reasonable. Yet it would suffice to read the passage just quoted to debunk this idea: the two aspects of Plato's philosophy—the calm, systematic exercise of dialectics alongside the relatively mythical construction of a metaphysics that is strongly marked by ontological dualism—always go together and it can neither be said that they are in contradiction with one another, nor that at some point Plato has traded one for the other" (Trabattoni 2012:313–314).

Yet there is an important difference. Whereas recollection, in the *Phaedrus* and the *Symposium*, is a dramatic process brought about by the shock of beauty, dialectics, as sketched in the *Republic* and in other dialogues, is a long and pains-taking procedure. In other words, the goal is the same, but love may provide a kind of shortcut to the Form(s). Moreover, this short passage tells us implicitly that recollection entails contempt, and, by implication, oblivion, of earthly realities, which have no real existence. So the question arises, could a good form of forgetfulness be part of the picture? And can one be sure that Memory is the hero of the story, and Oblivion the villain?

## Sappho's Helen

In order to address the problem, we shall turn to the section of the *Phaedrus* that immediately follows Socrates' "Hymn to Memory." To begin with, we encounter a distinction between the corrupt man and the initiated, who has seen much of the Forms in his prenatal wanderings. The former "does not move keenly from here to there, to beauty itself" (250e), so that the sight of beauty makes him "surrender to pleasure" in an attempt to cover his beloved as a beast. By contrast, the initiated is overwhelmed by beauty and stands in awe, shuddering, sweating, highly feverish, until he grows divine wings (251a–e). It is generally agreed that this list of symptoms is inspired by Sappho 31.[67] Other Sapphic elements include a strong emphasis on sight—Sapphic love is first and foremost a desire to contemplate the beloved—and on the power of memory, which, when the lover's soul cannot contemplate the youth, causes a mixture of pain and pleasure, since memory retains the sight of beauty even when the latter is absent.[68] This brings us to the climax of the entire passage, which I quote in full:

> ... πᾶσα κεντουμένη κύκλῳ ἡ ψυχὴ οἰστρᾷ καὶ ὀδυνᾶται, <u>μνήμην δ' αὖ</u>
> <u>ἔχουσα τοῦ καλοῦ</u> γέγηθεν. ἐκ δὲ ἀμφοτέρων μεμειγμένων ἀδημονεῖ
> τε τῇ ἀτοπίᾳ τοῦ πάθους καὶ ἀποροῦσα λυττᾷ, καὶ ἐμμανὴς οὖσα
> οὔτε νυκτὸς δύναται καθεύδειν οὔτε μεθ' ἡμέραν οὗ ἂν ᾖ μένειν, θεῖ
> δὲ ποθοῦσα ὅπου ἂν οἴηται <u>ὄψεσθαι τὸν ἔχοντα τὸ κάλλος</u>· ἰδοῦσα
> δὲ καὶ ἐποχετευσαμένη ἵμερον ἔλυσε μὲν τὰ τότε συμπεφραγμένα,
> ἀναπνοὴν δὲ λαβοῦσα κέντρων τε καὶ ὠδίνων ἔληξεν, ἡδονὴν δ' αὖ
> ταύτην γλυκυτάτην ἐν τῷ παρόντι καρποῦται. ὅθεν δὴ ἑκοῦσα εἶναι οὐκ
> ἀπολείπεται, οὐδέ τινα τοῦ καλοῦ περὶ πλείονος ποιεῖται, ἀλλὰ <u>μητέρων</u>
> <u>τε καὶ ἀδελφῶν καὶ ἑταίρων πάντων λέλησται</u>, καὶ οὐσίας δι' ἀμέλειαν
> ἀπολλυμένης παρ' οὐδὲν τίθεται, νομίμων δὲ καὶ εὐσχημόνων, οἷς

---

[67] Cf. e.g. Yunis 2011:152.
[68] Cf. e.g. the excellent discussion in the introduction of Di Benedetto 1987.

πρὸ τοῦ ἐκαλλωπίζετο, πάντων καταφρονήσασα δουλεύειν ἑτοίμη καὶ
κοιμᾶσθαι ὅπου ἂν ἐᾷ τις ἐγγυτάτω τοῦ πόθου· πρὸς γὰρ τῷ σέβεσθαι
τὸν τὸ κάλλος ἔχοντα ἰατρὸν ηὕρηκε μόνον τῶν μεγίστων πόνων.
τοῦτο δὲ τὸ πάθος, ὦ παῖ καλέ, πρὸς ὃν δή μοι ὁ λόγος, ἄνθρωποι μὲν
ἔρωτα ὀνομάζουσιν ...

... the entire soul, stung all over, goes mad with pain; but then, *remembering the beautiful*, it rejoices again. The mixture of both these states makes it despair at the strangeness of its condition, raging in its perplexity, and in its madness it can neither sleep at night nor keep still where it is by day, but runs wherever it thinks it will see *the possessor of the beauty* it longs for; and when it has seen the possessor and channeled desire in to itself it releases what was pent up before, and finding a breathing space it ceases from its stinging birth-pains, once more enjoying this for the moment as the sweetest pleasure. This it does not willingly give up, nor does it value anyone above the one with beauty, but quite *forgets mother, brothers, friends, all together*, not caring about the loss of its wealth through neglect, and with contempt for all the accepted standards of propriety and good taste in which it previously prided itself it is ready to act the part of a slave and sleep wherever it is allowed to do so, provided it is as close as possible to the object of its longing; for in addition to its reverence for *the possessor of beauty*, it has found him the sole healer of its greatest sufferings. This experience, my beautiful boy, men term love ...

Plato Phaedrus 251d–252b, trans. Rowe

As two critics have put it, "the body moves into the very substance of the soul," so that "l'âme est entièrement somatisée."[69] In fact, Plato's powerfully eroticized description of the soul contemplating beauty could easily be mistaken for a page of erotic mysticism from the Middle Ages.[70] Remarkably, both the subject and the object of love are presented as abstract, barely individual entities, even though there are overtones that evoke erotic intercourse. Moreover, the lover's contempt for earthly things, a consequence of his recollection of the Forms, results in his values being turned upside down, a reversal that takes the form of oblivion, thus making the case for a good form of forgetfulness

---

[69] Loraux 1995:144 and Stella 2006:142.

[70] As Belfiore 2012 notes: "Socrates' image of the wing recalls, throughout his second speech, the images of winged phalloi frequently represented in Greek art and graffiti" (226). Eros "is described in physical terms" (227). Cf. also Ferrari 1987:150–159, who gives the passage a Freudian interpretation.

explicit.[71] The lover is someone who forgets everyday values—mother, brothers, friends, riches—only to devote himself exclusively to what Plato refers to as "the possessor of beauty," that is, the embodiment of the relevant Form. The beloved, in turn, will undergo a similar experience, as he realizes that "not even all his other friends and his relations together" can match the lover. Consequently, he devotes himself to the lover and "is in love, but with what, he does not know" (ἐρᾷ μὲν οὖν, ὅτου δὲ ἀπορεῖ).[72] What is the source of this dramatic change? At a metapoetic level, an answer is readily available: Sappho and Helen. Socrates calls his speech a palinode because Helen had received such compensatory praise from Stesichorus, who, like so many other poets, had attacked her as a symbol of lust and guilt (243a–b). At this point, it is enlightening to read the poem Sappho dedicated to Helen (additional supplements are emphasized):[73]

> o]ἰ μὲν ἰππήων ϲτρότον οἰ δὲ πέϲδων
> οἰ δὲ νάων φαῖϲ' ἐπ[ὶ] γᾶν μέλαι[ν]αν
> ἔ]μμεναι κάλλιϲτον, ἔγω δὲ κῆν' ὄτ-
>    τω τιϲ ἔραται·
> πά]γχυ δ' εὔμαρεϲ ϲύνετον πόηϲαι
> π]άντι τ[ο]ῦτ', ἀ γὰρ πόλυ περϲκέθοιϲα
> κάλλοϲ [ἀνθ]ρώπων Ἐλένα [τὸ]ν ἄνδρα
>    τὸγ[    ἄρ]ιϲτον
> καλλ[ίποι]ϲ' ἔβα' ϲ Τροΐαν πλέοι[ϲα
> κωὐδ[ὲ πα]ῖδοϲ οὐδὲ φίλων το[κ]ήων
> πά[μπαν] ἐμνάϲθ⟨η⟩, ἀλλὰ παράγαγ' αὔταν
>    οὐδὲ θέλοι]ϲαν
>    ]αμπτον γὰρ [
>    ]...κούφωϲτ[          ]οη.[.]ν
> ..]με νῦν Ἀνακτορί[αϲ ὀ]νέμναιϲε
>    ϲ' οὐ ] παρεοίϲαϲ,

---

[71] This reversal is in some ways reminiscent of the conversion of the soul as described in the myth of the cave. As Vallejo Campos rightly notes: "La situación del enamorado es muy semejante a la del prisionero que vuelve a la caverna después de haber salido al exterior y haber tenido una visión de lo verdaderamente real. Cuando este hombre vuelve a la morada de sus antiguos compañeros de prisión se ha producido una transformación en él que le hace despreciar todos los honores y elogios que allí se tributaban. Este cambio no consiste sólo e una nueva concepción teórica del mundo sino en lo que nosotros describiríamos como una transformación de la voluntad: han cambiado sus valores y, en consecuencia, también sus deseos (cfr. [Plato] *Rep[ublic]* 515d3–4), porque aspira a tener contacto con el mundo superior y desprecia ocuparse de los asuntos humanos" (Vallejo Campos 2007:93–94).

[72] 255b–c.

[73] The supplement suggested by Martinelli Tempesta 1999—οὐδὲ θέλοι—at line 12 is almost certainly right, on palaeographical grounds.

τᾶ]ς ⟨κ⟩ε βολλοίμαν ἔρατόν τε βᾶμα
κἀμάρυχμα λάμπρον ἴδην προσώπω
ἢ τὰ Λύδων ἄρματα κἀν ὄπλοισι
    πεσδομ]άχεντας.

Some say an army on horse, some say on foot,
or borne by sea, is the most beautiful thing
upon the black earth—but I say most beautiful
    is the thing one loves.
And nothing is more easily made plain
to all, for even she who surpassed in beauty
all that is human, Helen, abandoned
    the best of men
when she departed for Troy by sail,
and neither child nor beloved parent
did she remember at all, but was led astray
    —*far from willing*—
for by
lightly
brings to my mind now Anaktoria,
    who is gone
and her beloved step, the spark
of her lambent eyes I would rather see
than the chariots of Lydia, than any march
    of soldiers at arms.

Sappho 16 Voigt

This is the only time in the extant fragments that Sappho tries to "demonstrate" a general thesis to an equally general audience (π]άντι),[74] which may give the impression of a proto-philosophical turn.[75] As in Socrates' speech, the poem

---

[74] Cf. e.g. des Bouvries Thorsen 1978:13.

[75] Accordingly, scholars have labeled Sappho's stance as sophistic (e.g. Race 1989–1990, who stresses Sappho's arguments for subjective and emotional choices), aesthetic (e.g. Koniaris 1967, who takes τὸ κάλλιστον as the pivotal element of the ode), relativist (Zellner 2007, arguing that the poem is an instance of "Inference to the Best Explanation"), political (Svenbro 1984, arguing for a feminist interpretation), logical/rhetorical (Most 1981, who interprets the poem in the light of Aristotle *Rhetoric* 1398b19–1398a6). Other scholars have indeed resisted the temptation to interpret 16 Voigt from a philosophical standpoint, either by claiming that the poem is obscure (e.g. Page 1955:53) and discontinuous (Fränkel 1955:92), or by stressing its religious (e.g. Privitera 1967), performative (e.g. Dodson-Robinson 2010), or ritualistic dimensions (e.g. Bierl 2003, who also offers a good survey of previous interpretations).

seems to entail a full *Umwertung aller Werte*[76] in what is ostensibly an inquiry into the ultimate object of human love (compare Sappho's ὄττω τις ἔραται and Plato's ἐρᾷ μὲν οὖν, ὅτου δὲ ἀπορεῖ). Sappho's Helen, referred to as the "hyper-possessor of beauty" (6–7), undergoes a complete reversal of values and forgets relatives and riches. At the same time, Helen's story, moving from the general to the particular, brings back to Sappho the vision of Anactoria's shining face (κἀμάρυχμα λάμπρον ἴδην προσώπω), [77] which calls to mind the *Phaedrus'* shining form of Beauty (κάλλος ἰδεῖν λαμπρόν) and its radiant incarnation as the lover's vision of a divine face (ὅταν θεοειδὲς πρόσωπον ἴδη).[78] Apart from the interesting dialectics between memory and oblivion, there is also the striking juxtaposition of the verb *memnêmai*, "remember," and *anamimnêsko*, "(cause somebody to) recollect," which also sounds somewhat "proto-philosophical."[79] Anactoria is absent, but her radiant memory is quite vivid, just as Socrates' beauty on earth is "shining" or "glittering" (250d, 254b). Whether Sappho was a proto-philosopher or not—I am in fact skeptical—her Helen poem certainly had enough to attract someone like Plato.[80]

As we have seen, Socrates' speech is compared to a palinode to Helen, and Plato conjures up both Gorgias' and Isocrates' Helen, who becomes "physically" present as a plane-tree. All of this makes Plato's allusion to Sappho's poem a powerful one, though no scholar, to the best of my knowledge, has ever noticed it.[81] Sappho is a model for the reversal of values brought about by the trau-matic experience of falling in love, and, more specifically, for the oblivion this provokes: because of beauty, the lover forgets all her usual pursuits, while her mind is fully taken up by the recollection of love. Yet what is the *content* of this memory?

The evocation of the beloved has a shining quality in both Sappho and Plato, but perhaps the two texts have more than this in common. In Sappho's extant

---

[76] Such is the title of Wills 1967, who stresses the strongly assertive tone of Sappho's poem.

[77] Cf. Dane 1981.

[78] 250b and 251a.

[79] Before Plato, there is just one more instance in another poem by Sappho (Sappho 94.10, cf. Burnett 1979:18) and one in Sophocles (*Oedipus the King* 1133).

[80] In Capra 2009, I have expressed my reservations about the teleologism often implicit in such reconstructions.

[81] This is all the more surprising because the poem was very famous. Not only was it well known to a number of prose writers, as we have seen, but allusions to it by the tragedians are a clear sign of its popularity. Cf. Casali 1989 (on Euripides *Bacchae* 881), Di Marco 1980 (on Euripides *Cyclops* 182–186), Scodel 1997 (on Euripides' *Hypsipyle* and *Phoenician Women* 88–177, and *Iphigenia in Aulis* 185–302), and Calder 1984 (on Aeschylus *Agamemnon* 403–419). The poem continued to be imitated in the Hellenistic Age (cf. Livrea 1968 on Apollonius Rhodius 1.538–539) and the Imperial Age. (Bierl 2002 argues that Chariton's novel can be construed as a development of Sappho's thesis as expressed in the Priamel of 16 Voigt.)

poetry, whenever a character longs for her beloved, the poet evokes a moment of performance, like the dance and music practiced by Sappho and her companions.[82] This is implicit in our poem as well: Sappho remembers Anactoria's "lovely step," which alone is evocative of dance, and even the "shining spark of her face" seems to suggest movement: *amarugma* or *amaruga* are used in early Greek poetry either to describe shining gestures or as an epithet for the Graces, who were, of course, dancing goddesses.[83] As for Plato, the lover, when struck by beauty, remembers the time when he followed his god as a *choreutês*, that is, member of a chorus (252d).[84] Thus, Sappho's lesson for Socrates is one of memory and oblivion: forget earthy things, remember beauty in the divine sparkle of dance.

## The "Mother" of Socrates' Speech

Ultimately, what are we to make of Plato's Sappho? As I mentioned earlier, this question, though a very old one, has recently given rise to a lively debate. The text quoted on the cover page of this chapter has Maximus of Tyrus going so far as to equate Sapphic with Platonic love, and claiming that Sappho should be recognized as the "mother" of Socrates' palinode. Building on Maximus, Helen Foley argues that in both authors "both masculine and feminine erotics are represented as not exclusively about bodies." Thus, Foley "counters a tendency in recent feminist criticism that pits Sappho as the paradigmatic celebrant of the materiality of the body against Plato's philosophic aim to transcend it."[85]

---

[82]  Lardinois 2008.

[83]  On *amarugma*, cf. Brown 1989. In some fragments, Sappho seems to aspire to an afterlife that takes the form of eternal dance and song (see Lardinois 2008), whereas in one of her most famous (and discussed) lines she claims that her love of the sun has granted her splendor and beauty, as opposed, it would seem, to other people's inglorious aging and death. The latter she does through a reference to the myth of Tithonus, who became so decrepit that he could not move, though his divine voice continued to flow, until—according to one version of the story that Sappho and her audience were likely to have known—he was eventually turned into an ever-singing cicada. This, of course, is not the place to discuss the problems raised by the recent publication of P. Köln XI 429 (inv. 21376), in particular, whether or not the final lines of fr. 58 Voigt belong to the poem about old age, i.e. fr. 58 1–24 Voigt. For a discussion of the so-called new Sappho, see e.g. Aloni 2008, as well as Green and Skinner 2011.

[84]  Lebeck 1972 examines the palinode "as if it were choral lyric" (267). One may add that after the end of the palinode Socrates chooses sun-mad cicadas as a symbol for the true pursuit of philosophy, the cicadas being a *choros* (dancing team, 238d) who, because of their passion for music—a passion that eventually persuaded the gods to grant them eternal song—had forgotten to eat and drink. This is possibly one more Sapphic echo: see previous note.

[85]  The quote is from page 6 of M. Wyke's incisive introduction to the edited volume, *Parchments of Gender: Deciphering the Bodies of Antiquity*, which includes Foley's 1998 article.

The latter is, indeed, the dominant view on the whole, but Elizabeth Pender has very recently published the most thorough discussion of the subject so far, and this has resulted in a more balanced assessment.[86] I fully share Pender's view, already quoted,[87] that "Plato draws directly on the poetic language of the lyric poets, but he sets against them a need for self-control to redirect the soul's energy from physical beauty to the Forms." Moreover, she claims that "in *Phaedrus* [unlike in Sappho's poetry] memory does not serve as a consolation but as a spur to further effort—it is merely the beginning of an arduous task ... Thus through his love story of recollection Plato challenges the lyric tradition by placing *eros* within a much larger framework of experience and understanding."[88]

Sappho idolizes her beloved ones, while Anacreon, Plato's other lyric model, goes so far as to state that "Boys are my gods."[89] By contrast, Plato's lover and beloved are abstract creatures, without names or individual traits. Through what he refers to as "enthusiasm through memory" (253a), Plato's lover transcends earthly beauty and attains to divine beauties *behind* the divine face of beautiful boys, as if their radiant faces were iconic windows open to Beauty. Sappho is fond of closeups: she likes to blow up poignant details of the past, particularly when they involve moments of dance and performance. Again by contrast, Plato's eye captures no less poignant and breathtaking a view of the metaphysical, prenatal world with extreme long shots that reveal the hyperuranion dance of the souls. Both experiences, however, entail the severing of everyday memories.

What one finds in certain lyric poems is undiluted *eros* manifesting itself in devastating ways. As is the case with Sappho's Helen, this brings about a complete reversal of values, resulting in the severing of all ties that bind us to everyday life—which is precisely what makes "lyric oblivion" attractive to Plato. But oblivion of earthly values goes hand in hand with the scintillating memory of the beloved, and it is memory, rather than oblivion, that opens up the gap between Plato and Sappho. Sappho's Helen poem "shows a tendency towards particularization,"[90] and Sappho's memory, as in other nostalgic poems, is obsessed with particular details: she intensifies the light shining on the face of a dancer, magnifies the hand playing a lyre, and so on.[91] Somehow, Sappho makes a sad fetish of her beloved ones, and this is precisely where Plato is not

---

[86] See Pender 2007 and 2011.
[87] Pender 2007:54, quoted above at page 32.
[88] Pender 2007:55.
[89] Testimonium 7 Campbell.
[90] Dane 1981:192.
[91] Discussions of Sappho's "memory" can be found in Burnett 1979, Jarratt 2002, Rayor 2005, and Lardinois 2008.

willing to follow her. One cannot fail to recall how in *Republic* 10 he attacks poetry precisely because it indulges in "recollections of *pathos*" (ἀναμνήσεις τοῦ πάθους) and "lamentations" (ὀδυρμούς).[92]

To conclude our discussion of memory and oblivion, we may say that Plato's "hymn to memory" incorporates and radically transforms Sappho's references to memory in a way that parallels Socrates' reply to Aristophanes in the *Symposium*. In the playwright's myth, the lovers can never forget their lost half and are obsessed with the individual. On the other hand, for Socrates, who openly refers to Aristophanes, that same poignant nostalgia can be channeled upwards in such a way as to transcend the individual in a search for Beauty.[93] Nevertheless, Sappho remains the undisputed, matchless *master of oblivion*, without which no true memory is possible. Moreover, as I shall now argue, she is a model in the appropriation of past texts, or, to put it more simply, a model of memory at work in texts.[94]

## Mobilizing the Poetry of the Past

My own discussion confirms Pender's interpretation. However, Pender's very sensible conclusions can be explored further and explained in greater depth. Elsewhere, Plato makes it very clear that it is no use scrutinizing texts in the absence of their authors.[95] Why then does he feel the need to argue through lyric poetry? Two passages from the *Phaedrus* may provide a credible answer. The first is in the *explicit* of the palinode (257a), when Socrates claims his palinode "was forced to use somewhat poetical language because of Phaedrus."[96] Not only do these words declare openly Plato's intention to echo lyric poetry, but they also suggest that good speech must be fashioned to meet the needs of the listener. Authentic, philosophical rhetoric is an erotic form of discourse that takes notice of the individual nature of its addressee—which is why lyric poetry may be useful for such an interlocutor as Phaedrus.

The second passage is from the myth of Theuth (275a–b), when the pharaoh describes writing as "an elixir not of memory but of reminding."[97] Whether read or recited, written composition is not true memory, but rather an aid to remembrance. The latter point is in itself ambiguous: on the one hand, Plato is probably

---

[92]  604d.

[93]  For a good account of the relationship between the speeches of Aristophanes and Socrates in the *Symposium*, see Fussi 2008.

[94]  Implicitly, this anticipates the enthusiasm prompted by the reading of poetry as described by Pseudo-Longinus 13. For other relevant parallels, cf. e.g. Manieri 1998:68 and *passim*.

[95]  *Protagoras* 347e is the *locus classicus*.

[96]  τά τε ἄλλα καὶ τοῖς ὀνόμασιν ἠναγκασμένη ποιητικοῖς τισιν διὰ Φαῖδρον.

[97]  οὔκουν μνήμης ἀλλὰ ὑπομνήσεως φάρμακον.

attacking the rhetorical practice of learning written speeches by heart, which is precisely what Phaedrus had set out to do at the beginning of the dialogue; on the other hand, however, written aids may work in a different way, and poetic myth can work as a "trigger for intuitive recollection," as Daniel Werner aptly puts it.[98] Let us have one last look at Helen's poem.

A favorite among early poets, Helen's story was probably perceived to be the very stuff of epics. The story of Helen is one of war and destruction, which may account for the martial images that form the background to the poem. But as Sappho composes her poem, Helen serves as a reminder of Anactoria. This is a different mode of poetic recollection. It might be interesting at this point to look back at the image reproduced on the cover page of this chapter. This painting, from a hydria dating from ca. 440–430 BCE, shows Sappho sitting on a chair in the company of three young women who hold a crown and a lyre.[99] As Franco Ferrari has suggested, "the iconographic scheme whereby a famous poet is on the point of playing and is surrounded by young female figures clearly does not recall a performance in action but a moment in preparation for the same. Hence the iconography shows Sappho holding a papyrus roll in her hands in keeping with a well-attested tradition of joint scenes and reading ... It is worth noting that the two recognizable sequences of letters on the roll, ἔπεα πτερόεντα, refer to a frequent epic formula and hence do not allude to a text that the poet has composed or is in the act of composing. Instead, they refer to an epic episode that has come to her memory."[100]

Ferrrari's perceptive reading does not extend, however, to another sequence of letters, namely the column Sappho is actually looking at (ἔπεα and πτερόεντα are written on the external margins of the roll). In this column, the sequence ΘΕΟΙ ΗΕΡΙΩΝ ΕΠΕΩΝ is clearly visible.[101] ΘΕΟΙ ("GODS") is a dedicatory

---

[98]  Werner 2012:264.

[99]  The name of Nikopolis, as well as the presence of a wreath, suggests a musical contest, thus highlighting Sappho's status as a (winning) poet (cf. Bundrick 2005:101–102). This, I believe, rules out the interpretation put forward by Glazebrook, who, building on the work of Snyder McIntosh (1997), claims that "the female figure with book roll, interpreted in the context of an oral culture like Athens, highlights the absence of a female voice and even alludes to the erasure or temporary muting of the female voice" (Glazebrook 2005:35).

[100]  Cf. Ferrari 2010:106–107. For a thorough discussion of this and other vases representing Sappho, see Chapter 2 of Yatromanolakis 2007.

[101]  This is perhaps followed by ΑΡΧΟΜΑΙ (cf. the image on the cover page), but the first letter is far from clear as it is partly covered by the poet's thumb, which might also cover a letter in the following line. I doubt whether the painter ever intended this to be read as ΑΡΧΟΜΑΙ (by contrast, the first five lines are perfectly clear). What follows is even more debatable, and I cannot agree with Edmonds, who reads the sequence as ἠερίων ἐπέων ἄρχομαι ἀλλ᾽ ὀνάτων (Edmonds 1922:3). More plausibly, Sider 2010 does not strive to reconstruct a continuous text and puts forward a number of suggestions pointing to dactylic sequences (n17).

formula,[102] possibly "intrusive from the language of official documents,"[103] or, I would add, from the usage of ΘΕΟΙ as a heading in private graffiti, a practice that began to spread in Athens very early in the fifth century BCE.[104] If this is so, the "extratextual" formula is followed by the "text" proper, namely, ΗΕΡΙΩΝ ΕΠΕΩΝ. And, if this is so, I suggest that the "text" should be read as the first half of an *epic* hexameter.[105] This reading accords perfectly with both the epic formula ἔπεα πτερόεντα ("winged words"), of which ΗΕΡΙΩΝ ΕΠΕΩΝ may be regarded as a rephrasing,[106] and with comparable representations of papyri from other vases which feature the beginnings of epic or quasi-epic poems,[107] as opposed to lyric beginnings. (The latter do not appear on vases in the form of book rolls, but as streams of letters flowing directly from the performer's mouth.[108])

---

[102] Cf. e.g. Herzog 1912:22–23 and Edmonds 1922:2. For other references, cf. Yatromanolakis 2007:160. However, Yatromanolakis considers ΘΕΟΙ, together with the following lines, to be part of a *lyric* poem (cf. below, note 101).

[103] Immerwahr 1964:39. ΘΕΟΙ is frequently found at the head of a given text, as in both of the epigraphic decrees (the earliest example dates from 448–447).

[104] Graffiti featuring ΘΕΟΙ as a heading include lists of gods (National Epigraphic Museum of Athens 5949), a private letter and a list of *kalos* names (cf. Lang 1976, C21), the last two from the first half of the fifth century BCE. Another private letter (lead tablet from the Pnyx, cf. Jordan 2003 VII:33), and a curse (cf. Strÿd 1903:58) date from a later time, between the fifth and the fourth centuries. These items are discussed in a doctoral dissertation by R. Pounder (1975), who later provided a brief summary of his work (not including our headings) in Pounder 1984. I was not able to see the dissertation by Traywick (1968).

[105] On the contrary, the line is considered to be a lyric fragment by Campbell and Page (printed as fr. 938d PMG). Note, however, that the adjective is very often found at the beginning of a hexameter, which surely adds to the epic note of ΗΕΡΙΩΝ ΕΠΕΩΝ.

[106] "In *Iliad* 3.7 the cranes are called ἠέριαι, which despite LSJ and a variant in the scholia probably means 'high in the air' ... Thus the phrase ἠέρια ἔπεα may be connected with the bird metaphor for speech" (Immerwahr 1964:47n1). This is now confirmed by the recently published Posidippus 23.1 (ἠερίην αἴθυιαν). For a different interpretation, see Yatromanolakis 2007, who, however tentatively, interprets the rephrasing as a "metonymic juxtaposition of epic discourse to an *écriture féminine* associated with an East Greek song-maker like Sappho" (163).

[107] On book rolls on Attic vases, cf. Immerwahr 1964 and 1973. Edmonds summarizes the comparative evidence as follows: "We have a close parallel in a vase-picture by Euphronios ... which belongs to a date not much more, perhaps, than a generation earlier than our present vase, and shows a rolled-up book with the title written across the back as it is here, Χιρώνεια, an epic poem presumably on Chiron the centaur ... The parallels from other vase-pictures cannot be proved to be first lines of *books*, but if we may include citations represented as coming from the lips of singers, the majority of them are the first lines of *poems*, some of them otherwise extant, for instance Theognis 1365 and Praxilla 5 PMG. And in spite of their difficulties the words inscribed on the book which figures in the famous school-scene of Douris, Μοῖσά μοι ἀμφὶ Σκάμανδρον κτλ., are undoubtedly intended for the first words of an epic poem" (Edmonds 1922:4–5). Note, however, that the last example comes in the context of a school scene: according to Sider 2010, the verse visible on the papyrus is the result of an awkward attempt at composition by an incompetent schoolboy.

[108] Cf. Immerwahr 1964:47. Overall, monodic texts are *never* shown on depicted book rolls. These feature mostly epic lines (including the beginning of one minor Homeric hymn),

The epic past seems to be integral to Sappho's own poetic practice as depicted by the painter.[109] Before she begins to sing her own songs, Sappho "consults" an epic poem, or else the papyrus is there to symbolize Sappho's poetic memory.[110] I believe that, in either case, this constitutes the creative paradigm for poetic memory that Plato fully endorses. It is through his poetic memory, which includes lyric poetry as well as other genres, or even "written aids," that Plato composes his own hymn to memory and depicts the hyperuranion world "as no other poet has previously done."[111]

## Conclusions

The *Phaedrus* is inextricably interwoven with the works of Gorgias and Isocrates dedicated to Helen. Both interact playfully with Sappho's Helen poem, and Plato readily plays along with them. Far from being a rhetorical embellishment, however, Plato's Helen is integral to the palinode. Not only is Helen "physically" present as Helen *dendritis*, the goddess of the plane-tree, but, more importantly, it is through Sappho's Helen that Plato elaborates his theory of oblivion and recollection. Gorgianic rhetoric explicitly takes advantage of the weakness of human memory and mind, and, in so doing, overwhelms and "drags" the listener's mind around. Plato, too, characterizes rhetoric as a form of "psychagogy" (dragging of souls), clearly hinting at Gorgias and Isocrates. But it is through Sappho's Helen that he reverses the role of memory: the emotional shock provoked by beauty, so integral to lyrical discourse, brings about the oblivion of mundane things and at the same time triggers off the bright recollection of more precious things. In Plato's case, the latter coincides with a long shot of the prenatal world of the Forms, as opposed to the "closeups" so typical of

---

dactylo-epitrites, and, in one exceptional case from a school scene, a prose mythological text (cf. Immerwahr 1973).

[109] In fact, much has been written on Sappho's appropriation of epic motives. For 16 Voigt in particular, see e.g. Bowie 2010 and Rosenmeyer 1997.

[110] Immerwahr 1964 concludes his survey of book rolls on Attic vases with the important remark that "none of the pictures shows a single figure engaged in individual reading, but the book roll is always used in a larger social context, although this context is sometimes merely suggested. The book roll is thus a mnemonic device facilitating recitation, not a real 'book' for reading alone" (36–37). He then comments on the only exception he found, in the famous Grottaferrata funerary relief.

[111] Τὸν δὲ ὑπερουράνιον τόπον οὔτε τις ὕμνησέ πω τῶν τῇδε ποιητὴς οὔτε ποτὲ ὑμνήσει κατ' ἀξίαν. ἔχει δὲ ὧδε—τολμητέον γὰρ οὖν τό γε ἀληθὲς εἰπεῖν, ἄλλως τε καὶ περὶ ἀληθείας λέγοντα; "As for the region above the heavens, no earthly poet has ever yet sung it as it deserves, nor will he ever sing it. But it is like this—for one must be bold enough to say what is true, especially when speaking about truth" (*Phaedrus* 247c, trans. Rowe, modified).

Sappho's poignant memories. Plato, moreover, evokes Sappho's active, creative reworking of epic themes, which led to a different model of intertextuality.

## Endnote: New "Facts"

- Building on a number of previous studies, this chapter offers a new survey of the intertextual relations between the *Phaedrus* and the two prose works dedicated to Helen by Gorgias and his pupil Isocrates. Echoes from Sappho 16 Voigt prove to be essential components of the intertextual play.

- A careful comparison shows that the *Phaedrus* reproduces, even in points of detail, the quadripartite argument of Gorgias' *Helen*, while it also appropriates the idea of rhetoric as a playful activity that can stir and mobilize the listener's soul. At the same time, by attacking the εἰκός while advocating truth, the *Phaedrus* reverses Gorgias' approach.

- Whereas Isocrates criticizes Gorgias by attacking *psykhagôgia*, Plato appropriates and transforms the notion. *Psykhagôgia* acquires a sublime status, thanks to the fundamental contribution of lyric poetry. Far from being an embellishment, as is the case with Gorgias and Isocrates, lyric echoes in the *Phaedrus* are integral to the discourse of philosophy. This is true for both Stesichorus, as discussed in Chapter 1, and for Sappho, as discussed in the current chapter.

- In the *Phaedrus*, Helen functions as a kind of "stone guest": she is only mentioned once, but her presence is made evident through a web of allusions to a number of works dedicated to her (by Stesichorus, Sappho, Gorgias, and Isocrates). Her relevance is confirmed by a detail that has been passed over until now: at 236d–e, the plane-tree is in fact addressed as a goddess. A survey of the relevant poetic and cultic traditions offers an explanation for this striking detail: the plane-tree, which ancient readers felt to be metonymic for the *Phaedrus*, or even for Plato as a writer (see Introduction), was closely associated (or even identified) with Helen, who emerges with a pivotal role in the dialogue.

- At 250c, Plato appropriates the traditional feature of the hymn in order to praise memory, which is addressed as a goddess. This "hymn" to memory provides a convenient introduction to a major (and unnoticed) poetic allusion. Not only is Sappho 16 Voigt a vital weapon in Plato's intertextual battle of wits; it also proves to be a crucial subtext at *Phaedrus* 251d and other key points of the palinode, while contextual and lexical elements make for a very powerful allusion. Sappho 16 Voigt is exceptional in its demonstrative character, which takes the form of a semantic opposition between memory and recollection, while at the same time introducing oblivion of earthly things as the most striking symptom of *eros*. Plato was clearly interested in this paradigm, to the extent that he adopts and transforms all these elements: he makes the idea of oblivion as a crucial step in the transcending of earthly pursuits his own, but turns Sappho's erotic remembrances into the no less erotic recollection of the Forms.

- The role of text and writing, as discussed at *Phaedrus* 275a–b, is also inspired by Sappho 16 Voigt. In the poem, the epic past functions as a form of poetic memory that prompts the creation of original poetry. This interpretation is supported by pictorial evidence: a close examination of the inscription visible on the Sappho hydria attributed to the group of Polygnotus (Athens National Archaeological Museum 1260) shows that the notion of reception that the painter had in mind was precisely this—especially if my interpretation of the words depicted on the papyrus roll as the beginning of an epic hexameter proves to be valid.

# 3

## CALLIOPE AND OURANIA

*... and to Calliope, the eldest, and to Ourania who comes after her (τῇ μετ᾽ αὐτῇ), the cicadas report those who spend their time in philosophy and honor the music that belongs to them—who most of the all the Muses have as their sphere the heaven (οὐρανόν) and the logoi, both divine and human, and utter the most beautiful voice (καλλίστην φωνήν)*

Phaedrus 259d

From the third frieze of the François vase, ca. 570 BC (cf. Chapter 1, cover page). In this section of the procession, the Muses Ourania and Calliope form a couple. The other seven Muses (not visible in this frame) follow them and Zeus from the left. On the right, a number of figures (the Horae, Dionysus, Hestia, Chariclo, Iris, Chiron and Peleus) stand in front of the *Thetideion* (one of the Horae is visible at the far right of the frame). Calliope, then, is at the head of the procession.

- Calliope and Ourania lead the procession, the boundaries of which are marked by the signature of the potter (ΕΡΓΟΤΙΜΟΣΜΕΠΟΙΕΣΕΝ), running parallel with the horses' forelegs. The two muses are thus framed by Zeus on Ourania's left and, on Calliope's right, by the author's name, which marks the culmination of the procession. This gives the couple an exceptional emphasis, suggestive of author(ial)ity.

- Calliope is unique in that she is seen frontally. In contrast with the other Muses, who are arranged in two groups of four and three and represented as parallel "synchronized" figures, Ourania and Calliope diverge from (and potentially interact with) each other.

# 3

# Calliope and Ourania
## The Initiation to Dialogue

A S EMMANUEL LÉVINAS SO GRANDLY PUT IT, in the *Phaedrus* "delirium does not have an irrationalistic significance … it is reason itself, rising to the ideas, thought in the highest sense."[1] But how can one reconcile this with the attacks on poetic (and erotic) "delirium" found in the *Ion* and the *Republic*? I have already mentioned Martha Nussbaum's evolutionary approach.[2] Other interpretations suggest that Plato's "poetic" soul somehow got the upper hand in the *Phaedrus*.[3] This accords with the common view of Plato as something of a schizophrenic, which often results in the alleged existence of two Socrateses.[4] As for Plato's poetry, this is often read in the light of a Freudian return of the repressed, as in Julia Annas's influential interpretation.[5] A more satisfactory explanation would be found if one were to reconstruct the cultural code that informs the *Phaedrus*—something that seems to have escaped modern readers. Besides poetic inspiration, already discussed in Chapters 1 and 2, the Greek tradition of poetic initiation is also part of the background of the dialogue and is essential for a proper understanding of it.

## *Mimêsis* and *Enthousiasmos*:
## A Very Short Introduction

First of all, we must enter into a brief discussion of two key Platonic "doctrines": *mimêsis* and *enthousiasmos*.[6] In books 2 and 3 of the *Republic*, Plato attacks poetry

---

[1] Cf. Lévinas 1969:50, reported in Fussi 2006:53.
[2] Nussbaum 1986. Cf. Chapter 1 in the current volume.
[3] Cf. e.g. the very influential commentary by Hackforth 1952:61
[4] Notable and influential examples are Vlastos 1991 and Blondell 2002.
[5] Annas 1982, according to whom "within the *Republic* [...] Plato's attitude is split, and he is not like the socialist realists, or Tolstoy, who think that it is both possible and necessary to throw out ephemeral, entertainment art and to promote deep, truth-promoting art" (23).
[6] Giuliano 2005 provides an excellent discussion of both doctrines, complete with bibliographic guidance. Distinguishing between two separate doctrines is a common activity among scholars,

on the grounds that people tend to sympathize with morally dubious characters, and this results in devastating side effects for their soul—or, in modern terms, for their psychology. In this context, *mimêsis* is taken to mean identification, and Plato's point of view may be broadly described as sociological. The word *mimêsis*, however, can also mean reproduction: this is how Plato seems to use the word in *Republic* 10, which puts forward the notorious idea that poetry is twice removed from truth. In this new context, Plato's critique may be labeled as ontological, though the effects of poetry on the soul continue to focus his interest.[7]

On close inspection, both meanings of *mimêsis* leave the door open for a more favorable understanding of poetry. For one cannot rule out in principle the possibility that audiences may identify with noble characters, and this is precisely what can be read between the lines of Plato's otherwise ruthless attack in the first books of the *Republic*.[8] Reproduction, moreover, might bypass

---

but can be questionable at times. Murray 1996:1–12 maintains that the two doctrines eventually and exceptionally merge in the *Laws* (719c), but this is probably not the whole story. Giuliano 2005:191–204 further develops the point in the light of earlier poetic traditions, and Morgan 2010 has argued that inspired *mimêsis* is found in *Phaedrus* 252d. Moreover, Palumbo 2011, in what she aptly refers to as "un gesto decisamente controcorrente" (166), plausibly suggests that the two doctrines are generally complementary rather than distinct. Büttner 2000, too, is a theo-retically sustained, if excessively dogmatic, attempt to reconcile *mimêsis* and *enthousiasmos*. Cf. the sensible criticism provided by Halliwell 2002b.

[7] The term is, in fact, extremely complex: given that identification, in ancient performative prac-tices, entails the reproduction of exterior postures known as *skhêmata*, the two meanings of *mimêsis* can in fact be reconciled. See Leszl 2007, especially 254–255. Halliwell 2002a:46–50 distin-guishes among no fewer than six different semantic areas pertaining to Platonic *mimêsis*. With its theatrical pedigree, *mimêsis* is integral both to Plato's cave and to Plato's hypothesis of the Forms, as Palumbo 2008 has put forward.

[8] See in particular *Republic* 397c–d, where we learn that the best performer for a *polis* is τὸν τοῦ ἐπιεικοῦς μιμητὴν ἄκρατον, i.e. as we find out at 398b, ὃς ἡμῖν τὴν τοῦ ἐπιεικοῦς λέξιν μιμοῖτο. Lapini 2003 suggests that this must refer to the performer/poet who imitates only (purely) the decent man (ἐπιεικοῦς, he rightly argues, cannot possibly be neuter, as most scholars believe). Plato's Socrates, moreover, seems to encourage young people to imitate him (see Blondell 2002:86). The same conclusion broadly applies to the previous discussion as well, as we learn from *Republic* 395c–d and 396c–d (cf. e.g. Asmis 1992:347 and Lapini 2003). As scholars have often noted, however, these two passages from the *Republic* are complicated by an apparent contra-diction. As Murray writes: "In the light of all that is said here we would expect S[ocrates] to advocate the virtues of poetic mimesis in his discussion of lexis at 392d5–398b4. But in fact he concludes (a) that potential guardians should imitate only good men (396c5-d3), and (b) that they should imitate as little as possible, using the mixed style exemplified by Homer, but with a small amount of mimesis (396e4, cf. 395c3–7). These views are not incompatible, but there is a certain ambivalence in P[lato]'s attitude ... P[lato] seems to be caught between the view that mimesis is beneficial provided that its object is suitable, and the feeling that there is something potentially harmful about mimesis in itself" (Murray 1996:13). However, Plato himself seems to suggest that an appropriate filter, such as playful narration and contextualization, can be an effective means in making the imitation of indecent things harmless, which is an important point: such imitation is to some extent desirable in that one has to know evil in order to avoid it (cf. 396a), a principle that is likely to have inspired Plato himself in composing his dialogues.

the physical world and draw directly on intelligible realities, as do the divine painters described in the *Republic*[9]—and as do, in their respective spheres, Timaeus and the demiurge, both described as painters in the sequel to the *Republic*, namely the *Timaeus-Critias*.[10] An argument may also be made for an explicit, and therefore non-deceptive, use of poetic images.[11] It would seem that Plato's dialogues suggest precisely this dual kind of good *mimêsis*: Plato's principal hero, Socrates, is a most noble character,[12] who invites identification; and Plato's myths, by openly presenting themselves as fictional, are not meant to deceive the readers, but to direct them towards the noetic world.[13]

I shall now turn to *enthousiasmos*. This is an equally ambiguous notion, which surfaces in a number of dialogues: *Meno, Apology, Laws,* and particularly in the *Ion* and the *Phaedrus*.[14] The *Ion* ridicules a rhapsode who knows Homer by

---

(Cf. Capra 2003 and Lapini 2003. See also Tsouna 2013, and, more generally, Elias 1984 for Plato's "poetry"—mainly his myths—as a kind of writing wholly in accord with Plato's own theories.)

[9] 471c–473b, with Gastaldi 1998. The paradigm of the divine painter is consistent with the ὀρθότης of *mimêsis* as discussed in *Laws* 667a–668c (see Tulli 2007c) and seems to look forward to the author of the *Republic*. Cf. also Reydams-Schils 2011 and Regali 2012 (Chapter 3) who argue for such an interpretation of the *Timaeus-Critias*.

[10] M. Regali aptly notes that the *Timaeus-Critias* is conceptualized as a hymn-cum-*egkômion*, i.e. the one type of poetry approved of in the *Republic*. (See *Republic* 607a and *Timaeus* 20e–21a, and compare *Republic* 388e with *Timaeus* 29d, where reference is made to "accepting"—ἀποδέχομαι—poetry. See Regali 2012, especially 33, 40–41.) Regali also argues that "la μίμησις di Timeo è priva … degli aspetti negativi che Socrate denuncia nella *Repubblica* in relazione alla μίμησις dei poeti: il racconto di Timeo non è copia inferiore di un modello tradito, ma è un racconto verosimile sviluppato nel segno dell'εἰκός, unica via per attingere ad un modello altrimenti non raggiungibile perché appartenente alla sfera del divino" (Regali 2012:10). Cf. Chapter 3 of Regali 2012 for the close relationship between the *Timaeus-Critias* and *mimêsis* as discussed in the *Republic*).

[11] Cf. Allen 2010 and Werner 2012. For a thorough treatment of the subject, cf. Gonzalez 1998, Chapter 5. Ferrari 1990 also notes that Plato is "careful to mark with caveats the various poetic resources to which he is nevertheless driven within the dialogues (myths, allegories and images)" (144). In the history of scholarship devoted to Platonic *mimêsis*, attempts to identify good forms of imitation can be found earlier as well. See Le Moli 2012 for a good survey, including the influence of the debate on twentieth century hermeneutics.

[12] Cf. Erler 2011. In *Letter 7*, which is in his own voice, Plato calls Socrates "the most rightful man of his time" (δικαιότατον … τῶν τότε, 324e); this closely parallels the *Phaedo*'s concluding praise of Socrates at 118a.

[13] This point is implicit in *Republic* 604e, where "Socrates is describing himself, which is to say that Plato … is describing the subject of his own dramatic imitations" (Clay 2000:146).

[14] For a lucid and succinct account, see e.g. the excellent article by Carter 1967, who includes *Timaeus* 72a and who suggests "that one who is possessed, divinely or naturally, is unable to evaluate the results of such madness and that the task of evaluation ought to be left to one who is sound of mind. This passage suggests that truth is not a necessary quality of any kind of madness; it must be judged by rational means" (113). My account is, of course, a simplified one. For example, Leszl has recently noted that apparently "when Plato talks inspiration in the *Ion*, he has two different views in mind. One of these views is suggested by the parallel with the oracle-teller (*mantis*) which is propounded (implicitly) in 534c–e, where it is said that the poets are used

heart, since this leads him to believe he is omniscient, or at least very knowl-edgeable in important matters, such as warfare. It turns out, however, that Ion is not even a competent poet, let alone militarily competent.[15] The only ability he has consists in a form of divine enthusiasm, which originates in the Muse and is then transmitted to humans, an idea conveyed in the famous image of the magnet: the Muse transmits her progressively declining magnetic force to a chain of "rings," namely the poet, the rhapsode, and the audience. Since it depends on divine mania, as opposed to rational knowledge, Ion's wisdom is partial and intermittent. Even more alarming, it does not encompass the whole of poetry, but only Homer. By Plato's standards, this is a sure indication of its irrational nature.[16] Moreover, Ion proves pathetically unable to answer a few simple questions related to Homer's "encyclopedia," and he eventually gives up any pretense of knowledge.

*Enthousiasmos* is equally important in the *Phaedrus*, even though here Plato's viewpoint seems to be radically different, since Socrates embarks on a "recan-tation" that results in an unprecedented appraisal of madness, including *poetic* madness. Madness is now said to be either human or divine, and the latter, unlike its human counterpart, is the source of the greatest good for us humans. As we now know, on performing his palinode, Socrates adopts the persona of a divinely inspired poet claiming to have access to a level of truth that is not commonly available to other men.[17]

Socrates' palinode raises a series of problems. What happened between the *Ion*, supposedly an early work, and the *Phaedrus*? Did Plato reconvert to the Muse of Poetry, after famously rejecting her in his youth? A full discussion of this vexing question is beyond the scope of the present study, not least because of

---

by the god as his servants or ministers, just as oracle-tellers and divine prophets are used by him and that it is the god himself who talks through them ... The other view is that of 535b, where the poet is 'out of himself'—and brought to this condition by his 'enthusiasm' (thus, it would seem, because of some divine intervention)—not because 'invaded' or 'possessed' by a god, in the way in which an oracle-teller like the Pythia is possessed, but because he travels with his mind to the place where events happened in the distant past. In this way the poet communicates what he has seen, and what he has seen by divine intervention, but does not directly communicate what the divinity tells him to communicate, using him as a mere instrument of intermediary" (Leszl 2006:345).

[15] The first explicit references to poetry as a rational expertise (τέχνη) date from the late fifth century BCE (cf. Aristophanes *Peace* 749; *Frogs* 762 and *passim*), although the idea is implicit earlier, especially in the *Hymn to Hermes*, which was probably composed in Athens between the sixth and the fifth century. See Nobili 2011, especially 160–165.

[16] On Plato's notion of *tekhnê*, cf. the incomparable work of Cambiano 1991.

[17] Some scholars and philosophers have, however, interpreted an important detail that distin-guishes Socrates' enthusiasm from that of the "simple" poets: namely, it does not entail the loss of rational thought; nor is it, like Ion's, occasional or intermittent. Besides Lévinas, cf. Giuliano 2005:205–216, who carries out a careful examination of the matter.

the sheer vastness of the relevant bibliography.[18] In our case, it is more sensible merely to reproduce the crucial passage from the *Ion*:

{ΙΩΝ.} Τί οὖν ποτε τὸ αἴτιον, ὦ Σώκρατες, ὅτι ἐγώ, ὅταν μέν τις περὶ ἄλλου του ποιητοῦ διαλέγηται, οὔτε προσέχω τὸν νοῦν ἀδυνατῶ τε καὶ ὁτιοῦν συμβαλέσθαι λόγου ἄξιον, ἀλλ' ἀτεχνῶς <u>νυστάζω</u>, ἐπειδὰν δέ τις περὶ Ὁμήρου μνησθῇ, εὐθύς τε ἐγρήγορα καὶ προσέχω τὸν νοῦν καὶ εὐπορῶ ὅτι λέγω; {ΣΩ.} ... ἔστι γὰρ τοῦτο τέχνη μὲν οὐκ ὂν παρὰ σοὶ περὶ Ὁμήρου εὖ λέγειν, ὃ νυνδὴ ἔλεγον, θεία δὲ δύναμις ἥ σε κινεῖ, ὥσπερ ἐν τῇ λίθῳ ἣν Εὐριπίδης μὲν Μαγνῆτιν ὠνόμασεν, οἱ δὲ πολλοὶ Ἡρακλείαν. καὶ γὰρ αὕτη ἡ λίθος οὐ μόνον αὐτοὺς τοὺς δακτυλίους ἄγει τοὺς σιδηροῦς ... οὕτω δὲ καὶ ἡ Μοῦσα ἐνθέους μὲν ποιεῖ αὐτή, διὰ δὲ τῶν ἐνθέων τούτων ἄλλων ἐνθουσιαζόντων ὁρμαθὸς ἐξαρτᾶται ... καὶ οἱ μελοποιοὶ οἱ ἀγαθοὶ ὡσαύτως, ὥσπερ οἱ <u>κορυβαντιῶντες</u> οὐκ ἔμφρονες ὄντες ὀρχοῦνται, οὕτω καὶ οἱ μελοποιοὶ οὐκ ἔμφρονες ὄντες τὰ καλὰ μέλη ταῦτα ποιοῦσιν, ἀλλ' ἐπειδὰν ἐμβῶσιν εἰς τὴν ἁρμονίαν καὶ εἰς τὸν ῥυθμόν, βακχεύουσι καὶ <u>κατεχόμενοι</u> ... Ἔχε δή μοι τόδε εἰπέ, ὦ Ἴων, καὶ μὴ ἀποκρύψῃ ὅτι ἄν σε ἔρωμαι· ὅταν εὖ εἴπῃς ἔπη καὶ <u>ἐκπλήξῃς</u> μάλιστα τοὺς θεωμένους ... τότε πότερον ἔμφρων εἶ ἢ ἔξω σαυτοῦ γίγνῃ καὶ παρὰ τοῖς πράγμασιν οἴεταί σου εἶναι ἡ ψυχὴ οἷς λέγεις ἐνθουσιάζουσα, ἢ ἐν Ἰθάκῃ οὖσιν ἢ ἐν Τροίᾳ ἢ ὅπως ἂν καὶ τὰ ἔπη ἔχῃ;{ΙΩΝ.} Ὡς ἐναργές μοι τοῦτο, ὦ Σώκρατες, τὸ τεκμήριον εἶπες· οὐ γάρ σε ἀποκρυψάμενος ἐρῶ. ἐγὼ γὰρ ὅταν ἐλεινόν τι λέγω, <u>δακρύων</u> ἐμπίμπλανταί μου <u>οἱ ὀφθαλμοί</u>· ὅταν τε φοβερὸν ἢ δεινόν, ὀρθαὶ αἱ τρίχες ἵστανται ὑπὸ φόβου καὶ ἡ <u>καρδία πηδᾷ</u> ... {ΣΩ.} Οἶσθα οὖν ὅτι οὗτός ἐστιν ὁ θεατὴς τῶν δακτυλίων ὁ ἔσχατος, ὧν ἐγὼ ἔλεγον ὑπὸ τῆς Ἡρακλειώτιδος λίθου ἀπ' ἀλλήλων τὴν δύναμιν λαμβάνειν; ὁ δὲ μέσος σὺ ὁ ῥαψῳδὸς καὶ ὑποκριτής, ὁ δὲ πρῶτος αὐτὸς ὁ ποιητής· ... καὶ ὁ μὲν τῶν ποιητῶν ἐξ ἄλλης Μούσης, ὁ δὲ ἐξ ἄλλης ἐξήρτηται—ὀνομάζομεν δὲ αὐτὸ κατέχεται, τὸ δέ ἐστι παραπλήσιον· ἔχεται γάρ—ἐκ δὲ τούτων τῶν πρώτων δακτυλίων, τῶν ποιητῶν, ἄλλοι ἐξ ἄλλου αὖ ἠρτημένοι εἰσὶ καὶ ἐνθουσιάζουσιν, οἱ μὲν ἐξ Ὀρφέως, οἱ δὲ ἐκ Μουσαίου· οἱ δὲ πολλοὶ ἐξ Ὁμήρου <u>κατέχονταί</u> τε καὶ ἔχονται.

ION. Why then, Socrates, do I lose attention and *nod off* and have absolutely no ideas of the least value, when any one speaks of any other poet; but when Homer is mentioned, I awake at once and am all attention and have plenty to say? SOCRATES. It's not hard to imagine, it's

---

[18]   I shall just mention Gonzalez 2011, whose interpretation is very close to mine, as expressed in Capra 2007b. Capuccino 2005:208–249 provides a detailed discussion and a massive bibliography.

crystal-clear. The gift which you possess of speaking excellently about Homer is not an art, but, as I was just saying, an inspiration; there is a divinity moving you, like that contained in the stone which Euripides calls a Magnet, but which is commonly known as the stone of Heraclea. This stone not only attracts iron rings, but also imparts to them a similar power of attracting other rings [...] In like manner the Muse first of all inspires men herself; and from these inspired persons a chain of other persons is suspended, who take the inspiration [...] And *as the Corybantian revelers* when they dance are not in their right mind, so the lyric poets are not in their right mind when they are composing their beautiful strains: but when falling under the power of music and meter they are inspired and *possessed* [...]. I wish you would frankly tell me, Ion, what I am going to ask of you: When you *carry* the audience *away* in the recitation of some striking passage [...] are you in your right mind? Are you not beside yourself and does not your soul in an ecstasy seem to be among the persons or places of which you are speaking, whether they are in Ithaca or in Troy or whatever may be the scene of the poem? ION. That proof strikes home to me, Socrates. For I must frankly confess that at the tale of pity, *my eyes are filled with tears*, and when I speak of horrors, my hair stands on end *and my heart leaps* (ἡ καρδία πηδᾷ). [...] SOC. Do you know that the spectator is the last of the rings which, as I am saying, receive the power of the original magnet from one another? The rhapsode like yourself and the actor are intermediate links, and the poet himself is the first of them. [...] And every poet has some Muse from whom he is suspended, and by whom he is said to be possessed, which is nearly the same thing; for he is taken hold of. And from these first rings, which are the poets, depend others, some deriving their inspiration from Orpheus, others from Musaeus; but the greater number are possessed and held by Homer

Plato *Ion* 532b–536b, trans. Jowett (modified)

The longer the chain, the weaker the force of the magnet. The process may be represented as follows:

The force that binds the rings together is called "divine possession," the Greek word being *katekho*, which commonly referred to religious forms of madness.[19] The poet's madness resembles the ecstatic fury of Bacchus' initiates. His emotional instability is described in quite dramatic terms: "my heart leaps," says Ion, "my eyes are filled with tears." Other poets make Ion "nod off," but Homer leaves him "unhinged": all of a sudden, he has "plenty to say," and he dances "like the Corybantian revelers." Needless to say, the outer "rings" of the poetic chain, that is, the audience, share the very same symptoms.

Magnetism, possession, Bacchic fury: at first sight, nothing could be more remote from Plato's alleged sobriety or from Socrates' celebrated intellectualism.[20] Ion is usually regarded as a quintessentially non-philosophic character. He seems to be a helpless, gullible fellow, who succumbs all too easily to Socrates' mocking questions. On second thought, however, Ion cannot be dismissed so lightly. Let us just reflect for a moment on *Socratic* discourse. In the *Symposium*, Alcibiades gives a full and ultimately reliable description of it.[21] Socrates and his speeches are compared to a mesmerizing Silenus, a Marsyas, and to the satyrs. Unlike these mythological doubles, however, Socrates can captivate the soul of his listeners through the sheer magic of his words, whose power of enchantment rival Marsyas' flutes and Olympus' melodies.[22] This comparison calls to mind the Bacchic and enthusiastic music that involved chains of delirious dancers. Socrates' words, moreover, induce a kind of possession:

---

[19] Cf. LSJ s.v. II.10.

[20] Plato is sometimes described as anti-Homeric even in the way he describes emotions. See Bouvier 2011.

[21] Alcibiades' description of Socrates is usually considered a "faithful" one, that is, one fully endorsed by Plato himself (see e.g. Brisson 1998b:51–54 and Zanker 1995:32–39), though its relationship to Socrates' speech is debated (see Destrée 2012 for a brief discussion of the better known interpretative approaches). Nevertheless, some distinguished scholars have tried to undermine its credibility by suggesting, for example, that Alcibiades is "the last person to understand the ironic Socrates," something that "cannot but compromise his praise" (Nightingale 1995:120 and cf. e.g. Narcy 2008). There is no doubt as to Alcibiades' ambiguous character, and the *Symposium* hints maliciously at the notorious scandals he was allegedly involved in (see Cornelli 2013). Does this affect the credibility of his description of Socrates (and, therefore, my present argument)? The question was variously debated at the 2013 Symposium Platonicum of the International Plato Society, which was entirely dedicated to the *Symposium*. The traditional view seems to predominate on the whole, though a few scholars share Nightingale's doubts. Interestingly, some scholars strike a middle ground: Petrucci 2013 and Nucci 2013 argue that Alcibiades gives us a faithful description of the *manifestations* of Socrates' virtue, even though he probably does not understand its philosophical foundation. My own argument is wholly compatible with this convincing interpretation.

[22] The comparison with Olympus calls to mind Socrates' reenacting of Stesichorus' song (see Chapter 2). Stesichorus' poems were also said to resemble Olympus' melodies (Plutarch *On Music* 1133f, with Barker 2001:11–12).

ἡμεῖς γοῦν ὅταν μέν του ἄλλου ἀκούωμεν λέγοντος καὶ πάνυ ἀγαθοῦ ῥήτορος ἄλλους λόγους, οὐδὲν μέλει ὡς ἔπος εἰπεῖν οὐδενί· ἐπειδὰν δὲ σοῦ τις ἀκούῃ ἢ τῶν σῶν λόγων ἄλλου λέγοντος, κἂν πάνυ φαῦλος ᾖ ὁ λέγων, ἐάντε γυνὴ ἀκούῃ ἐάντε ἀνὴρ ἐάντε μειράκιον, <u>ἐκπεπληγμένοι</u> ἐσμὲν καὶ <u>κατεχόμεθα</u>. ἐγὼ γοῦν, ὦ ἄνδρες, εἰ μὴ ἔμελλον κομιδῇ δόξειν μεθύειν, εἶπον ὁμόσας ἂν ὑμῖν οἷα δὴ πέπονθα αὐτὸς ὑπὸ τῶν τούτου λόγων καὶ πάσχω ἔτι καὶ νυνί. ὅταν γὰρ ἀκούω, πολύ μοι μᾶλλον ἢ τῶν <u>κορυβαντιώντων</u> ἥ τε <u>καρδία πηδᾷ</u> καὶ <u>δάκρυα ἐκχεῖται</u> ὑπὸ τῶν λόγων τῶν τούτου, ὁρῶ δὲ καὶ ἄλλους παμπόλλους τὰ αὐτὰ πάσχοντας·

As for us, when we hear the speeches of someone else, even if he's a very good orator, well, let's face it: we couldn't care less. But if one listens to you or hears your words as repeated by others, even if the speaker is no good, then it's totally different. Men, women, children: we all get *carried away, we are possessed.* And if I weren't afraid that you would think me hopelessly drunk, I would have sworn as well as spoken to the influence they have always had and still have over me. For *my heart leaps* more than that of any *Corybantian reveler,* and *my eyes rain tears* when I hear them.

Plato Symposium 215d–e

Socratic discourse would seem to provoke the same symptoms described in the *Ion*:

- Unhinged mind:     ἔκπληξις ~ ἐκπεπληγμένοι
- Palpitations:     καρδία πηδᾷ ~ καρδία πηδᾷ
- Tears:     δακρύων ... οἱ ὀφθαλμοί ~ δάκρυα ἐκχεῖται
- Possession:     κατεχόμενοι ~ κατεχόμεθα
- Corybantism:     κορυβαντιῶντες ~ κορυβαντιώντων

These striking parallels are hardly ever noticed, let alone explained.[23] Just like Homer, Socrates is unique in his capacity to spark passion in his listeners, a passion that manifests the very same symptoms: ecstasy, palpitations, tears, Corybantic frenzy. More importantly, the same effects are provoked whenever

---

[23] Fabio Massimo Giuliano sketches most of the parallels in his 2005 work, *Platone e la poesia: Teoria della composizione e prassi della ricezione* (see a "Note to Plato's *Symposium*," pages 216–218, cf. Giuliano 2004:176–179). The analogy receives no more than a passing remark in Asmis 1992:347 and Crotty 2009:xix. My own arguments develop a previous article of mine, cf. Capra 2007b, though I would like to emphasize that Giuliano's "Note," however sketchy, was a fundamental starting point for my own work.

people reproduce Socrates' words at second hand, even if they do so imperfectly. Consequently, Socrates' words result in a magical, or should we say magnetic, chain of effects. Remarkably, this is prefigured by the very structure of the *Symposium*, which features a famously complex narrative framework. The *Symposium* is, in fact, the narration of a narration of a narration:[24]

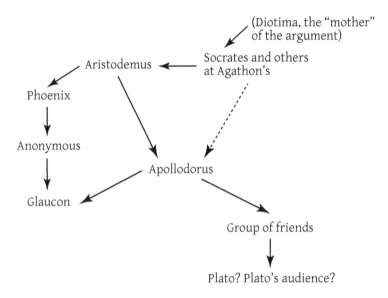

The core of the *Symposium* is allegedly what Socrates remembers of an amusing lecture given him by the priestess Diotima.[25] Socrates, in turn, tells the story again during a symposium. Aristodemus then reports it to Apollodorus, who eventually recounts it once more for the benefit of a group of friends. This amounts to three levels of narrative; but the picture is even more complicated. Prompted by philology, I would describe the narrative process as an "open" and "ramified" "recension." The "text" that Plato purports to reproduce is

---

[24]  For a good narratological account of the *Symposium*, see e.g. Scarcella 1987. Halperin 1992 has rapidly become a classic of sorts, and has made its way into the Oxford University Press's "Critical Assessments" of Plato (Smith 1998). In Halperin's clever interpretation, the chinese-box structure of the *Symposium* is an instance of what he refers to as the "erotics of narrativity," a literary procreation that both endorses and undermines the *Symposium*'s theory of reproduction as a human path to immortality. Blondell 2002 makes the interesting point that the narrators of the *Symposium* are meant to remind us of the danger of idolizing Socrates (106–112).

[25]  That Diotima's words are "the core" does not imply that they express the totality, or even the climax, of the *Symposium*'s philosophical message. Gonzalez 2012, for example, argues that "there is a tension between the mortal knowledge of the philosopher, continually demanding to be reborn by its continual retreat into oblivion, and that secure knowledge and possession of divine reality that the philosopher can only dream of" (51, from the abstract).

Apollodorus' account, but Apollodorus has taken some of the details of his story from Socrates himself (see dotted line). Moreover, the "textual tradition" has a rival offshoot in Glaucon, who, interestingly, was himself an author of Socratic dialogues.[26] It is probably no coincidence that Apollodorus dismisses Glaucon's account as unreliable, almost as if Plato were trying to discredit a rival.

The narrators are not especially talented, and yet Socrates' words do not lose their magic. This would seem to confirm Alcibiades' point that "even if the speaker is no good, we all get carried away, we are possessed" by Socrates' words, "even at secondhand, and however imperfectly repeated." The narrative structure of the *Symposium* clearly adds further evidence to Alcibiades' claim:

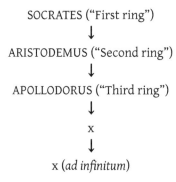

SOCRATES ("First ring")
↓
ARISTODEMUS ("Second ring")
↓
APOLLODORUS ("Third ring")
↓
x
↓
x (*ad infinitum*)

The intermediators in this process of storytelling are Socrates' fans, who are prone to the kind of frenzied possession so well epitomized by Alcibiades' image of a mesmerizing Silenus.[27]

To conclude, it is remarkable how Plato's dialogues seem to share the same genetic features of Homer's rhapsodies: in both cases, enthusiasm leads to a chain of multiple, successive appropriations. The emotional symptoms are strikingly similar, though, ultimately, Socratic discourse produces opposite effects: rhapsodic performances induce complacency and the dangerous presumption of knowing; Socrates' words, on the other hand, though arousing the same symptoms, are prompted by the recognition of one's ignorance and result in

---

[26] Diogenes Laertius 2.124 lists the titles of nine dialogues by Glaucon.

[27] Of Plato's dialogues, only the *Parmenides* features a similarly complicated framework, though the similarity only highlights the considerable difference between the two. Most telling of all is the way Plato depicts the effects of Eleatic discourse. Rather than create a mesmerizing, multiplying chain of narrations, as is the case with the Socratic *logoi* in the *Symposium*, those in the *Parmenides* backfire disastrously: the last "ring" of the chain, Antiphon, who, as a boy, was repeatedly exposed to Eleatism, ends up abandoning philosophy altogether; and the same is probably true of Pythodorus. As we show in Capra and Martinelli Tempesta 2011, the narrative chain of the *Symposium* dramatizes the protreptic force of Socratic discourse, whereas the narrative chain of the *Parmenides* reveals the *apotreptic* character of Eleatic discourse.

deep dissatisfaction.[28] Alcibiades lingers emphatically on the shame he experiences whenever he is exposed to Socrates' words, and this reminds one of the *Meno*, in which Socrates is humorously compared to an electric ray. Like the Homeric Muse, Socrates is "electric," but the ultimate effects of his words are beneficial (79e–80d).

Moreover, when Socrates replaces the Muse as the magnetic force, the flux of energy is unaffected by the progressive weakening typical of Homeric rhapsodies. The chain becomes potentially infinite: the magnetism does not fade as a result of the audience's passive reception. In Socratic chains, there is no such thing as a passive spectator as opposed to an active performer, for each "ring" takes an active role in the transmission of the *logoi*. Philosophy must differ from the passive reception of rhapsody, which in fact—as Isocrates seems to suggest—took place in gatherings of half-sleeping people.[29] These entranced and "enchained" people resemble the prisoners of Plato's cave and can be seen as an anti-model for the "free chain" of Socratic discourse.

One can conclude, therefore, that though Plato remained deeply attached to poetic tradition, he nevertheless transformed it profoundly. The dialogues can be seen as a kind of poetry because their very genesis and elaboration were conceptualized along recognizably rhapsodic lines. Plato strongly disapproved of the passive attitude he regarded as constitutive of his contemporaries' consumption of poetry. Nevertheless, his criticism was not aimed at every conceivable kind of poetry, and far less at emotional involvement as such, which plays a crucial role in the circulation of Socratic *logoi*.

It is now time to return to the *Phaedrus*, in which a similar pattern is clearly discernible. In Socrates' "palinode," we hear that on being "struck" by the beauty of the beloved (250a), the lover gains access to the divine realm of the Forms. His experience is described in terms that bring to mind an electric shock; something that sets in motion a kind of mimetic flux, including a *verbal* flux described in Bacchic terms.[30] The process binds three poles together, namely the Forms, the lover, and the beloved:

---

[28] The reversal emerges also from another interesting detail. In the *Symposium*, Alcibiades weeps while people around him burst out laughing (222c). Conversely, in a truly hilarious passage, Ion says that, ultimately, if he succeeds in bringing his audience to tears, he'll make a lot of money, and so *he* will be the one to laugh (535e). I owe this observation to Alexandra Pappas.

[29] *Panathenaicus* 12.263, with Graziosi 2010:113.

[30] Cf. 253a–b, where reference is made to Bacchic frenzy and *mimêsis*.

GODS/FORMS
↓
LOVER ("First ring")
↓
BELOVED ("Second ring")
↓

Once again, differences are no less important than similarities. The flux is akin to the poetic chain of the *Ion*, but two things stand out in particular. Firstly, the process is triggered off by the beloved rather than by the lover. Secondly, it includes a kind of rebound effect: when the lover is struck, the flow of beauty "rebounds" as if from a mirror and strikes the beloved, who then goes through the same experience as the lover, albeit in a milder form.[31] This prefigures an endless process, which ultimately blurs the boundaries between the traditional roles of lover and beloved, as well as those of poet and audience.[32] Once again, the conclusion is that the "rings" take a clearly active role in the process. This is evident from the final pages of the *Phaedrus*, when Socrates emphasizes the superior quality of oral dialogue to fixed and written speech. Not on any papyrus scroll, but in the soul of the beloved does the philosopher write, and his speech germinates in that soul, producing new speech that will fecundate more souls. In other words, philosophy brings about a long, uninterrupted chain of erotic speech, all carefully fashioned for the soul of the beloved.

Just like the *Symposium*, the *Phaedrus* rivals and appropriates the very fabric of poetic dissemination. Of course, such a pattern is only one of the "poetic" features of the *Phaedrus*. As I argued in the first two chapters, Socrates' "inspiration" has deep roots in the Greek poetic tradition. However, there is much more to it than this, for Socrates is not only inspired—he actually undergoes what can only be described as a poetic initiation. In order to demonstrate this, I shall examine two passages that, to the best of my knowledge, have never been

---

[31] For a good account of the mirror image in the *Phaedrus*, see Belfiore 2012.

[32] Role reversal is typical of Socratic *eros* as described in the *Symposium*. Edmonds rightly points out that "it is the lover himself, already pregnant by virtue of his stage in life, who gives birth with the assistance of the beloved. In the *Symposium*, Plato depicts his teacher not as the progenitor and begetter of ideas upon beautiful youths but as Socrates the Beautiful, the beloved who assists as a midwife at the labor of the fertile young men, helping them bring their spiritual progeny to light" (Edmonds 2000:266). The scholar also notes that "this confusion over the roles of the lover and beloved is a theme that recurs throughout the *Symposium*, and Plato includes a number of hints that this pattern is significant for his ideas of philosophic education" (Edmonds 2000:272). Besides the obvious example of Alcibiades, who famously ends up being the lover rather than the beloved, Edmonds points to Aristodemus, who behaves like a beloved but at 173b is called the lover of Socrates. Agathon, too, takes the initiative of sharing his couch with Socrates, thus contradicting Alcibiades' claim that Socrates is always on the hunt for beautiful boys (contrast 175c–d and 213c).

considered in this light before:[33] the first is Socrates' apotropaic prayer at the end of the palinode, which has the function of a negative foil; the second is the celebrated myth of the cicadas, which may be construed as the complementary *pars construens.*[34]

## Averting Poetic "Termination": Socrates and Thamyris

Socrates' prayer to Eros brings the palinode to a close:

Αὕτη σοι, ὦ φίλε Ἔρως, εἰς ἡμετέραν δύναμιν ὅτι καλλίστη καὶ ἀρίστη δέδοταί τε καὶ ἐκτέτεισται παλινῳδία, τά τε ἄλλα καὶ τοῖς ὀνόμασιν ἠναγκασμένη ποιητικοῖς τισιν διὰ Φαῖδρον εἰρῆσθαι. ἀλλὰ τῶν προτέρων τε συγγνώμην καὶ τῶνδε χάριν ἔχων, εὐμενὴς καὶ ἵλεως <u>τὴν ἐρωτικήν μοι τέχνην</u> ἣν ἔδωκας <u>μήτε ἀφέλῃ μήτε πηρώσῃς</u> δι' ὀργήν, δίδου τ' ἔτι μᾶλλον ἢ νῦν παρὰ τοῖς καλοῖς τίμιον εἶναι. ἐν τῷ πρόσθεν δ' εἴ τι λόγῳ σοι ἀπηχὲς εἴπομεν Φαῖδρός τε καὶ ἐγώ, Λυσίαν τὸν τοῦ λόγου πατέρα αἰτιώμενος <u>παῦε τῶν τοιούτων λόγων.</u>

This, dear Eros, is offered and paid to you as the finest and best palinode of which I am capable, especially given that it was forced to use some-what poetical language because of Phaedrus. Forgive what went before and regard this with favor; be kind and gracious—do not in anger *take away or maim the erotic expertise* which you gave me, and grant that I be valued still more than now by the beautiful. If in our speech Phaedrus and I said anything harsh against you, blame Lysias as the father and *make him cease from speeches* of this kind.

Plato Phaedrus 257b–c, trans. Rowe (modified)

With its sole Platonic instance of the verb "to maim" (*pêroô*), the prayer expresses Socrates' concern for his somewhat elusive *ars amatoria.*[35] As I noted in the first

---

[33] Gutzwiller 1991 suggests that "the movement of the dialogue as a whole is governed by the paradigm of a herdsman's conversion to poet or seer" (75). She does not develop this brilliant intuition, however, perhaps because the *Phaedrus* is not, after all, her main concern. Thus, she limits herself to applying the analogy to the progression of the three speeches in the first half of the *Phaedrus.*

[34] A third passage is Socrates' prayer to Pan at the end of the dialogue, which could be read as "poetic license." This is discussed in Chapter 4.

[35] In the *Symposium*, Socrates famously states that love is the only field in which he can claim some kind of knowledge (177d and *passim*). That love is something divine and potentially fruitful for pedagogy is also clear from the *Alcibiades* by Aeschines (fr. 11 = SSR vi A 53): cf. Ioppolo 1999 for a useful comparison with the *Symposium* and Belfiore 2012 (especially 1–12) for an overview of

chapter, the maiming refers back to the blinding of Stesichorus. But this is not the whole story: Socrates also alludes to the archetypal "incident" of this kind. I am thinking of Thamyris, the Thracian poet who was famously maimed by the Muses and who became a very popular subject in classical Athens.[36]

In the *Iliad*, the poetic "termination" of Thamyris—included as it is in the emphatically Muse-inspired Catalogue of Ships—seems to provide a negative foil for "Homer" himself.[37] Homer's blindness was synonymous with inspiration, as if blindness were the price he had to pay for his prodigious song (one thinks of Demodocus in the *Odyssey*).[38] By contrast, Thamyris is trapped in a somewhat unexpected "lose-lose situation," for after suffering physical damage, he is *also* deprived of his song.[39] It is worth revisiting the relevant passage in the *Iliad*:

> ... ἔνθά τε Μοῦσαι
> ἀντόμεναι Θάμυριν τὸν Θρήϊκα παῦσαν ἀοιδῆς
> Οἰχαλίηθεν ἰόντα παρ' Εὐρύτου Οἰχαλιῆος·
> στεῦτο γὰρ εὐχόμενος νικησέμεν εἴ περ ἂν αὐταὶ
> Μοῦσαι ἀείδοιεν κοῦραι Διὸς αἰγιόχοιο·
> αἳ δὲ χολωσάμεναι πηρὸν θέσαν, αὐτὰρ ἀοιδὴν
> θεσπεσίην ἀφέλοντο καὶ ἐκλέλαθον κιθαριστύν

> ... where the Muses
> met Thamyris the Thracian and made him cease from his song

---

Socrates' erotic art. However, the only other instance of *erôtikê tekhnê* as such is found in the *Sophist* (222e), where according to the Stranger it refers to a despicable knack in conquering young boys by way of presents and flattery. In the *Phaedrus* itself, *erôtikê tekhnê* is twice paralleled by the similar expression *erôtikê mania*, which marks the unusual overlapping of the two otherwise very different notions of *mania* and *tekhnê*. Other Platonic passages relevant to the problem of Socrates' knowledge of things erotic include *Charmides* 155d, *Lysis* 206a, and *Theagenes* 128b. All in all, the Socrates of the *Phaedrus* is very similar to the Socrates of the *Alcibiades*, who is equally fascinated by the notion of divine, dionysian enthusiasm.

[36] Note that Plato mentions Thamyris no fewer than three times: *Ion* 533b, *Republic* 620a, and *Laws* 829e. Thamyris became very popular in fifth-century Athens, probably because Sophocles dedicated an early tragedy to him, the *Thamyras* (see Meriani 2007 and Wilson 2009), in which, according to the *Vita Sophoclis*, he also performed as an actor. The Athenian pictorial record is also very interesting, and Thamyris was famous enough outside Athens to feature in Polygnotus' *Nekyia* in the Cnidian *leskhe* at Delphi (Pausanias 10.30.8): see Cillo 1993, who cautiously assigns to Polygnotus a similar image, which, according to the *Vita Sophoclis*, was also in the *Stoa Poikilê* (212). In the fourth century, no fewer than two theatrical plays were dedicated to him, namely Antiphanes' *Thamyris* (fr. 104 PCG) and the *Rhesus*. As Biles 2011 has argued, Thamyris' influence was so strong that it shaped the poetics of competition between comic playwrights (12–55). See also Wilson 2009:59–70.

[37] Cf. e.g. Ford 1992:97; Martin 1989:229–230; Nagy 1990:376.

[38] *Odyssey* 8.62–64. Cf. Graziosi 2002:143–144.

[39] *Iliad* 2.599, αὐτὰρ ἀοιδὴν, seems to "introduce a contrast," that is a compensation (Wilson 2009:50).

as he was journeying from Oechalia, from the house of Eurytus the
Oechalian:
for he vaunted with boasting that he would conquer, were the Muses
themselves
to sing against him, the daughters of Zeus that bears the Aegis;
but they in their wrath maimed him, and took away
his wondrous song (ἀοιδὴν ≈ τέχνην), and made him forget his
minstrelsy

Homer Iliad 2.594–600 trans. Murray (modified)

It seems to me that the verbal similarities with Socrates' prayer are striking.[40]
With an apotropaic shift, Socrates depicts himself as a potential Thamyris, with
two interesting qualifications. The first is that the Muses and song are replaced
by Eros and erotic expertise. The replacement of song makes perfect sense:
Socrates is promoting a form of erotic rhetoric in which speech is prompted by
love—and it should be noted that in the Euripidean *Rhesus,* Thamyris is blinded,
and song and *tekhnê* are mentioned together.[41] Moreover, by Plato's time the
myth had acquired sexual overtones, which made it even more suitable for the
erotic context of the *Phaedrus.* Thamyris, who had since been credited with the
discovery of pederasty, was unable to contain his sexual appetite, and so struck
a bargain with the Muses: were he to prevail, they would let him lie with them
all[42]—which, rather predictably, proved impossible.

Unlike Thamyris, Socrates wishes to retain both his art *and* his integrity.
In other words, he wishes and prays for a "win-win" outcome, which would
make him superior to both Homer and Stesichorus, not to mention Thamyris,
who, interestingly, seems to have had a cultic role as a musical anti-paradigm.
As Timothy Power points out, circumstantial evidence suggests that in the
fourth century BCE the "Thamyrists" (Θαμυρίδδοντες) "served as organizers of
competitive choral performances for Thespian youths" perhaps "in connection

---

[40] And, to the best of my knowledge, unnoticed.

[41] Euripides *Rhesus* 921–925. Cf. also Hesiod fr. 65 M-W.

[42] The complete version can be found in Apollodorus 1.16. Sexual overtones are implicit, however,
as early as in Timaeus (FGrH 566 F 83), and possibly in the myth of Er at the end of the *Republic*
(620a). The latter also mentions Orpheus' metamorphosis into a nightingale right after the
account of his death at the hands of women, which might possibly be related to the crude myth
and well-known metamorphoses of Procne, Tereus, and Philomela. Even more importantly, the
story is given almost in full, complete with the spicy detail of Thamyris' erotic proposal, by
Isocrates' pupil Asclepiades (FGrH 12 F 10), whose work *Tragodumena* was based on versions of
the myths known from tragedy: thus it is very probable that the proposal appeared as early as in
Sophocles' *Thamyras* (see Meriani 2007:48). For different reasons, Brillante 2009 also concludes
that "il mito di Thamyris ... doveva essere compiuto in tutte le sue parti già in età arcaica (*Iliade,*
*Catalogo* esiodeo, *Minyas*)" (20).

with a hero cult for Thamyris in the Valley of the Muses, which the Thamyrists apparently managed. These performances likely had an initiatory function, for which the suffering of Thamyris at the hands of the Muses—a failed rite of passage, broadly speaking—could have served as a mythic anti-model."[43] This reconstruction would considerably reinforce my suggestion that Socrates' prayer alludes to the "termination" of Thamyris as a convenient "anti-model."

## The Gift of the Muses

Having examined the averted *termination* of Socrates, I shall now move on to the myth of the cicadas and to the *initiation* proper. The myth binds together the first part, devoted to *eros*, and the second, which discusses rhetoric.[44] Socrates describes the story as something that no "friend of the Muses" should ignore, thus strongly conjuring up the idea of *mousikê*.[45] Almost the whole passage reads as follows:

> Σχολὴ μὲν δή, ὡς ἔοικε· καὶ ἅμα μοι δοκοῦσιν ὡς ἐν τῷ πνίγει ὑπὲρ κεφαλῆς ἡμῶν οἱ τέττιγες <u>ᾄδοντες</u> καὶ <u>ἀλλήλοις διαλεγόμενοι</u> καθορᾶν καὶ ἡμᾶς. εἰ οὖν ἴδοιεν καὶ <u>νὼ</u> καθάπερ τοὺς πολλοὺς ἐν μεσημβρίᾳ μὴ διαλεγομένους ἀλλὰ <u>νυστάζοντας</u> καὶ κηλουμένους ὑφ' αὑτῶν δι' ἀργίαν τῆς διανοίας, δικαίως ἂν <u>καταγελῷεν</u>, ἡγούμενοι ἀνδράποδ' ἄττα σφίσιν ἐλθόντα εἰς τὸ καταγώγιον ὥσπερ <u>προβάτια</u> <u>μεσημβριάζοντα</u> περὶ τὴν κρήνην εὕδειν· ἐὰν δὲ ὁρῶσι διαλεγομένους καὶ παραπλέοντάς σφας ὥσπερ Σειρῆνας ἀκηλήτους, ὃ <u>γέρας</u> παρὰ θεῶν ἔχουσιν ἀνθρώποις διδόναι, τάχ' ἂν δοῖεν ἀγασθέντες ... λέγεται δ' ὥς ποτ' ἦσαν οὗτοι ἄνθρωποι τῶν πρὶν Μούσας γεγονέναι, γενομένων δὲ Μουσῶν καὶ φανείσης ᾠδῆς οὕτως ἄρα τινὲς τῶν τότε <u>ἐξεπλάγησαν</u> ὑφ' ἡδονῆς, ὥστε ᾄδοντες <u>ἠμέλησαν σίτων τε καὶ ποτῶν</u>, καὶ ἔλαθον τελευτήσαντες αὑτούς· ἐξ ὧν τὸ τεττίγων γένος μετ' ἐκεῖνο φύεται, <u>γέρας τοῦτο παρὰ Μουσῶν</u> λαβόν, μηδὲν τροφῆς δεῖσθαι γενόμενον, ἀλλ' ἄσιτόν τε καὶ ἄποτον εὐθὺς ᾄδειν, ἕως ἂν τελευτήσῃ, καὶ μετὰ ταῦτα ἐλθὸν παρὰ Μούσας ἀπαγγέλλειν τίς τίνα αὐτῶν τιμᾷ τῶν ἐνθάδε. Τερψιχόρᾳ μὲν οὖν τοὺς ἐν τοῖς χοροῖς τετιμηκότας αὐτὴν ἀπαγγέλλοντες ποιοῦσι προσφιλεστέρους, τῇ δὲ Ἐρατοῖ τοὺς ἐν τοῖς

---

[43] Power 2010:208, with further bibliography. The evidence amounts to an inscription (SEG.503) and a fragment of Amphion of Thespiae (FGrH 387 F 1).

[44] The rather mysterious "pleasant bend" (γλυκὺς ἀγκών), which appears a few lines earlier (257d), has been plausibly interpreted as a metaliterary reference to a turning point in the dialogue. See Segoloni 2007.

[45] "It certainly isn't appropriate for a man who loves the Muses (φιλόμουσον ἄνδρα) not to have heard of things like this" (259b).

ἐρωτικοῖς, καὶ ταῖς ἄλλαις οὕτως, κατὰ τὸ εἶδος ἑκάστης τιμῆς· τῇ δὲ
πρεσβυτάτῃ Καλλιόπῃ καὶ τῇ μετ᾽ αὐτὴν Οὐρανίᾳ τοὺς ἐν φιλοσοφίᾳ
διάγοντάς τε καὶ τιμῶντας τὴν ἐκείνων μουσικὴν ἀγγέλλουσιν, αἳ δὴ
μάλιστα τῶν Μουσῶν περί τε οὐρανὸν καὶ λόγους οὖσαι θείους τε καὶ
ἀνθρωπίνους <u>ἱᾶσιν καλλίστην φωνήν</u>. πολλῶν δὴ οὖν ἕνεκα λεκτέον τι
καὶ οὐ καθευδητέον <u>ἐν τῇ μεσημβρίᾳ</u>.

We have plenty of time, it seems; and I think, too, that as the cicadas
*sing* above our heads [i.e. *on the plane-tree*] in their usual fashion in the
heat, and *dialogue* with each other, they look down on us too. So if they
the *two of us* as well, just like most people *at midday*, not dialoguing
but *nodding off* under their spell through lazy-mindedness, they would
justly *laugh at us*, thinking that some slaves had come to their retreat
and were having their *midday sleep* around the spring, *like sheep*; but
if they see us dialoguing and sailing past them un-bewitched by their
Siren song, perhaps they may respect us and give us that *gift* which they
have from the gods to give to men [...] The story is that these cicadas
were once men, belonging to a time before the Muses were born, and
that with the birth of the Muses and the appearance of song some of
the men of the time they *got carried away* by pleasure, so much that in
their singing they *neglected to eat and drink*, and failed to notice that
they had died; from them the race of cicadas was afterwards born, with
this *gift from the Muses*, that from their birth they have no need of suste-
nance, but immediately sing, without food or drink, until they die, and
after that go and report to the Muses which among those here honors
which of them. To Terpsichore they report those who have honored her
in the choral dance, and make them dearer to her; to Erato, those who
have honored her in the affairs of *eros*; and to the other Muses similarly,
according to the form of honor belonging to each; but to Calliope, the
eldest, and to Ourania who comes after her, they announce those who
spend their time in philosophy and honor the music which belongs to
them—who most of all the Muses have their sphere both the heavens
and talk, both divine and human, and *pour the most beautiful voice*. So
there are many reasons why we should say something, and not sleep
*in the midday heat*.

Plato *Phaedrus* 258e–259d, trans. Rowe (modified)

A very familiar pattern is clearly evident here too. The cicada song is expected
to inspire Socrates and Phaedrus just as Homer inspires Ion: they should be
both alert and "carried away"; instead of "nodding off" (the same word used

for Ion), they should be loquacious and yield to the power of their own Muses, just as Ion is carried away exclusively by Homer. However, the solar gift of the cicadas amounts to an ultimately *positive* paradigm, as should be clear from the following scheme:

1(a)   Cicadas sing and *dialogue* (ἀλλήλοις διαλεγόμενοι).

1(b)   Socrates suggests he and Phaedrus should dialogue (διαλεγομένους).

2(a)   Cicadas ignore bodily needs.

2(b)   Socrates suggests he and Phaedrus ignore sleep.

3(a)   The cicadas' perseverance earned them a gift (γέρας) from the Muses.

3(b)   Socrates' and Phaedrus' perseverance may earn them a gift (γέρας) from the cicadas.

In the *Phaedrus*, then, cicadas stand for music *and* philosophy, in that they both sing *and* dialogue, and it is Socrates' wish that he and Phaedrus may receive the same *geras* the cicadas once received from the Muses (including Calliope and Ourania, who are explicitly credited with a philosophical nature).[46] Once again, the result is a chain of inspired, and inspiring, *logoi:*[47]

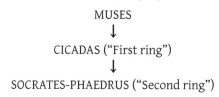

MUSES
↓
CICADAS ("First ring")
↓
SOCRATES-PHAEDRUS ("Second ring")

---

[46]   This should be enough evidence to discourage readers from construing the cicadas as a negative paradigm, and it is worth mentioning that Hermias Alexandrinus had no hesitation in identifying them as divine creatures, whose metamorphosis and devotion to music he ascribes to their philosophical nature. (Cf. on 259b, p. 226.5–30 Lucarini-Moreschini) Among modern critics, however, "negative" interpretations seem to be predominant. cf. de Vries 1969:193; Griswold 1986:166; Ferrari 1987:57 (where the cicadas stand for Phaedrus' excessive *philologia*); Burger 1980:73–74 (where they stand for the deceitful fascination of the written word); White 1993:190; De Luise 1997:26–27; Carson 1986:138–140; Nicholson 1999:220–21 (where their metamorphosis is a sign of degradation); Männlein-Robert 2012:92 and 100 (where they stand for "rein ästhetischen Sinne" and "produzieren nun Klang"); and Werner 2012:133–152 (where they stand for the potentially bewitching power of Socrates' own palinode). Nor should the cicadas' *ekplêxis* and the comparison with the sirens prove the point, for neither yields any negative meaning: as we have seen in the second chapter, *ekplêxis* is the hallmark of philosophical love (above, page 72), and sirens are depicted in a clearly positive light in the dialogues (cf. *Republic* 617c, *Symposium* 216a, and *Cratylus* 403d, with Capra 2000). In a nutshell, "Zoals de Cicade is de filosoof een muzenvriend" (Pinnoy 1986–1987:111).

[47]   One may add a third ring, namely that of Socrates' and Phaedrus' companions as mentioned at 279a: the two friends will report to them the message they have received from the local gods.

Yet again, there are important differences to be noted: rather than listen passively to the cicadas, Socrates and Phaedrus should take an active role and fashion their own dialogic song, just as the cicadas did in the past. As we have already seen, Plato constantly plays with the rhapsodic tradition in order to appropriate and transform it. As a result, the myth ultimately confirms the difference between the passivity of rhapsodic chains, with their numbing effect, and Socratic chains, which require alertness and active participation on the part of the "rings." Yet the myth has even more in store than this.

One may wonder why Plato decided to mention the cicadas at all. Very briefly, there are three traditions behind this apparently surprising choice. To begin with, cicadas were regarded as quintessentially poetic creatures: a paradigm of exclusive devotion to *mousikê*.[48] Secondly, earthborn cicadas were a powerful symbol of Athenian autochthony, which makes perfect sense in the religious context of Plato's *Phaedrus*.[49] Finally, "cicada" had seemingly become a slanderous nickname for poking fun at miserable, garrulous philosophers, so that Plato's choice, as so often is the case, looks like another instance of his self-deprecating humor.[50] Instead of refuting the popular accusation that philosophers resembled idle cicadas, Plato appropriates the image ironically and turns it into a sublime myth conveying the idea of philosophical *autarkeia* and of exclusive devotion to the "music of philosophy."[51]

The cicadas have another important function besides the three just mentioned. One detail is particularly arresting: what the cicadas receive from the Muses, only to pass it on to humans, is a "gift" (Greek *geras*), the gift of the Muses. Within the Greek tradition, this term was used to signify poetic inspiration, or some material object that symbolized it: the gift of the Muses is, of course, the culminating moment of poetic initiation,[52] and it is from this perspective that I interpret the passage.[53] The following initiation narratives would all appear to support my argument:

---

[48] Cf. e.g. Borthwick 1966, Lelli 2001, Cunha Corrêa 2010 (179–200), and Bodson 1976, the last of whom encapsulates the idea by noting that "les poètes grecs ont tous, ou peu s'en faut, chanté les cigales et, à travers elles, exalté les charmes des Muses ou la grâce souveraine d'Apollon" (Bodson 1976:93).

[49] Cf. e.g. Aristophanes *Knights* 1331, with Dušanić 1992:25, and especially Hoffmann 1988 for the archaeological and numismatic evidence.

[50] See Capra 2000.

[51] As early as Hesiod, the cicada, both an idler and a singer, "could both represent the poet and be a foil for him." I owe this suggestion to Lilah-Grace Fraser Canevaro, whose PhD dissertation (Durham UK, discussed September 2012) is an interpretative commentary on Hesiod's *Works and Days*.

[52] For the equation gift of the Muses = poetic inspiration, cf. e.g. Tarditi 1989 and Aloni 2011.

[53] That γέρας refers to inspiration is made quite clear from its further use at 262d, when Socrates refers back to his inspired palinode and attributes its efficacy to the inspiration provided by the local gods and by the cicadas.

## Chapter Three

### a) HESIOD

And one day the Muses taught Hesiod glorious song while he was shep-
herding his lambs under holy Helicon, and this word first the goddesses
said to me [...]: "Shepherds of the wilderness, wretched things of shame,
mere bellies, we know how to speak many false things as though they
were true; but we know, when we will, to utter true things." So said the
ready-voiced daughters of great Zeus, and they plucked and gave me a
rod, a shoot of sturdy laurel, a marvelous thing, and breathed into me
a divine voice to celebrate things that shall be and things there were
aforetime; and they bade me sing of the race of the blessed gods that
are eternally, but ever to sing of themselves both first and last. But why
all this about oak or rock?

Hesiod Theogony 22–35, trans. Finley

### b) EPIMENIDES[54]

Epimenides—when his father sent him to the countryside to fetch a
sheep—made a detour about midday: he fell asleep in a cave, and slept
for 57 years. When he woke up, he looked for the sheep, for he was
certain he had had just a quick sleep [...]

Diogenes Laertius 1.109

he claimed he had met, in his dream, the gods ... Aletheia and Dike

Maximus of Tyrus Dissertations 10.1

[the gods told him?] "Cretans [are] always liars, evil beasts, lazy
gluttons."

"Paul of Tarsus" Letter to Titus 1.12

Epimenides is turned into a seer, endowed with "enthusiastic and
telestic wisdom," which the Athenians put down to his being the son
of a nymph.

Plutarch Life of Solon 12.4

---

[54] For a good overall reconstruction of Epimenides' initiation, based on a number of various
fragmentary sources, see Brillante 2004. For a sensible account of Epimenides' place in the epic
tradition, see Arrighetti 2006:109–118. The collection provided by Federico and Visconti 2001
offers a number of valuable insights on different aspects of this elusive figure.

## c) ARCHILOCHUS RECOUNTED

They recount that Archilochos, when he was still a young man, was sent by his father Telesikles to the fields, to the district called the Meadows, to bring a heifer down for sale. He got up at night before sunrise, while the moon was still bright, to lead the heifer to the city. As he came to the place called Slippery Rocks, they say that he thought he saw a group of women. And, since he thought that they were leaving work for the city, he approached them and made fun of them. But they greeted him with good humor and laughter, and asked him if he intended to sell the cow he had in tow. When he answered that he did, they said that they would give him a good price. But, once they had said this, neither they nor the heifer could be seen, but lying before his feet he saw a lyre. He was dumb-founded and, after he had the time to regain his wits, he realized that the women who had appeared to him were the Muses ...

> "*Mnesiepes* inscription," E1 II 22–38, trans. Clay[55]

## d) ARCHILOCHUS DEPICTED[56]

"The *pyxis* divides into two panels. In the first a cowherd and a draped female figure flank a cow, whose four legs are still just visible. The female figure framing this composition to the right holds a *plektron* and a strap in her hand. Turn the vase and the scene that next appears represents a poet seated on a *diphros* holding a lyre. He is flanked by two Muses. I say "he," recognizing that this seated figure has universally been identified as a Muse. As I read the narrative, Archilochus is shown in the first panel as young cowherd; in the second he is shown holding the Muses' gift of a lyre, flanked by two Muses. To the right of this grouping are two more Muses. [...] The dividers of the two panels are a tree and the back of a standing Muse."

These and similar stories were no doubt well known to Plato's contemporaries,[57] and they were thought to describe a state of being akin to nympholepsy,

---

[55] See Clay 2004:109.

[56] This is Clay's reading (2004:14, 55) of the picture that appears in the current volume on page 119 of Chapter 4.

[57] Hesiod is mentioned and discussed countless times in Plato's dialogues: see Boys-Stones and Haubold 2010 (and Graziosi 2010 for the Athenians' acquaintance with Hesiodic performances). Epimenides was said to have purified Athens and is mentioned a couple of times by Plato himself: see *Laws* 644d and 677d. Finally, Corso 2008 comments: "Archilochus is remembered by Herodotus (1.12), and Sophocles (*Electra* 96), Euripides (*Medea* 679), and Aristophanes (*Acharnenses* 119–120,

which is precisely the state of possession Socrates claims he is in.[58] They clearly share a recurrent pattern,[59] which, in more or less complete form, is found throughout Greek literature—be it the result of direct imitation or of the constant adaptation of an archetypal blueprint.[60] The pattern can be said to consist of ten common features:

1. Man in the in countryside: a, b, c, d.

2. Noontime: a? (as at *Palatine Anthology* 9.64[61]), b, possibly c and d.[62] Cf. Aesop's noon initiation.[63]

---

278; *Pax* 603–604, 1148; *Aves* 1764; *Lysistrata* 1254–1256; *Ranae* 704; *Plutus* 476) quote Archilochean expressions ... That an oligarch like Critias condemned Archilochus because of his low social rank and unethical behavior suggests that the poet may have found further favor within Pericles' radical democratic party, since he did not comply with aristocratic desiderata. It is quite likely that this period saw the erection of the portrait that would become the template for later images of the poet" (Corso 2008:271–273). For a full account of the ancient reception of Archilochus, ranging from Pindar and Cratinus to the Roman poets, cf. Gerber 2008. Alexis, Plato's contemporary, wrote the *Archilochos* or *Archilochoi*, a title that suggests this comedy may have dealt with Archilochus' biography.

58 Cf. 279b with my Introduction to the current volume. As Kathryn Gutzwiller perceptively remarks, "Maximus of Tyre tells of a Melesagoras, an Eleusinian prophet, who was "possessed by the nymphs" (ἐκ νυμφῶν κάτοχος, 38.3a). This information immediately follows a discussion of Hesiod's conversion from shepherd to poet (γενόμενον ποιητὴν ἐκ ποιμένος, 38.2a) and precedes a discussion of Epimenides, who was converted from herdsman to seer during a sleep that began at noon. The order of the list shows that the divine encounter of the herdsman was conceived of as a form of possession by the gods that, if not actually called nympholepsy, was equivalent to it" (Gutzwiller 1991:77).

59 Grottanelli 1992 has an excellent discussion of stories 1–3, to which he adds, quite appropriately, the initiation story recounted in the *Romance of Aesop*. Caillois 1988 provides other fascinating parallels, including modern lore.

60 Cf. e.g. the proem of Callimachus' *Aetia*, which is consciously modeled on that of the *Theogony*, and cf. Theocritus 7, which presents even more clearly most of the elements I list below. The story of Aesop, on the contrary, does not seem to be constructed in the same literary way, that is, as a self-conscious attempt at a subtle imitation of a given model. Note, moreover, that there are significant differences in the way Archilochus is initiated: the version provided by Mnesiepes' inscription does not coincide completely with that visible on the *pyxis*.

61 Cf. the discussion in Kambylis 1965. In the light of *Palatine Anthology* 9.64 and of other parallels involving noon inspiration, he concludes that "dass diese Vorstellung auch in der Zeit des Hesiodos und besonders unter den Landleuten verbreitet war, ist nach den bereits angeführten Beispielen durchaus wahrscheinlich. Man wird sich heute noch umso leichter davon überzeugen lassen, wenn man einmal im Sommer diese geheimnisvolle und wirklich göttliche Stunde des Mittags im Süden erlebt hat" (Kambylis 1965:60–61). Cf. also Sens 2011 for more parallels related to noontime inspiration (312).

62 Most scholars assume that Archilochus' encounter with the Muses takes place at night or very early in the morning, but the inscription is vague on the point, and the *pyxis* certainly does not support a nocturnal setting. Brillante 1990 makes a strong case for noon as the implicit time of the encounter as recounted in the inscription.

63 *Life of Aesop* 6. Two more examples are worth mentioning. In the Homeric *Hymn to Hermes*, the child god plays the first ever lyre at midday (17). Secondly, Pausanias tells the story of a shepherd

3. Livestock animal present: a, b, c, d.

4. Tree and/or rock present: a? (cf. the "riddle" at line 35[64]), b, c, d.

5. Man meets gods: a, b, c, d.

6. Gods make fun of man: a, b, also vice versa in c.

7. Metamorphosis, of either man or animal: c, d. Implicit in a, b?

8. Man loses control: b, c. Implicit in d?

9. Gods bestow a symbolic gift on man: a, c, d.

10. Gods bestow inspiration on man: a, b, d.

With these points in mind, it is well worth looking at the cicada myth again, paying particular attention to the underlined words. We are in the middle of the dialogue, and Socrates and Phaedrus are talking under a plane-tree. They listen to the cicadas, who sing and *dialogue* in the midday heat—a very unusual detail. Both Socrates and Phaedrus (note the striking and exceptional form of the dual pronoun)[65] should do the same, because if they fail to do so and nod off like sheep, the cicadas, who are in fact the prophets of the Muses, will laugh at them. On the other hand, if they keep dialoguing, the cicadas will give them a divine gift. The cicadas were once men, but then the Muses were born, and the men got carried away by *mousikê*, to the point that they forgot to eat or drink, and died without even realizing it. The Muses were amazed and turned them into cicadas, who now spend their entire lives singing as prophets of the Muses. As such, they report to the Muses on the behavior of men. Each Muse has her own followers: lovers follow Erato, choral dancers follow Terpsichore, and Calliope and Ourania preside over philosophers, since philosophy is the most beautiful kind of *mousikê*.

Whether concretely, potentially, or in an otherwise oblique form, the elements of traditional initiation scenes are all present in the cicada myth: 1. countryside; 2. noontime; 3. sheep; 4. plane-tree; 5. Muses; 6. mocking gods;

---

who fell asleep by the tomb of Orpheus around midday and suddenly started singing Orpheus' poems while sleeping (9.30.10). On the latter, see Grottanelli 1992:233.

[64] The mention of oak and rock at *Theogony* 35 (ἀλλὰ τίη μοι ταῦτα περὶ δρῦν ἢ περὶ πέτρην;) is a notorious *crux* (cf. the thorough discussion of West 1966 *ad loc.*). For my purpose, it is important to note that the *Phaedrus* mentions both oak and rock at 275b–c. He clearly understands them in a literal sense, as part of the prophetic landscape of Dodona. "Oak and rock" are, of course, part of a formula found in Homer as well, and Labarbe 1949 reads 275b as an "evocation ... fugace," so that "Homère ne peut guère avoir été mis en cause. On pensera à l'association proverbiale de l'arbre (du chêne) et du rocher (de la pierre)" (305n2). However, the emphasis on truth, together with the context of the dialogue as a whole, suggests that Plato had the *Theogony* in mind.

[65] In classical prose, νώ, a poetic form, is found only in the *Phaedrus* (in the cicada myth and at 278b) and in the *Greater Alcibiades* (124d).

7. metamorphosis; 8. unhinged mind; 9.–10. gift(s) from the Muses. It is also worth noting that cicadas are a prominent feature of Hesiod's summer landscape in the *Works and Days*,[66] and that in the *Theogony*, Calliope's gift takes the form of dew (ἐέρση),[67] which both poets and philosophers recognized as the sole, distinctive nourishment of cicadas.[68] An element of frugality too seems to be essential: Hesiod is turned into an inspired poet when he ceases to be a "mere belly,"[69] and singing cicadas were traditionally (and favorably) contrasted with gluttonous asses.[70] As for Archilochus, it is worth mentioning that he explicitly identified himself with a cicada, and was eventually associated with a hero named Tettix (Cicada).[71] Even more interestingly, the *pyxis* depicts him, after his metamorphosis from cowherd to poet, in the company of four Muses.

Plato's myth follows a traditional pattern while echoing specific texts. As one would expect, however, he handles it in his own way. Deviations from the common pattern in any given initiation story are of paramount importance, because they highlight the specific characteristics of each particular author. Thus, for example, in Mnesiepes' story, Archilochus mocks the Muses, and they return his mockery. His role is exceptionally active, and it reverses the normal pattern whereby it is the Muses who ridicule the poet, the point being that Archilochus is an iambic and particularly aggressive poet.[72] In Plato's case, the initiation of Socrates remains potential: it is not clear whether Socrates and Phaedrus will undergo it in this life, and the distinction between inspiration and symbolic gift seems to collapse. I shall return to this crucial point in the next chapter. For now we shall address two other important variations that have a direct bearing on the argument of the current chapter.

---

[66] Aesop, too, meets the Muses in a *locus amoenus* full of cicadas (*Life of Aesop* 6).

[67] Cf. Hesiod *Theogony* 79–84.

[68] Poets: Hesiod *Shield* 393–397; Callimachus *Aetia* 1.29–34; *Anacreontea* 34. Philosopher: Aristotle *The History of Animals* 532b10–13. For further details and parallels, cf. Borthwick 1966:103–104, 107–108.

[69] For the importance of this connection, see Nagy 2009b. Haubold 2010 interprets the episode as the first stage of a "narrative of cultural and intellectual progress" (11), which spans the three major works of the Hesiodic corpus.

[70] Cf. e.g. Aesop 195 Hausrath-Hunger and Callimachus *Aetia* 1.29–34, with the useful discussion provided by Lelli 2001. The same contrast can be found in a *griphos*, which Athenaeus, citing Chamaeleon's *On Simonides*, ascribes to Simonides (10.457a). Livrea 2012 argues convincingly that Simonides is in fact the author of the *griphos*, which in turn inspired Callimachus.

[71] Cf. Archilochus 223 W as commented on by Lucian (*The Liar* 1), and see Petropoulos 1994, Chapter 5, who provides illuminating parallels with modern Greek folklore. As for Tettix, cf. Plutarch *On the Delays of Divine Vengeance* 560d–f and Suda s.v. *Archilochos*. Cf. the useful discussions of Nagy 1999, Chapter 18, Clay 2004:25–26, and Cunha Corrêa 2010:200–209. The Roman Phaedrus, too, implicitly identifies with a cicada (cf. 3.16 with Lelli 2001:247).

[72] As Aloni 2011 notes.

Firstly, there is the motif of sleep, which is loaded with cultural significance: the Muses even had a cultic association with the god Hypnos,[73] and midday sleep was traditionally associated with poetic inspiration. Yet Socrates is determined to fight back midday sleep, which is surely a meaningful detail. In the *Sophist*, Plato describes imitation as a shadowy and oneiric activity,[74] and I have mentioned the testimony of Isocrates, who claims that in panegyric gatherings "those who sleep are more numerous than those who listen."[75] By contrast, Socrates' (or Plato's) own "poetry" must reverse this tendency, and be a lucid, wakeful experience.[76]

Secondly, the song of the cicadas is referred to as dialogue. Nor is this initiation that of a poet wandering in the countryside all by himself, as is the case in the other stories. This initiation involves two dialoguing friends. Hesiod singles out one Muse, namely Calliope, with her etymologizing "beautiful voice," and Empedocles does the same by associating Calliope with good *logos* rather than with a beautiful voice.[77] On the other hand, Plato, who likewise implicitly etymologizes the Muses' names, appropriates the motif in a particularly significant manner. Not only do the Muses favor philosophers, as opposed to Hesiod's princes,[78] but Plato singles out *two* Muses, namely Calliope and Ourania. Interestingly, these two Muses form a leading (and potentially conversing?) pair in the François vase too, as is clear from the procession depicted on the cover page of this chapter. And again like the painter, Plato has Ourania come "after" Calliope (μετ' αὐτήν). Thus, Calliope and Ourania stand for a new, superior form of dialogic poetry. Put in a nutshell, the four Muses of the myth embody the old-yet-new inspiration of Plato's dialogues, both in their mythical components—such as myths, allegories, fairytales—and in their dialectical, argumentative character.

## Conclusions

In the first part of this chapter, I took my cue from the *Ion* and the *Symposium* to argue that the discourse of philosophy is genetically akin to that of poetry: Plato

---

[73] At Troezen, whose close connections with Athenian cult are well known, people used to worship Hypnos and the Muses together, as the former was especially dear to the latter: cf. Pausanias 2.31.3.

[74] *Sophist* 266b–267b (in all likelihood, *mimêsis* as mentioned at 267a includes poetry as well).

[75] *Panathenaicus* 263.

[76] That the inspiration of Socrates, unlike that of the poets, is rational and vigilant is something that scholars have sometimes argued on different grounds. Cf. e.g. Morgan 2010:59 and Männlein-Robert 2012.

[77] Cf. Hardie 2013.

[78] As Ryan 2012 aptly notes (247).

conceptualizes Socratic *logoi* as a chain of speech, which closely parallels that of poetry as described in the famous magnet simile of the *Ion*. The modes of transmission and the "symptoms" experienced by the human "rings" are identical, and yet the very similarity between the two phenomena, poetry and philosophy, is meant to highlight a number of significant differences. "Philosophic" chains are never-ending and imply the collapse of all distinctions between performer and audience: Socrates' *logoi* stir the speech of other people in a never-ending process that is fully vigilant and retains its strength when passing from one ring to another. By contrast, "poetic" chains entail self oblivion and a gradual weakening of the original "magnetic" strength. The discourse of philosophy is best described as reformed song and poetry in that it shares the same genetic process, which explains *why* poetry is so crucial to Plato's dialogues.

After the *Ion* and the *Symposium*, I returned to the *Phaedrus*, where a similar process of word chains can be seen at work. In particular, I showed how Socrates adopts the persona of a poet by adapting a number of archetypal features from the lives of the poets. Thus, for example, in his prayer to Eros, Socrates distances himself from the mythical paradigm of Thamyris, the singer who had famously undergone the tragic experience of poetic un-initiation, or "termination." The culmination of this process, however, is the myth of the cicadas, which closely parallels a number of different scenes of poetic initiation, and thus neatly complements Socrates' allusion to Thamyris: for, after averting poetic termination, Socrates then undergoes a proper, albeit potential, initiation. Once again, the differences are as significant as the similarities. By projecting philosophical discourse on to the traditional pattern of poetic initiation, Plato highlights the distinctive character of philosophy, which now emerges as a vigilant, unending, personal form of discourse. Above all, philosophy stands out because of its dialogical nature, which is why the list of Plato's Muses culminates in the dialoguing *pair* of Ourania and Calliope. Their voices embody philosophy as dialogue, as opposed to philosophy as continuous speech (Terpsichore and Erato), which is the mode adopted by Socrates in the first part of the *Phaedrus*. A turning point in the *Phaedrus*, the myth of the cicadas signals the memorable birth of a new genre, the dialogue.

## Endnote: New "Facts"

- Scholars have on occasion suggested that the discourses of poetry and philosophy as developed in the *Ion* and the *Symposium* (when read together) reveal a number of surprising analogies. This chapter features a first comprehensive study of what has previously been suggested. Through a careful analysis of the vocabulary and structure of the *Symposium*, it can be shown that Socratic *logoi* share the following features with Ion's poetry: an unhinged mind (ἐκπλήξης ~ ἐκπεπληγμένοι), palpitations (καρδία πηδᾷ ~ καρδία πηδᾷ), tears (δακρύων ... οἱ ὀφθαλμοί ~ δάκρυα ἐκχεῖται), possession (κατεχόμενοι ~ κατεχόμεθα), and Corybantism (κορυβαντιῶντες ~ κορυβαντιώντων). The discourse of both philosophy and poetry is conceptualized as a chain of *logoi*, but in philosophic chains the rhapsodic distinction between performer and audience is collapsed: philosophy is an active engagement, which should be "performed" by everyone. The same image can also be seen at work implicitly in the *Phaedrus*.

- By examining a number of lexical peculiarities, including the Platonic *hapax legomenon* πηρόω ("to maim"), I have shown that Socrates' prayer to Eros in the *Phaedrus* (257b–c) is composed in such a way as to evoke the story of the contest between Thamyris and the Muses, first attested in the *Iliad*, 2.594–560. Sophocles revived the story in his *Thamyras*, and a close examination of the relevant evidence allows me to conclude that Sophocles' more eroticized version is also clearly discernible between the lines of the *Phaedrus*.

- The initiation scene in Hesiod's *Theogony* exercised a considerable influence on Greek literature and may itself be an instance of a much more common mythologeme: roughly the same features can be found in the initiation stories of such diverse figures as Archilochus, Epimenides, Callimachus, and Aesop. The myth of the cicadas (*Phaedrus* 258e–259d) can be read, I argue, as yet another instance of this mythologeme, complete with a number of hitherto unnoticed echoes from earlier poetry. The encounter with the daemons, their disparaging comments, the magic gift of song, all these features make up the traditional pattern of the initiation scene, which is given a particularly epic flavor by means of allusions to Homer and Hesiod.

# 4

# THE MUSES AND THE TREE

*Having returned to Athens, Plato lived in the Academy, which is a gymnasium outside the walls, in a grove named after a certain hero, Hecademus, as is stated by Eupolis in his play entitled Shirkers "In the shady walks of the divine Hecademus." Moreover, there are verses of Timon which refer to Plato "Amongst all of them Plato was the leader, a big fish, but a sweet-voiced speaker, musical in prose as the cicala who, perched on the trees of Hecademus, pours forth a strain as delicate as a lily."*

Diogenes Laertius 3.7, trans. Ricks modified

*Platanus haec est ... Celebratae sunt primum in ambulatione Academiae Athenis, cubitorum XXXIII radice ramos antecedente*

Pliny *Natural History* 12.3–5

*Velut ego nunc moueor. Venit enim mihi Platonis in mentem, quem accepimus primum hic disputare solitum; cuius etiam illi hortuli propinqui non memoriam solum mihi adferunt sed ipsum uidentur in conspectu meo ponere*

Cicero *On the Ends of Good and Evil* 5.1.2

*Pyxis* by the Hesiod painter. Museum of Fine Arts, Boston, Inv. no. 98.887.

- "The *pyxis* divides into two panels. In the first a cowherd and a draped female figure flank a cow, whose four legs are still just visible. The female figure framing this composition to the right holds a *plektron* and a strap in her hand. Turn the vase and the scene that next appears represents a poet seated on a *diphros* holding a lyre. He is flanked by two Muses [...] Archilochos is shown in the first panel as young cowherd: in the second he is shown holding the Muses' gift of a lyre, flanked by two Muses. To the right of this grouping are two more Muses." (Clay 2004:14 and 55).

# 4

# The Muses and the Tree

## The Academy and the Heroization of Socrates

IN THE THIRD CHAPTER, I argued that Plato's dialogues project the discourse of philosophy onto the magnetic chains of rhapsody described in the *Ion*. The emotional impact they aroused in their respective audiences was almost identical, though certain significant *differences* were emphasized. Perhaps the most revealing of these emerges in the cicada myth: the Muses pass on their dialogic song to the cicadas, who are expected to do the same with Phaedrus and Socrates, who in turn will pass on the dialogue to other people in an unending chain. Unlike rhapsodic chains, their philosophical counterpart entails that every "ring" is both the recipient and the producer of ever-new *logoi*. As we have seen, the *Phaedrus* epitomizes such a process with the image of "writing in the soul."

The myth is then modeled on initiation scenes that can be found throughout the Greek poetic tradition. However, again, it is the differences that count, for it is these that mark the memorable birth of philosophic *dialogue* as opposed to monologic forms of discourse. Given that the myth comes in the middle of the *Phaedrus*, sandwiched between the erotic speeches of the first half and the dialectical discussion of the second, one might be tempted to regard it as a moment of transition, as if it were meant to suggest that dialectics must eventually supersede myth, or poetry, or at least continuous speech.[1] This line of argument could be continued in such a way as to interpret the cicada myth as a turning point in Plato's career; this would tally with some influential readings of the *Phaedrus*. For example, Charles Kahn reads the *Phaedrus* as a "Janus dialogue":[2] according to this interpretation, the self-referential reminiscences of the first half of the dialogue refer back to Plato's earlier output, while the

---

[1]  See e.g. Scott 2011, who argues that the second part of the dialogue corrects the thesis that philosophy is a form of madness.

[2]  Kahn 1996:372.

second half points forward to the "dialectical" dialogues of Plato's later career.[3] However, I cannot subscribe to such an explanation. Regardless of my personal dislike of developmentalism,[4] the cicada myth clearly highlights dialectics as *dialogue* rather than as the more specific procedure, based on the systematic division of concepts, typical of Plato's "late" works (or at least of some of them). Moreover, the myth appears to authorize both dialectics and myth: the cicadas and, indeed, any philosophers (potentially at least) who receive the "Muses' gift," *both sing and dialogue.*[5]

One peculiarity of the cicada myth is particularly relevant for my present argument. Initiation narratives are traditionally recounted in the past mode, after the poet has already received the gift of poetry, which, in turn, may serve to "motivate the cult of a poet as a hero."[6] By contrast, the initiation adumbrated in the *Phaedrus* remains potential: Socrates and Phaedrus, we are told, will receive the gift of the cicadas-Muses only if they fight back sleep and are willing to dialogue untiringly in the midday heat.[7] Moreover, the *Phaedrus* does not specify the precise nature of the gift, which in the traditional stories takes the form of divine inspiration *and* of a symbolic object. What is the reason for this?

Dialoguing in the midday heat is precisely what Socrates and Phaedrus do in the second half of the *Phaedrus*, when they discuss all forms of speech and writing. Socrates criticizes traditional rhetoric in favor of a form of personal, erotic discourse, which is best exemplified by his second speech in the first half of the dialogue. (Again, the *Phaedrus* seems to authorize forms of discourse other than Plato's "late" dialectic.) While famously criticizing writing, moreover, he describes good authors as those who know more than they write and who are aware that their works are ephemeral (like the "gardens of Adonis"), in contrast to the enduring effects of oral, personal speech (the "real crops").[8]

---

[3] Cairns 2013, too, argues that the *Phaedrus* "encapsulates Plato's career" (234) by juxtaposing its three phases: early, middle, and late.

[4] Cf. the Introduction to the current volume.

[5] Pinnoy rightly stresses the twofold nature of the cicadas' gift: "Daze gave is inets anders dan de kunst van het dichten (of zingen) en van het dialogeren. De Cicaden zijn van beide activiteiten de inspratiebron (ἐπιπεπνευκότες ἂν ἡμῖν εἶεν τοῦτο τὸ γέρας, 262d); immers, deze gave betekent niet alleen natuurlijke, aangeboren begaafdheid maar is een blijvende gunst, op voorwaarde dat de filosoof, naar het voorbeeld van de Cicaden, twee eigenschappen ontwikkelt: waakzaamheid (οὐ καθευδητέον) en onthechting (μηδὲν τροφῆς δεῖσθαι). Daarom zien de Cicaden nauwlettend toe" (Pinnoy 1986–1987:113). Cf. also Görgemanns 1993:145. One may add that the process of division is integral to the "mythic" section of the *Phaedrus* as well (e.g. 249b–c, discussed in Chapter 2 of this volume).

[6] Nagy 1990:49.

[7] 259b.

[8] 276b.

Thus the *Phaedrus* draws to its conclusion, though its finale has proved difficult to interpret. I shall start with a close examination of Socrates' puzzling prayer to Pan, before moving on to a careful reconstruction of its general background. As we shall see, the conclusion of the *Phaedrus* does not point so much to the "gold of wisdom", or to a polemical skirmish with Isocrates. Rather, it prefigures the heroization of Socrates and provides insights into the life of the Academy and the role of Plato as a Socratic writer, both within and against the cultural practices of the Athenian *polis*.

## Praying to Pan: The Riddle

A number of prayers can be found in Plato's dialogues,[9] but that of Socrates to Pan, which coincides with the last words of the *Phaedrus*, is by far the most famous and puzzling:

> ΣΩ. Ὦ φίλε Πάν τε καὶ ἄλλοι ὅσοι τῇδε θεοί, δοίητέ μοι καλῷ γενέσθαι τἄνδοθεν· ἔξωθεν δὲ ὅσα ἔχω, τοῖς ἐντὸς εἶναί μοι φίλια. πλούσιον δὲ νομίζοιμι τὸν σοφόν· τὸ δὲ χρυσοῦ πλῆθος εἴη μοι ὅσον μήτε φέρειν μήτε ἄγειν δύναιτο ἄλλος ἢ ὁ σώφρων. Ἔτ' ἄλλου του δεόμεθα, ὦ Φαῖδρε; ἐμοὶ μὲν γὰρ μετρίως ηὗκται. ΦΑΙ. Καὶ ἐμοὶ ταῦτα συνεύχου· κοινὰ γὰρ τὰ τῶν φίλων. ΣΩ. Ἴωμεν.

> SOCRATES: Dear Pan, and ye other gods who dwell in this place, grant that I may become beautiful within, and that such outward things as I have may be in agreement with the things within. May I count rich the wise; as for the amount of gold, may I have so much of it as no one but the temperate man should be able to bear and carry. Do we still need anything else, Phaedrus? For me that prayer is enough. PHAEDRUS: Let me join in prayer; for what friends have they share. SOCRATES: Let's go.

> Plato *Phaedrus* 279b–c[10]

Socrates' words are mysterious enough, yet the problem received "practically no attention" until the 1960s.[11] In the last few decades, however, scholars have become increasingly interested in their significance, so that the passage is now a notorious Platonic *crux*.[12] Indeed, the only thing scholars can agree

---

[9]  Jackson 1971 collects and discusses the 21 prayers (some of them mere hints) found in Plato's dialogues.

[10]  The translation combines those by Rosenmeyer (1962:34) and Rowe (1988).

[11]  Rosenmeyer 1962:34.

[12]  Gaiser 1989, itself a very long, dense work, provides an impressive list of relevant contributions.

upon is its enigmatic nature, so it is generally considered to be a "riddle."[13] Nevertheless, as Konrad Gaiser and others have sensibly remarked, the prayer must have some "logographic necessity,"[14] since Socrates has made it amply clear that each part of a good *logos* must have its unique and meaningful place in relation to the other parts. Yet how is the prayer related to the rest of the dialogue? At least three points are worth mentioning, and can serve as the basis for my own discussion.

Firstly, Diskin Clay has noted that the opening words of the prayer, *ô phile Pan*, are meant to recall the very beginning of the dialogue as well as Socrates' prayer to Eros at the end of the palinode, i.e. halfway through the *Phaedrus*. The very first words of the *Phaedrus* are *ô phile Phaidre* and, even more importantly, Socrates' prayer to Eros opens with the words *ô phile Erôs*. Socrates' prayer(s), then, must be of some importance for the structure of the *Phaedrus* as a whole and would, therefore, be consistent with the principle of "logographic necessity."[15]

A second point, developed by Konrad Gaiser in particular, is that the "gold" in question is a metaphor for wisdom, and that the phrase "bear and carry" conveys the idea of looting.[16] Thus the "temperate man," somewhat paradoxically, is put forward as a philosopher who successfully performs the Sack of Wisdom. I doubt whether there is any compelling evidence to bear out such an interpretation. Nevertheless, since Gaiser's exegetical *tour de force* is widely accepted, I will take it as my own starting point.

The third point is the paradoxical nature of the prayer: Socrates, the man who famously refuted the notion of *kalokagathia* as that of a correspondence between inner and outer, now seems to be making a plea for overall harmony. However we may interpret the expression "bear and carry," the emphasis on temperance results in an odd choice: of all the gods, Socrates addresses his prayer to Pan, possibly the least temperate divinity of the entire Greek pantheon. As we know from Socrates' palinode, this must mean that temperance and (divine) madness must coincide at some higher level. Yet what is the precise role of Pan and the local gods?

---

[13] E.g. Clay 1979:353, Griswold 1986:289, Gaiser 1989:109, Yunis 2011:248, and Stavru 2011:271.

[14] 264b–e, with Gaiser 1989: "Im *Phaidros* war zu lesen, eine gut gemachte Rede sei in ihrem Aufbau nicht willkürlich, sondern Anfang, Mitte un Ende müssten wie bei einem lebendigen Organismus aufeinander und auf das Ganze abgestimmt sein" (108). Cf. e.g. Clay 1979:345. For a recent discussion of the principle itself, with interesting parallels both in Plato and in the Hippocratic corpus, see Marino 2011.

[15] Clay 1979. I may add that a not altogether different stance can be found in Hermias Alexandrinus (on 279b, p. 279.5–8 Lucarini-Moreschini).

[16] A hendiadys or "Doppelausdruck," for which there are parallels. See e.g. Gaiser 1989:123.

Let us suppose for a moment that gold might indeed stand for wisdom: what kind of golden knowledge would Socrates be hinting at? Does gold allude to some secret doctrine, as the Tübingen followers of the "esoteric" interpretation have maintained? Or is it the superior, "royal" knowledge of the philosopher? Both options are hard to accept, since the equation, philosophy = wisdom, was explicitly rejected a few lines earlier (279d).[17] Consequently, "the wise" (τὸν σοφόν, which tends to be translated wrongly as "the wise *man*") is either god, or else an ideal projection of the philosopher's striving for knowledge, which more or less amounts to the same thing. At least, one can accept that the wealth referred to is metaphorical—surely "the wise" is not rich in any material sense—and that Socrates is not begging for money, but asking for something more "spiritual."[18] However, this is little more than a platitude.

Perhaps the key to the problem lies elsewhere. I shall start by submitting that the link between Socrates' two prayers (to Eros and to Pan) is even stronger than Clay has suggested. On praying to Eros to avert "termination," Socrates, among other things, asks him "not to take away or maim (*mête ... mête*)" his erotic expertise, and Phaedrus joins in the prayer (*suneuchomai*). The same structure is found in the prayer to Pan, in that Socrates asks for a pile of gold that nobody else but the temperate man could bear or carry (*mête ... mête*), and Phaedrus readily joins in the prayer (*suneuchou*).[19] Thus, the reader is more than authorized (by the author himself) to compare the two prayers. Likewise, I invite my own reader to look at the prayers side by side, that is, to look back at the text of Socrates' prayer to Eros and to its crucial message: by alluding to the story of Thamyris, *Socrates is anxious to avert "poetic termination,"* or, as the cicada myth makes clear in positive terms, to obtain poetic initiation. This, perhaps, is the key to a correct understanding of the meaning of the two most controversial points: namely the word "gold," and the phrase "bear and carry."

I shall begin with gold. In the light of numerous parallels, including some Platonic ones, scholars have made it amply clear that gold *can* be understood metaphorically. Nevertheless, there are two other important details that need to be clarified if we are to have a proper understanding of the term's connotations.

---

[17] *Sophos* and its cognates are constantly used ironically when applied to men, and with good reason. (See Stavru 2011, and cf. Despotopoulos 1999 for a good survey of Plato's use of *philosophos*, including our passage.) Despite what the esoteric interpreters say (e.g. Lavecchia 2006:86), as far as Plato was concerned, no mortal could possibly be described as *sophos* (wise), but, at the very most, *philosophos* (lover of wisdom), which is precisely what Socrates says just before uttering his prayer.

[18] The best Platonic parallel is possibly *Republic* 521a. Others are listed e.g. by Gaiser 1989:112n19.

[19] Note the exceptional repetition of this rare verb. Plato only uses it here and in the *Laws*, at 687e, 909e, and 931e.

Firstly, the expression is preceded by a definite article: "as for *the* amount of gold" (τὸ δὲ χρυσοῦ πλῆθος). Why is there an article? This is an arresting, though neglected, detail, for it is as if Socrates were talking about something we are supposed to know. The word order also contributes to this impression, as "the amount of gold" is placed emphatically in a front position.[20] In fact, this is not the first time that "gold" appears as a motif in the *Phaedrus*. Almost at the beginning of the dialogue, Phaedrus declares that he would rather be able to learn Lysias' speech by heart than possess a vast amount of gold, with the Greek *polu khrusion* closely paralleling Socrates' final words (228a). Not much later (235d–e), Phaedrus commits himself to a jocular promise: should Socrates succeed in outsmarting Lysias, he, Phaedrus, will set up a life-sized golden statue of Socrates at Delphi. Phaedrus' promise has been rightly interpreted as "the product of his own habitual vanity and inclination toward hyperbole,"[21] which explains why Socrates replies ironically, saying that Phaedrus really is a "golden boy."[22] Gold, then, is a recurrent motif, one that is associated with Phaedrus, and with rhetorical competition.[23] Secondly, it is worth noting that "(the) amount of gold" is a fairly common expression. Most of the time, "amount of gold" refers to *excessive* wealth,[24] which is often compared with something nobler, such as wisdom.[25] This will prove to be an important point, as I shall argue in the next section.

[20] Although he does not comment on either the article or the wording, Dušanić 1980:20, puts forward an explanation that would account for gold: namely that "Isocrates saw material profit from the Samian expedition [366–365], which is probably the immediate explanation of Socrates' mention of gold at 279c." Such topical allusions are as hard to disprove as they are to prove, and at best can only provide an added option. When available, internal evidence should be preferred as being more immediate.

[21] Ryan 2012:130. Phaedrus' words call to mind the oath the Athenian archons had to swear upon taking office: ἀναθήσειν ἀνδριάντα χρυσοῦν, ἐάν τινα παραβῶσι τῶν νόμων (Aristotle *The Athenian Constitution* 7.1).

[22] At 236b Phaedrus reiterates his promise, although this time he imagines a votive offer at Olympia, possibly cast in bronze.

[23] Cf. 240a (Socrates' first speech), where it designates material riches. There are no other instances of the word in the *Phaedrus*.

[24] A TLG survey of the relevant terms leaves little doubt, and the skeptics should take a look for themselves. For example, Plutarch's *Aristides* (10.5) says the following: "Go and tell the Spartans that for no amount of gold, such as that one may find either upon or underneath the earth, shall we ever surrender the freedom of the Greeks." This defiant declaration clearly demonstrates the note of contempt the expression conveyed.

[25] Particularly illuminating is Plutarch *How the Young Man Should Study Poetry* 20c–d. The passage features two poetic quotations. In both quotes, a "bad" line is immediately followed by a "good" one, which, according to Plutarch, "corrects" the former, and rehabilitates the poetic work. The second example, taken from an unknown play by Euripides, features the very same vocabulary of Socrates' prayer, reproducing the same contrast whereby the idea of rejoicing in "amounts of gold" (χρυσοῦ ... πλήθει) is corrected by the claim that it is shameful to be rich and ignorant (σκαιὸν τὸ πλουτεῖν κἄλλο μηδὲν εἰδέναι). Another passage bearing striking resemblances

# The Gift of Poetry

Given the connotations of the phrase "amount of gold," Gaiser's reading begins to look less promising: in our passage, gold is *prima facie* unlikely to be an unqualified good, or something that the temperate man would be eager to put his hands on.[26] On the contrary, Socrates would seem to be aspiring to something radically *different* from a vast amount of gold. However, Gaiser's interpretation would still stand were Socrates' prayer to be seen as self-consciously paradoxical, though it would still seem very odd that the "lover of wisdom" (*philosophos*), who was by definition distinct from the accomplished "wise [man]," could ever wish and pray for the "Sack of Wisdom." Be that as it may, the really vital question is the meaning of "bear-and-carry," the second controversial expression in the prayer. Are there any compelling reasons why we should understand it in the sense Gaiser declares, namely, as something akin to looting? A passage from the *Laws* helps to shed light (and cast serious doubts) on any reason why we should:

> τῶν δὲ σπουδαίων, ὥς φασι, τῶν περὶ τραγῳδίαν ἡμῖν ποιητῶν, ἐάν ποτέ τινες αὐτῶν ἡμᾶς ἐλθόντες ἐπανερωτήσωσιν οὑτωσί πως· "Ὦ ξένοι, πότερον φοιτῶμεν ὑμῖν εἰς τὴν πόλιν τε καὶ χώραν ἢ μή, καὶ τὴν ποίησιν φέρωμέν τε καὶ ἄγωμεν, ἢ πῶς ὑμῖν δέδοκται περὶ τὰ τοιαῦτα δρᾶν;"

> And, if any of the serious poets, as they are termed, who write tragedy, come to us and say "O strangers, may we go to your city and country or may we not, and shall traffic our poetry, what is your will about these matters?"

> Plato *Laws* 817a, trans. Jowett (modified)

The answer to the above question is, of course, in the negative: the lawmakers are themselves tragedians and "authors of the most beautiful tragedy," i.e. the laws, and, by extension, Plato's dialogue itself, the *Laws*. My immediate purpose in quoting the above words, however, is to draw attention to the phrase "traffic

---

to Socrates' prayer is an epigram, which, according to Athenaeus (11.465c–e), is reported by Harmodius from Leprea. Commenting on the licentiousness of the Arcads from Phigaleia, the epigram makes a sinister and overtly impious association between a man who is ironically called σώφρων in that he owned riches and πλῆθος ἀπειρέσιον ... χρυσοῦ. The epigram is possibly meant to recall Socrates' prayer.

26    Moreover, there are two more clear instances that witness against it. The first comes in Hermias Alexandrinus, who in his commentary on the *Phaedrus* interprets the expression in the "normal" way (on 279c, p. 279.25–27 Lucarini-Moreschini). The second, more important example comes from Plato himself, who, at the beginning of the probably authentic *Letter 6*, suggests that good friends are no match for any "amount of gold" (322c–d).

our poetry" (τὴν ποίησιν φέρωμέν τε καὶ ἄγωμεν), which proves Gaiser wrong, for this is the same pair of verbs we encounter in Socrates' prayer, and they certainly cannot mean loot or anything similar in this passage.[27] Of particular interest too, is that the object of the two verbs is "poetry," which, in the context of Socrates' prayer, reminds one of Pindar's *Nemean Ode* 8.36–39: some men pray for gold, but the poet's prayer is that he may give pleasure to his fellow citizens by "praising things worthy of[ praise while blaming the wicked,"[28] that is, by practicing poetry.

As Gaiser himself notes, throughout the *Phaedrus* the role of the gods is to provide Socrates with poetic inspiration, and it is precisely to this effect that Pan gets his only other mention a little earlier in the dialogue: Socrates credits "Pan son of Hermes" and the "nymphs daughters of Achelous" with granting him the "enthusiastic element" that enabled him to outsmart Lysias.[29] This is hardly surprising, given that nymphs often "act as rustic counterparts of the Muses"[30] in Greek tradition. Even more importantly, at 262d Socrates claims that the local gods, together with the "prophets of the Muses," i.e. the cicadas, were responsible for his inspiration, and at 278b he mentions the water and the *Mouseion* of the nymphs, which may be a possible allusion to the local Ilisiades or Ilissides, the Muses of the Ilissus.[31] Finally, we should not forget that the Muses' gift in the cicada myth was conditional upon Socrates' and Phaedrus' willingness to dialogue untiringly in the heat; by the end of the dialogue, this condition has been met.

Bearing these points in mind, we can now reformulate our question: what is Socrates asking from Pan and the local gods? At this point, Socrates has proved

---

[27] As Rosenmeyer points out: "the notion intended is that of doing business, of give and take, of setting up and taking down, of some kind of compound and commutative activity" (Rosenmeyer 1962:39). Gaiser himself, of course, knows this passage, yet he does not discuss it directly and merely says that the two verbs are "nicht allzu weit von der üblichen Bedeutung" (Gaiser 1989:123).

[28] ... χρυσὸν εὔχονται, πεδίον δ᾽ ἕτεροι ἀπέραντον, ἐγὼ δ᾽ ἀστοῖς ἁδὼν καὶ χθονὶ γυῖα καλύψαι, αἰνέων αἰνητά, μομφὰν δ᾽ ἐπισπείρων ἀλιτροῖς.

[29] 263d. The inspiring role of Pan and the Nymphs is not surprising. Note that, according to Pausanias, Pan used to utter oracles through the nymph Erato, his prophet (8.37.11; the tradition is, of course, Arcadian). A nymph Erato is found in the *Theogony* as well (246), and there are other cases where the names of the Muses overlap with those of the nymphs. Cf. Kambylis 1965:38–47. As for Pan, *Cratylus* 408b–d connects it with *logos* (cf. the useful discussion in Werner 2012:230–235).

[30] Larson 2001:52, quoting Theocritus 7.91–92 and referring to 1.12, 4.29, and 5.140.

[31] Cf. Marchiandi 2011: "Anche le Muse erano annoverate tra le divinità dell'Ilisso, con l'epiclesi locativa *Ilisiades* o *Ilissides*. Un altare è ricordato da Pausania (1.19.5); nel II secolo d.C. il loro sacerdote aveva un seggio riservato nel teatro di Dioniso (IG II2 5067; cf. F17). Il loro culto, tuttavia, parrebbe già attestato negli anni '20 del V secolo a.C. in un rendiconto delle finanze sacre ateniesi (IG I3 369.66,86, cf. Pl[ato] *Ph[ae]dr[us]* 262d, 237a, 259b; H[ero]d[ia]n[us] *De prosodia catholica* 3.1.102.20 Lentz; Him. 69.9 Colonna; St.Byz. s.v. Ilissos)" (Marchiandi 2011:482).

to be a better orator than Lysias, and a better poet than such venerable figures as Sappho, Anacreon, Ibycus, and Stesichorus—almost as if he had triumphed in some kind of poetic contest. As Phaedrus suggests, he deserves to be rewarded with gold. But Socrates' indifference to riches is well known, so the statue mentioned by Phaedrus—indeed a vast amount of gold—is of no interest to him. There is, however, another gift he would find much more appealing, but has not yet received: Socrates still awaits the "gift of the Muses." Like Pindar, whose prayer contrasts gold and poetry, Socrates is asking for a definitive consecration.

In short, my suggestion is that Socrates is asking the gods to complete his incomplete initiation, and that he is possibly hinting at some kind of symbolic gift, which is the missing detail with respect to the cicada myth, since all the other elements of poetic initiation are there. Thus, everything comes full circle, for Socrates' prayer brings together the various parts of the *Phaedrus* and leads to one final, crucial step. In the cicada myth, an important characteristic of Socrates' initiation is its potential status as against the actual experiences of the poets. At this later point, however, Socrates has met the cicadas' conditions and is ready to ask the gods to grant him an actual "poetic license," in order to "bear-and-carry" (that is, to practice) what in the *Laws* is denied to the tragedians: namely poetry, and perhaps the honors that poets traditionally enjoy.

## Heroism in the Making

So far, my argument may be described as fundamentally *textual* in that I have tried to penetrate the meaning of Socrates' final words by means of a new set of parallels, taken from both Plato and other sources. The notion of poetic honor, however, calls for broader consideration. Traditional stories of initiation are essentially linked with the idea of heroism: as Aristotle records, Archilochus enjoyed "honors" from his fellow citizens (Ἀρχίλοχον ...τετιμήκασι),[32] and the story told by Mnesiepes in the *Archilocheion* is part of this hero cult. Mnesiepes refers to the initiation of Archilochus as a story of the past: Mnesiepes' role, as suggested by the Delphic oracle, was to monumentalize the *Archilocheion* in honor of an indisputably authoritative poet. It is possible, though by no means certain, that Archilochus himself had referred to his initiation, or even to his potential heroization, in some lost poem.[33] However that may be, such a

---

[32] *Rhetoric* 1398b10–12.

[33] Cf. Aloni 2011. It is possible that another moment of Archilochus' initiation, namely his bargaining with the Muses, was the theme of one of Archilochus' own poems, i.e. fr. 35 W. See Cunha Corrêa 2008. The exchange is possibly: "la trasposizione narrativa di un evento sacrificale, ovvero la trasfigurazione del sacrificio dell'animale in onore delle dee tesmoforiche" (Ornaghi 2009:144–145).

potential heroization is clearly recognizable in the case of Socrates, who looks like a poet (and a hero?) in the making: his initiation story is not recounted *ex post*, but is seen as a potential outcome, one that Socrates himself prays for, as the final scene of the *Phaedrus* makes quite clear. How are we to assess this situation? Is there any clear parallel for it?

Unexpected help in contextualizing Socrates as a poet-hero *in statu nascenti* may be found in a document of exceptional interest. I am referring to the so-called seal of the Hellenistic poet Posidippus (ca. 310–240 BCE), who staged himself as an aspirant hero.[34] Many details of the text, preserved by two precarious wax tablets from the first century CE, remain uncertain, but the overall meaning of the poem, as well as its importance, have now been firmly established.[35] Here is Colin Austin's improved text, together with his beautiful translation:[36]

> εἴ τι καλόν, Μοῦσαι πολιήτιδες, ἢ παρὰ Φοίβου
> χρυσαλύρεω καθαροῖς οὔασιν ἐκλ[ύ]ετε
> Παρνησοῦ νιφόεντος ἀνὰ πτύχ[α]ς ἢ παρ' Ὀλύμπωι
> Βάκχωι τὰς τριετεῖς ἀρχόμεναι θυμέλα[ς
> νῦν δὲ Ποσε[ι]δίππωι στυγερὸν συναείρατε γῆρας
> γραψάμεναι δέλτων ἐν χρυσέαις σελίσιν.
> λιμπάνετε σκοπιὰς Ἑλικωνίδας, εἰς δὲ τὰ Θήβης
> τείχεα Πιπ[λ]ε̣ίης βαίνετε, Κασταλίδες.
> καὶ σὺ Ποσείδιππόν ποτ' ἐφίλαο; Κύνθιε, Λητοῦς
> υἱ' ἑκάε[ργ]ε̣, βέλο̣ς (vacat)
> [..].[......].. ραγ[.]γω̣............
> φήμη τις νιφόεντ' οἰκία τοῦ Παρίου·
> τοίην ἐκχρήσαις τε καὶ ἐξ ἀδύτων καναχήσαι[ς
> φωνὴν ἀθανάτην, ὦ ἄνα, καὶ κατ' ἐμοῦ
> ὄφρα με τιμήςωςι Μακηδόνες, οἵ τ' ἐπὶ γ[ήςων
> οἵ τ' Ἀςίης πάσης γείτονες ἠϊόνος.
> Πελλαῖον γένος ἀμόν· ἔοιμι δὲ βίβλον ἑλίςςων
> ἄφνω λαοφόρωι κείμενος εἰν ἀγορῆι.
> ἀλλ' ἐπὶ μὲν Παρίηι δὸς ἀηδόνι λυγρὸν ἐφ.[
> νῆμα κατὰ γληνέων δάκρυα κε̣ι̣νὰ χέ̣ω[ν

---

[34] Cf. Clay 2004:83–86, where he also discusses another example of an aspirant hero (Clay's own epithet), namely, Antigonos of Knidos, known to us only through an inscription (IKnidos no. 303). In an earlier age, Theodectas of Phaselis (ca. 375–334 BCE) "conceived a plan to honor himself in death that is more elaborate than the later ambitions of Poseidippos of Pella. At the site of his grave along the Sacred Road to Eleusis, he set up statues of the most famous poets along with a statue of himself" (Clay 2004:89).

[35] See Di Nino 2010:61–65, for a *status quaestionis* (with bibliography).

[36] Austin and Bastianini 2002 (118).

καὶ στενάχων, δι' ἐμὸν δὲ φίλον στόμα [ –‿‿ –‿
    αϲτ[...]..............
[..]...........[
    μηδέ τις οὖν χεύαι δάκρυον· αὐτὰρ ἐγὼ
γήραϊ μυστικὸν οἶμον ἐπὶ Ῥαδάμανθυν ἱκοίμην
    δήμωι καὶ λαῶι παντὶ ποθεινὸς ἐών,
ἀσκίπτων ἐν ποσσὶ καὶ ὀρθοεπὴς ἀν' ὅμιλον
    καὶ λείπων τέκνοις δῶμα καὶ ὄλβον ἐμόν.

If, Muses of my city, you have with pure ears
    heard anything beautiful, either from Phoebus of the golden lyre,
in the glens of snowy Parnassus, or near Olympus,
    as you start for Bacchus his triennial ceremonies,
now help Posidippus to bear the burden of hateful old age,
    writing down the song on the golden columns of your tablets.
Leave your Heliconian peaks, and come to the walls
    of Piplean Thebes, Muses of Castalia.
You also loved Posidippus once, Cynthian god, of Leto
    the far-shooting son [...] a dart [... ... ...]
an oracle to the snow-white house of the man from Paros.
May you send forth and sound out from your holy shrine
    such an immortal voice, O Lord, even for me,
so that the Macedonians may honor me, both the [islanders]
    and the neighbours of all the Asiatic shore.
Pellaean is my family. May I find myself unrolling a book,
    placed[37] all at once in the crowded marketplace.
For the Parian nightingale grant [...] a mournful
    thread, with empty tears streaming down the eyelids,
and groaning, while through my friendly mouth [... ... ...]
    and let no one shed a tear. But in old age
may I travel the mystic path to Rhadamnthys,
    longed for by my people and all the community,
on my feet without a stick, sure of speech among the crowd,
    and leaving to my children my house and my wealth.

                        Posidippus 118 AB, trans. Austin

---

[37]  Greek κείμενος. I have substituted "placed" for Austin's "standing," since the verb, as Dickie
    points out: "denotes placing a statue. A brief perusal of Pausanias' usage settles the meaning of
    the term and makes it quite clear that Posidippus is talking about a statue of himself. The term
    tells us nothing about how Posidippus will be represented" (Dickie 1994:381).

Posidippus envisages himself as a statue in the agora, honored by his fellow citizens thanks to Apollo and the local Muses, who are summoned to come to his hometown (Piplean Thebes).[38] For this purpose, he reminds the gods of an earlier oracle: in all probability, "the well-known one to Archilochus' father, to the effect that his son would be 'immortal and renowned in song among men.'"[39] The poet wishes for himself nothing less than heroization: he envisages himself as a poet-hero in the making, and refers to Archilochus as an important antecedent.

Posidippus' wish features a number of details that recall the cicada myth and Socrates' prayer to Pan. Firstly, Posidippus addresses his distinctly *local* divinities with cultic formulae (the optative mode, translated with "may," and the request to "give").[40] Secondly, he envisages the possibility of escaping old age through never-ending performance, albeit in the form of a statue unrolling a book. Thirdly, he mentions gold in connection with his poetic achievement. Fourthly, he asks for corporal, as well as "spiritual," well being. Finally, and most importantly, he superimposes his story onto a pattern of poetic initiation by referring to Archilochus.

Despite the many obvious differences, the Socrates of the *Phaedrus* shares all these five features.[41] Moreover, in adopting the persona of an inspired poet, he describes the blessed future that awaits the initiated after their death, something that closely resembles Posidippus' mystical voyage,[42] while it is also relevant that both Poseidippus' elegy and the myth of the cicadas stress the relationship of *philia* between man and the Muses.[43] Finally, as we have seen, Phaedrus makes a deliberate hint at the possibility of erecting a statue to

---

[38]  "Piplea was a place in Macedonia associated with the Muses, so 'Piplean Thebes' must surely be a poetic description of Pella itself, the poet's own birthplace" (Austin 2002:17).

[39]  Clay 2004:30, cf. Klooster 2011:180. This oracle figures in Mnesiepes' account too. Moreover, as Clay points out, "in his desire for heroic status in death, Poseidippos might be echoing the earlier vision of Simonides, who in fragment 23 of P. Oxy. 2327 seems to imagine himself travelling by ship to the Islands of the Blest, where not only the young Echekratides of Thessaly awaits him but perhaps Achilles and Patroklos as well" (Clay 2004:30). According to Lloyd-Jones 1963, the oracle referred to by Posidippus is the same as that which persuaded Mnesiepes to monumentalize the Archilocheion (178–179). (This seems less likely, nor would it change my point significantly.)

[40]  Local or made such, like the Muses. On the strongly local color of the elegy and its references to Pellaean cultic practices, see Rossi 1996.

[41]  To summarize: (1) Socrates reveres local divinities; (2) refers to dialectical teaching as a path to immortality (cf. 277a ἀθάνατον); (3) asks for a reward of gold; (4) asks for harmony between body and soul; (5) conforms to the pattern of poetic initiation.

[42]  Posidippus' "mystic path" (μυστικὸν οἶμον, 25) allows for a double meaning: "Così anche οἶμος, oltre ad indicare la 'via' che conduce a Radamanto, non può non mantenere la peculiarità che ha di indicare soprattutto il sentiero della poesia, la via del canto" (Angiò 1997:10).

[43]  Cf. verse 9 καὶ σὺ ... ἐφίλαο, which points to both Apollo and the Muses, and *Phaedrus* 259b φιλόμουσον ἄνδρα.

celebrate Socrates' achievements, which also matches Posidippus' expectations and requests.

Like Mnesiepes and Socrates, Posidippus resorts to familiar patterns in order to stress the specific features of his own poetry. Thus, by means of a contrast between mourning and serenity, he sets his own prospective status as a poet-hero against Archilochus'. It is also very likely that Posidippus would have been familiar, more or less directly, with the heroic statue of Archilochus that inspired an epigram usually attributed to Theocritus.[44] The epigram characterizes Archilochus as, like Posidippus, dear to Apollo and the Muses, and skilled in singing to the lyre, perhaps unlike Posidippus.[45] This strongly suggests that the Parian poet was represented with his famous instrument (the gift of the Muses) in his hands.[46] By contrast, Posidippus envisages himself holding a book roll, and his fellow citizens apparently fulfilled his wish: the Hellenistic statue of "Posidippus," quite possibly our poet, does in fact hold a book roll.[47]

Like other Hellenistic poets, though with a distinctly heroic tone, Posidippus "foresees, and to some extent constructs, his own passage into the pantheon of the 'great poets of the past.'"[48] At this point, mention of Callimachus' prologue to the *Aetia* becomes inevitable.[49] Here, the poet wishes to avert old age (γῆρας) by casting off his old skin (again γῆρας), as cicadas were known to do.[50] To this effect, he claims that Apollo and the Muses initiated him into poetry at an early age, and that this, in turn, allows him to avoid, or at least cope with old age. While probably alluding to both Plato's cicadas and Posidippus' seal,[51] Callimachus steers clear of the latter's mysticism and seems to opt for a more

---

[44] *Palatine Anthology* 7.664 = Gow 21 = Gow-Page 14. In the *Anthology*, the epigram is wrongly attributed to Leonidas. On the overall meaning of the epigram, see Aloni 1984, with further bibliography. On its "authenticity," whether it is a real inscription or a literary composition, see Rossi 2001, who favors the former (329–330).

[45] The little testimony we have of the life of Posidippus makes no mention of music. Instead, he seems to be called "maker of epigrams," ἐπιγραμματοποιός (*Testimonium* 3 AB).

[46] Cf. Corso 2008.

[47] A Roman copy of the statue, complete with an inscription bearing the name Posidippus, is preserved in the Vatican Museums, inventory number 735. See Dickie 1994:372–383 and Clay 2004:31–32.

[48] Hunter 2001:251. Hunter is concerned with Meleager (*Palatine Anthology* 7.419), but his article also discusses Posidippus and Callimachus.

[49] There is no space here to address any of the questions posed by this most troubled text. See Herder 2012, as well as Massimilla 1996, for a primary orientation.

[50] An echo from Plato's cicada myth is very likely. See e.g. Acosta-Hughes and Stephens 2012:36–39.

[51] Di Benedetto 2003 makes the case for Posidippus' priority and summarizes the analogy between Callimachus' proem and Posidippus' seal as follows: "Ma ecco l'elenco dei punti di contatto tra l'Elegia di Posidippo e la parte proemiale degli *Aitia* di cui abbiamo detto: 1) Invocazione delle Muse; 2) precedenti esperienze poetiche; 3) le tavolette; 4) canto e vecchiaia; 5) l'intervento di Apollo; 6) evocazione di regioni del Nord; 7) il culto bacchico; 8) l'isola di Paro; 9) αὐτὰρ ἐγώ a proposito di avviarsi" (Di Benedetto 2003:108). Cf. also Angiò 1997.

mundane, jocular form of poetic heroization, as his play on the word γῆρας suggests.[52]

Both Callimachus and Posidippus loosely follow the same mythological pattern found in the *Phaedrus* and in the initiation stories of Hesiod, Epimenides, and Archilochus.[53] Like Socrates, and possibly like Archilochus, they look to their poetic, even cultic future, which they deem to be a consequence of their devotion to the composition of poetry. This final detail cannot apply to Socrates, of course, since he is not a poet. This means we are confronted with the strange scenario of the poetic initiation of someone who is not a poet and who has never written anything. Posidippus has a vision of himself turned into a cultic statue and perpetually reciting his poems, as the book roll suggests.[54] Socrates, in a dialogue that famously criticizes writing, envisages himself as a cicada, perpetually pouring out his dialogic song. In other words, Plato aligns Socrates with a tradition that is structurally alien to him—a paradox that calls for some explanation.

## The Cult of Socrates in the Academy

It is important to recognize that Socrates *was* in fact a cultic figure. We happen to know that he "fell among the lesser deities or *daimones*, for a shrine dedicated to him (ἱερὸν χωρίον), the *Sokrateion*, lay outside the city gate on the road up from the Peiraeus (ἐπὶ τὴν πόλιν). A statue of Socrates marked the site (ἡ Σωκράτους στήλη), which also had a sacred spring not far away (οὐδὲ γὰρ πόρρω ἦν ἡ πηγή). Various rites were performed at the *Sokrateion*. Marinus of Neapolis refers to them as 'honors' (τιμαί), but Zosimus of Panopolis uses that expression as a euphemism for sacrifices. It was here that Proclus drank Attic water

---

[52] Theocritus 7 (cf. the following note) is also more mundane than Posidippus' seal (cf. Lombardi 2009). For Callimachus' reshaping of initiation stories, cf. Tulli 2008a.

[53] As does Theocritus 7, where, according to the general consensus, the figure bestowing the gift of poetry is "disguised" as a goatherd, namely Lycidas. The real identity of the goatherd is anyone's guess. The old hypothesis of a "mascarade bucolique" pointing to some fellow poet having now been discarded (see Gow 1952:129–130), scholars have recently suggested Pan (e.g. Clauss 2003), Dionysus (e.g. Moscadi 2007), Apollo (e.g. Williams 1971 and Livrea 2004), or perhaps no one in particular (e.g. Fantuzzi 2008:581) insofar as Lycidas is the "Musterbukoliker" (Puelma 1960:151). The idyll is strongly influenced by Plato, and by the *Phaedrus* in particular, as regards the landscape, the erotic motif, and the narrative technique: see Pearce 1988, Billault 2008, and Montes Cala 2009. On the other hand, it has been suggested that a pre-literary form of Sicilian bucolic poetry might have influenced the composition of the *Phaedrus*, as Murley 1940 famously argues.

[54] As for the actual statue, Posidippus does not seem to be portrayed in the act of reading the book roll. Rather, the position of the book roll points to "interrupted reading," according to an iconographic tradition that intimated intellectual prestige and was fully compatible with the representation of a *poeta recitans*. Cadario 2001 provides a perceptive survey of the "gesto della lettura interrotta."

(Ἀττικὸν ὕδωρ) for the first time upon his arrival in Athens, and entered the city after making the *proskynesis* to the deity."[55]

Admittedly, this is evidence from a later period.[56] However, Plutarch also mentions his own and his Platonic friends' custom of celebrating Socrates' birthday, which clearly points to a heroic cult.[57] In a seminal publication dedicated to "Reason and Religion in Socratic Philosophy," Donald White has argued convincingly that "the later Platonist practice of commemorating Socrates began a decade or two after his death, and [...] Plato alludes to the occasion and nature of those rites in the *Phaedo* by evoking their date, their form, and their function. This passion play ... presents Socrates as the founding father or ἥρως κτίστης, not of an educational institution, but of a new way of life devoted to the pursuit and cultivation of wisdom and virtue ... On the outskirts of Athens, Plato and his friends laid foundations for science and mathematics, drew plans for reforming education and society, and emulated their intellectual and moral model. They apparently also celebrated his life and memory in annual rites, which included a modest feast but centered on discussion, perhaps prompted by a reading of one of the dialogues that dramatically revive Socrates reasoning with his friends and many others."[58]

White's exceptionally well-documented and well-argued essay discusses a number of parallels between the portrayal of Socrates in Plato's dialogues and the cult of heroes, citing important antecedents and later examples, as well as Plato's own proposals for heroic rites in the *Republic* and in the *Laws*.[59] As he shows, the *Phaedo* seems to allude to the cult of Socrates much as the *Oedipus Coloneus* alludes to the cult of Oedipus,[60] a parallel that has a "spatial" dimension as well: as Cicero fondly recalled, the close proximity of the Academy to Colonus stirred "Platonic," as well as "Sophoclean," memories in the minds of the visitors.[61]

---

[55]   Trombley 1993:312, quoting Marinus *The Life of Proclus* 10.

[56]   Moreover, the site in question is on the road from Peiraeus to the city; thus, it could not have been Plato's Academy. Giannoulidou 1979, however, favors an early date and discusses the topography of the site. Masullo 1985 wonders whether or not "si tratti della statua di Lisippo" (131, on 251).

[57]   *Table Talks* 717b.

[58]   White 2000:168.

[59]   Wypustek 2013:65–95, provides an up-to-date, illuminating discussion of private hero cults. The evidence he has collected, together with his conclusions, are wholly compatible with White's interpretation.

[60]   The last days in the lives of both figures determine and (to a certain extent) prepare the way for their respective cults. This paradigm can be seen at work elsewhere too: Ajax's ambiguous speech in Sophocles' tragedy (646–692) can be construed precisely in this way (see Mambrini 2011).

[61]   *On the Ends of Good and Evil* 5.1.3, i.e. immediately after the passage quoted in the cover page.

White is also interested in the differences that distinguish Plato's "way" to heroization. By performing rites that were usually the prerogative of family members, Plato promoted the cult of Socrates in a potentially universal form, which stands in contrast to the traditionally parochial nature of heroic cults.[62] As such, the cult of Socrates may be said to be "philosophical," something by no means unknown in the Greek tradition, since figures ranging from Parmenides' teacher Ameinias to Pythagoras and Anaxagoras had long been the object of heroic worship.[63]

Unlike White's, my own discussion of the *Phaedrus* reveals a specific connection with the cults of poets in particular, whose traditions "have their own distinctive set of formulaic themes (initiation, inventions, pupils, poverty, power over nature, etc.)."[64] The coupling of poet and hero is not far-fetched. Socrates was not a poet, and, from this point of view, it might be better to place him in the company of more traditional heroes such as Oedipus. And yet Socrates inspired others to write. The figure of the *logos*-inspirer is explicitly and emphatically recognized in the *Phaedrus*, and elsewhere in Plato. And both Socrates, who helps his friends memorize and even write down Socratic conversations (as is clear for the framework of the *Symposium* and the *Theaetetus*), and others like Phaedrus, who are "divine" on account of their capacity to impel others to deliver speeches,[65] are such figures. The very boom of Socratic literature in the first half of the fourth century BCE testifies to the ability of the man to inspire composition: in some 50 years, no fewer than 250 Socratic works saw the light,[66] while Socrates' trial inspired the literary apologies of Plato, Xenophon, Lysias, and Isocrates, arguably the most important writers of their time.[67] Besides, no other thinker or writer was so influential in classical times as to give his name to a *literary* genre, so that, judged even by later standards,

---

[62] Heroic cults could be parochial and even explicitly exclusive. Cf. Ekroth 2009:138–139.

[63] Diogenes Laertius 9.21; Aristotle *Rhetoric* 1398b16–17. For Pythagoras, see the sources assembled and discussed by Boyancé 1937:233–241.

[64] Kivilo 2010:222. However, I do not share Kivilo's skepticism with regards to the heroic cults of poets in the archaic and classical ages.

[65] *Phaedrus* 242b. Cf. e.g. *Phaedo* 85c.

[66] See Vegetti 2006:119–120, who builds on a number of works by Livio Rossetti (see Rossetti 2011). Remarkably, the figures are adjusted downwards. Rossetti 2008 points out that *sokratikoi logoi* brought about "un sostanziale oscuramento di altri modi più tradizionali di fare filosofia" (39).

[67] Besides the *Apology* of Plato and that of Xenophon (see e.g. Danzig 2010:19–68) and the little we know about the speech composed by Lysias (cf. Rossetti 1975), I am of course referring to Isocrates' *Antidosis*. As Nicolai puts it: "Isocrate, che si presenta come educatore sommo, scrive per se stesso quella apologia—che è insieme solenne encomio—che Socrate, l'educatore degli Ateniesi nell'immaginario collettivo, non aveva mai scritto e che dopo la sua morte era stata redatta da Platone" (Nicolai 2004:99). It should be noted, moreover, that there is clear evidence of Socrates' direct influence on Isocrates, as Sarri 1974 has shown.

Socrates is no ordinary case.[68] Menippean satire was named after Menippus of Gadara, but Menippus *did* write satires, that is, works of the kind later named after him. By contrast, Socrates never wrote *sokratikoi logoi*.

With this background in mind, hardly any reader will be surprised to hear Socrates, the man who never wrote, describe the philosopher at the end of the *Phaedrus* as someone who is devoted to both oral dialectics (his serious concern, which he compares to agriculture) and written composition (his playful hobby, which he compares to the ephemeral gardens of Adonis).[69] Moreover, he puts an end to the discussion with a warning to Lysias and other prose writers and poets, including Homer, as well as Solon and other lawmakers. His warning is to the effect that they may rightly aspire to the title of *philosophos,* the highest honor achievable by a human being on this earth, provided they have stored within them a deeper knowledge than transpires from their writings—which was obviously not the case as far as Lysias and Homer were concerned.[70] These figures, however, are all labeled "mere poets,"[71] and clearly function as a foil for the true writer, that is, the philosopher, that is, ... Socrates? Most certainly not—Socrates is no writer. The man who combines serious agriculture with ephemeral gardening is clearly Plato, and this is confirmed by the quasi-anachronistic mention of Isocrates, Plato's rival, a few lines later.[72] Socrates is not a poet and does not write, and yet he juxtaposes himself and his own discourse to poets, writers, and even lawmakers. His status, then, may be described as that of a "half-poet."

White is once more on the right track when he makes the following observation:

> Through Plato's writing, Socrates thus attains the immortality that epic song awards its heroes. He also continues to exert a potent force at once similar to and very different from that ascribed to heroes in

---

[68]  Cf. Clay 1994, who notes that no other philosopher "has lent his name to a genre of literature that is the mimesis of a philosophical life" (23).

[69]  Ballériaux aptly points out that "dans les deux cas, ce que Socrate compare, ce sont des activités, différentes en sérieux et en valeur, d'un même homme" that is "Platon lui-même qui, à la fois, a écrit pour son plaisir—et pour le nôtre—et a, pour ensemencer leur âme, réunis des disciples choisis auxquels il prodiguait son enseignement à l'Académie" (Ballériaux 1987:163).

[70]  278b–d. Ford 2010 rightly compares this passage to Isocrates *Antidosis* 45, which features a list of prose genres that is "merely a foil to Isocrates' own oratory" (233). Ford goes on to say that "Lysias heads Plato's list because his ἐρωτικὸς λόγος had prompted the distinction, but here he represents the class of 'those who write prose' (συντίθησι λόγους) as distinct from poets. Next, with a formalistic thoroughness that is either prophetic or reminiscent of *Poetics*, Plato subdivides poets into composers of 'bare' poetry without melody and those of 'song.' Plato's categories are at bottom the same as Aristotle's; he differs in that he wants to set his own writing above all other texts and so takes in all artistic prose regardless of its mimetic nature" (Ford 2010:234).

[71]  Cf. 258b. Alcidamas does the same in his attack against writers. Cf. Roscalla 1997:69–72.

[72]  Cf. the Introduction to the current volume.

traditional cult, as his disembodied voice reasons dispassionately in the arguments of the dialogues. It is thus more than a humorous aside when Plato has him remark, in the middle of the final argument for immortality, that he is "talking like a book" (Hackforth's apt rendering of συγγραφικῶς ἐρεῖν, 102d3). It is likewise more than a poignant interlude when he pauses before that argument to advise Phaedo that unless they can "revive" the logos from its apparent state of death, the youth should cut his locks in mourning for its demise rather than for Socrates' imminent death (89b). Both remarks suggest that Socrates and the text speak as one.[73]

Though this may seem a bit far-fetched at first sight, I believe White's idea can be proven to be right.[74] One way to do so would be to find appropriate parallels in earlier works. For example, it has been argued that "an ideology reflecting the cult of the poet Hesiod is built into the poetry of Hesiod"[75] and that Empedocles' mention of the Muse refers to "the promise of mystic communion with the divinity of the Muse, and the poet's own future acquisition of divinity."[76] It is also pertinent to recall that "nympholepts"—Socrates claims he is becoming one—*were known as semi-poetic figures of cult* and were the object of pilgrimage, as Corinne Pache has recently argued on epigraphic and archaeological grounds.[77] However, this would be too long a path to follow, as it involves, among other things, delving into the elusive opacity of heroic cults in the archaic age,[78] and "Homeric reticence about cult."[79] Later texts, while preserving heroic traditions, tend to be more explicit, which is why I will continue to refer to the Hellenistic Age in this chapter.[80]

---

[73]  White 2000:161–162. Cf. Tomin 2001:172.

[74]  Boter 2013 (a provisional version of the author's ongoing research) also believes that "both the *Phaedo* and the *Symposium* can be regarded as monuments for Socrates." (91). Boter convincingly interprets *Symposium* 211e–212a as a reference to Socrates' posthumous immortality.

[75]  Nagy 1990:48. The argument is further developed, as regards *Works and Days* 42–105, by Bershadsky 2011 (quoting Nagy's words at page 6).

[76]  Hardie 2013:238–239.

[77]  Pache 2011 (see Chapter 2).

[78]  This opacity is due to the well-known "contrast ... between the literary (or poetic) and the archaeological record" (Clay 2004:65).

[79]  Bravo 2009:17, with a useful discussion that duly compares the classic (and conflicting) explanations provided by Martin West (1978) and Gregory Nagy (Bravo quotes from the original 1979 edition of Nagy 1999). In the second part, Bravo addresses the arduous "challenge" of "pinpointing the earliest examples of hero cult in the archaeological record" (Bravo 2009:18).

[80]  For example, Wypustek writes that "possible (and debated) evidence of heroization in the strict sense of the word, i.e. the hero-cult, consists of a wide array of testimonies, dated to Classical, Hellenistic, and Greek-Roman periods. It is sometimes thought to be found in heroic iconography on funerary reliefs. Later (Hellenistic) instances include the word ἥρως appearing on tombs and hero-cult foundations recorded in wills; funerary epigrams with heroic themes make

# Socratic Monuments

I shall begin with a curious document in the Platonic corpus, namely the *Second Letter*, which probably dates from the second or first century BCE.[81] Building on Plato's own authorial self-effacement as expressed in the *Seventh Letter* and in the *Phaedrus*, and possibly drawing on a tradition observed in the Academy, the letter concludes on an astonishing note, with "Plato" making the following claim:

> διὰ ταῦτα οὐδὲν πώποτ' ἐγὼ περὶ τούτων γέγραφα, οὐδ' ἔστιν σύγ-
> γραμμα Πλάτωνος οὐδὲν οὐδ' ἔσται, τὰ δὲ νῦν λεγόμενα Σωκράτους
> ἐστὶν <u>καλοῦ</u> καὶ νέου <u>γεγονότος</u>.

> For these reasons I have never written anything about such things, and there is no writing by Plato, and never will be: the ones that now bear his name belong to a Socrates *become beautiful* and young.

"Plato" Letter 3.314c

Interestingly, this authorial statement fulfills Socrates' prayer to Pan, since it was Socrates' precise request to become beautiful (καλῷ γενέσθαι). In the general Conclusion, we shall see how the *Phaedo* provides us with firm evidence for a construal of the dialogues as a monument designed to host the hero Socrates. Before moving on to Socrates' prison, however, I shall conclude this chapter with a further suggestion regarding Socrates' prayer to Pan.

As we have seen, Posidippus wished heroic immortality for himself, and that this took various forms: poetic, insofar as his poetry, written on golden columns, is an implicit defiance of time; mystic, in that the poet is a *mystês*, an affiliated, and imagines himself travelling to Rhadamanthys; civic, in that Posidippus asks for a statue that may be worshipped in the agora of Pella. Needless to say, these three forms, far from being mutually exclusive, are closely interconnected, and one could fairly say that Posidippus' heroic status was *trinus et unus*.

Let us see if this tripartite pattern fits Socrates.[82] "Writing in the soul" amounts to a form of immortality, in that authentic *logoi* will never cease to proliferate. Mysticism is also relevant in the *Phaedrus*, since Socrates lingers on

---

a slightly later (Greek-Roman period) phenomenon" (Wypustek 2013:65). As for archaic poetry, one can detect indirect allusions to hero cults. Thus, Dué and Nagy 2004 (with references to previous works by both authors) note that "the lamentation for heroes within epic is a reflection of ritual lamentation on the part of the community outside of epic," pointing to "hero cults of Achilles in the classical and even postclassical periods" (Dué and Nagy 2004:69).

[81] For the dating, see Isnardi Parente 2002:13.

[82] It is beyond my scope to discuss Socrates' immortality as referred to in other dialogues, notably in *Symposium* 212a (for two contrasting views, see Tuozzo 2013, who holds immortality to be educative talk, and Vegetti 2013, who believes it to be contemplation).

the blessed afterlife that awaits philosophic lovers.[83] As for the third point, we have seen how Phaedrus volunteers to have a golden statue sculpted for Socrates (235d–e). Almost immediately after, he reiterates his promise in a jocular, yet striking, manner:

τῶν δὲ λοιπῶν ἕτερα πλείω καὶ πλείονος ἄξια εἰπὼν τῶνδε [Λυσίου] παρὰ τὸ Κυψελιδῶν ἀνάθημα σφυρήλατος ἐν Ὀλυμπίᾳ στάθητι.

... when you've made a speech different from Lysias' in all other respects, which contains more and of greater value, then you'll stand in hammered metal beside the votive offering of the Cypselids at Olympia.

Plato Phaedrus 236b, trans. Rowe

Socrates is envisaged as a statue, and we know that Socrates did in fact receive such an honor. Scholars have long recognized that ancient portraits of Socrates are of two different types, conventionally called "A" and "B": "B" portraits are likely to derive from an official statue made by Lysippus, whereas "A" can be traced to a privately sponsored work, which has been identified with a bust of Socrates erected by Plato and his associates.[84] In type "B," Socrates is "normalized" and portrayed as a good citizen, whereas type "A" is more Silenus-like and wild. Paul Zanker has interpreted the latter as a deliberate provocation aimed at the ideal of the good citizen, by definition "good and beautiful" (*kalokagathia*). As he sees it, it was a paradoxical "example not of the confirmation of collective norms, but of their denial, in paying honors to Socrates."[85] The point is worth developing briefly.

In the *Apology*, Socrates comes up with an odd request: he asks the jury for public maintenance at the *Prytanaeum*.[86] This may sound outrageous, but it was not unheard of. We know of a number of such requests made by exceptional benefactors, who, according to the law, had to formulate the request in their own name. Lysias himself, a haunting "stone guest" in the *Phaedrus*, was said to have defended the general Iphicrates against a charge aimed at stripping him of the honors he had successfully asked for,[87] and the story was probably discussed

---

[83] Note that in the *Apology* Socrates expresses a desire to meet a just judge such as Rhadamanthys (41a). The *Apology* (along with its sequel the *Phaedo*) is full of Socrates' hopes for a blessed afterlife. (For references to eschatological ἐλπίς cf. *Apology* 40c, 41c; *Phaedo* 63c, 114c. Cf. *Phaedo* 114d and 114e.) See Slings's discussion on the relevant passages from the *Apology* (1994).

[84] Zanker 1995. See Charalabopoulos 2012:166–173, with added bibliography.

[85] Zanker 1995:32.

[86] 36d–37a.

[87] The authenticity of the speech (fr. 40–49 Carey) is disputed. Cf. Gauthier 1985:177–180, who concludes that "l'attribution à Lysias ne ferait guère de difficulté" (180). C. Carey summarizes the question concisely as follows: "Oratio in anno 371 habita est. De Lysia auctore ambigebatur apud

in a lost Socratic work that featured a dialogue between Socrates and Iphicrates himself.[88] Besides the maintenance, the request included *the making of a statue* and, as another token of honor, *a golden crown*.[89]

The archetypal benefactors were Harmodius and Aristogeiton, and in the fifth century the honor was reserved for generals only. In a later age, however, the orators Demades and Demosthenes obtained it.[90] The statue of the latter was placed in the agora beside a plane-tree, as Plutarch reports.[91] Later still, and outside Athens, similar honors were given to poets as well. In addition to Posidippus, who (successfully!) requested a statue in a way reminiscent of Athenian law, there is the famous example of Philitas, as recorded by his pupil Hermesianax:

Οἶσθα δὲ καὶ τὸν ἀοιδόν, ὃν Εὐρυπύλου πολιῆται
Κῷοι χάλκειον στῆσαν ὑπὸ πλατάνῳ
Βιττίδα μολπάζοντα θοήν, περὶ πάντα Φιλίταν
ῥήματα καὶ πᾶσαν τρυόμενον λαλιήν.

You also know, (Leontion) for whom the townsmen of Eurypylus,
the Coans, raised a bronze statue under a plane-tree,
Philetas, who sang his love for tall Bittis,
whilst rescuing all the love terms and all the rare words.

Hermesianax fr. 7.75–78 Powell, trans. Kobiliri

scriptores antiquos. Propter tempus a Lysia abiudicante Dionysio, Paulus Germanus authentiam vindicabat. Iudicium non dat Aelius. Lysiae sine dubitatione tribuit auctor vitarum decem oratorum, sed Aristotelem quidem ut Dionysius apparet existimasse ipsum Iphicratem scipsisse orationem" (Carey 2007:336).

[88] The existence of such a Socratic work is suggested by a remark made by Iphicrates in Diogenes Laertius 2.30, where a list of people who had been exposed to Socrates' protreptic or apotreptic influence is drawn up. All the examples seem to be linked with Socratic works, so this is probably the case with Iphicrates as well. See Patzer 1985. For a reconstruction of Iphicrates' career, see Bianco 1997.

[89] For a detailed discussion of this tradition, see Gauthier 1985, who defines this institution as "une procédure assez répandue" (112). Gauthier discusses both the literary and epigraphic evidence. As regards Athens in the Classical and Hellenistic Ages, he examines all the known cases, namely Harmodius and Aristogiton, Cleon, Conon, Iphicrates, Chabrias, Timotheus, Demades, Lycurgus, Philippides of Paiania, Philippides of Cephale, Demosthenes, Callias of Sphettos, Phaedrus of Sphettos, and Cephisodorus (Gauthier 1985:79–112).

[90] "Plutarch" *Lives of the Ten Orators* 847a.

[91] *Life of Demosthenes* 31.2. For an analysis of the statue, sculpted by one Polyeuktos and easily recognizable in certain Roman copies, see Zanker 1995:83–87, with added bibliography. The statue was meaningfully close to that of Lycurgus with Eirene holding their child Plutus. Demosthenes had in fact pleaded the cause of Lycurgus' children. See Worthington 1986.

This statue is probably the same as that described in one of Posidippus' "new" epigrams, where the idea of heroic status is clearly implied,[92] and scholars have argued that the context must have been that of a *Mouseion*.[93] Philitas himself seems to have suggested preemptively the placing of his statue under a plane-tree, since a fragment of his poetry has a curious reference to "the sitting under a plane-tree."[94] His pupil may well have made sure that his master's wish for a heroic statue under a plane-tree was fulfilled.[95]

Now, a simple question arises: where did Plato and his friends place the statue of Socrates? Zanker suggested that "the statue might have been intended to stand in the *Mouseion* of Plato's Academy ... where we know a statue of Plato himself, put up by the Persian Mithradatas and made by the sculptor Silanion, later stood (Diogenes Laertius 3.25)."[96] Thanks to the testimony of Philochorus, as recorded in a Philodemus papyrus from Hercolanum, we can now confirm Zanker's idea that an early type "A" really did exist. We can even determine its date with a fair degree of accuracy, for given that Philochorus mentions it in his fifth book, the statue could not date from any later than 359–358 BCE and must have belonged to the Academy's *Mouseion*.[97] At this point, it should

---

[92] Posidippus 63 AB. As Clay 2004 remarks, "before the definitive publication of Poseidippos' epigram on a statue of Philitas on Kos, it had been suggested that Propertius' mysterious invocation to the sacred rites of Philitas (*Coi sacra Philitae*) was an indication of Philitas' wish to be honored by a hero cult in his native island. Line 4 of the new epigram might well strengthen this conjecture. Here Poseidippos says of the sculptor, Heketaios, that he conveyed nothing of the form of heroes in rendering the old man in bronze (ἀφ'ἡρώων δ'οὐδὲν ἔμειξ{ε} ἰδέης), a description that seems to indicate a new manner of representing the poet as *heros*" (Clay 2004:30–31).

[93] See Hardie 1997, and, after the publication of the new Posidippus, Prioux 2007:23–27. The statues of aspirant heroes from the so-called "*Mouseion* of Epiktêta" constitute an interesting parallel (see Clay 2004:72–74).

[94] Fr. 14 Powell θρήσασθαι πλατάνῃ γραίῃ ὕπο.

[95] It is not clear, however, whether the text implies that the statue represented Philitas in the act of singing, i.e. whether μολπάζοντα is governed by στῆσαν or by οἶσθα. Scholars are divided on this point. A positive answer would amount to a stronger case for a heroic context, in that the analogy with the seal of Posidippus would be greater. (Cf. Hollis 2006 and, for the style, Kobiliri 1998 *ad loc.*)

[96] Zanker 1995:38. The exact location of the *Mouseion* is not known. See Billot 1983:743–744 and Charalabopoulos 2012:173n46, with more bibliography.

[97] The existence of type A was previously posited on merely stylistic grounds (this is the reconstruction still found in Zanker 1995:57–63). PHerc 1021 Col. II puts the case for the new reconstruction, as is clear from Augustin Speyer's translation: "'But [according] ... to others ... philanthropy ... to the ....' Whilst Dikaiarchos was writing such things, Philochorus joked laughingly in the sixth book of the Atthis: 'He, Plato, obtains that all more or less in passing, and does not take it ... knowing ...' And in the fifth book of the Atthis, he writes, 'And they put up an image of Socrates, a bronze bust, on which was written: SOTES MADE IT. On the sides ... there were inscribed numerous names [words?] ... that he has ordered to put up at Athens an image, a bronze bust, on which was written THIS IMAGE... besides the Museion, but he [ = Plato] was from the demos Kollytos. He [ = Philodemus' source] says, he [ = Plato] died in the year of Theophilos, having lived 82 years." (Speyer 2001:85–86. The crucial supplements at lines 13–15, ἀνέθε[σε]ν εἰκό[να / Σ[ω]

be remembered that the Academy was renowned for its shady trees, and for its plane-trees in particular.[98] In other words, the portrait was placed in a context very similar to that of Philitas', and in an ambient closely resembling that of the landscape in *Phaedrus*, where Socrates is promised an honorary statue and where he prays to Pan and the nymphs of the *Mouseion* "under a plane-tree."[99] I find it hard to believe that all this is coincidental. Let us look once more at Timon's hilarious description of the Academy:

> τῶν πάντων δ' ἡγεῖτο πλατίστακος, ἀλλ' ἀγορητὴς
> ἡδυεπής, τέττιξιν ἰσογράφος, οἵ θ' Ἑκαδήμου
> δένδρει ἐφεζόμενοι ὄπα λειριόεσσαν ἱεῖσιν.

And a plate-fish was leading them all, though it was a speaking one, and sweet-voiced at that! In his writings, he matches the cicadas, pouring out their lily song from the tree of Academos.

Timon of Phlius fr. 30 Di Marco

On first discussing the uniquely self-referential quality of the *Phaedrus* in the Introduction, we found that the plane-tree was constantly associated with Plato, and that Timon made a pun out of "Plato" and "platanos," a typically Academic tree. We also saw that Timon closely echoes, or parodies rather, the myth of the cicadas in the dialogue.[100] What is even more striking is that the distinction between *the setting of the dialogue and the site of the Academy collapse into each other*, the unifying element being the plane-tree inhabited by the cicadas.[101] This is all the more interesting insofar as the *Phaedrus*, as we have seen in the second chapter, conjures up the arboreal cult of Helen.[102] "Helen of the Trees" was strongly associated with plane-trees and she was worshipped both

---

κράτους π[ροσω]πον [χαλ / κο]ῦν are made possible by the fact that the phrase is found again at lines 26–28: ἀναθή / [σ]ειν Ἀθ[ηνε]σ[ι]ν [εἰ]κόνα πρό / σωπον χαλκοῦν). Besides Speyer 2001 and Dorandi 1991:30–31 and 86–87, see Méndez-Angeli 1992:250–251. (On palaeographical grounds, they rule out the previous reconstruction whereby the statue portrayed Isocrates rather than Socrates.) See also Voutiras 1994, who concludes that the very same portrait is referred to twice. Charalabopoulos 2012:171–174 provides a full interpretation.

[98] Cf. the Introduction to the current volume.

[99] 278c. Cf. Gaiser 1989:133.

[100] Cf. Di Marco 1989 *ad loc.*

[101] As Vallozza 2011 notes, Timon "trasferisce nell'Accademia gli alberi e le cicale del *Fedro*" (122). A conflation of the two settings is also implicit in Diogenes Laertius 3.8, who resorts to Timon's lines, as well as to Eupolis 36 PCG, in order to introduce Praxiphanes' *On the Poets*, where, says Diogenes, Plato hosted Isocrates in a field. Vallozza thus suggests that the setting of Praxiphanes' *On the Poets* was the Academy, described through the words of the *Phaedrus*. In her edition of Praxiphanes, Matelli 2013 fully endorses this view (281–284).

[102] Cf. Chapter 2 in the current volume.

at Therapne, where Helen's plane-tree stood by the river, and near Platanistas, whose very name points to the suburban wood of plane-trees that was found on the opposite side of the river and which hosted a famous gymnasium.[103] The rustic cult at Therapne was earlier, and its suburban counterpart near Platanistas has been interpreted as its complement.[104]

All of this becomes meaningful once it is realized that the Academy and its suburban gymnasium owed their name to Hecademus, a relatively minor figure, whose sole exploit involved Helen: he saved her by helping her brothers to find her, which explains why the Spartans spared the Academy when they invaded Attica.[105] Like Platanistas, the Academy must have had numerous "trees of Academus," that is, many plane-trees;[106] yet Timon surprisingly uses a singular form. So why just *one* plane-tree? This may be a result of Timon's echoing *Iliad* 3.152, or of his conflating two settings (the Academy and the *Phaedrus*). There is, however, another possible explanation. As we have seen, a plane-tree was a feature of the natural setting for statues of heroes. Given his close connections with two heads of the Academy, namely Arcesilaus and Lacydes,[107] Timon was certainly familiar with the school, so his lines, rather than the result of confusion,[108] may be a reference to just a very simple fact: that the portraits of Socrates and Plato, like those of Demosthenes and Philitas, were placed near a plane-tree.[109] Timon clearly identifies the plane-tree and *Mouseion* of the *Phaedrus* with the plane-tree and *Mouseion* of the Academy, and, in so doing, becomes our

---

[103] Cf. *Scholia on Theocritus* 18.22–25 (p. 322 Wendel).

[104] See the illuminating discussion in Arrigoni 2008:70–76 (originally published in 1985).

[105] See Plutarch *Life of Theseus* 32, with Billot 1989:733–735 and Caruso 2013:48.

[106] On the arrangement of the Academy's plane-trees, cf. Arrigoni: "Ὡς πρὸς τὴν διάταξιν τῶν δένδρων εἶναι δυνατὸν νὰ βεβαιωθῇ μετ' ἀρκούσης ἀσφαλείας ὅτι οἱ δενδρόφυτοι δρόμοι (περίπατοι) τῆς Ἀκαδημίας περιεβάλλοντο κατὰ τὰς πλευράς τῶν ὑπὸ μακρῶν σειρῶν πλατάνων, συμφώνως πρὸς συνήθειαν ἐπικρατήσασαν κατὰ τὸν ε' αἰ. π.Χ. Κατὰ τὰ ἄλλα ὁ Κίμων εἶχεν ἐπίσης κοσμήσει τοὺς χώρους τῆς ἀγορᾶς μὲ πλατάνους" (Arrigoni 1969–1970:359).

[107] Diogenes Laertius 9.115; Athenaeus 10.438a. As Caruso makes clear, no significant change marked the arrangement of the Academy "per tutto il periodo compreso dalla fondazione alla direzione di Filone di Larissa (110–87 a.C.)" (Caruso 2013:193).

[108] As Reale 1998 apparently believes (xxv–xxvi).

[109] As Billot 1989 aptly notes, "Favorinus dit qu'un certain Mithradatès, fils d'un Orontobatès également inconnu, dédia aux Muses, à l'Académie, une statue de Platon réalisée par Silanion (fr. 43 Amato). Ce que nous savons de la carrière de Silanion permet de dater l'érection de la statue aux environs de 360. Le "chaldéen" qui, selon Philppe d'Oponte, reproduit par Philodème, adoucit de ses chants les derniers moments de Platon (PHerc 1021, col. III, 34–43, et col. V, 1–22 Gaiser [pages 13–14 Mekler]) était peut-être, d'après K. Gaiser ... Mithradates lui-même. Dans ce cas, conformément à l'éthique de Platon, Silanion n'aurait exécuté son portrait qu'après la mort du philosophe en 348/7 ... cette statue-portrait ne pouvait alors se dresser que dans le *mouséion* de la propriété privée de Platon" (Billot 1989:781–782).

first testimony of a long-lived tradition whereby plane-trees served as a symbol for Plato's activity and writings.[110]

My reading of the *Phaedrus*, like White's reading of the *Phaedo*, reflects the cultic reality of the Academy. In short, what I am proposing is a figural or typological reading of the *Phaedrus*' setting, which, I believe, Plato's contemporaries would have been well aware of. In figural reading, be it applied to the Scriptures, the *Divine Comedy*, or any other work, "the figure itself is real in its own place, time, and right and without any detraction from that reality it prefigures the reality that will fulfill it. This figural relation not only brings into coherent relation events in biblical narration, but allows also the fitting of each present occurrence and experience into a real, narrative framework or world."[111] The plane-tree and *Mouseion* of the *Phaedrus* really existed, and the Athenians knew their whereabouts.[112] At the same time, in Plato's *Phaedrus*, they serve the purpose of prefiguring the plane-tree(s) and *Mouseion* of the fourth-century Academy, which were no less real, but had yet to become a Socratic-Platonic site at the time of the fifth-century "events" of the *Phaedrus* (the so-called dramatic date). Thus, the relationship between the two sites recalls that between Helen's two places of worship at Sparta. At the end of the *Phaedrus*, Socrates prays and bids farewell to the rustic gods before crossing the river to go to the city. In so doing, he points ideally to the future of the Academy and provides a kind of *aition* for its foundation.[113]

Socrates' prayer and his potential initiation as a poet-hero in the cicada myth are realized only through the writings of Plato, and, presumably, through the placing of Socrates' portrait under the plane-tree(s) of the Academy. In the foreshadowing "figure" provided by the *Phaedrus*, Socrates and his friend read Lysias in the shade of the plane-tree by the local *Mouseion*; in the foreshadowed "reality" of the Academy's *Mouseion*, however, Plato and his associates were likely to have read and recited the cicada-like words of their hero Socrates, as embedded in Plato's dialogues. In the spirit of the Greek cult of poets, the relevant book rolls must have been integral to the *Mouseion*,[114] as was the case later

---

[110] Cf. the Introduction to the current volume, pages 16–18.

[111] Frei 1974:153.

[112] It was in fact a sacred area, "a grove next to the Callirrhoe spring on the Agrae side of the Ilissus River," a setting designed "to evoke the Lesser Mysteries of Eleusis, which were celebrated there" (Nelson 2000:43). Nelson shows that the *Phaedrus* resonates with the lesser mysteries in a number of ways. Rinella argues that the *Phaedrus* entails "the superimposition of philosophy's metaphysical *epopteia* on top of the original, drug-induced Eleusinian *epopteia*" (Rinella 2000:75–76).

[113] The crossing of the river is emphatically mentioned at 242a and again at 242b, when Socrates claims that his daemonic sign has persuaded him to postpone his return to the city. The Academy, of course, was not near the Ilissus.

[114] As Clay 2004 reminds us, "poetry was also preserved in places associated with the cult of the poets" (82).

for a sacred space marked by a metrical inscription that seems to have a Platonic echo:[115]

> ἄλcoc μὲν μούcαιc ἱερὸν λέγε τοῦτ' ἀνακεῖcθαι
> τὰc βύβλουc δείξαc τὰc παρὰ ταῖc πλατάνοιc
> ἡμᾶc δὲ φρουρεῖν· κἂν γνήcιοc ἐνθάδ' ἐραcτὴc
> ἔλθῃ τῷ κιccῷ τοῦτον ἀν[α]—cτέφομεν.

Say that this grove is sacred to the Muses,
  show the books that lie by the planes,
and add that we guard them. And if a true lover
  comes by, we crown him with heather.

In all likelihood, the Academy was not equipped with a proper library.[116] Perhaps it is not too fanciful to imagine that the book rolls containing the dialogues, together with Socrates' portrait, and later Plato's, lay by that majestic plane-tree of the Academy, which Pliny recalls in the passage reproduced on the cover page.[117]

---

[115] CLE 886 and CIG III 6186 = Kaibel 829 = IG XIV 1011. The relevant stele ("*Il fere saeculi*," according to Kaibel), was found in the eighteenth century in the area of Colonna, ancient Labicum ad Quintanas (see the entry in CIG) along with a second one inscribed with a Latin version (*Hunc · sacrum · Aoniis · lucum dic · esse · Camoenis, / ostendens · libros · heic ·prope sub · platanis. / Nos · agere · excubias · atque huc · si · dignus · amator / se · ferat · huic · hederae mollia · serta · damus*). Of particular interest is the motif of the "authentic" lover. The phrase γνήcιοc ἐραcτήc was originally a Platonic *iunctura* (*Lysis* 222a) and, according to the TLG, is not to be found elsewhere in poetry. Moreover, it recurs mainly in the Platonic tradition, and is explicitly associated with Plato and Socrates. Such a phrase, in conjunction with the plane-trees and the *Mouseion*, makes it very likely that the author has Plato and the *Phaedrus* in mind.

[116] Caruso 2013 cautiously concludes that "per la scuola di Platone ... l'esistenza stessa di una biblioteca ... è un fatto ancora da dimostrare" (116).

[117] References to "Platonic" plane-tree(s) are found in Cicero (cf. *De Oratore* 1.7.28, with González Rendón 2012) and intensify in second-century Roman culture. Not only literary texts (see the Introduction to the current volume), but even everyday objects can serve as evidence of Plato's Academy. Thus, Simon 2002 discusses what she refers to as a "*lychnouchos platonikos*," i.e. a bronze putto representing Eros and crowned with plane-tree leaves, which Simon dates to the second century and interprets as an allusion to Plato's plane-trees. In such an atmosphere of revival, at a time when "tourism" in Greece was a long-established phenomenon, the epigram may well have been a reproduction of an Academic original. If so, the otherwise elusive pronoun of the third line of the epigram (ἡμᾶc-*nos*) could stand for the portraits of Socrates and Plato, the "guardians" of the *Mouseion* and of the book-rolls. However, one should not forget that plane-trees were also a prominent feature of Pompey's portico, where "stately plane trees as living colonnades dominated ordered boxwood topiaries, myrtle and palm and laurel trees and vines, and living birds brought to life the *paradeisos* conceit enacted in the theater's beast shows" (Kuttner 1999:347; Kuttner discusses a number of poems probably related more or less to Pompey's plane-trees).

# Conclusions

We have seen that Socrates' prayer to Pan is really a request for the "poetic license" required to fulfill the potential initiation of the cicada myth. Viewed in the light of a number of parallels, this points to poetic heroization, and suggests that a cult of Socrates was practiced at the Academy. Hence, his monumentalization in both literary terms (Plato's dialogues) and in more tangible ways (Socrates' portrait by a plane-tree). Nevertheless, the many affinities with the cult of poets lead to a strange paradox, for whereas Socrates was not so much a poet as a maieutic *logos*-inspirer, Plato, Socrates' complement and mirror-image, is a writer constantly disavowing authorship through stubborn anonymity. As we shall see in the Conclusion, the *Phaedo* can be seen as the meeting point where these two complementary half-poets merge to form a whole.

# Endnote: New "Facts"

- Socrates' prayer to Pan is a notorious riddle, which can be better understood in the light of certain neglected data. Firstly, the article in the expression τὸ δὲ χρυσοῦ πλῆθος emphasizes the negative connotations of gold throughout the *Phaedrus*. Secondly, an examination of the use of χρυσοῦ πλῆθος reveals that it carries equally negative overtones, usually in contrast to other good ones. Thirdly, contrary to Gaiser's widely accepted interpretation, the hendiadys ἄγω-φέρω may mean something quite different from looting: in the instance found in *Laws* 817a, it signifies the practice of poetry. Fourthly, the local divinities Socrates prays to are mentioned earlier as capable of conferring poetic inspiration. All this suggests that Socrates is really asking the gods to grant him the status of poet. Socrates' request for heroic status may be fruitfully compared to those made by other poets, such as that found in Posidippus 118 AB.

- A new reading of PHerc 1021 has confirmed that a statue representing Socrates was placed in the Academy's *Mouseion* between 385 and 359–358 BCE, possibly near a plane-tree. Comparative material such as Hermesianax 75–78 (which mentions the statue of Philitas under a plane-tree) suggests that the *Phaedrus'* references to the envisaged erection of a statue to celebrate Socrates' rhetorical accomplishments (235d–e; 236b) should be read against that historical background. Specifically, the fifth-century setting of the *Phaedrus* (*Mouseion* and plane-tree) prefigures the fourth-century cult of Socrates within the precinct of the Academy. Additional evidence (IG XIV 1011) suggests that a plane-tree within the Academy was likely to be the natural place where the book rolls containing Plato's dialogues were preserved as part of an ongoing cultic tradition.

# Conclusion

IN THE INTRODUCTION, I searched Plato's corpus for what I called his "self-disclosures": Plato consistently, albeit implicitly, refers to his dialogues as a form of *mousikê*, as opposed to other forms of discourse. The book's four chapters focus on the *Phaedrus* with such a purpose in mind, and from a number of different perspectives suggested by Socrates' meaningful mention of four Muses in the cicada myth. Each chapter (or perspective) deals with a particular example of "self-disclosure." Together, they yield a rich description of philosophical discourse—precisely what Andrea Nightingale's illuminating discussion found lacking in the dialogues.[1] If my reconstruction were to prove correct, the unraveling of certain cultural codes that have hitherto puzzled modern readers would finally enable us to understand many interesting facets of Plato's authorial voice. As is often the case, however, the solution of one problem breeds a number of others. I shall now consider some of the questions that arise from my book, and, at the same time, address three fundamental issues.

Firstly, there is the problem posed by what I may refer to as the "return" of *mousikê*. The *Phaedrus* and its encoded description of philosophy may be construed as a self-conscious appropriation and reconfiguration of traditional *mousikê*, as opposed to non-musical forms of discourse, such as sophistry and rhetoric. But why does Plato feel the need to "musicalize" philosophy? Secondly, my reading of the *Phaedrus* has given rise to a strange paradox: it is well known that Socrates did not write anything, and yet Plato has him go through a process of poetic initiation in the dialogue. Why did Plato adopt this cultural code to monumentalize someone who was clearly not a writer, let alone a poet? Last but not least, there is the status of Plato's writings. Does Plato's involvement with poetry detract from the philosophic status of the dialogues? And are the dialogues the new, all-encompassing opus designed to supersede all previous literature in Plato's ideal city? These questions will eventually take us back to Plato's entire corpus, as opposed to the four chapters' narrower focus on the *Phaedrus*.

---

[1] As I mentioned in the Introduction, page 23.

# Socrates' Anti-Intellectualism

Socrates' intellectualism is a much celebrated and discussed milestone in the history of philosophy, so the above heading may sound like a provocation. Nevertheless, I believe I can say, although not without some reservation, that the present study reveals a surprisingly anti-intellectualistic strand in the *Phaedrus*, and in Plato more generally. I am referring not only to the fact that the *Phaedrus* appropriates the devastating manifestations of Eros found in lyric poetry (Chapter 2), or to the genetic, cultic kinship of poetic and philosophical discourse (Chapters 3 and 4), but also to a thematic undercurrent that was first dealt with in the Introduction and Chapter 1: that is, the recurrent tension between philosophy and prose. I must, therefore, bring my argument to a close by exploring the ultimate reasons for Plato's return to *mousikê*.

That the *Phaedrus* criticizes contemporary rhetoric is obvious enough, but that Socrates should take sides with "musical" inspiration against "human" prose writing is puzzling, and demands some explanation. On the one hand, I argue that Socrates' attitude can be explained as an apologetic move on the part of Plato, that is, as a means to counter wide-spread allegations against philosophy. On the other, Socrates' move helps to define the discourse of philosophy as against the negativity of rhetoric, which adds weight to my previous conclusions.

I shall begin with the apologetic element.[2] By the end of the fifth century BCE, Socrates' public image, as portrayed by comic playwrights, was more or less the same as that criticized by Nietzsche. The *Clouds*, which both Plato and Xenophon refer to so often, depicts Socrates as a pointy-headed intellectual who encourages young Athenians to disparage traditional *mousikê*.[3] Thus, for example, it is after attending Socrates' "classes" that Pheidippides rejects the time-honored tradition of sympotic music and beats his father for asking him to sing. The chorus comments that this serves the father right, given that he wanted his son to be a "clever orator" (δεινὸν ... λέγειν).[4] In the *Frogs*, Socrates' alleged propensity for rhetoric makes him Euripides' accomplice in the murder of tragedy:[5]

---

[2]  Apologetic traits are ubiquitous in the writings of both Plato and Xenophon. Danzig 2010 offers a good discussion.

[3]  Polycrates, in turn, seems to have suggested that Socrates has perversely distorted the meaning of a number of influential poems. Cf. Lasserre 1987 for a lucid reconstruction.

[4]  1314–1315.

[5]  See Brancacci 2004. Socrates was not always represented as an enemy of *mousikê* in Greek comedy; for a thorough discussion of the relevant passages, see Segoloni 2003. The *Frogs*, however, was comedy's last word on Socrates, as well as being an extraordinarily successful play, which resulted in new productions in the fourth century BCE (see the Introduction to the

χαρίεν οὖν μὴ Σωκράτει / παρακαθήμενον λαλεῖν, / ἀποβαλόντα
μουσικὴν / τά τε μέγιστα παραλιπόντα / τῆς τραγῳδικῆς τέχνης. / τὸ
δ' ἐπὶ σεμνοῖσιν λόγοισι/ καὶ σκαριφησμοῖσι λήρων / διατριβὴν ἀργὸν
ποιεῖσθαι, / παραφρονοῦντος ἀνδρός.

It's an elegant thing not to sit by Socrates and chat or cast the Muses'
work aside, forgetting the most vital skills of writing tragedies. Wasting
time with pompous words, while idly scratching verbal bits that suits a
man who's lost his wits.

Aristophanes Frogs 1491–1499, trans. Johnson (modified)

The accusation that Socrates was "unmusical" helps us to understand why
the *Phaedrus* aligns Socrates with musical Stesichorus and Sappho (cf. Chapters
1 and 2), and why Socrates asks for poetic initiation while seeming to expect
poetic heroization (Chapters 3 and 4). The other allegation, that he was an
overly subtle rhetorician, also figures prominently in the dialogues. I shall turn
my attention briefly, therefore, to the phrase "clever speaker."[6]

Remarkably, this is the first accusation Socrates addresses at the beginning
of the *Apology*:

Ὅτι μὲν ὑμεῖς, ὦ ἄνδρες Ἀθηναῖοι, πεπόνθατε ὑπὸ τῶν ἐμῶν
κατηγόρων, οὐκ οἶδα· ἐγὼ δ' οὖν καὶ αὐτὸς ὑπ' αὐτῶν ὀλίγου ἐμαυτοῦ
ἐπελαθόμην, οὕτω πιθανῶς ἔλεγον. καίτοι ἀληθές γε ὡς ἔπος εἰπεῖν
οὐδὲν εἰρήκασιν. μάλιστα δὲ αὐτῶν ἓν ἐθαύμασα τῶν πολλῶν ὧν
ἐψεύσαντο, τοῦτο ἐν ᾧ ἔλεγον ὡς χρῆν ὑμᾶς εὐλαβεῖσθαι μὴ ὑπ' ἐμοῦ
ἐξαπατηθῆτε ὡς <u>δεινοῦ</u> ὄντος <u>λέγειν</u>. τὸ γὰρ μὴ αἰσχυνθῆναι ὅτι αὐτίκα
ὑπ' ἐμοῦ ἐξελεγχθήσονται ἔργῳ, ἐπειδὰν μηδ' ὁπωστιοῦν φαίνωμαι
<u>δεινὸς λέγειν</u>, τοῦτό μοι ἔδοξεν αὐτῶν ἀναισχυντότατον εἶναι, εἰ μὴ
ἄρα <u>δεινὸν</u> καλοῦσιν οὗτοι <u>λέγειν</u> τὸν τἀληθῆ λέγοντα· εἰ μὲν γὰρ τοῦτο
λέγουσιν, ὁμολογοίην ἂν ἔγωγε οὐ κατὰ τούτους εἶναι ῥήτωρ.

How you, Athenians, have been affected by my accusers, I don't know;
but certainly they made even me almost forget about myself, they were

---

current volume). As such, and coming in the aftermath of Athens' final defeat in 404, Athenians
would have naturally taken it to imply that Socrates, together with Euripides, was responsible
for the decline of the city. And this explains why the Socratics were particularly anxious to rebut
the *Frogs*. As a *vir Socraticus*, Panaetius, too, was very concerned about this passage, as the ancient
*scholia* testify (cf. Lapini 1999 for a thorough discussion of the text and meaning of the *scholia*).

6 For a general discussion of *deinos* and *deinotês*, see e.g. Lombardo 2003. Cf. also North 1988.
Despite its title ("Socrates *Deinos Legein*"), the article does not address the issue I discuss in this
paragraph. Rather, it draws attention to rhetorical clichés, which are found both in rhetorical
speeches and in Plato's *Apology*.

speaking so persuasively. And yet they have said virtually nothing *true*. The one I found most surprising among their many falsehoods was this, when they were saying that you ought to be careful I don't deceive you, because I'm a *clever speaker*. Their failure to be ashamed at the immediate prospect of my refuting them in practice, when it becomes apparent I'm not at all a *clever speaker*, this struck me as the very height of their shamelessness—unless after all my opponents give the title of *"clever speaker"* to one that tells the truth; if that's what they are saying I should agree that I'm an orator in a different league from them.

Plato Apology of Socrates 17a–b, trans. Stokes (modified)

Repeated no less than three times at the very beginning of Socrates' plea, the phrase "clever speaker" (δεινὸς λέγειν) sounds very much like a catchword employed deliberately to rebut the accusation voiced by Aristophanes. One may recall how the *Apology* singles out Aristophanes as being somehow responsible for Socrates' distorted image,[7] which seems to have continued to haunt both Plato and Xenophon.[8]

The passage from the *Apology* plays on the ambiguity of the phrase "clever speaker;" δεινός is in fact notoriously ambiguous, its meaning hovering between positive and negative connotations, between "terrific" and "terrible," as in the famous choral song from Sophocles' *Antigone*. Even more remarkable is Socrates' suggestion that the term might easily be turned in his favor. Were "clever" to mean truthful, for example, then he could claim to be clever. This, however, never seems to happen in Plato's dialogues.

---

[7]  This is, of course, an oversimplified account. I agree with Stephen Halliwell that in "the relevant passages of the *Apology*—passages whose one-sided interpretation has become one of the stalest received opinions in classical scholarship—a *distinction* is indicated between the comedian Aristophanes (and by extension other comic poets too who wrote plays about Socrates) and those who over the years have maligned Socrates with real 'malice and denigration' (φθόνῳ καὶ διαβολῇ, 18d)" (Halliwell 2008:254–255).

[8]  Cf. Guthrie 1971: "Xenophon and Plato make several references to the treatment of Socrates by the comic poets, though not all are certainly to Aristophanes. In the *Oeconomicus* (11.3) he says he is 'supposed to be a poor man' and in the *Symposium* (6.6) Xenophon makes a direct reference to the *Clouds* when the impresario rudely asks Socrates not only whether he is 'the one they call *phrontistes*' but also whether he can tell him how many feet away a flea is, 'for this is the sort of geometry they say you do' (cf. *Clouds* 145f.). At *Phaedo* 70b–c Socrates says drily that if, as a man condemned to death, he discusses the possibility of immortality, 'not even a comic poet could say that I am a chatterer about things that don't concern me', and the remark in the *Republic* (488e) that in the 'democratic' ship the skilled steersman will be called a 'sky-gazer, a chatterer, and useless' is a fairly obvious reference to the Socrates of comedy. In Plato's *Symposium* (221b) Alcibiades quotes the actual words from the *Clouds* about his 'swaggering and rolling his eyes.' But the most striking allusion is in Plato's *Apology* (18b, 19b–c)" (Guthrie 1971:54).

Usually, it was the sophists, like Protagoras and the two brothers of the *Euthydemus*, who taught their pupils how to become "clever speaker(s)."[9] Yet the "clever speaker" *par excellence* was Gorgias, as a brilliant pun in the *Symposium* makes clear. Having spotted ample traces of Gorgianic rhetoric in Agathon's speech, Socrates says:

> ... ὑπ' αἰσχύνης ὀλίγου ἀποδρὰς ᾠχόμην, εἴ πη εἶχον. καὶ γάρ με Γοργίου ὁ λόγος ἀνεμίμνησκεν, ὥστε ἀτεχνῶς τὸ τοῦ Ὁμήρου ἐπεπόνθη· ἐφοβούμην μή μοι τελευτῶν ὁ Ἀγάθων <u>Γοργίου κεφαλὴν δεινοῦ λέγειν</u> ἐν τῷ λόγῳ ἐπὶ τὸν ἐμὸν λόγον πέμψας αὐτόν με λίθον τῇ ἀφωνίᾳ ποιήσειεν. καὶ ἐνενόησα τότε ἄρα καταγέλαστος ὤν, ἡνίκα ὑμῖν ὡμολόγουν ἐν τῷ μέρει μεθ' ὑμῶν ἐγκωμιάσεσθαι τὸν Ἔρωτα καὶ ἔφην εἶναι <u>δεινὸς τὰ ἐρωτικά</u>, οὐδὲν εἰδὼς ἄρα τοῦ πράγματος, ὡς ἔδει ἐγκωμιάζειν ὁτιοῦν. ἐγὼ μὲν γὰρ ὑπ' ἀβελτερίας ᾤμην δεῖν τἀληθῆ λέγειν περὶ ἑκάστου τοῦ ἐγκωμιαζομένου.

> I was ready to run away for shame, if there had been a possibility of escape. For I was reminded of Gorgias, and at the end of his speech I fancied that Agathon was shaking at me *the Gorginian head of that clever speaker*, which was simply to turn me and my speech, into stone, as Homer says, and strike me dumb. And then I perceived how foolish I had been in consenting to take my turn with you in praising love, and saying that I too was *clever in things erotic* when I really had no conception how anything ought to be praised. For in my simplicity I imagined that the topics of praise should be true.

> Plato *Symposium* 198c, trans. Jowett (modified)

Socrates again hints at the possibility of turning the meaning of "clever" to his advantage. Gorgias, who is compared to the Homeric Gorgo, is of course "terrible" (δεινός), whereas Socrates describes himself as "terrific" in things erotic, that is, where praising Eros means telling the truth.

Socrates' disambiguation of the term "clever" calls to mind the semantic distinctions of Prodicus, and it is no coincidence that one of the instances in the *Protagoras* makes a direct reference to this adjective. In this case, Socrates proclaims himself to be a pupil of Prodicus, who, he says, has taught him how

---

[9] Only once does Socrates apply the phrase to himself, in the highly ironic context of the *Menexenus*, where he mentions a woman, Aspasia, as his teacher of rhetoric. In the same text, however, he closely associates cleverness *with the knowledge of "music,"* that is, with the quintessentially traditional art that Aristophanes had maliciously accused Socrates of rejecting so deplorably. For the occurrences of the phrase in Plato's dialogues, cf. *Euthydemus* 272a, *Protagoras* 312d (twice) and 312e (twice); see also *Menexenus* 95c.

to use the notion of *deinos* so as to retain its exclusively negative connotations ("terrible" as opposed to "terrific").[10] Socrates must surely be joking when he calls Prodicus his teacher, and yet the above-mentioned examples suggest that he is being serious in some way. Let me summarize the evidence collected so far:

- Aristophanes accuses Socrates of rejecting "music" and teaching his acolytes how to become "clever speaker(s)."
- Socrates denies he is a "clever speaker," unless this means telling the truth.
- In Socrates' view, the sophists, and especially Gorgias, are "clever speakers."
- A pupil of Prodicus, Socrates often hints at the possibility of a different notion of cleverness.

What we find in the *Phaedrus* is precisely such a one-sided notion of cleverness, with Socrates erasing all the positive connotations of the word in order to distance "musical" philosophy from "clever" rhetoric.[11]

Before reaching the plane-tree, Socrates and Phaedrus discuss the story of Oreithyia, who, it was alleged, was abducted by Boreas on a hill nearby. Phaedrus is skeptical and asks Socrates if he thinks the story is true. To the surprise of modern readers, Socrates emphatically refuses to fall in with the rationalistic doubts of Phaedrus. Unlike the "smart ones" (οἱ σοφοί), he has no inclination to "try and reduce myth to what is likely" (κατὰ τὸ εἰκός), on the grounds that "such explanations are 'elegant' things" (χαρίεντα) and "belong to an over-clever (δεινοῦ) and laborious person, who is not altogether fortunate."[12] Socrates prefers to stick with tradition (τῷ νομιζομένῳ) and bids farewell (χαίρειν) to such ingenious explanations.[13]

Socrates uses the word "clever" in a wholly pejorative sense, thus activating only one of its two major semantic fields.[14] Socrates' reply is far from innocent, in that it implicitly makes fun of Phaedrus' enthusiasm for Lysias, whom Phaedrus had called "the cleverest (δεινότατος) of present writers" (228a). He

---

[10] *Protagoras* 341a–b. *Deinos*, says Prodicus, is synonymous with *kakos* (τὸ γὰρ δεινόν, φησίν, κακόν ἐστιν).

[11] It is interesting to see that, on proclaiming himself a pupil of Prodicus, Socrates calls his art a form of *mousikê* (*Protagoras* 340a).

[12] 229c–d. Socrates describes this form of rationalism as a "rude kind of wisdom" (ἄγροικός τις σοφία, 229e). Apparently, the adjective χαρίεις "was used in the classical era with reference to measuring various different degrees of sophistication in the practice and understanding of the verbal arts" (Nagy 2011 §95, cf. §112, and §117).

[13] 230a. Socrates also mentions the Delphic motto, "know thyself."

[14] The pejorative use of σοφός is also exceptional. Cf. *Ion* 532d, with the commentary of Rijksbaron 2007 *ad loc.*

is deliberately poking fun at the rationalism of the "clever," "smart" orators and sophists, as is clear from his use of "likely," which, as the final pages of the dialogue make clear, was one of their favorite catchwords.[15] His defense of traditional myth against rationalism may also be a pointed reply to Aristophanes, who had his chorus declaim that it was a "elegant thing" (χαρίεν) to steer clear of Socrates' rationalistic nonsense. By way of a riposte, Plato has Socrates declare he has no time for such "elegant things" (χαρίεντα), which are the prerogative of the overly clever.

The *deinos* motif reappears later, after Socrates has delivered his first speech and begins to feel the pangs of remorse. On that occasion, he had deprecated his own speech by twice calling it "terrible" (δεινόν, δεινόν). Now he feels he must make atonement, for nothing could be more terrible than such a silly, impious speech.[16] In the second half of the dialogue, the adjective is variously used to qualify the clever tricks of orators and the shortcomings of writing,[17] but the culmination of the motif must surely come near the beginning of the palinode, when Socrates introduces the notion of an immortal soul and its prenatal vision of the Forms:

Τοσαῦτα μέν σοι καὶ ἔτι πλείω ἔχω μανίας γιγνομένης ἀπὸ θεῶν λέγειν καλὰ ἔργα. ὥστε τοῦτό γε αὐτὸ μὴ φοβώμεθα, μηδέ τις ἡμᾶς λόγος θορυβείτω δεδιττόμενος ὡς πρὸ τοῦ κεκινημένου τὸν σώφρονα δεῖ προαιρεῖσθαι φίλον· ἀλλὰ τόδε πρὸς ἐκείνῳ δείξας φερέσθω τὰ νικητήρια, ὡς οὐκ ἐπ' ὠφελίᾳ ὁ ἔρως τῷ ἐρῶντι καὶ τῷ ἐρωμένῳ ἐκ θεῶν ἐπιπέμπεται. ἡμῖν δὲ ἀποδεικτέον αὖ τοὐναντίον, ὡς ἐπ' εὐτυχίᾳ τῇ μεγίστῃ παρὰ θεῶν ἡ τοιαύτη μανία δίδοται· ἡ δὲ δὴ ἀπόδειξις ἔσται <u>δεινοῖς μὲν ἄπιστος, σοφοῖς δὲ πιστή</u>.

All these and still more are the fine achievements which I am able to relate to you of madness which comes from the gods. So let us have no fears about that, and let us not be alarmed by any argument that tries to frighten us into supposing that we should prefer the sane man as friend to the one who is disturbed; let it carry off the prize of victory only if it has shown this too—that love is not sent from the gods for the benefit of lover and beloved. We in our turn must prove the reverse, that such madness is given by the gods to allow us to achieve the greatest good fortune; and the proof will be *disbelieved by the clever, believed by the wise.*

Plato *Phaedrus* 245b–c, trans. Rowe

---

[15]  Cf. Chapter 2 in the current volume.
[16]  242a Εὐήθη καὶ ὑπό τι ἀσεβῆ· οὗ τίς ἂν εἴη δεινότερος;.
[17]  260c, 267c, 275d. Cf. 272a (δεινώσεως) and 273c (δεινῶς).

Here, the contrast is so radical that Socrates ends up pitting wisdom (philosophy) against cleverness (rhetoric). As we saw in Chapter 3, Socrates ends his speech by asking the god to "terminate" Lysias, an implicit reference to the poetic "termination" of Thamyris, the archenemy of the Muses. To sum up, Socrates' use of δεινός in the *Phaedrus* is unusually and consistently pejorative, and it highlights the dichotomy between the "musical" discourse of philosophy and that of "clever" rhetoric seen as a manipulative form of rationalism.

Paradoxically, the emphatic re-signification of *deinotês* is not only a means of acquitting Socrates and philosophy of the allegations insinuated by Aristophanes; it also becomes the *conditio sine qua non* of any authentic discourse. True philosophy is exercised only insofar as it pursues a form of wisdom that keeps "cleverness" at bay.

# The Death of Socrates and the Birth of Philosophical Writing

As we have seen, Plato clearly "musicalizes" philosophy, and he does so by aligning Socrates with a number of poetic traditions: Stesichorus' "re-vision" (Chapter 1); Sappho's memory (Chapter 2); the pattern of poetic initiation (Chapter 3); and the heroic cults of poets (Chapter 4). This is quite puzzling to say the least, given that Socrates was neither a poet nor a writer. In fact, he never wrote anything at all. Even so, he was a remarkable inspirer of *logos*, and as such may be regarded as a kind of poet manqué. It is now time to explore this paradox within a broader framework, that is, beyond the limits of the *Phaedrus* and Socratic biography.

Plato has Socrates undergo a proper, albeit potential, initiation into poetry in the *Phaedrus*, and the final prayer to Pan should be interpreted, as we have seen in Chapter 4, as a request for poetic consecration, or even poetic heroization. In the *Phaedo*, however, *potency* comes close to becoming *act*. Almost at the beginning of the dialogue, once Xanthippe is taken away and the chains removed, Socrates bends down and rubs his legs with a mixed feeling of pleasure and pain. He remarks that the two feelings, however different, are interrelated. Aesop, Socrates claims, "would have made a myth (μῦθον ἂν συνθεῖναι) about God trying to reconcile their strife, and how, when he could not, he fastened their heads together; and this is the reason why when one comes the other follows" (60c).[18]

---

[18]  McPherran 2012 tries to imagine which of Aesop's extant fables might have inspired Socrates' versifying, as mentioned immediately afterwards. Betegh 2009 notes that the tale shares a number of structural features with other fables found in the dialogues, such as Aristophanes' in the *Symposium* and the myth of origins recounted in the *Protagoras*. According to Betegh, by

Socrates' "mythological" remark reminds Cebes that the sophist-poet Evenus is eager to know why on earth (ὅτι ποτὲ διανοηθείς) Socrates, once in prison, tried his hand at poetry, "turning Aesop's fables into verse, and also composing that hymn in honor of Apollo." Socrates replies that he had no intention of rivaling Evenus or his poetic output. Rather, he did it in order to "make expiation":

ἐνυπνίων τινῶν <u>ἀποπειρώμενος τί λέγοι</u>, καὶ <u>ἀφοσιούμενος</u> εἰ ἄρα πολλάκις ταύτην τὴν μουσικήν μοι ἐπιτάττοι ποιεῖν. ἦν γὰρ δὴ ἄττα τοιάδε· πολλάκις μοι φοιτῶν τὸ αὐτὸ ἐνύπνιον ἐν τῷ παρελθόντι βίῳ, ἄλλοτ' ἐν ἄλλῃ ὄψει φαινόμενον, τὰ αὐτὰ δὲ λέγον, "Ὦ Σώκρατες," ἔφη, "μουσικὴν ποίει καὶ ἐργάζου." καὶ ἐγὼ ἔν γε τῷ πρόσθεν χρόνῳ ὅπερ ἔπραττον τοῦτο ὑπελάμβανον αὐτό μοι παρακελεύεσθαί τε καὶ ἐπικελεύειν, ὥσπερ οἱ τοῖς θέουσι διακελευόμενοι, καὶ ἐμοὶ οὕτω τὸ ἐνύπνιον ὅπερ ἔπραττον τοῦτο ἐπικελεύειν, μουσικὴν ποιεῖν, ὡς φιλοσοφίας μὲν οὔσης μεγίστης μουσικῆς, ἐμοῦ δὲ τοῦτο πράττοντος. νῦν δ' ἐπειδὴ ἥ τε δίκη ἐγένετο καὶ ἡ τοῦ θεοῦ ἑορτὴ διεκώλυέ με ἀποθνῄσκειν, ἔδοξε χρῆναι, εἰ ἄρα πολλάκις μοι προστάττοι τὸ ἐνύπνιον ταύτην τὴν δημώδη μουσικὴν ποιεῖν, μὴ ἀπειθῆσαι αὐτῷ ἀλλὰ ποιεῖν· ἀσφαλέστερον γὰρ εἶναι μὴ ἀπιέναι πρὶν <u>ἀφοσιώσασθαι</u> ποιήσαντα ποιήματα [καὶ] πιθόμενον τῷ ἐνυπνίῳ. οὕτω δὴ πρῶτον μὲν εἰς τὸν θεὸν ἐποίησα οὗ ἦν ἡ παροῦσα θυσία· μετὰ δὲ τὸν θεόν, ἐννοήσας ὅτι τὸν ποιητὴν δέοι, εἴπερ μέλλοι ποιητὴς εἶναι, <u>ποιεῖν μύθους</u> ἀλλ' οὐ λόγους, καὶ αὐτὸς οὐκ ἦ μυθολογικός, διὰ ταῦτα δὴ οὓς προχείρους εἶχον μύθους καὶ ἠπιστάμην τοὺς Αἰσώπου, τούτων ἐποίησα οἷς πρώτοις ἐνέτυχον.

... for I wanted to *put to the test* certain dreams so as to understand *what they are saying*, and I also wanted to *make expiation*, in case this was the kind of music that the dreams intimated me to compose. In the course of my life I have often had intimations in dreams that I should compose music. The same dream came to me sometimes in one form, and sometimes in another, but always saying the same or nearly the same words: "*Cultivate and make music*," said the dream. And hitherto I had imagined that this was only intended to exhort and encourage me in the study of philosophy, which has been the pursuit of my life, and is the noblest and best of *mousikê*. The dream was bidding me do what I was already doing, in the same way that the competitor in a race is bidden by the spectators to run when he is already running. But I was not certain of

---

presenting the gods as "rational and benevolent agents" (91) these tales meet Plato's conditions for ethical narratives.

this, for the dream might have meant *mousikê* in the popular sense of the word, and being under sentence of death, and the festival giving me a respite, I thought that it would be safer for me in obedience to the dream, to compose a few verses and *make expiation* before I departed. And first I made a hymn in honor of the god of the festival, and then considering that a poet, if he is really to be a poet, should not only put together words, but should *make myths*, and that I have no invention, I took some fables of Aesop, which I had ready at hand and which I knew—they were the first I came upon—and turned them into verse.

Plato *Phaedo* 60e–61b, trans. Jowett (modified)

It is clear that the passage, by warning Socrates against the excesses of rationalism,[19] introduces the theme of *mousikê* in a way that closely parallels the *Phaedrus*.

In the *Phaedrus*, Socrates delivers an impious speech, which would have put an end to the dialogue had not his divine sign prevented him from crossing the river—before returning home, Socrates had to "make expiation" (ἀφοσιώσομαι).[20] This results in the rehabilitation of divine madness (including Muse-inspired poetry) and in Socrates' great "enthusiastic" speech, whereby the philosopher averts Homeric blindness and delivers a myth that "will be disbelieved by the clever, believed by the wise" (245c). As in the *Phaedo*, the notion of purification is conveyed by the rather unusual verb ἀφοσιοῦμαι, which in both dialogues presages some kind of musical experience.[21] It is probably no coincidence, therefore, that Socrates identifies with singing and holy animals (sacred to Apollo and the Muses) in both dialogues;[22] indeed, it has often been remarked that the swans in the *Phaedo* are in many ways the equivalent of the singing cicadas.[23] Yet the analogy goes even deeper.

In the *Phaedo*, Socrates turns his back on natural science and declares that the study of natural phenomena nearly made him "blind," so that he had to

---

[19] And pointing to what *Letter* 7.340a refers to as the "weakness of *logos*." For this interpretation of Socrates' dream, see Roochnik 2001, who concludes that the dream is a crucial warning for Socrates: without myth, philosophy "would present itself in the misleading guise of hyper-wakefulness, of pure or systematic rationality" (257).

[20] Cf. Chapter 3 in the current volume.

[21] These are the only two passages in the entire corpus where the verb is referred to Socrates. Like the *Phaedrus*, the *Phaedo* displays a number of poetic features, including a number of lines that scan like verse (cf. Bacon 1990).

[22] "A cigarra é protegida não só pelas Musas, mas também por Apolo, como evidenciam moedas de Camarina, Caulonia e de Atenas, nas quais ela figura ao lado do deus" (Cunha Corrêa 2010:195).

[23] Cf. e.g. Pinnoy 1991. The *Phaedo*'s swans embody the anti-tragic nature of Plato's philosophical discourse, as Susanetti 2002 has argued. Castrucci 2013 offers further fascinating insights.

resort to what he famously refers to as the "second sailing."[24] The *Phaedrus* tells a similar story. Socrates risks becoming blind like Homer, but then feels the need to deliver a second speech. He then turns to musical Stesichorus and renounces all forms of narrow rationalism, thus preserving his sight.[25] This is accompanied by a suitably analogous anti-intellectualistic stance, which results in him contrasting "wisdom" and "cleverness." As we have already seen, Socrates questions the "clever" (*deinos*) rationalism of Phaedrus, who, in disbelieving the myth of Oreithyia, stings Socrates into making an unfavorable comparison between the clever (*deinoi*) and the wise (*sophoi*) (245c). The conclusive eschatological myth of the *Phaedo* also follows what is basically a similar pattern:

Τὸ μὲν οὖν ταῦτα διισχυρίσασθαι οὕτως ἔχειν ὡς ἐγὼ διελήλυθα, οὐ πρέπει <u>νοῦν ἔχοντι ἀνδρί</u>· ὅτι μέντοι ἢ ταῦτ' ἐστὶν ἢ τοιαῦτ' ἄττα περὶ τὰς ψυχὰς ἡμῶν καὶ τὰς οἰκήσεις, ἐπείπερ ἀθάνατόν γε ἡ ψυχὴ φαίνεται οὖσα, τοῦτο καὶ πρέπειν μοι δοκεῖ καὶ ἄξιον κινδυνεῦσαι οἰομένῳ οὕτως ἔχειν—καλὸς γὰρ ὁ κίνδυνος—καὶ χρὴ <u>τὰ τοιαῦτα ὥσπερ ἐπᾴδειν ἑαυτῷ</u>, διὸ δὴ ἔγωγε καὶ πάλαι <u>μηκύνω τὸν μῦθον</u>.

A *man of sense* ought not to say, nor will I be very confident, that the description which I have given of the soul and her mansions is exactly true. But I do say that, inasmuch as the soul is shown to be immortal, he may venture to think, not improperly or unworthily, that something of the kind is true. The venture is a glorious one, and one should *charm himself with words like these*, which is the reason why *I lengthen out the myth*.

Plato *Phaedo* 114d, trans. Jowett (modified)

As in the *Phaedrus*, a sensible man is not likely to believe Socrates' "charming" myth, but the truly wise will.[26]

---

[24] There should be no room left for doubt as to the meaning of δεύτερος πλοῦς ("second sailing"). Martinelli Tempesta 2003b has provided an extensive analysis of the phrase that amounts to conclusive evidence.

[25] The equivalence between blindness and rationalism probably had poetic precedents (cf. Pindar *Paean* 7b 11–22, with Ferrari 2004).

[26] However, there is a notable difference in the way this same idea is formulated. In the *Phaedrus*, Socrates uses δεινός, which refers back to a rhetorical catchword, rhetoric being one major target of the dialogue. In the *Phaedo*'s perfectly parallel statement, the expression is "a man of sense," that is, someone equipped with *nous*. This is hardly coincidental: Anaxagoras' *nous* is Socrates' major polemical target in the *Phaedo*, and Socrates tries hard to distance himself from it, in an attempt to clear his name from the accusations voiced by Aristophanes and others that he was a natural philosopher.

The parallels with the *Phaedrus* are extremely interesting from the point of view of Plato's implicit poetics. In both dialogues, Plato compares rationalistic forms of discourse unfavorably with *mousikê* and clearly identifies his own activity with the latter.[27] The *Phaedo* passage, however, would seem to have a more specifically poetological import. Socrates' conversion to poetry takes place on a day sacred to Apollo, whose "festivity" (ἑορτή) is explicitly mentioned.[28] This is, of course, perfectly consistent with Socrates' "serious" composition, namely his hymn (προοίμιον) to Apollo.[29] However, an Apollonian connection is equally plausible as regards Aesop, who enjoyed a Delphic cult,[30] founded upon what may be described as a ritual antagonism with Apollo. Historically, this antagonism took the form of a polarity between high and low discourse,[31] which recalls Plato's "self-disclosures" as discussed later in the Appendix. I am thinking, in particular, of the *Symposium*, in which Socrates advocates an art capable of combining comedy and tragedy, something scholars are increasingly willing to accept as pertinent to Plato's own dialogues.

It is in this Apollonian context that the *Apology* depicts Socrates as a "soldier of Apollo," who will never desert the post assigned to him by the god.[32] In fact, Socrates' philosophical life is entirely the product of the Delphic oracle, as he famously recounts in the *Apology*: when Chaerephon "asked the oracle to tell him whether there was anyone wiser than I was," the Pythian prophetess answered in the negative (21a). Consequently, Socrates wondered what the god might mean (τί ποτε λέγει) and resolved to put the oracle to the test (ἐλέγξων τὸ μαντεῖον) by examining people who were said to be wise. Thus, Socrates chose the life of philosophy, something that turned him into a potential rival of Athens' self-proclaimed educators. This explains why, just before telling the story of Chaerephon's visit to Delphi, Socrates cites the case of Evenus of Parus, who charged fees for his lessons.

It would seem to be no coincidence, therefore, that Evenus of Paros should resurface in the *Phaedo* passage, which again introduces him as a potential rival of Socrates. This time, however, the rivalry is different, since it involves the art

---

[27] According to Acosta-Hughes and Stephens 2012 (31–29), both the cicada myth and *Phaedo* 60e–61b are echoed in Callimachus' proem to the *Aetia*. If true, this is a further connection.

[28] 61a, and cf. 58a–c.

[29] It should be noted that the meaning and etymology of the word προοίμιον are discussed in relation to whether it is formed after οἴμη, as is generally believed, or after οἶμος, as argued by Maslov 2012.

[30] The clearest testimony is P. Oxy. 1800 fr. 2 ii 32–63 = Aesop *Testimonia* 25 Perry.

[31] See Nagy 2011, with added bibliography (including references to Nagy's own previous work and to Kurke 2011, who articulates the polarity between Apollo and Aesop in ways that significantly differ from Nagy's). For the parallels between Plato's Socrates and the life of Aesop, see the Introduction to the current volume

[32] Cf. 28d–29a and 33c.

of poetry much more specifically. Another important similarity between the two situations, however, is that the Socrates of the *Phaedo* puts his dreams to the test (ἐνυπνίων τινῶν ἀποπειρώμενος) in an attempt to find out what they might mean (τί λέγει). The *déjà vu* effect should alert us. The testing of the divine dreams in the Apollonian context of the *Phaedo*, just like the testing of the Apollonian oracle in the *Apology*, is a sign intended to mark a new beginning. When Socrates was young, the oracle determined his conversion to a life of enquiry. Now, in the *Phaedo*, the divine dream marks Socrates' conversion to music and poetry.[33] Thus, Socrates' Apollonian turns call to mind those of the "man of Paros," who of course is not Evenus: I am referring to the poet and soldier Archilochus of Paros, whose Apollonian initiation, as we saw in the third and fourth chapters, provides a striking parallel to the poetic initiation of Socrates.

Two philosophical beginnings are juxtaposed in Plato's narrative of Socrates' trial and death, and both seem to be inspired by the god.[34] It is interesting to note that the external setting of the *Phaedo*, the locality where Phaedo meets Echecrates and tells him the story of Socrates' last day, is Phlius, a relatively insignificant town in the Peloponnese. Is there any particular reason for this? Blessed with the "immemorial shadow" and "poetic seclusion" of the surrounding hills,[35] Phlius had become a martyr city by the time Plato wrote the *Phaedo*, famous for the virtue of its temperate, courageous citizens, who had paid for their faithful commitment to the declining Peloponnesian League with their lives.[36] This already resonates with the fate of "Apollo's soldier," but there is even more to Plato's choice of site. At the time of the *Phaedo*'s dramatic setting (as opposed to its date of composition), Phlius had become a kind of "philosophical refuge," harboring "the last of the Pythagoreans," as Aristoxenus is reported to have claimed.[37] Echecrates, the speaker in the *Phaedo* who is particularly

---

[33] This is probably part of a broader strategy. In many ways, Plato has crafted both the *Apology* and the *Phaedo* in such a way that on close inspection they prove to be perfectly complementary, despite some alleged discrepancies. See the excellent discussion of Jedrkiewcsz 2011.

[34] Quarch 1994 has dealt with this juxtaposition sensitively, and interprets it as a mythological turn in Socrates' philosophical career: "An die Stelle der rationalen Rechenschaftsgabe, des *logon didonai*, ist die mythische Rede getreten, das *mythologein*. Beide sind von Apollon verordnet: erstere für den freien Sokrates in der Polis, letztere für den gefesselten im Kerker" (114).

[35] I owe these phrases to Geddes 1863:175. Geddes also quotes Pindar's reference to Phlius' hills and shade (*Nemean Odes* 6.45–46).

[36] On Xenophon's lengthy excursus on Phlius, see Daverio Rocchi 2004, who refers to Phlius as "la città martire, che ha offerto un tributo pesantissimo ... alla coerenza delle sue idee" (51).

[37] F 12 τελευταῖοι τῶν Πυθαγορείων. In the words of Nails: "In Aristoxenus' list of the last of the Pythagoreans, nine or ten generations after Pythagoras, Xenophilus of Chalcidice, Phanton, Echecrates, Diocles, and Polymnastus are from Phlius. The Phlius area consisted of a valley with a settlement of the same name on its eastern side; it was something of a Pythagorean refuge, lying on the way from Athens to Elis" (Nails 2002:138). Cf. also Horky 2013:107–108. The identity

interested in the details of Socrates' death, is one of these, and we are invited to imagine his thoughts as he listens to the report of Socrates' last words, which include a challenging discussion of several Pythagorean doctrines.[38]

Besides being what was soon perceived to be the site of the virtual extinction of authentic Pythagoreanism,[39] Phlius was also famous for the "beginnings" of philosophy as such, for it was here, according to the famous account of Plato's pupil Hereclides Ponticus, that Pythagoras, himself of Phliasian origin, invented the word *philosophos*—to the astonishment of the local ruler.[40] Pythagoras, whom Socrates credits with the invention of philosophy as a way of life in the *Republic*, had probably been the first to suggest the identification of philosophy with *mousikê*.[41] Like Socrates, he had never written anything either.[42] Socrates' poetic

---

of Echecrates, and his Pythagorean affiliation, is a thorny question. For a skeptical view, besides the issues and scholarly objections discussed critically in Horky 2013, cf. Prontera, who argues for the existence of "due Echecrati ... un fliasio legato alla cerchia socratica, lontano dal maestro il giorno della sua morte, cui Platone immaginò che Fedone raccontasse le ultime ore di Socrate, ed un pitagorico locrese" (Prontera 1974:19).

[38] As Sedley 1995 puts it, the *Phaedo*, while suggesting Plato's debt to Pythagoreanism, exposes "the shortcomings of Simmias' and Cebes' Pythagorean training" (11). Needless to say, the choice of the characters is no less important. Phaedo's biography and philosophy resonate in important way with Socrates' and Plato's, as Boys-Stones 2004 and Kamen 2013 have shown.

[39] This is another thorny problem. For a clear introduction, see Huffman 2010:3.4.

[40] Heraclides Ponticus 87–88 Wehrli, discussed in the Introduction to the current volume. From a different, but fully compatible, perspective, Notomi highlights the Phliasian setting as well: "The audience who listen to Phaedo's report include some famous Pythagoreans, above all Echecrates. But again, why did those Pythagoreans reside in this country place? It is probably because Phlius is (according to legend) the birth place of the 'philosopher Pythagoras.' Pausanias tells us that an ancestor of Pythagoras was a citizen of Phlius who flew the native land to Samos for political reasons. I associate this report with another famous anecdote: when Pythagoras moved to South Italy to found his own community (against the tyranny of Polycrates), he stopped in Phlius (or Sikyon, the neighbor city) and had a conversation with a local lord; it is in that conversation that the word 'philosopher' (*philosophos*) was used for the first time in the history. The small city Phlius is remembered as the home land of Pythagoras' family and as the birthplace of the notion of 'philosopher.' Phaedo, by telling the people in Phlius the memory of Socrates on his last day, sets out his new life as a philosopher, probably back in his native city, where he is reported to have founded his school of philosophy. The author Plato (who Phaedo says was absent) confronts Socrates with the Pythagorean ideal of the philosopher and depicts his master as the model philosopher, who died without fear. Narrating about the life of Socrates is not just a pleasure, but a great stimulus and encouragement for people—first speakers and listeners, then readers of the dialogue—to start philosophy" (Notomi 2008:357). Cf. also Peterson 2011:166–167. Geddes 1863, however, had already made the connection between Pythagoras' invention and the setting of the *Phaedo*.

[41] As explicitly stated by Strabo 10.468. According to Caruso 2013, the Academy's *Mouseion* "si pone in linea con la tradizione dei *mouseia* pitagorici di cui lo stesso Platone aveva fatto esperienza a Taranto" (193, with further bibliography).

[42] Socrates' reference to Pythagoras and Pythagorean life is found in the *Republic* (600b). It is the only mention of Pythagoras in the dialogues.

turn, introduced with what one critic has described as "a sacramental tone,"[43] has all the solemnity of a new beginning aimed at changing philosophy forever;[44] and it may even shed new light on Socrates' involvement with Pythagoras in the *Phaedo*.[45] It is all the more interesting, therefore, that the heroic cult of Socrates in the Academy involved the commemoration of Socrates' death as his birthday, as if to suggest that everything did eventually come full circle.[46]

As we saw earlier, Socrates experiences a second conversion, one that issues in his prayer to Pan and distances him from his previous self, as well as from Pythagoras' invention of philosophy. But what kind of a new beginning can one hope to actuate on the eve of one's death? A possible clue lies in Socrates' emphasis on myth, which he describes as the *conditio sine qua non* of poetry. This reminds one of Aristotle. In the *Poetics*, *muthos* is by far the most important part of tragedy, that which in some way subsumes all the others: without myth, tragedy cannot even be conceived of. The very beginning of the work has a strange, though hitherto unnoticed, Platonic air about it.[47] Aristotle is intent on exploring the power and inner workings of *muthoi*, which are so integral to poetry (1447a 9–10 πῶς δεῖ συνίστασθαι τοὺς μύθους εἰ μέλλει καλῶς ἕξειν ἡ ποίησις). This closely parallels the beginning of the *Phaedo*, when Socrates claims that *muthos* is fundamental for the very definition of poetry (61b ... τὸν ποιητὴν δέοι, εἴπερ μέλλοι ποιητὴς εἶναι, ποιεῖν μύθους and cf. 60c μῦθον ἂν συνθεῖναι).

Admittedly, Aristotle ends by giving *muthos* an entirely new meaning in the *Poetics*, similar to plot or structure. Nevertheless, his terminology and certain turns of phrase clearly call to mind the *Phaedo*. I take this as evidence that Aristotle sensed the poetological import of the passage in question, or that he may have had firsthand knowledge of its intended meaning. Whatever the case, he seems to have construed it as Plato's own "poetics." The fact that Aristotle's *Poetics* takes into consideration *Sokratikoi logoi*, including the dialogues, is equally

---

[43] Bacon 1990:151.

[44] For a classic discussion of the sources related to Pythagoras' "silence," see Burkert 1972, who deals convincingly with the few texts that appear to attribute writings to Pythagoras (218–220).

[45] Scholars have always debated the extent to which the *Phaedo* can be described as "Pythagorean" (cf. for example the well-known views of Burnet 1911, later criticized by Hackforth 1955). Yet even a radical scholar such as Theodor Ebert, who argues for the paradoxical thesis that the *Phaedo* is meant to discredit Pythagoreanism and to expose the fallacies of Pythagorean arguments, registers a "Stilisierung des Sokrates auf einen Pythagoreischen φιλόσοφος" (Ebert 1994:17)

[46] All the relevant evidence is admirably collected and discussed in White 2000.

[47] Gilead 1994 has an entire chapter on "The *Phaedo* in the Light of Aristotle's *Poetics*" (109–127), though this point is never actually addressed. Interestingly, however, Gilead concludes that Aristotle's conditions for good poetry are fully met by the *Phaedo*, and he also observes that Socrates' interpretation of the dream "well serves the purposes of Plato also. It entitles him to describe the last day of his master in such a poetic and dramatic manner, just as Socrates himself composes poems at the terminal stage of his mundane life" (Gilead 1994:57).

interesting. Plato's dialogues, in turn, contain many myths. It follows that the dialogues were thought of in both Plato's and Aristotle's "poetics" as a form of poetry by definition.

In the very moment in which he claims he is incapable of composing myths, Socrates is in fact fashioning one, as is evident from the Aesopic image he creates to express the intimate bond between pain and pleasure. This seems to argue for Socrates' new status as an accomplished poet, and is at variance with the manner he usually adopts in other dialogues. Most of the time, when it comes to recounting myths, Plato's Socrates disclaims authorship: the myths he recounts are not of his own making, so he says, but reflect time-honored traditions.[48] In the *Phaedo*, however, Socrates refers to his own discourse as myth (*muthos*) and charm (*epaidô* and cognates), while the very subject of the dialogue, namely the immortality of the soul, is introduced through the two verbs "to enquire" (διασκοπεῖν) and "to tell myths" (μυθολογεῖν).[49] Thus, the *Phaedo* is conceptualized not only as an intellectual enterprise, but as a "mythological" one too. Yet the *Phaedo* is, almost literally, Socrates' swan song, as he implies when he explicitly identifies himself with Apollo's birds. What would happen after his death? This is how the question was put to him by his anxious friends:

Καὶ ὁ Κέβης ἐπιγελάσας, Ὡς δεδιότων, ἔφη, ὦ Σώκρατες, πειρῶ ἀναπείθειν· μᾶλλον δὲ μὴ ὡς ἡμῶν δεδιότων, ἀλλ' ἴσως ἔνι τις καὶ ἐν ἡμῖν παῖς ὅστις τὰ τοιαῦτα φοβεῖται. τοῦτον οὖν πειρῶ μεταπείθειν μὴ δεδιέναι τὸν θάνατον ὥσπερ τὰ μορμολύκεια. Ἀλλὰ χρή, ἔφη ὁ Σωκράτης, <u>ἐπᾴδειν αὐτῷ ἑκάστης ἡμέρας ἕως ἂν ἐξεπᾴσητε</u>. Πόθεν οὖν, ἔφη, ὦ Σώκρατες, τῶν τοιούτων <u>ἀγαθὸν ἐπῳδὸν</u> ληψόμεθα, ἐπειδὴ σύ, ἔφη, ἡμᾶς ἀπολείπεις;

Cebes answered with a laugh: "Then, Socrates, you must argue us out of our fears—and yet, strictly speaking, they are not our fears, but there is a child within us to whom death is a sort of hobgoblin; him too we must persuade not to be afraid when he is alone with him in the dark." Socrates said: "*Let the voice of the charmer be applied daily until you have charmed him away.*" "And where shall we find a *good* charmer of our fears, Socrates, when you are gone?"

Plato *Phaedo* 77e–78a, trans. Jowett (modified)

---

[48] See the convincing discussion by Latona 2004. Among other things, he argues that: "Plato does not see his own use of myth as inconsistent with his critique of poetic myth largely because he views knowing as an act of memory as opposed to a creative act" (184).

[49] 61c, and cf. 70b.

After Socrates' death, a "good charmer" will have to be found somewhere. We have seen in the Introduction that "charming" (ἐπᾴδω) is a key element in Plato's meta-poetic strategy, pointing to the "serious" side of his writing. Here, we encounter the exceptional verbal form ἐξεπᾴσητε (from ἐξεπᾴδω, "charm away"), which probably puns on the word *pais*, triggering the secondary meaning of "get rid of one's childish fear." Be that as it may, Socrates' reply is somewhat mysterious:

Πολλὴ μὲν ἡ Ἑλλάς, ἔφη, ὦ Κέβης, ἐν ᾗ ἔνεισί που ἀγαθοὶ ἄνδρες, πολλὰ δὲ καὶ τὰ τῶν βαρβάρων γένη, οὓς πάντας χρὴ διερευνᾶσθαι ζητοῦντας τοιοῦτον ἐπῳδόν, μήτε χρημάτων φειδομένους μήτε πόνων, ὡς οὐκ ἔστιν εἰς ὅτι ἂν εὐκαιρότερον ἀναλίσκοιτε χρήματα. ζητεῖν δὲ χρὴ καὶ αὐτοὺς μετ' ἀλλήλων· ἴσως γὰρ ἂν οὐδὲ ῥᾳδίως εὕροιτε μᾶλλον ὑμῶν δυναμένους τοῦτο ποιεῖν.

Hellas, he replied, is a large place, Cebes, and has many good men, and there are barbarous races not a few: seek for him among them all, far and wide, sparing neither pains nor money; for there is no better way of using your money. And you must not forget to seek for him among yourselves too; for nowhere are you more likely to find someone to do it.

Plato *Phaedo* 78a, trans. Jowett

Socrates' answer is carefully crafted along the lines of a rhetorical *Priamel*, which, decoded, reads something like: You can search Greece, you can search far-away countries, you can spend a lot of money on your quest. Nevertheless, the best thing you can do is to look for the good charmer among yourselves, for only there are you likely to find somebody "to do it," that is, to do the charming; "among yourselves," says Socrates, pointing to his acolytes. Socrates' main interlocutors in the *Phaedo*, starting with Phaedo himself and the "Theban couple" Simmias and Cebes, were writers in the genre of *Sokratikoi logoi*.[50] In Platonic terms, composing a dialogue might well be described as "to do the charming" (*poiein epôidas*), a phrase that combines Plato's poetological *epôidê* with the verb *poiein* ("to do," but also "to compose" or "be a poet"). However, Cebes and Simmias feel lost and have no clue as to where they might find the good charmer: Where is he? And, we might add, *who* is he?

Only in his last days did Socrates become a "real" poet by trying his hand at a hymn to Apollo and at some of Aesop's fables. His poetic initiation was completed at last, but there was no time left for him to practice the art. As we learn at the beginning of the *Phaedo*, "Plato was ill" (59c) and so could not visit

---

[50] Diogenes Laertius 2.105, 2.121–124.

## Conclusion

his dying master.[51] This is the one and only time that the name Plato appears in the dialogues,[52] and I believe the reason for this is that he is in fact the "good charmer," who, though not physically present at Socrates' deathbed, was most certainly among his friends.[53] As in the *Phaedrus*, then, Socrates' late metamorphosis into a fully fledged poet merely *prefigures* the reality of Plato.[54]

At the moment of his death, Socrates passed his poetic status on to Plato, who, in his *Seventh Letter*, famously declares that he has never written his philosophy down on paper. Just as Plato and Socrates were portrayed together in a double herm from the Hellenistic Age,[55] so the two complementary half-figures formed a single poetic entity, which may be seen as a circumspect attempt to effect a partial transition from oral to written philosophical dialogue.[56] The end product of this strategic turn was, of course, destined to become the most read and most studied corpus in the history of philosophy and literature: in terms of authorship, there could hardly have been a more radical, or, indeed, more astonishing result.

---

[51] Plato's reference to his own absence has given rise to much discussion. An extreme example of fanciful interpretation is Tomin 2001, who suggests that Plato was part of a plot to spring Socrates from prison: Plato's alleged role was to "secure his safe passage out of Athens," and a "supposed illness was to be his alibi in case a witch-hunt was unleashed after Socrates' escape from prison" (Tomin 2001:145). More plausibly, Most 1993 reads the passage in the light of Socrates' last words, "we owe a cock to Asclepius" (116a), which he interprets as a prophecy that the god intended to cure Plato's no doubt serious illness.

[52] Discounting the *Apology*, where Socrates mentions the name at 34a–b.

[53] In the published version of a "Corso di storia della filosofia antica" held at the University of Milan, F. Decleva Caizzi rightly observes that: "per quanto riguarda i Greci, l'invito ai discepoli a cercare al loro interno può essere inteso come un cenno allo stesso Platone o, più in generale, alla 'scuola' che raccoglierà l'eredità del maestro; un esplicito riferimento ai discepoli, che saranno 'ancor più rigorosi' di lui verso gli errori del popolo ateniese, si legge in *Apol.* 39c–d" (Decleva Caizzi 1986–1987:64). One should bear in mind the fact that Plato was a relatively minor figure in the eyes of Socrates and his followers (cf. Xenophon *Memorabilia* 2.6.1, with Clay 1994:27, who notes that Plato was "a minor Socratic" at the moment of Socrates' death). Consequently, Socrates' words would have had a different meaning for Socrates' interlocutors and for Plato's audiences, a common literary device in both tragedy and Platonic dialogue.

[54] This includes his new interpretation of Pythagoreanism. It must be remembered that the cult of the Muses as practiced by Pythagoras and his acolytes was the obvious model for Plato's own, so that when Plato, unlike Pythagoras, accepted the idea of writing, he was making a momentous and potentially dangerous move that would have exposed him to allegations of betrayal. As Horky 2013 judiciously concludes his discussion of "exoteric" Pythagoreans, "the early heresiological traditions that derive from Timaeus of Tauromenium and Neanthes describe Pythagorean exoterics as those who made available the unwritten teachings of Pythagoras to the wider public and, in certain cases, incurred punishment for having done so: Perillus of Thurii, Cylon and Ninon of Croton, Empedocles of Agrigentum, Diodorus of Aspendus, Epicharmus of Syracuse, Cleinias and Philolaus of Heraclea, Theorides and Eurytus of Metapontum, Archytas of Tarentum, and possibly Plato of Athens" (Horky 2013:119).

[55] Cf. Lippold 1956:3.2, reported in Clay 2000:ii, iv.

[56] Sedley 1989 addresses Socrates' and Plato's authorial cohabitation in the *Phaedo*.

# The Status of Plato's Dialogues

Plato "musicalizes" the discourse of philosophy in carrying out an apologetic maneuver: Plato defends Socrates (and to some extent himself) from the widespread accusation of being an enemy of musical *paideia*. At the same time, he attacks all forms of discourse—be they sophistic, rhetorical, historiographical, or other—that present themselves as purely human and dispense with the divine. When it comes to the really important divide between the musical and non-musical arts, Plato adopts a provocatively old-fashioned attitude and crucially opts for the former. Musical philosophy, moreover, implies philosophical composition, as against Socrates' and Pythagoras' rejection of writing. Thus, Socrates, the poet who never wrote, and Plato, the writer who never acknowledged his own authorship, form an unprecedented complementary pair in embodying a new form of *mousikê*.

So far so good. But what are the implications of hypothesizing a new attitude on the part of Plato towards the divide that separated the musical arts, such as poetry, from the non-musical arts, such as the various forms of scientific prose, for example? One possible objection—one that philosophers have often raised with respect to my present thesis—may be summed up as follows: are we to believe that Plato's dialogues are poems rather than philosophical arguments? My answer is that such an opposition is misplaced and stems from modern habits of thought (one might even say from hardened prejudices).[57] It is not my intention to diminish the importance of argument in Plato's dialogues in any way, and there are very good reasons for not doing so, as I shall now try to make clear.

When he compares philosophical discourse with poetry, Plato clearly emphasizes the irrational nature of the latter, as well as its inability to put forward credible arguments. When he compares philosophical discourse with non-musical prose writing, however, Plato does the opposite: indeed, he frequently underlines the musical (mythical, poetic ...) nature of his own philosophical writing. Thus, his attitude would appear to be ambivalent, though even this may be the result of modern misunderstanding. In the Introduction, I repeatedly stressed the extent to which the Greeks, including those like Aristotle, tended to unite, rather than separate, poetry and knowledge. More pertinent still is the fact that Plato's Socrates assumes that to *argue for a given thesis* is a normal function of poetry: the poets are said to claim, maintain, and

---

[57]  Gerson's thesis that "representation is not argumentation" (Gerson 2000:205), in other words, that the analogy between (the playwrights') *mimêsis* and (Plato's) arguments "is misleading," epitomizes the kind of objection I have in mind.

argue for something.[58] This is hardly surprising, since Plato's contemporaries had no difficulty in crediting poetry with "philosophical" procedures such as demonstration (*apodeixis*).[59] Nevertheless, even as he implicitly conceptualizes the dialogues as poetry, Plato is taking a crucial step towards what *we* would call philosophy. And in the very moment in which he highlights essential differences between the two activities, he is careful to emphasize how these differences, bound as they are to poetic tradition, are also essential to the unprecedented philosophical nature of the dialogues. For the sake of clarity, and at the risk of both repetition and significant omission, I shall summarize these differences very briefly.

Firstly, Socrates adopts the persona of Stesichorus, but points out that *mousikê*, unlike Homeric poetry, entails the "knowing of the cause" (Chapter 1). Secondly, the *Phaedrus* appropriates the extraordinary role played by memory and recollection in Sappho. However, these faculties, while preserving the emotional power they had in lyric poetry, are now redirected towards the universal (the Form of the beautiful), as opposed to Sappho's particular memories (beautiful forms, as discussed in Chapter 2). Thirdly, Plato aligns Socrates with the traditional pattern of poetic initiation, but he makes it quite clear that *philosophical* initiation amounts to vigilant and dialectic "dialogue and song," as opposed to the hypnotic nature of traditional poetry (Chapter 3). Fourthly, Plato appropriates the tradition of the heroic cult of poets, but his heroization of Socrates is construed as a potentially universal phenomenon, as opposed to the parochial nature of the cults of "normal" poets (Chapter 4).

Plato's remodeling of tradition is apparent even at the level of vocabulary.[60] In the *Phaedrus*, Socrates adopts the persona of an inspired poet who proves superior to both poets (Homer, Thamyris, Stesichorus, Sappho, etc.) and prose writers (Lysias and, implicitly, Isocrates). It is interesting to note, however,

---

[58] Nowhere is this made clearer than in the *Protagoras*. The sophist begins his discussion of Simonides by claiming that a very important part of *paideia* is to be "clever" (*deinos*) in evaluating poetry: one must be able to tell the difference between good and bad in a poem, that is (and the point is a crucial one), to determine whether a poem contains good *arguments*. Socrates readily goes along with this and never challenges such a view. This is plainly clear in what follows: for both Socrates and Protagoras, the poet "argues" (*legei*) "as if he were telling a *logos*" (ὡς ἂν εἰ λέγοι λόγον, 344b). Consequently, he can be proven wrong if he contradicts himself.

[59] As in the passage from Lycurgus discussed in the Introduction. By contrast, Plato's *Timaeus* claims that the traditional poets do *not* have the capacity for "demonstration" (ἀποδείξεις, 40e), which is likely to point to Timaeus' own speech as a more accomplished account (cf. Regali 2012:173–174). Moreover, "demonstration" (ἀπόδειξις) is a key feature of the palinode (245c–246a, on the immortality of the soul), which, as we know from the previous chapters, is delivered by an "inspired" and "poetic" Socrates.

[60] Remodeling, or, to quote the definition made famous by August Diès (1927:400–449): "Transposition platonicienne."

that he reserves the phrase "mere poets" for poets and prose writers, whereas the true composer, who has more to say than he writes, is called *philosophos*, "philosopher."[61] In other words, there is absolutely nothing "anti-philosophical" in Plato's eagerness to remodel philosophy on music. Nevertheless, a serious, and possibly insoluble, dilemma remains. Are the dialogues, written as they are by the true poet, i.e. the philosopher, meant to educate the Kallipolis? Is this the new poetry for Plato's ideal city, or are the dialogues a mere approximation in the guise of a mold, blueprint, or paradigm of some kind? It is certainly not my intention to embark on a lengthy discussion of such an arduous problem at this point in the present study. I shall, however, sketch the outlines of a possible solution.

We have seen in the *Phaedo* how Socrates fashions a new myth in the very moment he confesses his incapacity to do so. Plato's proposals for a reformed kind of poetry in the ideal society of the *Republic* and of the *Laws* present another difficulty. On the one hand, the dialogues seem to meet many of the conditions laid down by these two works as indispensable for the creation of acceptable poetry, something I have already dealt with at length in the previous chapters. On the other hand, an essential requirement of Plato's reformed poetry, which he insists upon almost obsessively, is that it be pure and unmixed: there must be no mixing of genres or musical modes, nor indeed will any form of innovation be tolerated. And yet one of the few certainties we have regarding the dialogues is that they are an unprecedented and hugely experimental mixture of well-established genres, rivaled only by Isocrates' works.[62] Would Plato's dialogues be suitable for Plato's ideal city? And if that were not enough, the epic war between Atlantis and Athens in the *Critias*, which seems to meet all of Plato's conditions for good *mimêsis*,[63] breaks off suddenly and, it would seem, self-consciously, right at the beginning of the real "poem."[64]

Plato's ambivalence is even more apparent in two passages of the *Republic* and the *Laws*, both of which deal with the role of poets in the ideal city. In the first, Socrates draws an important distinction between poets and city founders:

Ὦ Ἀδείμαντε, οὐκ ἐσμὲν ποιηταὶ ἐγώ τε καὶ σὺ ἐν τῷ παρόντι, ἀλλ' οἰκισταὶ πόλεως· οἰκισταῖς δὲ τοὺς μὲν τύπους προσήκει εἰδέναι ἐν οἷς δεῖ μυθολογεῖν τοὺς ποιητάς, παρ' οὓς ἐὰν ποιῶσιν οὐκ ἐπιτρεπτέον, οὐ μὴν αὐτοῖς γε ποιητέον μύθους.

---

61 278b–e. Cf. Chapter 4 in the current volume.
62 The important book of Roberto Nicolai (2004) explores Isocrates' experimentalism in depth.
63 As Regali 2012 has most persuasively shown. Cf. Chapter 3 in the current volume.
64 See Capra 2010, with added bibliography.

Adeimantus, *we are not poets*, you and I at present, but founders of a state. And to founders it pertains to know the patterns on which poets must compose their fables and from which their poems must not be allowed to deviate; but the founders are not required themselves to compose fables.

Plato *Republic* 378e–379a, trans. Shorey

The second passage, from the *Laws*, follows the Athenian's claim that the legislator is the author of the most beautiful tragedy that can possibly be imagined. This was discussed in the Introduction when we broached the subject of Platonic "self-disclosure," since it would seem to be a reference to Plato's own production. Here are the Athenian's words:

ποιηταὶ μὲν οὖν ὑμεῖς, <u>ποιηταὶ</u> δὲ καὶ ἡμεῖς <u>ἐσμὲν</u> τῶν αὐτῶν, ὑμῖν ἀντίτεχνοί τε καὶ ἀνταγωνισταὶ τοῦ καλλίστου δράματος, ὃ δὴ νόμος ἀληθὴς μόνος ἀποτελεῖν πέφυκεν, ὡς ἡ παρ' ἡμῶν ἐστιν ἐλπίς.

*We are poets* of the same things as yourselves, we rival you as artists and actors of the most beautiful drama, which by nature is the nobly effective one, according to our hope.

Plato *Laws* 816b–c

Apparently, the two speakers express points of view that are comparable, and yet wholly incompatible. In expressing their views, Socrates and the Athenian are speaking as prospective legislators, and both have been looked upon as spokesmen for Plato himself in these instances. And yet one affirms the exact opposite of the other: we are *not* poets, says Socrates; we *are* poets, says the Athenian. How can such a blatant contradiction be resolved?

The question allows for different answers. Were one a developmentalist, one would claim that Plato, by the time he composed the *Laws*, had come to conceptualize his work as a form of poetry in spite of, or as a reaction to, the earlier views of the *Republic*. The reader will be well aware by now that this is a hypothesis the present author is never likely to subscribe to. Nevertheless, given certain premises, it may not seem entirely unreasonable, and many readers would probably be prepared to accept it. On the other hand, it should be quite clear that we are dealing here with two different speakers: Socrates never put pen to paper, so Plato could not possibly have had him making claims to being a poet; conversely, many see the Athenian as Plato himself, who, unlike Socrates, considered writing to be part of his philosophical activity. This interpretation may or may not seem reasonable; yet I am inclined to think that Plato is being self-consciously ambiguous on this point. Are we poets, he is asking? It all depends, is the answer.

Bidding my own farewell to any pretense of scholarly exhaustiveness, I shall conclude with one final, tentative comparison, which doubtless many will find surprising. As Stanley Mitchell once observed, Walter Benjamin saw "Brecht's epic theatre as a form not merely of 'Socratic', but of truly Platonic drama."[65] More recently, Slavoy Žižek has claimed that Brecht's anti-Aristotelian theater is in fact a fully "Platonist theatre."[66] At first, I was inclined to regard such statements as mere *boutades*, but, on closer inspection, I came to the conclusion that Benjamin and Žižek were fundamentally right and I undertook a detailed study of the analogies between Brecht and Plato.[67] What I found was wholly unexpected, for though there is no evidence whatsoever that Brecht had firsthand knowledge of the dialogues, his critique of the theater of his day, and his proposals for its reform, are very close to Plato's own, down to the minutest detail. For once one has to agree with Voltaire that "les beaux esprits se rencontrent."[68] Or perhaps Brecht's anti-Aristotelian theater, insofar as it was a reaction to Aristotle's ultimately anti-Platonic stance, turned the clock back to Plato's day.[69]

As Hellmut Flashar notes, Plato and Brecht share the same "structure of critical thought."[70] Indeed, the analogies are so strong that Brecht's writings on the theater—more numerous and detailed than Plato's, of course—could even serve to illuminate the elusive fabric of the dialogues. It could be argued, for example, that Plato resorts to narrated dialogue (as opposed to the purely dramatic form of most of his works) when he needs to "filter" morally dangerous content.[71]

---

[65] In the introduction of Benjamin 1998:xv. As Gruber points out: "Walter Benjamin ... alludes to Brecht's 'Platonic' drama in a lecture delivered at the Institute for the Study of Fascism, Paris 27 April 1934. Benjamin's address appears in his posthumous work *Versüche über Brecht* (Frankfurt: Suhrkamp, 1966)" (Gruber 1987:323n3).

[66] Žižek 2002 (from the "Afterword"): "This is what Brecht's 'non-Aristotelian' theatre ultimately amounts to: a *Platonist* theatre, in which the aesthetic charm is strictly controlled, in order to transmit the philosophico-political Truth which is *external* to it" (Žižek 2002:193).

[67] Capra 2010b, with added bibliography.

[68] Voltaire used the expression in the *Dictionnaire philosophique*, s.v. "Bacchus."

[69] Cf. Gruber 1987. Needless to say, Brecht's reading of the *Poetics* "is another reinterpretation of 'Aristotle', another creative reconstruction of 'Aristotle', another new and sublimely un-Aristotelian coherence" (Silk 2001:190).

[70] "... die Struktur des kritischen Gedankens bei Platon und Brecht ... die gleiche ist" (Flashar 1974:20).

[71] The *Republic* warns prospective city rulers against certain poetic subjects, unless the poet in question has resorted to the distancing filter of humor and narration (396c–e). In accordance with this view, many prohibited themes censored in the third book of the *Republic* are dealt with only in Plato's "narrative," as opposed to "dramatic" dialogues. Immoderate laughter, grief, and other instances of insufficient self-control, must be mitigated through narration, and,

## Conclusion

This insight derives from a reading of Brecht's anti-epic (i.e. narrative) theater and dramatic theory, and the Brechtian hypothesis, when tested on the Platonic corpus as a whole, proves to be correct: the "forbidden" contents censored in the *Republic* are found almost exclusively in the narrated dialogues.

Though he did not like to talk about the matter very much, Brecht had a clear idea of the difference between *his* theater, which he theorized as a "negative" form of resistance literature designed to question the status quo, and the "positive" education that the theater *ought to be* able to promote in a reformed society. In a secret fragment, he called the former "Minor Pedagogy" (*kleine Pädagogik*)—as opposed to the prospective "Major Pedagogy" (*große Pädagogik*) that ought to be implemented systematically in reformed societies.[72]

The distinction Brecht makes between these two forms of theatrical pedagogy is fluid and results in a certain overlapping. Yet its most valuable implication is that all distinction between performers and audience is destined to disappear in the "Major Pedagogy." This reminds one of Magnesia, Plato's (semi-)ideal city in the *Laws*. It has been suggested that the name Magnesia was a literal derivation from the Magnetic power of inspiration conferred by the Muses of philosophy, who were destined to replace the traditional Muses.[73] This power would then appropriate, and ultimately replace, the deficient magnetism of traditional poetry as described in the *Ion*, in which Plato again elaborates a distinction between true music and mere poetry. Magnesia was to feature revised festivals, twelve in all, corresponding to the twelve Olympian gods. In these new festivals, the distinction between existing poetic genres would be allowed to collapse, as if what Plato had in mind was a merging of all the major festivals of Athens—the "epic" Panathenaia and the "theatrical" and "lyric" Dionysia—into one. The purpose of this was to resurrect a very primal, undifferentiated *mousikê*, where the distinction between audience and performer would cease to exist.[74]

Besides fascinating suggestions of this kind, Plato tells us that "magnetism" (as we discussed it in Chapter 3) is no longer to be the exclusive prerogative of epic rhapsodes, but the distinguishing feature, albeit in a strikingly revised form, of Socratic *logoi* too, and, by extension, of his own dialogues. Revised "magnetism" is also present in the *Phaedrus*, where it occurs more than once. It characterizes the magic chain that binds together dialoguing men, dialoguing

---

occasionally, humor. See Capra 2003 for a full discussion. Some related points can be found in Tsouna 2013.

[72] The distinction is made in a fragment found in the Brecht archives. See Steinweg 1976:51.

[73] See the "Excursus on Plato's *Laws*" in Nagy 2009a:386–392 (§77–94).

[74] In fact, the description of Magnesia culminates in the extraordinary image of the whole citizenry depicted as a compact people busily engaged in *enchanting* itself (665c). For a convincing analysis, see Panno 2007.

cicadas, and the dialogical Muses; it also informs the relationship between the beloved, the lover, and one of the twelve gods (depending on the character of the couple).[75] Thus, Socrates' palinode envisages twelve-minus-one potential choruses and magic chains, which seem to foreshadow the twelve festivals of the *Laws*.[76]

These two examples of transposed magnetism, whereby the dialogues prefigure the dream of philosophy in a minor key, point to a fluid and dynamic relationship between Plato's actual production and the potential poetry of the philosophical *polis*. My final suggestion, therefore, comes in the form of a modest proposal aimed at stimulating discussion and shedding some light on Plato's baffling ambivalence: perhaps the dialogues are Plato's "minor pedagogy" as opposed to the "major pedagogy" that was to be foisted on reformed societies—even if, like Brecht, he preferred, understandably, not to talk too much about it. Philosophy shapes both, but identifies with neither. Writing is, and always will be, the ephemeral fruit of "Adonis' gardens." However, the "real crop" is what Aristotle, with a novel word possibly inspired by sweet memories from his "Platonic" youth, calls *sumphilosophein*: the everyday life and discussion shared among friends.[77]

---

[75]   Cf. Chapter 3 in the current volume.

[76]   On the curious twelve-minus-one number and on the relevant choruses, cf. *Phaedrus* 246e–247a and 252c–253c.

[77]   Cf. Aristotle *Nicomachean Ethics* 1272a1–7, with Berti 2012:vii–xii. (*Sumphilosophein* is the very title of Berti's beautiful book, which explores the liberal style of life and inquiry of Plato's Academy.) Plato's dialogues offer no definition of truth, but provide poetic glimpses of this ideal (cf. Casertano 2007). Besides portraying *sumphilosophein*, however, Plato's works—think of the elenctic dialogues—also depict the "Kampf in allen Spielformen, von der Feindschaft bis zum liebenden Ringen, die erste Stufe des Weges also, noch ganz in der Welt der Doxa, dort wo Sokrates allemal erst anfängt" (Gundert 1968:44).

# Appendix

## Plato's Self-Disclosures
### A Discussion of Gaiser's Interpretation

THE PRESENT APPENDIX is designed to integrate my discussion of Plato's self-referential statements and their references to Gaiser's work, which my general Introduction builds upon. It is also intended as a tribute to what I regard as a milestone in Platonic studies.

## Four Self-Disclosures

The sequence in which Gaiser (1984) examines Plato's self-disclosures, i.e. those passages in which Plato seems to allude to his own works, follows the lectures that provided the primary subject matter of the current book. However, I find it more useful to appraise these self-disclosures in accordance with their importance. I shall start, therefore, with the most obvious case, before dealing with the less straightforward ones.[1]

### Laws 811b–e and 817b[2]

The clearest instance of self-disclosure is found in the seventh book of the Laws, as Paul Friedländer noticed long ago.[3] At 811a–c we hear that good education needs good writings, but where can one find a good paradigm for the latter? The Athenian has no hesitation: the conversation he has been having with his two interlocutors resembles poetry and bears the signs of *divine inspiration* (οὐκ ἄνευ τινὸς ἐπιπνοίας θεῶν), thus making an appropriate paradigm. Such speeches should be written down, and any such conversation, either in prose or in verse, can be used as a proper and effective means for the education of young people. Later on, the Athenian engages in an imaginary conversation with prospective

---

[1]   I will omit Gaiser's discussion of *Ion* 541e–542a (Gaiser 1984:111–115), since he himself is very cautious on the subject and admits that his argument involves much speculation.

[2]   Gaiser 1984:107–111.

[3]   See Friedländer 1930:623, and cf. Cameron 1978.

playwrights about the ideal city, and famously adopts the persona of a tragic poet, in a passage we have already examined:

τῶν δὲ σπουδαίων, ὥς φασι, τῶν περὶ τραγῳδίαν ἡμῖν ποιητῶν, ἐάν ποτέ τινες αὐτῶν ἡμᾶς ἐλθόντες ἐπανερωτήσωσιν οὑτωσί πως· "Ὦ ξένοι, πότερον φοιτῶμεν ὑμῖν εἰς τὴν πόλιν τε καὶ χώραν ἢ μή, καὶ τὴν ποίησιν φέρωμέν τε καὶ ἄγωμεν, ἢ πῶς ὑμῖν δέδοκται περὶ τὰ τοιαῦτα δρᾶν;"—τί οὖν ἂν πρὸς ταῦτα ὀρθῶς ἀποκριναίμεθα τοῖς θείοις ἀνδράσιν; ἐμοὶ μὲν γὰρ δοκεῖ τάδε· "Ὦ ἄριστοι," φάναι, "τῶν ξένων, ἡμεῖς ἐσμὲν τραγῳδίας αὐτοὶ ποιηταὶ κατὰ δύναμιν ὅτι καλλίστης ἅμα καὶ ἀρίστης· πᾶσα οὖν ἡμῖν ἡ πολιτεία συνέστηκε μίμησις τοῦ καλλίστου καὶ ἀρίστου βίου, ὃ δή φαμεν ἡμεῖς γε ὄντως εἶναι τραγῳδίαν τὴν ἀληθεστάτην. ποιηταὶ μὲν οὖν ὑμεῖς, ποιηταὶ δὲ καὶ ἡμεῖς ἐσμὲν τῶν αὐτῶν, ὑμῖν ἀντίτεχνοί τε καὶ ἀνταγωνισταὶ τοῦ καλλίστου δράματος, ὃ δὴ νόμος ἀληθὴς μόνος ἀποτελεῖν πέφυκεν, ὡς ἡ παρ' ἡμῶν ἐστιν ἐλπίς."

And, if any of the serious poets, as they are termed, who write tragedy, come to us and say "O strangers, may we go to your city and country or may we not, and shall we bring with us our poetry, what is your will about these matters?" How shall we answer the divine men? I think that our answer should be as follows: "Best of strangers," we will say to them, "we also according to our ability are tragic poets, and our tragedy is the best and noblest; for our whole state is an imitation of the best and noblest life, which we affirm to be indeed the very truth of tragedy. You are poets and we are poets, both makers of the same strains, rivals and antagonists in the noblest of dramas, which true law can alone perfect, as our hope is."

Plato Laws 817a–c, trans. Jowett

From this passage one can deduce that the laws of the city, or rather the *Laws* as dialogue, are being equated with the finest tragedy, which leads Gaiser to conclude that Plato is here referring to his own work: the dialogues are meant to replace poetry, because they are themselves a kind of poetry (or a poem of sorts).[4]

---

[4]  Sauvé Meyer 2011 argues that the Athenian's mention of tragedy in the *Laws* does not point to an equation between tragedy and Plato's dialogues, but is limited to the legislative discourse *per se*: "the text of our passage makes it clear that it is not the philosopher but the legislator who lays claim to the title of tragedian," so that the truest tragedy should be identified with "the body of legislation being devised for the city of Magnesia" (Sauvé Meyer 2011:388). If that were so, however, the Athenian's reference to "divine inspiration" as a crucial factor in the discussion as a *whole* would make little sense. Moreover, a comparison with the passage from Lycurgus (*Against*

## *Phaedrus* 274b–279c[5]

The conclusion to the *Phaedrus* is a notorious battlefield. According to Socrates, no true philosopher would confide his "serious" thoughts to written works, since writings are intrinsically non-serious. Written *logoi* are a lifeless image (*eidôlon*) of authentic speech, and, in order to drive home his point Socrates resorts to a celebrated agricultural simile: a serious farmer would never entrust his most precious seeds to the so-called "gardens of Adonis," which grow quickly, but produce nothing substantial; on the contrary, he follows the longer process of proper agriculture.[6] From this perspective, writing is assimilated to the ephemeral gardens of Adonis, whereas true philosophy is like serious agriculture, in that the seeds sown in the pupil's soul will result in vigorous and solid growth.[7] Once detached from their "father," moreover, written *logoi* are not able to defend themselves, and are exposed to the abuse of all kinds of people, who may be incapable of understanding them properly.[8] As is well known, this is one of the most discussed passages in the entire Platonic corpus; does Socrates' critique of written work affect Plato's dialogues as well? This is not the place to revive an endless debate. Suffice it to say that Gaiser advances two important arguments that strongly suggest an affirmative answer.[9] Namely, that Plato's dialogues, at least to some extent, are indeed affected by Socrates' critique:

- That Plato's *Phaedrus* could in fact, like the writings referred to by Socrates, end up in the hands of careless people is a very likely possibility, given that Plato's intended audience is the general public. Whether or not we believe that Plato's authorial self-effacement is meant as a preemptive move against such risks, Socrates does not make any exception: all written works are exposed to this danger.

- Socrates' description of written works as a playful activity partially offsets his critique. Of course, oral speech is superior; nevertheless, playing with written words is a beautiful game. Such a game is the hallmark of a noble man, who, in his old age, can look at his written

---

*Leocrates* 103) further clarifies the issue: in themselves, laws are certainly different from poetry; whereas the *Laws*, just like poetry as described by Lycurgus, are superior in that they depict human life.

5  Gaiser 1984:77–101.

6  276a–e. Detienne's reading (1972, Chapter 5) remains a stimulating classic on Adonis' gardens. Balériaux 1987 provides a very useful discussion of the ways in which the *Phaedrus* suggests that Plato is both the serious farmer (i.e. devotes himself to oral dialectics) and the ephemeral gardener Adonis (i.e. the author of the dialogues). See now Grilli 2013.

7  276e–277a. Cf. A. Nightingale's discussion as outlined in the Introduction to the current volume.

8  275d–e.

9  The arguments put forth in Werner 2012:198–227 are very similar to those of Gaiser.

offspring with moderate pride. Remarkably, the end of the *Phaedrus* is announced by Socrates' comment that he and Phaedrus "have played enough" (278b), which, once again, gives the whole discussion a self-referential air.[10]

- Proper writing is described as the activity of a man who knows and who is able to "mythologize" (*muthologein*) about the good and the just (276e). As Gaiser remarks, this brings to mind the contents of the dialogues: the *Republic*, for example, is undoubtedly devoted to the good and the just. We may add two important details overlooked by Gaiser: Socrates' arguments in the *Republic* are repeatedly described as a form of mythology,[11] and the presence of myth, according to the *Phaedo*, is the defining quality of poetry (see below).

All in all, the *Phaedrus*, by referring to good writing (i.e. to Plato's dialogues) as a playful activity, introduces the notion of literature as *lusus*, and, of course, gives us important indications as to how we should approach Plato's works.[12]

## *Symposium* 212c–233d[13]

Gaiser deals with two passages from the *Symposium*. The first, discussed in detail in Chapter 3, contains the well-known comparison of Socrates to a statuette representing Silenus: once opened, the ugly, ridiculous statuette will reveal divine images within.[14] Such is Socrates, and such, especially, are his *logoi*. Commenting on this passage, Gaiser puts forth a series of arguments suggesting that Alcibiades' words have metaliterary implications. Here is a list of those that strike me as being the most convincing:

- According to Alcibiades, the twofold nature of Socrates' *logoi* is maintained, even when his words are reported by other speakers (or by

---

[10] Arguably through a comic formula recognizable as such. See Pedrique 2012.

[11] 378c and 501e. See Murray 1999.

[12] I find the following words of Elizabeth Asmis particularly lucid and illuminating: "if they [the writers] know the truth about what they composed, and can defend what they wrote by speaking about it, while showing that what they wrote is worthless, then they deserve the name of 'philosopher' rather than the name that corresponds to their compositions—that is, 'speechwriter,' 'poet,' or 'lawgiver' (278b–e). Plato's own dialogues may be regarded as attempts to exemplify this use of language. We may call them poetry as a tribute to Plato's literary skill. But from Plato's point of view it would be more accurate to regard them as adumbrations or 'semblances' of how all sorts of language—poetic, political, legal, and the rest—may be transformed into philosophical discourse" (Asmis 1992:360).

[13] Gaiser 1984:55–76.

[14] *Symposium* 215a–d (Socrates) and 221d–222a (Socrates' *logoi*). I discuss the reliability of Alcibiades' speech in Chapter 3 (page 97n3).

secondary narrators): the *Symposium* is clearly a narration of a narration of Socrates' words.

- Alcibiades' own speech is ridiculous and elicits the laughter of his companions, but at the same time it gives us the most detailed portrait we have of Socrates. Thus, his words, combining the serious with the jocular, are likely to have a self-referential quality.

- Plato's dialogues are, for the most part, nothing less than *sokratikoi logoi*, the name given them as early as Aristotle's *Poetics*. Thus, Socrates' *words* are, in a sense, Plato's *works*.

Gaiser's second passage concerns the dialogue's very last scene. In a somewhat mysterious manner, the *Symposium* ends with an argument about drama. Socrates forces his sleepy companions (only Aristophanes the comedian and Agathon the tragic poet are still awake) to admit that, contrary to contemporary conventions, a true poet should be able to compose both comedy and tragedy. This sounds like an analogue to Socrates' twofold speeches, which combine a ridiculous manner with serious content. Like other scholars,[15] Gaiser suggests that the "true poet" alluded to in the *Symposium*'s final scene is none other than Plato. However, Gaiser goes further in noting that this "true poetry," combining the serious and the ridiculous, corresponds rather neatly to the twofold nature of Socrates' *words* (alias Plato's *works*). Moreover, the *Symposium* singles out Socrates as the best speaker of the company, who easily prevails over such poets and rhetors as Agathon, Aristophanes, Pausanias, and Phaedrus. Consequently, Socrates' words and Plato's works are implicitly presented as a superior form of poetry, incorporating and superseding all previous genres.[16]

---

[15] E.g. Clay 1975. I draw attention to Adrados 1969, an important but rarely cited study in Spanish. Adrados argues that the end of the Symposium entails "una consideración del Teatro en bloque, como opuesto a la Filosofía, inferior a ella desde luego, pero esencialmente semejante en cuanto está bajo el patrocinio del mismo *eros*" (Adrados 1969:4). According to Mader 1977: "Die Herleitung des *Symposion*—Schlusses aus dem Dialogganzen hat ergeben, dass das Entscheidende an der platonischen Dialogfigur Sokrates, dem daimon, die Überwindung und Vermittlung der Gegensätze *geloion/spoudaion, paidia/spoude, doxa/aletheia* ist" (Mader 1977:78). "Die Identität von Tragödie und Komödie erweist sich an den platonischen Schriften, und zwar in dem Sinne, dass diese beide zugleich sind 'Antitragödie' und 'Metakomödie'" (Mader 1977:79).

[16] Belfiore summarizes the point: "In the *Symposium* ... Plato represents the poetic tradition about love as being inadequate. The first five speakers' use of quotations and allusions suggests that those who rely on the poets without questioning them are lacking in understanding. Socrates, on the other hand, is represented throughout the dialogue as directly challenging the poetic tradition. He famously wins a victory over the poets at the end of the *Symposium*, when he forces Agathon and Aristophanes to agree that the same person knows how to make both comedy and tragedy, and then puts both poets to bed" (Belfiore 2011:172). Cf. also Clay 2000:64 and Bacon 1959.

## *Phaedo* 60c–61b[17]

In the *Phaedo* we learn that Socrates, on the last day of his life, had second thoughts about *mousikê*. A recurrent dream had long been urging him to practice *mousikê*, something he had always understood to be an invitation to continue his untiring research, *philosophia* being the highest form of *mousikê* (a Platonic leitmotiv, as we know). On the eve of his death, however, Socrates suspects that the dream might have a more literal meaning: the god wants him to practice *mousikê* in the literal sense, which is why Socrates tries his hand at poetry while in prison. He works on a hymn to Apollo and tries to put some of Aesop's tales into verse. Gaiser points out two important facts:

- Socrates' first mention of Aesop (59a) recalls passage b) from the *Symposium*, in that Socrates refers to the strange mixture of pleasure and pain he felt from the relief of being released from his chains. The two feelings, he observes, always go hand in hand, and one of Aesop's tales on the subject might have been inspired by his envisaging a two-masked creature: the mask of pain necessarily follows that of pleasure, and vice versa. This also reminds one of the discussion of tragedy and comedy in the *Philebus* (47d–50a), where both genres are said to always involve a mixture of pleasure and pain.

- Socrates explicitly affirms that poetry, qua poetry, involves *muthos*, which is its hallmark and defining quality. Socrates himself, however, is not *muthologikos*, i.e. he is not able to create myths. This is why he merely puts Aesop's tales to verse, thereby utilizing a set of easily accessible, ready-made myths. Nevertheless, the *Phaedo* itself contains new myths (one thinks of the Apollonian swan song mentioned at 84e–85b, and, in particular, the eschatological myth that concludes the dialogue) and may be construed as a kind of hymn to Apollo. Moreover, Plato is certainly *muthologikos*, and, being *muthologikos*, he is most certainly a poet, according to Socrates' (i.e. Plato's own) definition.

Gaiser concludes that Socrates' poetic efforts should be read, therefore, as an allusion to Plato himself as a "philosophical poet," whose ambition is to engage with the most venerable tradition of Greek poetry.[18]

---

[17] Gaiser 1984:114–115.
[18] Cf. my own discussion in the (prior) Conclusion to the current volume.

# A Possible Objection

The cumulative force of the above four instances of "self-disclosure" is considerable, but therein lies a possible problem: *prima facie* Plato's self-disclosures may look confusingly disparate, even though it would be easy (and by no means implausible) to account for such a variety in the light of the dialogues' changing contexts, as I shall do in the case of the *Laws*. In the *Symposium*, on the other hand, they are an unprecedented form of drama combining comedy and tragedy. Yet only the former seems to play a role in the *Phaedrus*, where Socrates emphasizes the jocular nature of writing. Then again, in the *Phaedo,* we are confronted with a hymn. And if that were not enough, the other passages Gaiser discusses in his introduction suggest that the dialogues can be a form of both incantation (*epôidê*) and purification (*katharsis*). In other words, the landscape looks overly complicated. Unless we are prepared to think of Plato as a Protean flip-flopper, a better explanation is needed. And this is all the more necessary if one discards, as I do, chronological solutions to Plato's alleged, or apparent, contradictions.[19]

One has to realize above all that Plato's idea of poetic genres was different from our own (and from that of Alexandrian scholars, for that matter). Genres began to be perceived as rigid categories only when the social circumstances that gave them birth began to change, and when literature (as a bookish activity) came to replace poetry (as a social and largely oral phenomenon).[20] Ever since Havelock's studies, it has been generally accepted that Plato was a transitional author coming somewhere between the world of oral poetry and written literature.[21] This explains why the notion of genres is a very fluid one in

---

[19]  In Capra and Martinelli 2011, a sustained case is made against the tripartite chronology, and, more generally, against evolution as an interpretative paradigm. Our knowledge of Plato's dialogues ultimately depends on an Academic edition, which must have included the dialogues *in their final and revised form.* A number of sources—Dionysius of Halicarnassus *The Arrangement of Words* 25.32, Quintilian *Institutes of Oratory* 8.6.64–65, Diogenes Laertius 3.37, and *Anonymous Commentary on the Theaetetus* (CPF III.9 = P. Berol. inv. 9782) col. 3.28–49—inform us that Plato kept revising his dialogues throughout his lifetime. (On the subject of revision, cf. Thesleff 1982 and Capra 2003.) It has been argued that Plato's dialogues were not available by the booksellers at the time Plato directed the Academy: see Lucarini 2010–2011:350, with added bibliography. This perceptive, well-documented article also demonstrates that Aristophanes of Byzantium's trilogies were based on a preexistent tetralogic edition of the Academy, which was also the basis for the medieval tradition.

[20]  See Rossi 1971 for a classic discussion of the phenomenon. Rossi's seminal theory was the subject of a 2011 conference and is now published in a monographic issue of the "Seminari romani di cultura classica" (1.2, 2012).

[21]  The work of Havelock (1963) proved to be hugely influential. However, he underestimated the diffusion of literacy (cf. e.g. Harvey 1966) and argued that Plato was to all extent and purposes a supporter of writing against orality. This thesis is, of course, untenable, since it is contradicted by many explicit statements in the Platonic corpus. (Cf. e.g. Adkins 1980 reviewing Havelock

Plato's dialogues and why it reflects a number of points of view. In the *Republic*, for example, Plato puts forward the pioneering distinction between *mimêsis* and *diêgêsis*, but, at the same time, treats Homer and the tragedians as belonging in the same category.[22] Another example is lyric poetry: there was no such notion in archaic Greece, and Genette has famously argued that the very idea of lyric poetry is absent in both Plato and Aristotle.[23]

Part of the problem, then, lies in the fact that we tend to see as distinct categories a number of poetic phenomena that Plato would have considered, if not coincident, to be by and large overlapping. One should never forget that the basic classification of poetry in the Greek world was based on a binary opposition between praise and blame, something that is likely to have originated in Indo-European poetry and remains a fundamental criterion in Aristotle's *Poetics*.[24] Even more importantly, Plato ridicules the likes of Evenus of Paros, who developed more articulated distinctions.[25] Bearing this in mind, we can now try to form a clear idea of the generic distinctions that can be found throughout the whole corpus.

By way of summary, we can say that Gaiser's thesis is that Plato looked upon his own work as a form of poetry, which could take the general form of either enchantment or purification—or, more specifically, be construed as tragedy (*Laws*), as a mixture of tragedy and comedy (*Symposium*), as a hymn (*Phaedo*), or even as a jocular activity consisting in playful *muthologia* (*Phaedrus*). In Plato's dialogues, *humnos* refers to a variety of poems, or, as we moderns would say, genres. In his detailed study, Roberto Velardi has shown that the usage of *humnos* and its cognates in the dialogues is (as one would expect) very fluid.[26] At times the term seems to indicate a rather specific category of poems composed in honor of the gods,[27] though examples of this are not numerous and are

---

1978, and Werner 2012:204–206. Usener 1994 provides a careful examination of all passages involving reading in the corpus of Plato and Isocrates.)

[22] Cf. *Republic* 595c, 598d, 605c, 607a (and cf. e.g. Isocrates *To Nicocles* 48–49). See Herrington 1985:213–215. On the other hand, Halliwell 2002a argues persuasively that Plato is the one ancient author who saw tragedy as a form of Weltanschauung.

[23] Genette 1979. In my view, this is only partially true, for in some ways the *Phaedrus* "invents" lyric poetry against the background of epic, though this does not mean that the same distinction can be found in dialogues other than the *Phaedrus* (cf. Beecroft 2010:146). Still, we may regard the *Phaedrus* as a brilliant thought experiment aimed at serving the purposes of that specific dialogue.

[24] See Gentili 2006, Chapter 8. The opposition is crucial to Nagy's discussion of the hero in Greek poetry (1990). For a recent discussion, cf. West 2007:63–70.

[25] *Phaedrus* 267a.

[26] Velardi 1991. Cf. also Regali 2012 (particularly 34–37), who notes a more specialized usage: at times, *humnos* designates Plato's attempts to correct and integrate the poetic tradition (see *Symposium* 193c–d and *Phaedrus* 265b–c).

[27] Notably *Republic* 607a and *Laws* 709a–c.

curiously confined to the *Republic* and the *Laws-Epinomis* (i.e. to ideal as opposed to real cities on the whole).[28] On other occasions, the term is used for poems or speeches devoted to men (as opposed to gods) and can indicate very different genres, including tragedy, prose, and epic.[29] None of this, however, is surprising, given that Plato often uses the term(s) poet/poetry for prose compositions,[30] and, in the *Republic*, goes so far as to define poetry as a form of rhetoric "dressed up" in a beautiful fashion.[31]

The *Phaedo*'s self-disclosure, then, does not contradict those found in the *Laws* or in the *Symposium*, because the term *humnos* is general enough to accommodate tragedy as well. Or perhaps I should say, it comprises that kind of purified, pious tragedy, which, according to the *Laws*, coincides ultimately with philosophical discourse. In fact, the only consistent antinomy one finds throughout the dialogues is that between eulogy and blame. Both are fiercely criticized from a factual and historical point of view, and yet both discourses, if properly reformed, are admitted to a place in Plato's ideal cities. They are also crucial to Plato's own poetic fabric: comic and tragic elements, in different combinations and proportions, are a crucial subtext in much Platonic writing. From this point of view, it should be noted that the *Phaedo*, when referring to poetry, touches on Aesop's tales and on a hymn to Apollo. Aesop was, of course, a popular comic figure who closely resembled Socrates himself: he was notoriously ugly, and yet, just like Socrates, his unprepossessing appearance concealed a divine wisdom. Recent scholarship has led to the fascinating discovery that Socrates' trial, as depicted by Plato in the *Apology*, incorporates various elements of Aesop's biography, which makes the parallel an arresting one.[32]

---

[28] "Delle 56 occorrenze del semantema nel *corpus* delle sue opere soltanto 10, comprese quelle già citate di *Resp.* 10, 607a4 e *Leg.* 3, 700b2; d7, sono le attestazioni alle quali può essere attribuito il significato specifico di 'discorso rivolto alla divinità per celebrarla e per implorare la sua benevolenza verso gli uomini,' nel quale, cioè, la divinità sia contemporaneamente destinataria e argomento del canto: *Leg.* 7, 812c5; 822c5; 11, 931b6; 12, 960c4; *Resp.* 2, 372b7 (con riferimento ad inni simposiali); *Epin.* 980b1; b8" (Velardi 1991:218–219). Cf. also Giuliano 2005:118–129.

[29] The *Timaeus-Critias* is conceptualized as a hymn, which amounts to another example of self-disclosure (unnoticed by Gaiser). See Capra 2010a and Regali 2012, in particular 32–39.

[30] This is particularly obvious in the *Phaedrus*, which features a number of passages where *poiêtês* and its cognates are unambiguously referred to prose writers: cf. 234e, 236d, 258a, 258b, 278e. At the same time, as if to confirm Plato's fluid, non-technical usage of poetry-related terminology, at 258d Socrates contrasts *poiêtês* with *idiôtês*, the former signifying poet as opposed to prose writer (ἐν μέτρῳ ὡς ποιητὴς ἢ ἄνευ μέτρου ὡς ἰδιώτης.). Cf. also 257a.

[31] Cf. e.g. *Republic* 603a, with Murrray 2005 (on personification). A similar point is made in the *Gorgias* (502c).

[32] Chvatík 2001, Compton 2006:154–165, Kurke 2006, Clayton 2008. Given that Aesop's *bios* might have been a major influence on Aristophanes' *Wasps* (see Schirru 2009), this is not altogether improbable. Schauer and Merkle 1992 add the important detail that "Platons Hinweis auf Äsop impliziert eine Kritik an dessen mangelnder Todesbereitschafft" (96).

Thus, in conclusion, the *Phaedo* features a twofold self-disclosure, both serious and comic, which clearly echoes the *Symposium*. At the same time, it also tallies with the *Phaedrus*: there too, the jocular activity of writing is tantamount to the narration of myths (*muthologia*), and (as we have seen) the presence of myth is precisely the hallmark of poetry according to the *Phaedo*. In the *Phaedrus*, moreover, the writer's "game" is viewed favorably as a more dignified activity compared with sympotic pleasure, not to mention the fact that Socrates' "palinode" in the *Phaedrus*—itself another self-disclosure—is crucially described as "a jocular and mythological *hymn*."[33] In short, Plato's self-disclosures are connected by a network of multiple links.

By now, the "Protean" variety of Plato's self-disclosures should appear far less confusing. The *Phaedo*, the *Phaedrus*, and the *Symposium*, though bearing different labels, constitute a fairly unified viewpoint. Plato refers to his dialogues as a new kind of poetry made up of a peculiar blend of serious and jocular elements, and this twofold nature is a close reflection of the twofold nature of Plato's principal protagonist, Socrates, himself. Yet we still have to explain why the *Laws*, though not in contradiction with the other passages Gaiser discusses, is focused exclusively on tragedy, i.e. on the serious side of Plato's own meta-poetic self-characterization.[34] One does not have to look far for the answer however, for this is the one dialogue in the whole corpus that does not feature Socrates as a character. Accordingly, the uncharacteristically dogmatic dialogue lacks the peculiar mixture of serious and jocular that is the distinguishing characteristic of Socrates,[35] the daemonic man who combines physical ugliness with sublime wisdom.[36]

---

[33] 265c μυθικόν τινα ὕμνον προσεπαίσαμεν.

[34] The emphasis on poetry's serious side may also be due to the fact that the *Laws* discusses a reformed city. In comparison with "minor pedagogy," Plato's "major pedagogy" (i.e. the kind of poetry to be implemented in reformed cities; cf. my Conclusion) tends to be emphatically "serious," which explains why the *Republic*, too, points to hymns (i.e. serious poetry) as the appropriate kind of poetry for the Kallipolis.

[35] I stress the word *peculiar* because in other respects the notion of playfulness is crucial in the *Laws*, in that for Plato *paideia*, could not be conceived of without *paidia* (see Jouët-Pastré 2006). Moreover, Mouze 1998 rightly points out that "c'est à l'interieur du genre divertissant que la tragédie est comprise comme sérieuse" (99, cf. *Statesman* 288c).

[36] With her usual perceptiveness, Elizabeth Asmis remarks that: "One does not want to leave the last word on poetry to the *Laws*, where Plato reduces the poet once more to a servant of the law-maker. The old Athenian who has replaced Socrates as Plato's chief spokesman suggests that the discussion that he and his companions have had about the laws is a kind of 'poetry': it is, indeed, the most suitable of all poems and prose works for children to hear and teachers to approve (811c–e). In this rivalry with the poets, the lawmakers will surely lose if we appoint as judge the Socrates of the *Phaedrus*" (Asmis 1992:361).

## *Reductio ad Duo*: Plato's Seriocomic Poetry

The generic markers that feature in Plato's self-disclosures prove, therefore, to be consistent on the whole. Nevertheless, one must still account for Gaiser's more general categories: purification (*katharsis*) and enchantment (*epôidê*). As I have mentioned, these are two different, if complementary, modes of Plato's philosophy. But how do they relate to Plato's more specific self-disclosures? The answer is a relatively easy one, since Plato's various self-conscious moments can now be placed into two general categories: the jocular and the serious. It is my contention that purification and incantation can be broadly associated with the jocular and the serious, respectively. That "enchanting" is a basically "serious" procedure should not be controversial: the very usage of *epôidê* in the dialogues points to a focused state of mind, and the similarity between incantation on the one hand and tragedy or hymn on the other (that is, the serious side of Plato's self-disclosures) is obvious enough.[37] Thus, in what follows, my focus will be on the other, less obvious association of purification and the jocular.

Socratic elenchus can result in an entertaining spectacle, as Socrates plainly states in the *Apology*: young people experience pleasure in listening to him refuting his pompous interlocutors (χαίρουσιν ἀκούοντες, 23b). It is surely no accident, then, that the aporetic dialogues, in which Socrates demolishes various people's claims to knowledge and often deflates their egos in the process, are the richest in humor and comic elements. By contrast, fully "constructive" or dogmatic dialogues such as the *Laws* are much less entertaining, and it is not surprising that Socrates does not star in this dialogue, which is the one instance of Platonic self-disclosure where there are no jocular elements.[38]

One strategy to prove the basically jocular nature of Socratic elenchus might be to search the elenctic dialogues for comic elements. A thorough examination would reveal that comedy—even as a deliberate emulation of Aristophanes and other playwrights—is a very important ingredient in these dialogues.[39] This would require another book, however, so it might be better to follow a shorter, more theoretical path. With this in mind, we shall take a close

---

[37]  *epôidê* and *tragôidia* are both cognates of *ôide*, "song."
[38]  The *Laws* is also notable because of the paramount importance it confers on the idea of enchantment (see Panno 2007 and cf. the conclusion to the current chapter). This, I believe, strengthens the hypothesis that *epôidê* corresponds to the "serious" and constructive moment of philosophical discourse, whereas *katharsis* stands for the (predominantly jocular) Socratic elenchus. Of course, a number of dialogues feature both a *pars destruens* and a *pars construens*, and the *Symposium*, the *Phaedo*, and the *Phaedrus* clearly belong to this ambiguous group. Unsurprisingly then, the relevant instances of self-disclosure feature both the serious and the jocular.
[39]  See Capra 2001, with further bibliography. More recent work includes Beltrametti 2004, Trivigno 2009, and Buarque 2011.

look at the well-known passage from the *Sophist,* which, it is generally agreed, describes the effects of Socratic refutation:[40]

{ΞΕ.} Τί δὲ δὴ τῷ τῆς διδασκαλικῆς ἄρα μέρει τῷ τοῦτο ἀπαλλάττοντι λεκτέον; [...] Τὸ μὲν ἀρχαιοπρεπές τι πάτριον, ᾧ πρὸς τοὺς ὑεῖς μάλιστ' ἐχρῶντό τε καὶ ἔτι πολλοὶ χρῶνται τὰ νῦν, ὅταν αὐτοῖς ἐξαμαρτάνωσί τι, τὰ μὲν χαλεπαίνοντες, τὰ δὲ μαλθακωτέρως παραμυθούμενοι· τὸ δ' οὖν σύμπαν αὐτὸ ὀρθότατα εἴποι τις ἂν νουθετητικήν. [...] Τὸ δέ γε, εἴξασί τινες αὖ λόγον ἑαυτοῖς δόντες ἡγήσασθαι πᾶσαν ἀκούσιον ἀμαθίαν εἶναι, καὶ μαθεῖν οὐδέν ποτ' ἂν ἐθέλειν τὸν οἰόμενον εἶναι σοφὸν τούτων ὧν οἴοιτο πέρι δεινὸς εἶναι, μετὰ δὲ πολλοῦ πόνου τὸ νουθετητικὸν εἶδος τῆς παιδείας σμικρὸν ἀνύτειν. [...] Τῷ τοι ταύτης τῆς δόξης ἐπὶ ἐκβολὴν ἄλλῳ τρόπῳ στέλλονται [...] Διερωτῶσιν ὧν ἂν οἴηταί τίς τι πέρι λέγειν λέγων μηδέν· εἶθ' ἅτε πλανωμένων τὰς δόξας ῥᾳδίως ἐξετάζουσι, καὶ συνάγοντες δὴ τοῖς λόγοις εἰς ταὐτὸν τιθέασι παρ' ἀλλήλας, τιθέντες δὲ ἐπιδεικνύουσιν αὐτὰς αὑταῖς ἅμα περὶ τῶν αὐτῶν πρὸς τὰ αὐτὰ κατὰ ταὐτὰ ἐναντίας. οἱ δ' ὁρῶντες ἑαυτοῖς μὲν χαλεπαίνουσι, πρὸς δὲ τοὺς ἄλλους ἡμεροῦνται, καὶ τούτῳ δὴ τῷ τρόπῳ τῶν περὶ αὐτοὺς μεγάλων καὶ σκληρῶν δοξῶν ἀπαλλάττονται πασῶν [τε] ἀπαλλαγῶν ἀκούειν τε ἡδίστην καὶ τῷ πάσχοντι βεβαιότατα γιγνομένην. νομίζοντες γάρ, ὦ παῖ φίλε, οἱ καθαίροντες αὐτούς, ὥσπερ οἱ περὶ τὰ σώματα ἰατροὶ νενομίκασι μὴ πρότερον ἂν τῆς προσφερομένης τροφῆς ἀπολαύειν δύνασθαι σῶμα, πρὶν ἂν τὰ ἐμποδίζοντα ἐντός τις ἐκβάλῃ, ταὐτὸν καὶ περὶ ψυχῆς διενοήθησαν ἐκεῖνοι, μὴ πρότερον αὐτὴν ἕξειν τῶν προσφερομένων μαθημάτων ὄνησιν, πρὶν ἂν ἐλέγχων τις τὸν ἐλεγχόμενον εἰς αἰσχύνην καταστήσας, τὰς τοῖς μαθήμασιν ἐμποδίους δόξας ἐξελών, καθαρὸν ἀποφήνῃ καὶ ταῦτα ἡγούμενον ἅπερ οἶδεν εἰδέναι μόνα, πλείω δὲ μή. [...] Διὰ ταῦτα δὴ πάντα ἡμῖν, ὦ Θεαίτητε, καὶ τὸν ἔλεγχον λεκτέον ὡς ἄρα μεγίστη καὶ κυριωτάτη τῶν καθάρσεών ἐστι.

What name, then, shall be given to the sort of instruction which gets rid of this [ignorant stupidity]? [...] There is the time-honored mode which our fathers commonly practised towards their sons, and which is still adopted by many—either of roughly reproving their errors, or of gently advising them; which varieties may be correctly included under the general term of admonition [...] But whereas some appear to have arrived at the conclusion that all ignorance is involuntary, and

---

[40]  See e.g. Cornford 1935:181 and Kerferd 1986:24–25. The passage is too long to quote in its unabridged form.

that no one who thinks himself wise is willing to learn any of those things in which he is conscious of his own cleverness, and that the admonitory sort of instruction gives much trouble and does little good [...] Accordingly, they set to work to eradicate the spirit of conceit in another way [...] They cross-examine a man's words, when he thinks that he is saying something and is really saying nothing, and easily convict him of inconsistencies in his opinions; these they then collect by the dialectical process, and placing them side by side, show that they contradict one another about the same things, in relation to the same things, and in the same respect. He, seeing this, is angry with himself, and grows gentle towards others, and thus is entirely delivered from great prejudices and harsh notions, in a way which is most amusing to the hearer, and produces the most lasting good effect on the person who is the subject of the operation. For as the physician considers that the body will receive no benefit from taking food until the internal obstacles have been removed, so the purifier of the soul is conscious that his patient will receive no benefit from the application of knowledge until he is refuted, and from refutation learns modesty; he must be purged of his prejudices first and made to think that he knows only what he knows, and no more [...] For all these reasons, Theaetetus, we must admit that refutation is the greatest and chiefest of purifications.

Plato Sophist 229c–230d, trans. Jowett

This passage confirms the idea that Plato conceived of philosophical discourse as a two-stage process, whereby the individual must first be purified before more constructive "food for the soul" can be administered. It is the second stage that corresponds to the "serious" side of Plato's self-disclosure, whereas the first reflects the jocular. The very description in the *Sophist* bears this out: refutation is "most amusing to the hearer."

The form of "amusement" referred to in the *Sophist* fits other descriptions of Socrates' elenctic procedures perfectly.[41] That this is an intrinsically comic form of pleasure will become evident in the light of the *Philebus'* concise theory of comedy.[42] It is well to remember that Socratic *elenchos*, according to the *Sophist*, results in the purification from conceit and apparent knowledge (δοκεῖν

---

[41]  In the *Apology*, Socrates says that young people take pleasure in listening to Socrates question and refute conceited people. This is emphatically confirmed by Callicles in the *Gorgias*, when he tells us that Socrates' refutation of Gorgias and Polus was the most entertaining (funniest?) exchange he had ever witnessed. See *Apology* 23c, 33b–c and *Gorgias* 458d.

[42]  Cf. Cerasuolo 1980 and Munteanu 2011:95–97.

εἰδέναι). What is interesting for my present discussion is that it is precisely conceit and apparent knowledge (δοξοσοφία) that is singled out in the *Philebus* as the source of comic laughter (49a–50e).[43] Even more importantly, comic laughter is not limited to the stage but encompasses "the whole comedy and tragedy of life" (50b), as is plainly stated a few lines later. Socratic purification, in short, can be construed as something intrinsically comic, and this squares well with the jocular character of many elenctic dialogues.

Plato's dialogues are implicitly conceived as an unprecedented form of poetry mixing the serious with the ridiculous: a projection, in other words, of the exceptionally twofold nature of Socrates. As Alcibiades quite clearly states, not only is Socrates simultaneously ridiculous and sublime, but, more importantly, so are the Socratic *logoi*—that is, Plato's dialogues.

---

43 And provided this does not happen at the expense of one's friends, in which case it is labeled as a form of envy, resulting in a mixture of pleasure and pain.

# Bibliography

Acosta-Hughes, B., and S. A. Stephens. 2012. *Callimachus in Context: From Plato to the Augustan Poets*. Cambridge.

Adkins, A. W. H. 1980. Review of Havelock 1978. *Classical Philology* 75:256–268.

Adomenas, M. 2006. "Plato, Presocratics and the Question of Intellectual Genre." In *La costruzione del discorso filosofico nell'età dei Presocratici: The Construction of Philosophical Discourse in the Age of the Presocratics*, ed. M. M. Sassi, 329–353. Pisa.

Adrados, F. 1969. "El *Banquete* platónico y la teoría del teatro." *Emerita* 37:1–28.

Albersmeier, S. 2009. *Heroes: Mortals and Myths in Ancient Greece*. Baltimore.

Allen, D. 2010. *Why Plato Wrote*. Malden.

Aloni, A. 1984. "Un Archiloco 'epico' in Teocrito?" *Museum Philologicum Londiniense* 6:1–5.

———, ed. 2008. *Nuove acquisizioni di Saffo e della lirica greca: Per il testo di P. Köln inv. 21351+21376 e P. Oxy. 1787*. Alessandria.

———. 2011. "Il dono e i doni degli dèi: Sull'identità poetica di Archiloco." In *Tra panellenismo e tradizioni locali: Nuovi contributi*, ed. A. Aloni and M. Ornaghi, 141–153. Messina.

Andò, V. 1996. "Nymphe: La sposa e le ninfe." *Quaderni Urbinati di Cultura Classica* 52:47–79.

Angiò, F. 1997. "Posidippo di Pella e la vecchiaia (a proposito di P. Berol. inv. 142839)." *Papyrologica Lupiensia* 6:7–13.

Annas, J. 1982. "Plato on the Triviality of Literature." In *Plato on Beauty, Wisdom, and the Arts*, ed. J. Moravcsik and P. Temko, 1–28. Totowa.

———. 1985. Review of Gaiser 1984. *Classical Review* 35:401–402.

Arieti, J. A. 1992. *Interpreting Plato: The Dialogues as Drama*. Savage.

Arrighetti, G. 1994. "Stesicoro e il suo pubblico." *Materiali e Discussioni per l'analisi dei testi classici* 32:9–30.

———. 2006. *Poesia, poetiche e storia nella riflessione dei Greci*. Pisa.

Arrigoni, E. 1969–1970. "Στοιχεῖα πρὸς ἀναπαράστασιν τοῦ τοπίου τῆς Ἀττικῆς κατὰ τὴν κλασσικὴν ἐποχήν." *Athēna* 71:322–386.

# Bibliography

Arrigoni, G. 2008. "Donne e sport nel mondo greco: Religione e società." In *Le donne in Grecia*, ed. G. Arrrigoni, 55–201. Rome.

Asmis, E. 1986. "Psychagogia in Plato's *Phaedrus*." *Illinois Classical Studies* 11:153–172.

———. 1992. "Plato on Poetic Creativity." In *The Cambridge Companion to Plato*, ed. R. Kraut, 338–364. Cambridge.

Austin, C. 2002. "Posidippus and the Mysteries ... of the Text." In *Il papiro di Posidippo un anno dopo: Atti del convegno internazionale di studi, Firenze 13-14 giugno 2002*, ed. G. Bastianini and A. Casanova, 7–19. Florence.

Austin, C., and G. Bastianini, eds. 2002. *Posidippi Pellaei quae supersunt omnia*. Milan.

Austin, N. 1994. *Helen of Troy and Her Shameless Phantom*. Ithaca.

Bacon, H. 1959. "Socrates Crowned." *The Virginia Quarterly Review* 35:424–430.

———. 1990. "The Poetry of the *Phaedo*." In *Cabinet of the Muses: Essays on Classical and Comparative Literature in Honor of Thomas G. Rosenmeyer*, ed. M. Griffith and D. J. Mastronarde, 147–162. Atlanta.

Balériaux, O. 1987. "Des jardins d'Adonis au bosquet sacré d'Hékadèmos." In Servais, Hackens, and Servais-Soyez 1987:153–168.

Barfield, R. 2011. *The Ancient Quarrel between Philosophy and Poetry*. Cambridge.

Barker, A. 2001. "La musica di Stesicoro." *Quaderni Urbinati di Cultura Classica* 67:7–20.

Barnes, J. 1989. "Philodemus and the Old Academy." *Apeiron* 22:139–148.

Barrett, J. 2001. "Plato's *Apology*: Philosophy, Rhetoric, and the World of Myth." *Classical World* 95:3–30.

Bassi, K. 2000. "The Somatics of the Past: Helen and the Body of Tragedy." In *Acting on the Past: Historical Performance across the Disciplines*, ed. M. Franko and A. Richards, 13–34. London.

Baxter, E. 2007. "The 'New Sappho' and the *Phaedo*: Reflections on Immortality." *Dionysius* 25:7–19.

Beecroft, A. J. 2006. "'This is Not a True Story': Stesichorus's *Palinode* and the Revenge of the Epichoric." *Transactions of the American Philological Association* 136:47–69.

———. 2010. *Authorship and Cultural Identity in Early Greece and China: Patterns of Literary Circulation*. Cambridge.

Belfiore, E. S. 1980. "Elenchus, Epode, and Magic: Socrates as Silenus." *Phoenix* 34:128–137.

———. 2011. "Poets at the Symposium." In Destrée and Hermann 2011:155–174.

———. 2012. *Socrates' Daimonic Art: Love for Wisdom in Four Platonic Dialogues*. Cambridge.

Beltrametti, A. 2004. "La vena comica: *Extrema ratio o principium sapientiae?* Quando Euripide e Platone, nei loro dialoghi, fanno la commedia e non (solo) per far ridere." *Itaca* 20:87–113.

Benjamin, W. 1998. *Understanding Brecht.* Trans. A. Bostock, introduction S. Mitchell. London.

Bershadsky, N. 2011. "A Picnic, a Tomb, and a Crow: Hesiod's Cult in the *Works and Days.*" *Harvard Studies in Classical Philology* 106:1–45.

Berti, E. 2012. *Sumphilosophein: La vita nell'Accademia di Platone.* Rome.

Betegh, G. 2009. "Tale, Theology and Teleology in the *Phaedo.*" In *Plato's Myths,* ed. C. Partenie, 77–100. Cambridge.

Bettini, M., and C. Brillante. 2002. *Il mito di Elena: Immagini e racconti dalla Grecia a oggi.* Turin.

Bianco, E. 1997. "Ificrate, ῥήτωρ καὶ στρατηγός." *Miscellanea Greca e Romana* 21:179–207.

Bierl, A. 2002. "Charitons Kallirhoe im Lichte von Sapphos Priamelgedicht (Fr. 16 Voigt): Liebe und Intertextualität im griechischen Roman." *Poetica* 34:1–27.

———. 2003. "'Ich aber (sage), das Schönste ist, was einer liebt!': Eine pragmatische Deutung von Sappho Fr. 16 L-P./V." *Quaderni Urbinati di Cultura Classica* 74:91–124.

Biles, Z. P. 2011. *Aristophanes and the Poetics of Competition.* Cambridge.

Billault, A. 2008. "Théocrite et Platon: Remarques sur l'*Idylle* VII." *Revue des Études Grecques* 121:496–513.

Billot, M. F. 1989. "Académie—topographie et archéologie." In *Dictionnaire des philosophes Antiques.* I., ed. R. Goulet, 693–789. Paris.

Blondell, R. 2002. *The Play of Character in Plato's Dialogues.* Cambridge.

———. 2013. *Helen of Troy: Beauty, Myth, Devastation.* Oxford.

Bodson, L. 1976. "La stridulation des cigales: Poésie grecque et réalité entomologique." *L'Antiquité Classique* 45:75-94.

Bonazzi, M. 2011. *Platone. Fedro.* Turin.

Bonazzi, M., and F. Trabatonni, eds. 2003. *Platone e la traditione platonica.* Milan.

Borghini, A. 1996. "L'episodio petroniano di Circe e Polieno: Sul valore simbolico-rituale del platano." *Aufidus* 10:19–32.

Borthwick, E. K. 1966. "A Grasshopper's Diet: Notes on an Epigram of Meleager and a Fragment of Eubulus." *Classical Quarterly* 16:103–112.

Boter, G. 2013. "*Symposium* 212a6–7: The Most Immortal Men." *Proceedings of the X Symposium Platonicum on the Symposium.* I:88–92. http://platosociety.org/the-x-symposium-platonicum-platos-symposium-pisa/.

Bötticher, C. 1856. *Der Baumcultus der Hellenen: Nach den gottesdienstlichen Gebräuchen und den überlieferten Bildwerken.* Berlin.

*Bibliography*

Bouvier, D. 2011. "Du frisson (*phrikê*) d'horreur au frisson poétique: Interpretation de quelques emotions entre larmes chaudes et sueurs froides chez Platon et Homère." *Mètis* 9:15–35.

Bouvries Thorsen, S. des. 1978. "The Interpretations of Sappho's Fragment 16 L.P." *Symbolae Osloenses* 53:5–23.

Bowen, A. C. 1988. "On Interpreting Plato." In *Platonic Writings, Platonic Readings*, ed. C. L. Griswold, 49–65. New York.

Bowie, E. 1993. "Lies, Fiction and Slander in Early Greek Poetry." In *Lies and Fiction in the Ancient World*, ed. C. Gill and T. P. Wiseman, 1–37. Exeter.

———. 2010. "The Trojan War's Reception in Early Greek Lyric, Iambic and Elegiac Poetry." In *Intentional History: Spinning Time in Ancient Greece*, ed. L. Foxhall, H. J. Gehrke, and N. Luraghi, 57–87. Stuttgart.

Bowra, C. M. 1938. "Plato's Epigram on Dion's Death." *American Journal of Philology* 59: 399–404.

Boyancé, P. 1937. *Le culte des Muses chez les philosophes grecs: Études d'histoire et de psychologie religieuses*. Paris.

Boys-Stones, G. 2004. "Phaedo of Elis and Plato on the Soul." *Phronesis* 49:1–23.

Boys-Stones, G., and J. Haubold, eds. 2010. *Plato and Hesiod*. Oxford.

Brancacci, A. 2004. "Socrate, la musique et la danse: Aristophane, Xénophon, Platon." *Les Études Philosophiques* 2:193–211.

———. 2011. "L'elogio di Isocrate nel *Fedro*, la chiusa dell'*Eutidemo*, e la polemica isocrateo-antistenico-platonica." In Casertano 2011:7–38.

———. 2012. "Μίμησις, poesia e musica nella *Repubblica* di Platone." *Philosophia* 42:121–134.

Bravo, J. J., III. 2009. "Recovering the Past: The Origins of Greek Heroes and Hero Cult." In Albersmeier 2009:10–29.

Brillante, C. 1990. "Archiloco e le Muse." *Quaderni Urbinati di Cultura Classica* 35:7–20.

———. 2001–2002. "Elena: Da Stesicoro a Euripide." *Fontes* 4–5:15–58.

———. 2003. "Sull'*idillio* XVIII di Teocrito." In *Studi di filologia e tradizione greca in memoria di Aristide Colonna*. I., ed. F. Benedetti and S. Grandolini, 179–192. Naples.

———. 2004. "Il sogno di Epimenide." *Quaderni Urbinati di Cultura Classica* 77:11–39.

———. 2009. *Il cantore e la Musa: Poesia e modelli culturali nella Grecia arcaica*. Pisa.

Brisson, L. 1993. "La *Lettre VII* de Platon, une autobiographie?" In *L'invention de l'autobiographie d'Hésiode à Saint Augustin*, ed. M. F. Baslez, P. Hoffmann and L. Pernot, 37–46. Paris.

———. 1998a. *Plato the Mythmaker*. Trans. G. Naddaf. Chicago.

———. 1998b. *Platon. Le Banquet*. Paris.

Brown, C. 1989. "Anactoria and the Χαρίτων ἀμαρύγματα. Sappho fr. 16, 18 Voigt." *Quaderni Urbinati di Cultura Classica* 61:7–15.

Buarque, L. 2011. *As armas cômicas: Os interlocutores de Platão no Crátilo*. Rio de Janeiro.

Buchheim, T. 1989, ed. *Gorgias von Leontinoi. Reden, Fragmente und Testimonien*. Hamburg.

Bundrick, S. D. 2005. *Music and Image in Classical Athens*. Cambridge.

Burger, R. 1980. *Plato's Phaedrus: A Defense of the Philosophic Art of Writing*. Tuscaloosa.

Burkert, W. 1960. "Platon oder Pythagoras? Zum Ursprung des Wortes 'Philosophie.'" *Hermes* 88:159–177.

———. 1972. *Lore and Science in Ancient Pythagoreanism*. Cambridge, MA.

———. 1987. "The Making of Homer in the Sixth Century B.C.: Rhapsodes versus Stesichorus." In *Papers on the Amasis Painter and his World*, ed. J. Paul Getty Museum, 43–62. Malibu.

Burnet, J., ed. 1911. *Plato's Phaedo*. Oxford.

Burnett, A. 1979. "Desire and Memory (Sappho Frag. 94)." *Classical Philology* 74:16–27.

Burnyeat, M. F. 1997. "First Words: A Valedictory Lecture." *Proceedings of the Cambridge Philological Society* 43:1–20.

———. 1999. "Culture and Society in Plato's *Republic*." *The Tanner Lectures on Human Values* 20:215–324.

Butti de Lima, P. 2012. *Un'archeologia della politica: Letture della Repubblica di Platone*. Milan.

Büttner, S. 2000. *Die Literaturtheorie bei Platon und ihre anthropologische Begründung*. Tübingen.

———. 2011. "Inspiration and Inspired Poets in Plato's Dialogues." In Destrée and Hermann 2011:111–129.

Cadario, M. 2001. "Un intellettuale a teatro: Una statua togata lunense nel gesto della lettura interrotta." *Quaderni del Centro Studi Lunensi* 7:83–114.

Cairns, D. 2009. "Weeping and Veiling: Grief, Display and Concealment in Ancient Greek Culture." In *Tears in the Graeco-Roman World*, ed. T. Fögen, 37–57. Berlin.

———. 2013. "The Imagery of *Eros* in Plato's *Phaedrus*." In *Eros in Ancient Greece*, ed. E. Sanders, C. Thumiger, C. Carey, and N. Lowe, 233–250. Oxford.

Caillois, R. 1988. *I demoni meridiani*. Turin.

Calame, C. 1997. *Choruses of Young Women in Ancient Greece*. Trans. D. Burton Collins and J. Orion. Lanham. (Revised version of *Les choeurs de jeunes filles en Grèce archaïque*, 1977, Rome).

Calasso, R. 2005. *La follia che viene dalle Ninfe*. Milan.

# Bibliography

Calder, W. M. 1984. "An Echo of Sappho Fragment 16 L.P. at Aeschylus, *Agamemnon* 403–419?" *Estudios Clásicos* 87:215–218.

Calogero, G. 1957. "Gorgias and the Socratic Principle: *Nemo Sua Sponte Peccat.*" *The Journal of Hellenic Studies* 77:12–17.

Cambiano, G. 1991. *Platone e le tecniche.* Rome.

———. 2007. "Problemi della memoria in Platone." In *Tracce nella mente: Teorie della memoria da Platone ai moderni,* ed. M. M. Sassi, 1–23. Pisa.

Cameron, A. 1978. *Plato's Affair with Tragedy.* Cincinnati.

Cantilena, M. 1995. "Il ponte di Nicanore." In *Struttura e storia dell'esametro greco,* ed. M. Fantuzzi and R. Pretagostini, 9–67. Rome.

———. 2007. "Due versi di Platone." *Quaderni Urbinati di Cultura Classica* 85:143–149.

Capra, A. 2000. "Il mito delle cicale e il motivo della bellezza sensibile nel *Fedro.*" *Maia* 52:225–247.

———. 2001. *Agon logon: Il Protagora di Platone tra eristica e commedia.* Milan.

———. 2003. "Dialoghi narrati e dialoghi drammatici in Platone." In Bonazzi and Trabattoni 2003:3–30. Milan.

———. 2004. "Poeti, eristi, e innamorati: il *Liside* nel suo contesto." In Trabattoni 2003–2004, II:173–231.

———. 2007a. "Stratagemmi comici da Aristofane a Platone. II: L'invettiva (*Cavalieri, Gorgia, Repubblica*)." *Stratagemmi* 3:7–45.

———. 2007b. "Dialettica e poesia: Platone e il 'mesmerismo' di Socrate." In *La poesia filosofica,* ed. A. Costazza, 29–44. Milan.

———. 2009. "Lyric Poetry." In *The Oxford Handbook of Hellenic Studies,* ed. G. R. Boys-Stones, B. Graziosi, and P. Vasunia, 454–468. Oxford.

———. 2010a. "Plato's Hesiod and the Will of Zeus. Philosophical Rhapsody in the *Timaeus* and the *Critias.*" In Boys-Stones and Haubold 2010:200–218.

———. 2010b. "Teatro e libertà. Mimesi, stupore e straniamento fra Brecht e Platone." In *La filosofia a teatro,* ed. A. Costazza, 113–131. Milan.

———. 2013. "'... *Sed magis amica Voluptas*': le lettere 'platoniche' di Aristeneto (1.3 e 1.18)." In *Lettere, mimesi, retorica: Studi sull'epistolografia greca di età imperiale e tardo antica,* ed. O. Vox, 375–385. Lecce.

Capra, A., and S. Martinelli Tempesta. 2011. "Riding from Elea to Athens (*via* Syracuse). The *Parmenides* and the Early Reception of Eleatism: Epicharmus, Cratinus and Plato." *Méthexis* 24:153–193.

Capuccino, C. 2005. *Filosofi e Rapsodi: Testo, traduzione e commento dello Ione platonico.* Bologna.

Carey, C., ed. 2007. *Lysiae Orationes cum Fragmentis.* Oxford.

Carson, A. 1986. *Bittersweet Eros.* Princeton.

Carter, R. E. 1967. "Plato and Inspiration." *Journal of the History of Philosophy* 5:111–121.

Caruso, A. 2013. *Akademia: Archeologia di una scuola filosofica ad Atene da Platone a Proclo (387 a.c.-485 d.C.)*. Athens.

Casali, C. 1989. "Le *Baccanti* e l'esempio di Elena." *Lexis* 3:37–41.

Casertano, G. 2007. *Paradigmi della verità in Platone*. Rome.

———, ed. 2011. *Il Fedro di Platone: Struttura e problematiche*. Naples.

Cassio, A. C. 1999. "Futuri dorici, dialetto di Siracusa e testo antico dei lirici greci." In *Katà diálekton: Atti del III colloquio internazionale di dialettologia greca (Napoli-Fiaiano d'Ischia, 25-28 settembre 1996)*, ed. A. C. Cassio, 187–214. Naples.

———. 2002. "Early Editions of the Greek Epics and Homeric Textual Criticism in the Sixth and Fifth Centuries BC." In *Omero tremila anni dopo*, ed. F. Montanari con la collaborazione di P. Ascheri, 105–136. Rome.

———. 2012. "Epica orale fluttuante e testo omerico fissato: Riflessi su Stesicoro (PMGF 222b 229 e 275)." *Seminari Romani di cultura greca* 1.2:253–260.

Castrucci, G. 2013. "Il lago dei cigni di Delo: Dal threnos al peana." *Acme* 66.1-2:53–78.

Cerasuolo, S. 1980. *La teoria del comico nel Filebo di Platone*. Naples.

Cerri, G. 1984-1985. "Dal canto citarodico al coro tragico: La *Palinodia* di Stesicoro, l'*Elena* di Euripide e le sirene." *Dioniso* 55:157–174.

———. 1991. *Platone sociologo della comunicazione*. Milan.

———. 2008. *La poetica di Platone: Una teoria della comunicazione*. Lecce.

Chapouthier, F. 1935. *Les Dioscures au service d'une déesse: Étude d'iconographie religieuse*. Paris.

Charalabopoulos, N. 2012. *Platonic Drama and Its Ancient Reception*. Cambridge.

Cherniss, H. F. 1945. *The Riddle of the Early Academy*. Berkeley.

Chvatík, I. 2001. "Aisopou ti geloion: Erster Beitrag zu einem Kommentar von Platons *Phaidon*." In Havlíček and Karfík 2001:174–192.

Cillo, P. 1993. "La 'cetra di Tamiri': Mito e realtà musicale." *Annali di Archeologia e Storia Antica* 15:205–243.

Clauss, J. J. 2003. "Once upon a Time on Cos: A Banquet with Pan on the Side in Theocritus *Idyll 7*." *Harvard Studies in Classical Philology* 101:289–302.

Clay, D. 1975. "The Tragic and the Comic Poet in the *Symposium*." *Arion* 2:238–261.

———. 1979. "Socrates' Prayer to Pan." In *Arktouros: Hellenic Studies Presented to Bernhard M. W. Knox on the Occasion of His 65th Birthday*, ed. G. W. Bowersock, 345–353. Berlin.

———. 1992. "Plato's First Words." In *Beginnings in Classical Literature*, ed. F. M. Dunn and T. Cole. *Yale Classical Studies* 29:113–129.

————. 1994. "The Origins of the Socratic Dialogue." In *The Socratic Movement*, ed. P. A. Waerdt, 23–47. Ithaca.

————. 2000. *Platonic Questions: Dialogues with the Silent Philosopher*. University Park.

————. 2004. *Archilochos Heros: The Cult of Poets in the Greek Polis*. Hellenic Studies 6. Washington, DC.

Clayman, D. L. 2009. *Timon of Phlius: Pyrrhonism into Poetry*. Berlin.

Clayton, E. W. 2008. "The Death of Socrates and the Life of Aesop." *Ancient Philosophy* 28:311–328.

Cohon, R. 1991–1992. "Hesiod and the Order and Naming of the Muses in Hellenistic Art." *Boreas* 14–15:67–83.

Compton, T. M. 2006. *Victim of the Muses: Poet as Scapegoat, Warrior, and Hero in Graeco-Roman and Indo-European Myth and History*. Hellenic Studies 11. Washington, DC.

Connor, W. R. 1998. "Seized by the Nymphs: Nympholepsy and Symbolic Expression in Classical Greece." *Classical Antiquity* 7:155–189.

Constantinidou, S. 2004. "Helen and Pandora: A Comparative Study with Emphasis on the *Eidolon* Theme as a Concept of *Eris*." *Dodone* (*Philologia*) 33.2:165–241.

————. 2008. *Logos into Mythos: The Case of Gorgias' Encomium of Helen*. Athens.

Conte, G. B. 1986. *The Rhetoric of Imitation: Genre and Poetic Memory in Virgil and Other Latin Poets*, with a foreword by Ch. Segal. Ithaca.

Cornelli, G. 2013. "Alcibiades' Connection: Plato's *Symposium* Rewriting the Case on Socrates and Alcibiades." *Proceedings of the X Symposium Platonicum on the Symposium*. II:240–248. http://platosociety.org/the-x-symposium-platonicum-platos-symposium-pisa/.

Cornford, F. M. 1935. *Plato's Theory of Knowledge*. London.

————. 1950. *The Unwritten Philosophy and Other Essays*.

Corradi, M. 2011. "Un poeta senza Muse: L'*aletheia* di Protagora." In *L'autore pensoso: Un seminario per Graziano Arrighetti sulla coscienza letteraria dei Greci*, ed. M. Tulli, 71–109. Pisa.

Corso, A. 2008. "The Portraiture of Archilochos." In Katsonopoulou, Petropoulos, and Katsarou 2008:267–288.

Coulter, J. A. 1964. "The Relation of the *Apology of Socrates* to Gorgias' *Defense of Palamedes* and Plato's Critique of Gorgianic Rhetoric." *Harvard Studies in Classical Philology* 68:269–303.

Crotty, K. 2009. *The Philosopher's Song: The Poets' Influence on Plato*. Lanham.

Cunha Corrêa, P. da. 2008. "Archilochos 35 IEG: The Muses Buy a Cow?" In Katsonopoulou, Petropoulos, and Katsarou 2008:191–202.

———. 2010. *Um bestiário arcaico: Fábulas e imagens de animais na poesia de Arquíloco.* Campinas.

Curbera, J. B., and M. Galaz. 1995. "*Platanus Caesariana.*" *Habis* 26:153–158.

D'Alfonso, F. 1994. "Stesicoro *versus* Omero nel *Fedro* platonico." *Rivista di Cultura Classica e Medioevale* 36:167–175.

———. 2006. *Stesicoro e la performance: Studio sulle modalità esecutive dei carmi stesicorei.* Rome.

Dalfen, J. 1974. *Plato und Poiesis: Die Auseinendersetzung mit der Dichtung bei Plato und seinen Zeitgenossen.* Munich.

———. 1987. Review of Gaiser 1984. *Grazer Beiträge* 14:298–302.

Dane, J. A. 1981. "Sappho fr. 16. An Analysis." *Eos* 79:185–192.

Danzig, G. 2010. *Apologizing for Socrates.* Lanham.

Daverio Rocchi, G. 2004. "La città di Fliunte nelle *Elleniche*: Caso politico e modello letterario." In *Il Peloponneso di Senofonte,* ed. G. Daverio Rocchi and M. Cavalli, 41–56. Milan.

Decleva Caizzi, F. 1986–1987. *Lettura del Fedone.* Milan.

de Boo, E. L. 2001. *Ὁ θεὸς πλάττων: Puns on Plato's Name in the Republic.* PhD diss., Brown University.

De Luise, F., 1997. *Platone. Fedro.* Bologna.

De Martino, F. 1984. *Stesicoro, con un lessico dialettale.* Bari.

De Martino, F., and O. Vox, 1996. *Lirica greca.* Bari.

De Sanctis, D. 2007. "Il canto di Elena: Osservazioni sul rapporto di Teocrito con Omero e con Esiodo nell'*Epitalamio.*" In *La cultura letteraria ellenistica: Persistenza, innovazione, trasmissione,* ed. R. Pretagostini and E. Dettori, 33–47. Rome.

Del Mastro, G. 2012. "Altri frammenti dal P. Herc. 1691: Filodemo, *Historia Academicorum e Di III.*" *Cronache Ercolanesi* 42:277–292.

Delatte, A. 1915. *Études sur la littérature pythagoricienne.* Paris.

Demos, M. 1999. *Lyric Quotation in Plato.* Lanham.

Derrida, J. 1972. *La dissémination.* Paris.

Despotopoulos, K. 1999. "Ὁ κατὰ Πλάτωνα Φιλόσοφος." *Πρακτικὰ τῆς Ἀκαδημίας Ἀθηνῶν* 74:94–112.

Destrée, P. 2012. "The Speech of Alcibiades (212c4–222b7)." In *Platon. Symposion,* ed. C. Horn, 191–205. Berlin.

Destrée, P., and F. G. Hermann, eds. 2011. *Plato and the Poets.* Leiden.

Detienne, M. 1957. "La légende pythagoricienne d'Hélène." *Revue de l'Histoire des Religions* 152:129–152.

———. 1962. *Homère, Hésiode et Pythagore: Poésie et philosophie dans le Pythagoreisme ancien.* Brussels.

———. 1972. *Les jardins d'Adonis: La mythologie des aromates en Grèce.* Paris.

Di Benedetto, V. 1987. *Saffo. Poesie.* Milan.

———. 2003. "Posidippo tra Pindaro e Callimaco." *Prometheus* 29:97–119.

Di Marco, M. 1980. "Una parodia di Saffo in Euripide (*Cycl.* 182–186)." *Quaderni Urbinati di Cultura Classica* 34:39–45.

———, ed. 1989. *Timone di Fliunte. Silli.* Rome.

Di Nino, M. 2010. *I fiori campestri di Posidippo: Ricerche sulla lingua e lo stile di Posidippo di Pella.* Göttingen.

Dickie, M. W. 1994. "Which Posidippus?" *Greek, Roman, and Byzantine Studies* 35:373–383.

Diès, A. 1927. *Autour de Platon: Essais de critique et d'histoire.* Paris.

Dodson-Robinson, E. 2010. "Helen's 'Judgment of Paris' and Greek Marriage Ritual in Sappho 16." *Arethusa* 43:1–20.

Dorandi, T., ed. 1991. *Filodemo. Storia dei filosofi. Platone e l'Accademia (P. Herc. 1021 e 164). Edizione, traduzione e commento.* Naples.

Dover, K., ed. 1993. *Aristophanes. Frogs.* Oxford.

Dubois, P. 1985. "Phallocentrism and Its Subversion in Plato's *Phaedrus.*" *Arethusa* 18:91–103.

———. 1995. *Sappho is Burning.* Chicago.

Dué, C., and G. Nagy. 2004. "Illuminating the Classics with the Heroes of Philostratus." In *Philostratus's Heroikos: Religion and Cultural Identity in the Third Century C.E.*, ed. E. Bradshwaw Aitken and J. K. Berenson Maclean, 49–73. Atlanta.

Dušanić, S. 1980. "The Political Context of Plato's *Phaedrus.*" *Rivista Storica dell'Antichità* 10:1–26.

———. 1992. "Athenian Politics in Plato's *Phaedrus.*" *Aevum* 66:23–39.

———. 1999. "Isocrates, the Chian Intellectuals and the Political Context of the *Euthydemus.*" *The Journal of Hellenic Studies* 119:1–16.

Ebert, T. 1993. "A Pre-Socratic Philosopher Behind the *Phaedrus*: Empedocles." *Revue de Philosophie Ancienne* 11:211–227.

———. 1994. *Sokrates als Pythagoreer und die Anamnesis in Platons Phaidon.* Mainz.

Edmonds, J. M. 1922. "Sappho's Book as Depicted on an Attic Vase." *Classical Quarterly* 16:1–14.

Edmonds, R. G. 2000. "Socrates the Beautiful: Role Reversal and Midwifery in Plato's *Symposium.*" *Transactions of the American Philological Association* 130:261–285.

Edmunds, L. 2006–2007. "Helen's Divine Origins." *Electronic Antiquity* 10.2:2–45.

———. 2011. "Isocrates' *Encomium of Helen* and the Cult of Helen and Menelaus at Therapne." *Electronic Antiquity* 14.2:21–35.

Ekroth, G. 2009. "The Cult of Heroes." In Albersmeier 2009:120–143.

Elias, J. A. 1984. *Plato's Defence of Poetry*. Albany.

Ercoles, M. 2012. "Tra monodia e coralità: Aspetti drammatici della performance di Stesicoro." *Dionysus ex machina* 3:1–22.

———, ed. 2013. *Stesicoro: Le testimonianze antiche*. Bologna.

Ercoles, M., and L. Fiorentini. 2011. "Giocasta tra Stesicoro (PMGF 222(B)) ed Euripide (*Fenicie*)." *Zeitschrift für Papyrologie und Epigraphik* 179:21–34.

Erler, M. 1987a. *Der Sinn der Aporien in den Dialogen Platons*. Berlin.

———. 1987b. Review of Gaiser 1984. *Gymnasium* 94:82–85.

———. 2011. "The Happiness of Bees: Affect and Virtue in the *Phaedo* and in the *Republic*." In *Inner Life and Soul: Psychē in Plato*, ed. M. Migliori, L. M. Napolitano Valditara, and A. Fermani, 59–71. Sankt Augustin.

Fantuzzi, M. 2008. "Teocrito e l'invenzione della tradizione letteraria bucolica." In *Phileuripidès: Mélanges offerts à François Jouan*, ed. D. Auger and J. Peigney, 569–588. Paris.

Federico, E., and A. Visconti, eds. 2001. *Epimenide cretese*. Naples.

Ferrari, Franco (1). 2004. "La sapienza acerba e il dio-tutto: Pindaro e Senofane." *Prometheus* 30:139–147.

———. 2010. *Sappho's Gift: The Poet and Her Community*. Ann Arbor.

Ferrari, Franco (2). 2012. "Quando, come e perché nacque il platonismo." *Athenaeum* 100:71–92.

Ferrari, G. R. F. 1987. *Listening to the Cicadas: A Study of Plato's Phaedrus*. Cambridge.

———. 1990. "Plato and Poetry." In *The Cambridge History of Literary Criticism*, I, ed. G. A. Kennedy, 92–148. Cambridge.

Flashar, H. 1974. "Aristoteles und Brecht." *Poetica* 6:17–37.

Foley, H. P. 1998. "'The Mother of the Argument': *Eros* and the Body in Sappho and Plato's *Phaedrus*." In *Parchments of Gender: Deciphering the Bodies of Antiquity*, ed. M. Wyke, 39–70. Oxford.

Ford, A. 1992. *Homer: The Poetry of the Past*. Ithaca.

———. 1997. "The Inland Ship: Problems in the Performance and Reception of Homeric Epic." In *Written Voices, Spoken Signs*, ed. E. Bakker and A. Kahane, 83–109. Cambridge, MA.

———. 2008. "The Beginnings of Dialogue. Socratic Discourses and Fourth-Century Prose." In Goldhill 2008:29–44.

———. 2010. "Σωκρατικοὶ λόγοι in Aristotle and Fourth-Century Theories of Genre." *Classical Philology* 105:231–235.

Fortenbaugh, W. W. 1966. "Plato's *Phaedrus* 235c3." *Classical Philology* 61:108–109.

Fowler, R. L. 2011. "*Mythos* and *Logos*." *The Journal of Hellenic Studies* 131:45–66.

Frame, D. 2009. *Hippota Nestor*. Hellenic Studies 37. Washington, DC.

# Bibliography

Fränkel, H. 1955. *Wege und Formen frühgriechischen Denkens.* Munich.

Frede, M. 1990. "An Empiricist View of Knowledge: Memorism." In *Companions to Ancient Thought: 1, Epistemology,* ed. S. Everson, 225–250. Cambridge.

Frei, H. W. 1974. *The Eclipse of Biblical Narrative: A Study in Eighteenth and Nineteenth Century Hermeneutics.* New Haven.

Friedländer, P. 1930. *Platon, II. Die platonische Schriften.* Berlin.

Fussi, A. 2006. "'As the Wolf Loves the Lamb': Need, Desire, Envy, and Generosity in Plato's *Phaedrus.*" *Epoché* 11:51-80.

———. 2008. "Tempo, desiderio, generazione. Diotima e Aristofane nel *Simposio* di Platone." *Rivista di Storia della Filosofia* 1:1–27.

Gaiser, K. 1959. *Protreptik und Paränese bei Platon: Untersuchungen zur Form des platonischen Dialogs.* Stuttgart.

———. 1968. *Platons ungeschriebene Lehre.* Stuttgart.

———. 1974. "Ein Komödienwitz über Platon." In *Musa iocosa: Arbeiten über Humor und Witz, Komik und Komödie der Antike; Andreas Thierfelder zum 70. Geburtstag am 15. Juni 1973,* ed. U. Reinhardt and K. Sallmann, 62-67. Hildesheim.

———. 1980. *Die Philosophenmosaik in Neapel: Eine Darstellung der platonischen Akademie.* Heidelberg.

———. 1983. "La biografia di Platone: Nuovi dati dal P. Herc. 1021." *Bollettino del Centro Internazionale per lo Studio dei Papiri Ercolanesi* 13:53–62.

———. 1984. *Platone come scrittore filosofico: Saggi sull'ermeneutica dei dialoghi platonici.* Naples.

———. 1988. *Philodems Academica: Die Berichte über Platon und die Alte Akademie in 2 herkulanensischen Papyri.* Stuttgart.

———. 1989. "Das Gold der Weisheit: Zum Gebet des Philosophen am Schluss des *Phaidros.*" *Rheinisches Museum für Philologie* 132:105–140.

———. 2004. *Gesammelte Schriften.* Hrsg. von T. A. Szlezák, unter Mitw. von K. H. Stanzel. Sankt Augustin.

Gastaldi, S. 1998. *Paideia / Mythologia.* In *Platone. La Repubblica, II,* ed. M. Vegetti, 333–392. Naples.

Gauthier, P. 1985. *Les cités grecques et leurs bienfaiteurs (IVe-Ier siècle avant J-C.): Contribution à l'histoire des institutions.* Paris.

Geddes, W. D., ed. 1863. *The Phaedo of Plato. Edited with Introduction and Notes.* London.

Genette, G. 1979. *Introduction à l'architexte.* Paris.

Gentili, B. 2006. *Poesia e pubblico nella Grecia antica: Da Omero al V secolo.* Updated edition. Milan.

Gerber, D. E. 2008. "Archilochos and Tradition." In Katsonopoulou, Petropoulos and Katsarou 2008:17–21.

Gerson, L. P. 2000. "Plato *Absconditus*." In *Who speaks for Plato? Studies in Platonic Anonymity*, ed. G. A. Press, 201–210. Lanham.

Giannantoni, G. 1985. Review of Gaiser 1984. *Elenchos* 6:202–207.

Giannopoulou, Z. 2010. "Enacting the Other, Being Oneself: The Drama of Rhetoric and Philosophy in Plato's *Phaedrus*." *Classical Philology* 105:146–161.

Giannoulidou, K. 1979. "Ποῦ ἔκειτο τὸ Σωκρατεῖον;" *Platon* 31:123–127.

Gilead, A. 1994. *The Platonic Odyssey: A Philosophical-Literary Inquiry into the Phaedo*. Amsterdam.

Gill, C. 1992. "Dogmatic Dialogue in *Phaedrus* 276–7?" In Rossetti 1992:156–172.

Giuliano, F. M. 2004. *Studi di letteratura greca*. Pisa.

———. 2005. *Platone e la poesia: Teoria della composizione e prassi della ricezione*. Sankt Augustin.

Glazebrook, A. 2005. "Reading Women: Book Rolls on Attic Vases." *Mouseion* 5:1–46.

Goldhill, S., ed. 2008. *The End of Dialogue in Antiquity*. Cambridge.

Gonzalez, F. J. 1998. *Dialectic and Dialogue: Plato's Practice of Philosophical Inquiry*. Evanston.

———. 2011. "The Hermeneutics of Madness: Poet and Philosopher in Plato's *Ion* and *Phaedrus*." In Destrée and Hermann 2011:93–110.

———. 2012. "Il bello nel *Simposio*: Sogno o visione?" *Méthexis* 25:51–70.

González Rendón, D. 2012. "La metafora dell'ombra: Sullo stile filosofico di Cicerone." *Camenae* 10:1–10.

Görgemanns, H. 1993. "Zur Deutung der Szene am Ilissos in Platons *Phaidros*." In *Philanthropia kai Eusebeia: Festschrift für Albrecht Dihle am 70. Geburstag*, ed. G. W. Most, H. Petersmann, and A. M. Ritter, 122–147. Göttingen.

Görler, W. 1988. "From Athens to Tusculum: Gleaning the Background of Cicero's *De Oratore*." *Rhetorica* 6:215–235.

Gostoli, A. 1995. "L'armonia frigia in Platone e Aristotele." In *Mousike: Metrica e ritmica greca in memoria di Giovanni Comotti*, ed. B. Gentili and F. Perusino, 133–144. Rome.

Gottfried, B. 1993. "Pan, the Cicadas, and Plato's Use of Myth in the *Phaedrus*." In *Plato's Dialogues: New Studies and Interpretations*, ed. G. A. Press, 179–195. Lanham.

Gow, A. S. F., ed. 1952. *Theocritus*. Cambridge.

Graziosi, B. 2002. *Inventing Homer*. Cambridge.

———. 2010. *Hesiod in Classical Athens: Rhapsodes, Orators, and Platonic Discourse*. In Boys-Stones and Haubold 2010:111–132.

Greco, E. 2011. *Topografia di Atene: Sviluppo urbano e monumenti dalle origini al III secolo d.C. Tomo 2. Colline sud-occidentali — Valle dell'Ilisso*. Athens.

Greene, E., and M. Skinner., eds. 2009. *The New Sappho on Old Age: Textual and Philosophical Issues*. Hellenic Studies 38. Classics@ Issue 4. Washington, DC.

## Bibliography

Grilli, A. 2013. *Storie di Venere e di Adone: Bellezza, genere, desiderio.* Milan.

Griswold, C. L. 1986. *Self-Knowledge in Plato's Phaedrus.* New Haven.

Grottanelli, C. 1992. "La parola rivelata." In *Lo spazio letterario della Grecia antica, I, La produzione e la circolazione del testo. 1: La polis*, ed. G. Cambiano, L. Canfora and D. Lanza, 219–264. Rome.

Gruber, W. E. 1987. "'Non-Aristotelian' Theater: Brecht's and Plato's Theories of Artistic Imitation." *Comparative Drama* 21:199–213.

Guastini, D. 2010. *Aristotele. Poetica.* Rome.

Gundert, H. 1968. *Der platonische Dialog.* Heidelberg.

Guthrie, W. K. C. 1975. *Socrates.* Cambridge.

Gutzwiller, K. 1991. *Theocritus' Pastoral Analogies.* Madison.

Hackforth, R. 1952. *Plato's Phaedrus.* New York.

———. 1955. *Plato's Phaedo.* Cambridge.

Hadot, P. 2005. *What is Ancient Philosophy?* Trans. J. M. Chase. Cambridge, MA.

Halliwell, S. 2000. "The Subjection of *Muthos* to *Logos*: Plato's Citation of the Poets." *Classical Quarterly* 50:94–112.

———. 2002a. *The Aesthetics of Mimesis: Ancient Texts and Modern Problems.* Oxford.

———. 2002b. Review of Büttner 2000. *Zeitschfrit für philosophische Forschung* 56:476–480.

———. 2008. *Greek Laughter: A Study of Cultural Psychology from Homer to Early Christianity.* Cambridge.

———. 2011a. "Antidotes and Incantations: Is There a Cure for Poetry in Plato's *Republic*?" In Destrée and Hermann 2011:241–266.

———. 2011b. *Between Ecstasy and Truth: Interpretations of Greek Poetics from Homer to Longinus.* Oxford.

Halperin, D. M. 1992. "Plato and the Erotics of Narrativity." *Oxford Studies in Ancient Philosophy* suppl. vol. 1992:93–129.

Hardie, A. 1997. "Philitas and the Plane Tree." *Zeitschrift für Papyrologie und Epigraphik* 19:21–36.

———. 2013. "Empedocles and the Muse of *Agathos Logos*." *American Journal of Philology* 134 2:209–246.

Harvey, F. D. 1966. "Literacy in the Athenian Democracy." *Revue des Études Grecques* 79:585–635.

Haslam, M. W. 1976. "A Note on Plato's Unfinished Dialogues." *American Journal of Philology* 97:336–339.

———. 1991. "Kleitias, Stesichoros, and the Jar of Dionysos." *Transactions of the American Philological Association* 121:35–45.

Haubold, J. 2010. "Shepherd, Farmer, Poet, Sophist: Hesiod on His Own Reception." In Boys-Stones and Haubold 2010:11–30.

Havelock, E. A. 1963. *Preface to Plato.* Oxford.

———. 1978. *The Greek Concept of Justice: From Its Shadow in Homer to Its Substance in Plato*. Cambridge, MA.

Havlíček A., and F. Karfík, eds. 2001. *Plato's Phaedo: Proceedings of the Second Symposium Platonicum Pragense*. Prague.

Heath, M. 1989. "The Unity of Plato's *Phaedrus*." *Oxford Studies in Ancient Philosophy* 7:151–173 and 189–191.

———. 2013. *Ancient Philosophical Poetics*. Cambridge.

Heitsch, E. 1993. *Platon. Phaidros*. Göttingen.

Henderson Collins, J., II. 2012. "Prompts for Participation in Early Philosophical Texts." In *Orality, Literacy and Performance*, ed. E. Minchin, 151–182. Leiden.

Herder, A., ed. 2012. *Callimachus. Aetia. Introduction, Text, Translation and Commentary*. Oxford.

Herrington, J. 1985. *Poetry into Drama: Early Tragedy and the Greek Poetic Tradition*. Berkeley.

Herzog, R. 1912. *Die Umschrift der älteren griechischen Literatur in das ionische Alphabet*. Basel.

Hoffmann, H. 1988. "The Cicada and the *Omphalos*: An Iconological Excursion." *Antiquity* 62:744–749.

Hollis, A. S. 1996. "Heroic Honours for Philetas?" *Zeitschrift für Papyrologie und Epigraphik* 110:56–62.

Horky, P. S. 2013. *Plato and Pythagoreanism*. Oxford.

Huffman, C. A. 2010. "Pythagoreanism." In *The Stanford Encyclopedia of Philosophy* (Summer 2010 Edition). http://plato.stanford.edu/archives/sum2010/entries/pythagoreanism.

Hunter, R. 1996. *Theocritus and the Archaeology of Greek Poetry*. Cambridge.

———. 2001. "The Poet Unleaved. Simonides and Callimachus." In *The New Simonides: Contexts of Praise and Desire*, ed. D. Boedeker and D. Sider, 242–254. Oxford.

———. 2012. *Plato and the Traditions of Ancient Literature: The Silent Stream*. Cambridge.

Huxley, G. L. 1960. "A Poem of the Homeridae." *Greek, Roman, and Byzantine Studies* 3:29–30.

Ieranò, G. 2006. "Eschilo in Euripide." *Lexis* 24:77–93.

Imhoof-Blumer, F., and P. Gardner. 1886. "Numismatic Commentary on Pausanias, Part II. Books III–VII." *The Journal of Hellenic Studies* 7:57–113.

Immerwahr, H. R. 1964. "Book Rolls on Attic Vases." In *Classical, Mediaeval, and Renaissance Studies in Honor of B. L. Ullman: 1*, ed. C. Henderson Jr., 17–48. Rome.

———. 1973. "More Book Rolls on Attic Vases." *Antike Kunst* 16:143–147.

# Bibliography

Ioppolo, A. M. 1999. "Socrate e la conoscenza delle cose d'amore." *Elenchos* 20:53–74.

Isnardi Parente, M., ed. 2002. *Platone. Lettere.* Milan.

Jackson, B. D. 1971. "The Prayers of Socrates." *Phronesis* 16:14–37.

Jarratt, S. C. 2002. "Sappho's Memory." *Rhetoric Society Quarterly* 32:11–43.

Jedrkiewcsz, S. 2011. "The Platonic Socrates and the 'Science of Nature': A Parallel Reading of the *Apology* and the *Phaedo.*" *Lexis* 19:173–197.

Jesi, F. 1961. "Aspetti isiaci di Elena nell'apologetica pitagorica." *Aegyptus* 41:152–158.

Joly, R. 1970. "Platon ou Pythagore? Héraclide Pontique, fr. 87-88. Wehrli." In *Hommages à Marie Delcourt*, 136–148. Brussels.

Jordan, D. 2003. "A Letter from the Banker Pasion." In *Lettered Attica: A Day of Attic Epigraphy*, ed. D. Jordan and J. Traill, 24–39. Athens.

Jouët-Pastré, E. 2006. *Le jeu et le sérieux dans les Lois de Platon.* Sankt Augustin.

Kahn, C. 1996. *Plato and the Socratic Dialogue: The Philosophical Use of a Literary Form.* Cambridge.

Kambylis, A. 1965. *Die Dichterweihe und ihre Symbolik: Untersuchungen zu Hesiodos, Kallimachos, Properz, und Ennius.* Heidelberg.

Kamen, D. 2013. "The Manumission of Socrates: A Rereading of Plato's *Phaedo.*" *Classical Antiquity* 32:78–100.

Katsonopoulou, D, I. Petropoulos and S. Katsarou, eds. 2008. *Archilochos and his Age: Proceedings of the Second International Conference on the Archaeology of Paros and the Cyclades, Paroikia, Paros, 7-9 October 2005.* Athens.

Kelly, A. 2007. "Stesikhoros and Helen." *Museum Helveticum* 64:1–21.

Kennedy, J. B. 2011. *The Musical Structure of Plato's Dialogues.* Durham.

Kerferd, G. B. 1986. "Le sophiste vu par Platon: Un philosophe imparfait." In *Positions de la sophistique*, ed. B. Cassin, 13–25. Paris.

Kivilo, M. 2010. *Early Greek Poets' Lives: The Shaping of the Tradition.* Leiden.

Klooster, J. 2011. *Poetry as Window and Mirror: Positioning the Poet in Hellenistic Poetry.* Leiden.

Kobiliri, P. 1998. *A Stylistic Commentary on Hermesianax.* Amsterdam.

Koch, D., I. Männlein-Robert, and N. Weidtmann, eds. 2012. *Platon und die Mousiké.* Tübingen.

Koniaris, G. L. 1967. "On Sappho, fr. 16 L-P." *Hermes* 95:257–268.

Kraus, M. 2006. "Nothing to Do with Truth? Εἰκός in Early Greek Rhetoric and Philosophy." *Papers on Rhetoric* 7:129–150.

Kurke, L. 2006. "Plato, Aesop, and the Beginning of Mimetic Prose." *Representation* 94:6–52.

———. 2011. *Aesopic Conversations: Popular Traditions, Cultural Dialogue, and the Invention of Greek Prose.* Princeton.

Kuttner, A. L. 1999. "Culture and History at Pompey's Museum." *Transactions of the American Philological Association* 129:343–373.

Labarbe, J. 1949. *L'Homère de Platon*. Paris.

———. 1994 "Socrate épique dans le *Phèdre* de Platon." *L'Antiquité Classique* 63:225–230.

Lacourse Munteanu, D. 2011. "Comic Emotions: Shamelessness and Envy (Schadenfreude); Moderate Emotion." In *Emotion, Genre and Gender in Classical Antiquity*, ed. D. Lacourse Munteanu, 89–112. Bristol.

Lafrance, Y. 1992. "F. Schleiermacher lecteur du *Phèdre* de Platon." In Rossetti 1992:209–213.

Lamberton, R. 1992. "The Neoplatonists and the Spiritualization of Homer." In *Homer's Ancient Readers: The Hermeneutics of Greek Epic's Earliest Exegetes*, ed. L. Lamberton and J. J. Keaney, 115–133. Princeton.

Lang, M., ed. 1976. *Graffiti and Dipinti*. Athenian Agora 21. Princeton.

Lapini, W. 1999. "Panezio e l'altro' Socrate (T 144 Alesse)." *Elenchos* 20:345–358.

———. 2003. *Studi di filologia filosofica greca*. Florence.

Laplace, M. 2011. "Des rapports du *Phèdre* de Platon avec l'*Éloge d'Hélène* et le *Panégyrique* d'Isocrate." *Hermes* 139:165–178.

Lardinois, A. 2008. "'Someone, I Say, Will Remember Us': Oral Memory in Sappho's Poetry." In *Orality, Literacy, Memory in the Ancient Greek and Roman World*, ed. E. Anne Mackay, 79–96. Leiden.

Larson, J. 2001. *Greek Nymphs: Myth, Cult, Lore*. Oxford.

Lasserre, F. 1967. "*Mimésis* et mimétique." *Dioniso* 41:245–266.

———. 1987. "Platon, Homère et la cité." In Servais, Hackens, and Servais-Soyrez 1987:3–14.

Latona, M. 2004. "The Tale is not My Own (οὐκ ἐμὸς ὁ μῦθος): Myth and Recollection in Plato." *Apeiron* 37:181–210.

Lavecchia, S. 2006. *Una via che conduce al divino: La "homoiosis theo" nella filosofia di Platone*. Milan.

Lazzeri, M. 2002. "Imerio e la *Palinodia* di Stesicoro." *Seminari Romani di cultura greca* 5.2:169–179.

Lebeck, A. 1972. "The Central Myth of Plato's *Phaedrus*." *Greek, Roman and Byzantine Studies* 13:267–269.

Lehnus, L. 1975. "Note stesicoree: I poemetti minori (frr. 277-9 PMG)." *Studi Classici e Orientali* 24:191–196.

Lelli, E. 2001. "La polivalenza simbolica dell'opposizione asino / cicala nel prologo degli *Aitia* di Callimaco (fr. 1. 29 ss. Pf.)." *Seminari Romani di cultura greca* 4. 2:245–252.

Le Moli, A. 2012. "*Mimesis* e rappresentazione: Dal platonismo all'ermeneutica." In *Ermeneutica e filosofia antica*, ed. F. Trabattoni and M. Bergomi, 35–62. Milan.

# Bibliography

Leszl, W. 1985. "Il potere della parola in Gorgia e Platone." *Siculorum Gymnasium* 38:65–80.

———. 2006. "Plato's Attitude to Poetry and the Fine Arts, and the Origins of Aesthetics, Part II." *Études Platoniciennes* 2:285-351.

———. 2007. "Plato's Attitude to Poetry and the Fine Arts, and the Origins of Aesthetics, Part III." *Études Platoniciennes* 3:245–334.

Lévinas, E. 1969. *Totality and Infinity*. Trans. A. Lingis. Pittsburgh.

Lincoln, B. 1997. "Competing Discourses: Rethinking the Prehistory of *Mythos* and *Logos*." *Arethusa* 30:341-368.

Lippold, G. 1956. *Die Skulpturen des Vaticanischen Museums*. Berlin.

Livrea, E. 1968. "Un'eco saffica in Apollonio Rodio." *Helikon* 8:447.

———. 2004. "Lycidas and Apollo in Theocritus' *Thalysia*." *Eikasmos* 15:161–167.

———. 2012. "Simonidea." *Zeitschrift für Papyrologie und Epigraphik* 182:45–54.

Lloyd-Jones, H. 1963. "The Seal of Posidippus." *The Journal of Hellenic Studies* 83:75–99.

Lombardi, M. 2009. "La secolarizzazione dell'arte nella poetica teocritea." In *Semeion philias: Studi di letteratura greaca offerti ad Agostino Masaracchia*, ed. M. Di Marco and E. Tagliaferro, 147–170. Rome.

Lombardo, G. 2003. "Sublime et *deinótès* dans l'antiquité gréco-latine." *Revue Philosophique de la France et de l'Étranger* 193:403–420.

Long, A. 2008. "Plato's Dialogues and a Common Rationale for Dialogue Form." In Goldhill 2008: 45–59.

Loraux, N. 1995. *The Experiences of Tiresias: The Feminine and the Greek Man*. Princeton.

Lucarini, C. M. 2010–2011. "Osservazioni sulla prima circolazione delle opere di Platone e sulle *trilogiae* di Aristofane di Bisanzio (D.L. 3: 56-66)." *Hyperboreus* 16–17:346–361.

Luccioni, P. 1997. "Un éloge d'Hélène? (Théocrite, Id. XVIII, v. 29-31, Gorgias et Stésichore)." *Revue des Études Grecques* 110:622–626.

Ludwig, W. 1963. "Plato's Love Epigrams." *Greek, Roman and Byzantine Studies* 4:59–82.

Lynch, J. 1972. *Aristotle's School: A Study of a Greek Educational Institution*. Berkeley.

Mader, M. 1977. *Das Problem des Lachens und der Komödie bei Platon*. Stuttgart.

Mambrini, F. 2011. "Diventare eroe: Note per una lettura antropologica di Sofocle, *Aiace* 642-92." *Mètis* 9:165–191.

Manieri, A. 1998. *L'immagine poetica nella teoria degli antichi: Phantasia ed enargeia*. Pisa.

Männlein-Robert, I. 2012. "Die Musenkunst des Philosophen oder Sokrates und die Zikaden in Platons *Phaidros*." In Koch, Männlein-Robert, and Weidtmann 2012:83–103.

Marchiandi, D. 2011. "L'Ilisso e i culti lungo le sue rive." In Greco 2011:480–483.

Marignac, A. de. 1951. *Imagination et dialectique: Essai sur l'expression du spirituel par l'image dans les dialogues de Platon.* Paris.

Marino, S. 2011. "*Quot capita tot sententiae*: Il corpo del discorso tra fisiologia delle parti e genesi del senso in *Fedro* 264C2–5." In Casertano 2011:125–137.

Martin, R. 1989. *The Language of Heroes: Speech and Performance in the Iliad.* Ithaca.

Martinelli Tempesta, S. 1999. "Nota a Saffo, fr. 16: 12-13 V. (P.Oxy. 1231)." *Maia* 69:7–14.

———, ed. 2003a. *Platone. Liside. Edizione critica, traduzione e commento filologico.* Vol. 1 of Trabattoni 2003–2004.

———. 2003b. "Sul significato di δεύτερος πλοῦς nel *Fedone* di Platone." In Bonazzi and Trabattoni 2003:89–125. Milan.

Maslov, B. 2012. "The Real Life of the Genre of *Prooimion*." *Classical Philology* 107:191–205.

Massimilla, G. 1990. "*L'Elena* di Stesicoro quale premessa ad una ritrattazione." *La Parola del Passato* 45:370–381.

———, ed. 1996. *Callimaco. Aitia. Libri primo e secondo. Introduzione, testo critico, traduzione e commento.* Pisa.

Masullo, R., ed. 1985. *Marino di Neapoli. Vita di Proclo. Testo critico, introduzione, traduzione e commentario.* Naples.

Matelli, E., ed. 2013. *Prassifane. Testimonianze e frammenti. Filosofia e grammatica in età ellenistica.* Milan.

McAdon, B. 2004. "Plato's Denunciation of Rhetoric in the *Phaedrus*." *Rhetoric Review* 23:21–39.

McPherran, M. L. 2012. "Socrates and Aesop in Plato's *Phaedo*." *Apeiron* 45:50–60.

Méndez, E. A., and A. Angeli, eds. 1992. *Filodemo: Testimonianze su Socrate.* Naples.

Meriani, A. 2007. "Il *Thamyras* di Sofocle." In Volpe Cacciatore 2007:37–70.

Mesturini, A. 2001. *Ryhtmos: Percorsi (alternativi) della tradizione classica.* Genoa.

Michelini, A. N., ed. 2003. *Plato as Author: The Rhetoric of Philosophy.* Leiden.

Migliori, M., L. Napolitano Valditara, and A. Fermani, eds. 2007. *Interiorità e anima: La psychè in Platone.* Milan.

Miller, S. G. 2009. *The Berkeley Plato: From Neglected Relic to Ancient Treasure.* Berkeley.

Mionnet, T. E. 1829. *Description de médailles antiques, grecques et romaines.* Suppl. T. IV. Paris.

Monoson, S. 2000. *Plato's Democratic Entanglements.* Princeton.

Montes Cala, J. G. 2009. "El Diálogo platónico y los modos de enunciación del idilio teocriteo." *Cuadernos de Filología Clásica: Estudios griegos e indoeuropeos* 19:151–162.

Moors, K. F. 1978. "Plato's Use of Dialogue." *Classical World* 72:77–93.

# Bibliography

Morgan, K. A. 2010. "Inspiration, Recollection, and *Mimesis* in Plato's *Phaedrus*." In *Ancient Models of Mind: Studies in Human and Divine Rationality*, ed. A. Nightingale and D. Sedley, 45–63. Cambridge.

Moscadi, A. 2007. "*L'idillio* 7 di Teocrito: La doppia investitura." *Prometheus* 33:214–230.

Moss, J. 2012. "Soul-leading: The Unity of the *Phaedrus*, Again." *Oxford Studies in Ancient Philosophy* 43:1–23.

Most, G. W. 1981. "Sappho Fr. 16.6-7 L-P." *Classical Quarterly* 31:11–17.

———. 1993. "A Cock for Asclepius." *Classical Quarterly* 43:96–111.

———. 1994. "Simonides' Ode to Scopas in Its Contexts." In *Modern Critical Theory and Classical Literature*, ed. I. J. F. de Jong and J. P. Sullivan, 127–152. Leiden.

———. 1996. "Reflecting Sappho." In *Re-Reading Sappho: Reception and Transmission*, ed. E. Greene, 11–35. Berkeley.

Motte, A. 1963. "Le pré sacré de Pan et des nymphes dans le *Phèdre* de Platon." *L'Antiquité Classique* 32:460–476.

———. 1973. *Prairies et jardins de la Grèce antique*. Brussels.

Mouze, L. 1998. "La dernière tragédie de Platon." *Revue de Philosophie Ancienne* 16:79–101.

Murley, C. 1940. "Plato's *Phaedrus* and Theocritan Pastoral." *Transactions of the American Philological Association* 1940:281–295.

Murr, J. 1969. *Die Pflanzenwelt in der Griechischen Mythologie*. Groningen.

Murray, P. 1996. *Plato on Poetry: Ion, Republic 376e-398b, Republic 595-608b*. Cambridge.

———. 1999. "What is a *Muthos* for Plato?" In *From Myth to Reason? Studies in the Development of Greek Thought*, ed. R. Buxton, 251–262. Oxford.

———. 2005. "The Muses: Creativity Personified?" In *Personification in the Greek World: From Antiquity to Byzantium*, ed. E. Stafford and J. Herrin, 147–159. London.

Nagy, G. 1990. *Pindar's Homer: The Lyric Possession of an Epic Past*. Baltimore.

———. 1999. *The Best of the Achaeans: Concepts of the Hero in Archaic Greek Poetry*. Baltimore.

———. 2002. *Plato's Rhapsody and Homer's Music: The Poetics of the Panathenaic Festival in Classical Athens*. Cambridge, MA.

———. 2007. "Did Sappho and Alcaeus Ever Meet? Symmetries of Myth and Ritual in Performing the Songs of Ancient Lesbos." In *Literatur und Religion 1. Wege zu einer mythisch-rituellen Poetik bei den Griechen*, ed. A. Bierl, R. Lämmle, and K. Wesselmann, 211–269. Berlin.

———. 2008. "Convergences and Divergences between God and Hero in the Mnesiepes Inscription of Paros." In Katsonopoulou, Petropoulos, and Katsarou 2008:259–265.

————. 2009a. *Homer the Classic.* Hellenic Studies 36. Washington, DC.

————. 2009b. "Hesiod and the Ancient Biographical Traditions." In *Brill's Companion to Hesiod,* ed. F. Montanari, A. Rengakos, and C. Tsagalis, 271–311. Leiden.

————. 2011. "Diachrony and the Case of Aesop." *Classics@* 9: Defense Mechanisms in Interdisciplinary Approaches to Classical Studies and Beyond. http://nrs.harvard.edu/urn-3:hul.ebook:CHS_Classicsat.

Nails, D. 2002. *The People of Plato.* Indianapolis.

Napolitano Valditara, L., ed. *Antichi e nuovi dialoghi di sapienti e di eroi: Etica, linguaggio, dialettica fra tragedia greca e filosofia.* Trieste.

Narcy, M. 2007. "Che cosa è un dialogo socratico?" In *Il Socrate dei dialoghi,* ed. G. Mazzarra, M. Narcy, and L. Rossetti, 21–32. Bari.

————. 2008. "Socrate nel discorso di Alcibiade (Platone, *Simposio* 215a–222b)." In Rossetti and Stavru 2008:287–304.

Nehamas, A. 1990. "Eristic, Antilogic, Sophistic, Dialectic: Plato's Demarcation of Philosophy from Sophistry." *History of Philosophy Quarterly* 7:3–16.

Nelson, M. 2000. "The Lesser Mysteries in Plato's *Phaedrus.*" *Échos du monde classique* 19:25–43.

Nesselrath, H-G., ed. 2006. *Platon. Kritias. Platon Werke* VII, 4, 150–151. Göttingen.

Nicholson, G. 1999. *Plato's Phaedrus: The Philosophy of Love.* West Lafayette, IN.

Nicolai, R. 2004. *Studi su Isocrate: La comunicazione letteraria nel IV sec. a.C. e i nuovi generi della prosa.* Rome.

————. 2012. "Erodoto e la tragedia di Troia: A proposito di 2.112–120." In *Harmonia: Scritti di filologia classica in onore di Angelo Casanova,* ed. G. Bastianini, W. Lapini, and M. Tulli, 633–649. Florence.

Nietzsche, F. 1995. *Werke.* Kritische Gesamtausgabe, begründet von Giorgio Colli und Mazzarino Montinari, weitergeführt von Volfgang Müller-Lauter und Karl Pestalozzi, II,4 *Vorlesungsaufzeichnungen* (WS 1871/72 - WS 1874/75). Berlin.

Nightingale, A. 1995. *Genres in Dialogue: Plato and the Construct of Philosophy.* Cambridge.

Nikulin, D., 2012. *The Other Plato: The Tübingen Interpretation of Plato's Inner-Academic Teachings.* New York.

Nobili, C. 2011. *L' 'Inno omerico a Ermes' e le tradizioni locali.* Milan.

Nonvel Pieri, S. 2002. "Le Muse in dialogo: Ancora qualche spunto su tragedia e filosofia." In Napolitano Valditara 2002: 77–99.

Norden, E. 1923. *Die antike Kunstprosa.* I. 4th ed. Leipzig.

North, H. 1988. "Socrates *Deinos Legein.*" In *Language and the Tragic Hero: Essays on Greek Tragedy in Honor of Gordon M. Kirkwood,* ed. P. Pucci, 121–130. Atlanta.

Notomi, N. 2008. "The Birth of the Philosopher: People around Socrates." In Rossetti and Stavru 2008:355–370.

Nucci, M. 2013. "La bellezza dell'amante: La strada più lunga che Alcibiade non vide e i grandi misteri che finì per profanare." *Proceedings of the X Symposium Platonicum on the Symposium.* II:135–142. http://platosociety. org/the-x-symposium-platonicum-platos-symposium-pisa/.

Nuesser, O. 1991. *Albins Prolog und die Dialogtheorie des Platonismus.* Stuttgart.

Nussbaum, M. 1986. *The Fragility of Goodness.* New York.

Olson, D. S., ed. 2007. *Broken Laughter: Select Fragments of Greek Comedy.* Oxford.

Ornaghi, M. 2009. *La lira, la vacca e le donne insolenti: Contesti di ricezione e promozione della figura e della poesia di Archiloco dall'arcaismo all'ellenismo.* Alessandria.

Pace, C. 2008. "Tragedia, ἔκπληξις e ἀπάτη nell'anonima *Vita di Eschilo*." *Seminari Romani di cultura greca* 11.2:229–254.

Pache, C. O. 2011. *A Moment's Ornament: The Poetics of Nympholepsy in Ancient Greece.* Oxford.

Paganelli, L. 1989. "Il dramma satiresco: Spazio, tematiche e messa in scena." *Dioniso* 59.2:213–82.

Page, D. 1955. *Sappho and Alcaeus.* Oxford.

Pagliara, A. 2000. "Musica e politica nella speculazione platonica: Considerazioni intorno all'*ethos* del modo frigio (*Resp.* III 10:399a–c)." In *Synaulía: Cultura musicale in Grecia e contatti mediterranei,* ed. A. C. Cassio, D. Musti, and L. E. Rossi, 157–216. Naples.

Palumbo, L. 2008. *Μίμησις: Rappresentazione, teatro e mondo nei dialoghi di Platone e nella Poetica di Aristotele.* Naples.

———. 2011. "*Mimesis* ed *enthousiasmos* in Platone: Appunti sul *Fedro.*" In Casertano 2011:157–172.

Panno, G. 2007. *Dionisiaco e alterità nelle Leggi di Platone: Ordine del corpo e automovimento nell'anima della città tragedia.* Milan.

Papillon, T. L. 1995–1996. "Isocrates on Gorgias and Helen: The Unity of the *Helen*." *The Classical Journal* 91:377–391.

Pasquali, G. 1938. *Le lettere di Platone.* Florence.

Patzer, A. 1985. "Sokrates und Iphikrates." *Würzburger Jahrbücher für die Altertumswissenschaft* 11:45–62.

Pavese, C. O. 1972. *Tradizioni e generi poetici della Grecia arcaica.* Rome.

Pearce, T. E. V. 1988. "The Function of the *Locus Amoenus* in Theocritus' Seventh Poem." *Rheinisches Museum für Philologie* 113:276–304.

Pedrique, N. 2012. "Πεπαίσθω μετρίως ἡμῖν: Komödien-Exodoi und das Ende des Phaidros (278b7)." *Rivista di Filologia e di Istruzione Classica* 140:87–114.

Peixoto, M. 2011. "La psicagogica del *Fedro.*" In Casertano 2011:173–206.

Pelliccia, H. 1992. "Sappho 16, Gorgias' *Helen*, and the Preface to Herodotus' *Histories*." *Yale Classical Studies* 29:63–84.

Pelosi, F. 2010. *Plato on Music, Soul and Body.* Cambridge.

Pender, E. E. 2007. "Sappho and Anacreon in Plato's *Phaedrus*." *Leeds International Classical Studies* 6.4:1–57.

———. 2011. "A Transfer of Energy: Lyric *Eros* in *Phaedrus*." In Destrée and Hermann 327–348.

Penella, R. J. P. 2007. *Man and the World: The Orations of Himerius.* Berkeley.

Perine, M. 2011. "Il *Fedro*: Un invito alla filosofia." In Casertano 2011:207–221.

Peterson, S. 2011. *Socrates and Philosophy in the Dialogues of Plato.* Cambridge.

Petropoulos, J. C. B. 1994. *Heat and Lust: Hesiod's Midsummer Festival Scene Revisited.* London.

Petrucci, F. 2013. "Platone, la virtù è un gioco di specchi: Guardare il filosofo con gli occhi del φιλότιμος." In *Proceedings of the X Symposium Platonicum on the Symposium* I, 389–393. http://platosociety.org/the-x-symposium-platonicum-platos-symposium-pisa/.

Philip, A. 1981. "Récurrences thématiques et topologie dans le *Phèdre* de Platon." *Revue de Métaphysique et de Morale* 86:452–476.

Pieper, K. 2000. *Enthusiasm and Divine Madness: On the Platonic Dialogue Phaedrus.* New York.

Pinnoy, M. 1986–1987. "De mythe van de cicaden (Plato, *Phaedrus*, 258e–259d)." *Kleio* 16:107–113.

Pinnoy, M. 1991. "*Platonica minora*: Due miti originali nel *Fedro* di Platone." *Quaderni Urbinati di Cultura Classica* 37:29–43.

Pisani, V. 1928. "Elena e l'Εἴδωλον." *Rivista di Filologia e di Istruzione Classica* 56:489–499.

Pizzone, A. 2009. "*Ex epiboules phantazesthai*: Dal divino inganno di Timeo alla *phantasia* plotiniana." *Methexis* 22:127–150.

Pounder, R. L. 1975. *The Origin and Meaning of ΘΕΟΙ in Greek Inscription Headings.* PhD diss., Brown University.

———. 1984. "The Origin and Meaning of ΘΕΟΙ as Inscription Heading." In *Studies Presented to Sterling Dow on His Eightieth Birthday* (Greek, Roman, and Byzantine Monographs 10), ed. K. J. Rigsby, 243–250. Durham.

Power, T. 2010. *The Culture of Kitharôidia.* Hellenic Studies 15. Washington, DC.

Prioux, E. 2007. *Regards alexandrins: Histoire et théorie des arts dans l'épigramme hellénistique.* Leuven.

Privitera, G. A. 1967. "Su una nuova interpretazione di Saffo fr. 16 L-P." *Quaderni Urbinati di Cultura Classica* 4:182–187.

Prontera, F. 1974. "Echecrate di Fliunte un Pitagorico?" *Atti e memorie dell'Accademia Toscana di scienze e lettere La Colombaria* 39:1–19.

# Bibliography

Puelma, M. 1960. "Die Dichterbegegnung in Theokrits *Thalysien.*" *Museum Helveticum* 17:144–164.

Quarch, C. 1994. "Platons Konzept des *Diamythologein*: Philosophie und *Mythos* in Platons *Phaidon.*" In *Mythos zwischen Philosophie und Theologie*, ed. E. Rudolf, 113–141 and 212–221. Darmstadt.

Race, W. H. 1989–1990. "Sappho, Fr. 16 L-P. and Alkaios, Fr. 42 L-P. Romantic and Classical Strains in Lesbian Lyric." *Classical Journal* 85:16–33.

Rayor, D. J. 2005. "The Power of Memory in Erinna and Sappho." In *Women Poets in Ancient Greece and Rome*, ed. E. Greene, 59–71. Norman.

Reale, G. 1998. *Platone. Fedro.* Milan.

Regali, M. 2010. "Hesiod in the *Timaeus*: The Demiurge Addresses the Gods." In Boys-Stones and Haubold 2010:259–275.

———. 2012. *Il poeta e il demiurgo: Teoria e prassi della produzione letteraria nel Timeo e nel Crizia di Platone.* Sankt Augustin.

Repath, I. 2010. "Plato in Petronius: Petronius in Platanona." *Classical Quarterly* 60:577–595.

Reydams-Schils, G. 2011. "Myth and Poetry in the *Timaeus.*" In Destrée and Hermann 2011:349–360.

Ridgway, B. S. 1998. "An Issue of Methodology: Anakreon, Perikles, Xanthippos." *American Journal of Archaeology* 102:717–738.

Rijksbaron, A., ed. 2007. *Plato. Ion, or On the Iliad. Edited with Introduction and Commentary.* Leiden.

Rinella, M. A. 2000. "Supplementing the Ecstatic: Plato, the Eleusinian Mysteries and the *Phaedrus.*" *Polis* 17:61–78.

Robin, L. 1986. "Notice." In *Platon. Phèdre*, vii–ccxxv. Paris.

Rocconi, E. 2012. "The Aesthetic Value of Music in Platonic Thought." In *Aesthetic Value in Classical Antiquity*, ed. I. Sluiter and R. M. Rosen, 113–132. Leiden.

Roochnik, D. 2001. "The Deathbed Dream of Reason: Socrates' Dream in the *Phaedo.*" *Arethusa* 34:239–258.

Roscalla, F. 1997. "Lisia, Fedro e Isocrate: L'Atene di fine V secolo e la messin-scena platonica." *Quaderni di Storia* 23:59–85.

———. 1998. "Strategie letterarie a confronto: Isocrate e Platone." *Athenaeum* 86:109–132.

Rosenmeyer, P. A. 1962. "Plato's Prayer to Pan (*Phaedrus* 279b8–c3)." *Hermes* 90:43–44.

———. 1997. "Her Master's Voice: Sappho's Dialogue with Homer." *Materiali e Discussioni per l'analisi dei testi classici* 39:123–149.

Rossetti, L. 1975. "Alla ricerca dei *logoi sokratikoi* perduti." *Rivista di Studi Classici* 23:87–99 and 361–381.

———, ed. 1992. *Understanding the Phaedrus: Proceedings of the II Symposium Platonicum*. Sankt Augustin.

———. 2008. "I Socratici della prima generazione: Fare filosofia con i dialoghi anziché con i trattati o testi paradossali." In Rossetti and Stavru 2008:39–75.

———. 2011. *Le dialogue socratique*. Paris.

Rossetti, L., and A. Stavru, eds. 2008. *Socratica 2005: Studi sulla letteratura socratica antica presentati alle Giornate di studio di Senigallia*. Bari.

Rossi, L. E. 1971. "I generi letterari e le loro leggi scritte e non scritte nelle letterature classiche." *Bulletin of the Institute of Classical Studies* 18:69–94.

———. 1996. "Il testamento di Posidippo e le laminette auree di Pella." *Zeitschrift für Papyrologie und Epigraphik* 112:59–65.

———. 2001. *The Epigrams Ascribed to Theocritus: A Method of Approach*. Leuven.

Rowe, C. 1986. "The Argument and Structure of Plato's *Phaedrus*." *Proceedings of the Cambridge Philological Society* 32:106–125.

———, ed. 1988. *Plato. Phaedrus*. 2nd ed. Oxford.

———. 1989. "The Unity of the *Phaedrus*: A Reply to Heath." *Oxford Studies in Ancient Philosophy* 7:175–188.

———. 2007. *Plato and the Art of Philosophical Writing*. Cambridge.

Ryan, P. 2012. *Plato's Phaedrus: A Commentary for Greek Readers*. Norman.

Saïd, S. 2007. "Myth and Historiography." In *A Companion to Greek and Roman Historiography*, ed. J. Marincola, 76–88. Malden.

Sarri, F. 1974. "Isocrate come testimone del messaggio socratico." *Rivista di Filosofia Neo-scolastica* 66:40–58.

Sassi, M. M. 2007. "*Eros* come energia psichica: Platone e i flussi dell'anima." In Migliori, Napolitano Valditara, and Fermani 2007:275–292.

———. 2009. *Gli inizi della filosofia in Grecia*. Turin.

Sauvé Meyer, S. 2011. "Legislation as a Tragedy: On Plato's *Laws* VII, 817b–d." In Destrée and Hermann 2011:387–402.

Sbardella, L. 2012. *Cucitori di canti: Studi sulla tradizione epico-rapsodica greca e i suoi itinerari nel VI secolo a.C.* Rome.

Scarcella, A. M. 1987. "Attrezzi dell'officina platonica: Struttura narratologica e progetto ideologico del *Convito*." *Quaderni dell'Istituto di Filosofia, Università degli Studi di Perugia* 4:41–52.

Schauer, M., and S. Merkle. 1992. "Äsop und Sokrates." In *Der Äsop-Roman: Motivgeschichte und Erzählstruktur*, ed. N. von Holzberg, 85–96. Tübingen.

Schirru, S. 2009. *La favola in Aristofane*. Berlin.

Schörner, G., and H. Rupprecht Goette. 2004. *Die Pan-Grotte von Vari*. Mainz.

Schröder, F. R. 1953–1954. "Die Platane am Ilissos." *Germanisch-Romanische Monatschrift* 3–4:81–107.

# Bibliography

Scodel, R. 1997. "Teichoscopia, Catalogue, and the Female Spectator in Euripides." *Colby Quaterly* 33:76–93.

Scott, D. 2011. "Philosophy and Madness in the *Phaedrus*." *Oxford Studies in Ancient Philosophy* 41:169–200.

Scott, G. A. 2000. *Plato's Socrates as Educator*. New York.

Sedley, D. 1989. "Teleology and Myth in the *Phaedo*." *Proceedings of the Boston Area Colloquium in Ancient Philosophy* 5:359–383.

———. 1995. "The Dramatis Personae of Plato's *Phaedo*." *Proceedings of the British Academy* 85:3–26.

Segoloni, L. 2003. "Socrate 'musico' e poeta." In *Rhysmos: Studi di poesia, metrica e musica greca offerti dagli allievi a Luigi Enrico Rossi per i suoi settant'anni*, ed. R. Nicolai, 303–317. Rome.

———. 2007. "La 'dolce ansa' del Nilo (Platone, *Fedro* 257d–e): Un segnale di articolazione interno al testo platonico?" *Seminari Romani di cultura greca* 10.1:139–161.

———. 2012. "Un genere letterario privo di leggi scritte, legge a se stesso: Il dialogo." *Seminari Romani di cultura greca* 1.2:339–350.

Sens, A., ed. 2011. *Asclepiades of Samos. Epigrams and Fragments. Edited with Translation and Commentary*. Oxford.

Servais, J., T. Hackens, and B. Servais-Soyez, eds. 1987. *Stemmata: Mélanges de philologie, d'histoire et d'archéologie grecques offert a Jules Labarbe*. Liège.

Sgobbi, A. 2003. "Stesicoro, Falaride e la battaglia della Sagra." *Acme* 56.3:3–37.

Shapiro, H. A. 2005. "The Judgment of Helen in Athenian Art." In *Periklean Athens and Its Legacy: Problems and Perspectives*, ed. J. M. Barringer and J. M. Hurwit, 47–62. Austin.

———. 2009. "Helen: Heroine of Cult, Heroine in Art." In Albersmeier 2009:49–56.

———. 2012. *Re-fashioning Anakreon in Classical Athens*. Munich.

Sharp, K. 2008. "Socratic Discourse and the Second Person in Plato: Three Inside Views." In Rossetti and Stavru 2008:265–286.

Sider, D. 1980. "Plato's *Symposium* as Dionysian Festival." *Quaderni Urbinati di Cultura Classica* 4:41–56.

———. 1989. "The Blinding of Stesichorus." *Hermes* 117:423–431.

———. 2010. "Greek Verse on a Vase by Douris." *Hesperia* 79:541–554.

Silk, M. 2001. "Aristotle, Rapin, Brecht." In *Making Sense of Aristotle: Essays in Poetics*, ed. Ø. Andersen and J. Haarberg, 173–195. London.

Simon, E. 2002. "*Lychnouchos Platonikos*." In *Table ronde "Rites et cultes dans le monde antique,"* ed. P. Linant de Bellefonds, 77–95. Paris.

Skutsch, O. 1987. "Helen, Her Name and Nature." *The Journal of Hellenic Studies* 107:188–193.

Slings, S. R., ed. 1994. *Plato's Apology of Socrates: A Literary and Philosophical Study with a Running Commentary*. Leiden.

Snell, B. 1953. *The Discovery of the Mind: The Greek Origins of European Thought*. Oxford. English translation of *Die Entdeckung des Geistes: Studien zur Entstehung des europäischen Denkens bei den Griechen*, Hamburg 1946.

Snyder McIntosh, J. 1997. "Sappho in Attic Vase Painting." In *Naked Truths: Women, Sexuality and Gender in Classical Art and Archaeology*, ed. A. O. Koloski-Ostrow and C. L. Lyons, 108–119. London.

Speyer, A. 2001. "The Earliest Bust of Socrates? New Observations to Philochoros in P.Herc. 1021 Col.2." *Cronache Ercolanesi* 31:81–95.

Stanzel, K. H. 2012. "Dichtung, *Mousiké* und Philosophie: Zur Auseinandersetzung Platons mit der traditionellen Dichtung." In Koch, Männlein-Robert, and Weidtmann 2012:175–194.

Stavru, A. 2001. "Interiorità ed esteriorità nella preghiera conclusiva del *Fedro*." In Casertano 2011:269–284.

Steinweg R. 1976. *Brechts Modell der Lehrstücke: Zeugnisse, Diskussion, Erfahrungen*. Frankfurt a.M.

Stella, A. S. 1983. *L'illusion philosophique: La mort de Socrate; Sur la scène des Dialogues platoniciens*. Grenoble.

Stewart, J. 1997. "Stesichorus and the François Vase." In *Ancient Greek Art and Iconography*, ed. W. G. Moon, 53–74. Madison.

Strÿd, J. H. W. 1903. "Ἀττικὰ μετ' ἀρῶν μολύβδινα ἐλάσματα." *Ephemeris Archaiologike*:55–60.

Susanetti, D. 2002. "Il cigno antitragico: L'esperienza del teatro dall'*Alcesti* euripideo al *Fedone* platonico." In Napolitano Valditara 2002:53–76.

Svenbro, J. 1984. "La stratégie de l'amour: Modèle de la guerre et théorie de l'amour dans la poésie de Sappho." *Quaderni di Storia* 19:57–79.

Swift Riginos, A. 1976. *Platonica: The Anecdotes Concerning the Life and Writings of Plato*. Leiden.

Szlezák, T. A. 1985. *Platon und die Schriftlichkeit der Philosophie: Interpretationen zu den frühen und mittleren Dialogen*. Berlin.

———. 1991. *Come leggere Platone: Un nuovo canone per affrontare gli scritti platonici*. Milan.

Tarditi, G. 1989. "Le Muse e le Chariti tra fede del poeta ed *ethos poietikon*." *Aevum Antiquum* 2:19–45.

Tarrant, D. 1951. "Plato's Use of Quotations and Other Illustrative Material." *Classical Quarterly* 45:59–67.

Tarrant, H. 2008. "The Dramatic Background of the Arguments with Callicles, Euripides' *Antiope*, and an Athenian Anti-Intellectual Argument." *Anticthon* 42:20–39.

Tell, H. 2011. *Plato's Counterfeit Sophists.* Hellenic Studies 44. Washington, DC.

Thesleff, H. 1981. "Man and *locus amoenus* in Early Greek Poetry." In *Gnomosyne: Menschliches Denken und Handeln in der frühgriechischen Literatur,* ed. G. Kurz and D. Müller, 31–45. Munich.

———. 1982. *Studies in Plato's Chronology.* Helsinki.

———. 2009. *Platonic Patterns.* Las Vegas.

Thiercy, P. 1986. *Aristophane: Fiction et dramaturgie.* Paris.

Tomin, J. 2001. "Socrates in the *Phaedo.*" In Havlíček and Karfík 2001:140–173.

Trabattoni, F. 1994. *Scrivere nell'anima: Verità, dialettica e persuasione in Platone.* Florence.

———, ed. 2003–2004. *Platone. Liside,* I (Milan 2003) and II (Milan 2004).

———. 2011. "Un'interpretazione 'platonica' del primo discorso di Socrate nel *Fedro.*" In Casertano 2011:285–305.

———. 2012. "Myth and Truth in Plato's *Phaedrus.*" In *Plato and Myth: Studies on the Use and Status of Platonic Myths,* ed. C. Collobert, P. Destrée and F. Gonzalez, 305–321. Leiden.

Travlos, J. 1971. *Pictorial Dictionary of Ancient Athens.* London.

Traywick, J. P. 1968. *Theoi and Agathei Tuchei in Headings of Attic Inscriptions.* PhD diss., Harvard University.

Treu, M. 2003. "Il passaggio del fiume: Echi simbolici e tecniche narrative nel *Fedro.*" *Studi Italiani di Filologia Classica* 50:83–194.

Trivigno, F. V. 2009. "Paratragedy in Plato's *Gorgias.*" *Oxford Studies in Ancient Philosophy* 36:73–105.

———. 2011. "Is Good Tragedy Possible? The Argument of Plato's *Gorgias* 502b–503b." *Oxford Studies in Ancient Philosophy* 41:115–138.

Trombley, F. R. 1993. *Hellenic Religion and Christianization c[a]. 370–529.* Leiden and New York.

Tsouna, V. 2013. "Mimêsis and the Platonic Dialogue." *Rhizomata* 1:1–29.

Tulli, M. 1990. "Sul rapporto di Platone con Isocrate: Profezia e lode di un lungo impegno letterario." *Athenaeum* 78:402–422.

———. 1996. "La poesia nuova del *Carmide.*" *Studi Classici e Orientali* 46:377–383.

———. 2007a. "Epitafio e malia dell'anima: Gorgia nel *Menesseno.*" In Migliori, Napolitano Valditara, and Fermani 2007:321–329.

———. 2007b. "Il *Gorgia* e la lira di Anfione." In *Gorgias — Menon: Selected Papers from the Seventh Symposium Platonicum,* ed. M. Erler and L. Brisson. 2007:72–77. Sankt Augustin.

———. 2007c. "Platone fra musica e letteratura: Il II libro delle *Leggi.*" In Volpe Cacciatore 2007:129–142.

———. 2008a. "Esiodo e il sogno di Callimaco." *Seminari Romani di cultura greca* 11.2:185–198.

————. 2008b. "Isocrate storico del pensiero: Antistene, Platone, gli eristi nell'*Encomio di Elena*." In Rossetti and Stravru 2008:91–105.

Tuozzo, T. M. 2013. "Reproduction, Immortality, and the Greater Mysteries in Plato's *Symposium*." *Proceedings of the X Symposium Platonicum on the Symposium*. I:234–238. http://platosociety.org/the-x-symposium-platonicum-platos-symposium-pisa/.

Usener, S. 1994. *Isokrates, Platon und ihr Publikum: Hörer und Leser von Literatur im 4. Jahrhundert v. Chr.* Tübingen.

Valiavitcharska, V. 2006. "Correct λόγος and Truth in Gorgias' *Encomium of Helen*." *Rhetorica* 24:147–161.

Vallejo Campos, Á. 2001. "El fantasma de Helena: El papel de la razón en la concepción platónica del amor." *Er: Revista de filosofía* 30:83–109.

Vallozza, M. 2011. "Isocrate ospite di Platone nel dialogo sui poeti di Prassifane." *Studi Classici e Orientali* 57:119–136.

Vasilescu, M. 2004. "Stesicoro e il mito dorico." In *Italia e Romania: Storia, cultura e civiltà a cofronto; Atti del IV Convegno di studi italo-romeno (Bari, 21-23 ottobre 2002)*, ed. S. Santella, 79–97. Bari.

Vassallo, Ch. 2012. "Diatriba e dialogo socratico dal punto di vista della classificazione dei generi letterari." *Museum Helveticum* 69:45–61.

Vegetti, M. 2006. "La letteratura socratica e la competizione fra generi letterari." In *L'autore e l'opera: Attribuzioni, appropriazioni, apocrifi nella Grecia antica; Atti del Convegno internazionale* (Pavia 27-28 maggio 2005), ed. F. Roscalla, 119–131. Pisa.

————. 2013. "Immortalità personale senza anima immortale: Diotima e Aristotele." *Proceedings of the X Symposium Platonicum on the Symposium*. I:95–104. http://platosociety.org/the-x-symposium-platonicum-platos-symposium-pisa/.

Velardi, R. 1991. "Le origini dell'inno in prosa tra V e IV secolo a.c.: Menandro Retore e Platone." In *L'inno tra rituale e letteratura nel mondo antico*, ed. A.C. Cassio and G. Cerri. 1991:205–231.

————. 2006. *Platone. Fedro.* Milan.

Vlastos, G. 1991. *Socrates: Ironist and Moral Philosopher.* Cambridge.

Volpe Cacciatore, P., ed. 2007. *Musica e generi letterari nella Grecia di età classica*, 37–70. Naples.

Voutiras, E. 1994. "Sokrates in der Akademie: Die früheste bezeugte Philosophenstatue." *Mitteilungen des Deutschen Archäologischen Instituts* (Athenische Abteilung) 109:133–161.

Vries, G. J. de. 1969. *A Commentary on the Phaedrus of Plato.* Amsterdam.

Wachter, R. 1991. "The Inscriptions on the François Vase." *Museum Helveticum* 48:86–113.

# Bibliography

Wardy, R. 1996. *The Birth of Rhetoric: Gorgias, Plato and Their Successors*. London.

Watts, E. 2007. "Creating the Academy: Historical Discourse and the Shape of Community in the Old Academy." *Journal of Hellenic Studies* 127:106–122.

Werner, D. 2007. "Plato's *Phaedrus* and the Problem of Unity." *Oxford Studies in Ancient Philosophy* 32:91–137.

———. 2012 *Myth and Philosophy in Plato's Phaedrus*. New York.

West, M., ed. 1966. *Hesiod. Theogony. Edited with Prolegomena and Commentary*. Oxford.

———. 1969. "*Stesichorus Redivivus*." *Zeitschrift für Papyrologie und Epigraphik* 4:135–149.

———. 1975. *Immortal Helen: An Inaugural Lecture*. London.

———, ed. 1978. *Hesiod. Works and Days. Edited with Prolegomena and Commentary*. Oxford.

———. 2007. *Indo-European Poetry and Myth*. Oxford.

White, D. A. 1993. *Rhetoric and Reality in Plato's Phaedrus*. New York.

White, S. A. 2000. "Socrates at Colonus." In *Reason and Religion in Socratic Philosophy*, ed. N. D. Smith, and P. Woodruff, 140–164. Oxford.

Whitehead, A. N. 1929. *Process and Reality: An Essay in Cosmology*. New York.

Wide, S. 1893. *Lakonische Kulte*. Leipzig.

Wilamowitz-Moellendorff, U. von. 1881. *Antigonos von Karystos*. Berlin.

———. 1920. *Platon. I*. Berlin.

Williams, F. A. 1971. "Theophany in Theocritus." *Classical Quarterly* 21:137–145.

Wills, G. 1967. "The Sapphic Umwertung aller Werte." *American Journal of Philology* 88:434–442.

Wilson, P. 2009. "Thamyris the Thracian: The Archetypal Wandering Poet?" In *Wandering Poets in Ancient Greek Culture: Travel, Locality and Pan-Hellenism*, ed. R. Hunter and I. Rutherford, 46–79. Cambridge.

Worthington, I. 1986. "The Siting of Demosthenes' Statue." *The Annual of the British School at Athens* 81:389.

Wypustek, A. 2013. *Images of Eternal Beauty in Funerary Verse Inscriptions of the Hellenistic and Greco-Roman Periods*. Leiden.

Yatromanolakis, D. 2007. *Sappho in the Making: The Early Reception*. Hellenic Studies 28. Washington, DC.

Yunis, H., ed. 2011. *Plato. Phaedrus*. Cambridge.

Zanker, P. 1995. *The Mask of Socrates: The Image of the Intellectual in Antiquity*. Berkeley.

Zaslavsky, R. 1981. "A Hitherto Unremarked Pun in the *Phaedrus*." *Apeiron* 15:115–116.

Zellner, H. M. 2007. "Sappho's Alleged Proof of Aesthetic Relativity." *Greek Roman and Byzantine Studies* 47:257–270.

Žižek, S., ed. 2002. *Revolution at the Gates: Selected Writings of Lenin from 1917.* London.

Zuckert, K. 2009. *Plato's Philosophers: The Coherence of the Dialogues.* Chicago.

# Index of Passages

Italicized page numbers indicate that a given passage is reproduced in Greek and in translation in the main text.

# Index of Passages

Aristotle
The Athenian Constitution 7.1, 26
The History of Animals 532b10–13, 114
Nicomachean Ethics 1272a1–7, 173
Poetics 1447a9–10, 163;
1447a28–1447b14, 8
Politics 1265a12–14, 8
Rhetoric 1393b8–1394a1, 29;
1398b10–12, 129; 1398b16–17,
136; 1398b19–1398a6, 78;
1408b12–20, 45; 1414b24–28, 62
Asclepiades
FGrH 12 F 10, 105
Athenaeus
4.186b, 68; 10.438b, 144; 10.457a, 114;
11.465c–e, 127
Callimachus
Aetia 1.29–34, 114
Hymns 6.38, 66
Chamaeleon
fr. 29 Wehrli, see Stesichorus 193 PMG
Chrysippus
fr. 83.3–5 Arnim, 23
Cicero
De Oratore 1.7.28, 146
On the Ends of Good and Evil 5.1.2, 119;
5.1.3, 135
Conon
FGrH 26 F 1 18, 37
FGrH 26 F 1 42, 29
Corpus Paroemiographorum Graecorum
I 268, 82
Dicaearchus
fr. 40 Wehrli, 5
Diogenes Laertius
1.109, 110; 2.30, 141; 2.105, 165;
2.121–124, 165; 2.124, 100; 3.4, 18;
3.7, 119; 3.8, 143; 3.25, 142; 3.37,
8, 181; 3.38, 18; 6.25, 18; 9.21, 136;
9.115, 144
Dionysius of Halicarnassus
The Arrangement of Words 25.32, 181
On the Style of Demosthenes 7.9–19, 45

Epicrates
5 PCG, 12
Eupolis
36 PCG, 143
148 PCG, 1–2, 29
395 PCG, 30
Euripides
Bacchae 881, 79
Cyclops 182–186, 79
Electra 524–537, 10
Iphigenia in Aulis 185–302, 79
Medea 679, 111
Phoenician Women 88–177, 79;
734–753, 10
Rhesus 921–925, 101
Eustathius
Commentary on the Odyssey 4.121 (I
p. 154.30–36 Stallbaum), 29
Favorinus
fr. 43 Amato, 144
Gorgias
Helen 5, 60; 11, 60; 13, 61; 15, 61;
15–16, 60; 20–21, 61
Heraclides Ponticus
87–88 Wehrli, 4, 162
157 Wehrli, 47
Hermesianax
fr. 7. 75–78 Powell, 141
Hermias Alexandrinus
p. 59.29–31 Lucarini-Moreschini (on
Phaedrus 238d), 31
p.186.3–4 Lucarini-Moreshini (on
Phaedrus 250b), 19
p. 187.3 Lucarini-Moreschini (on
Phaedrus 250c), 73
p. 187.10 Lucarini-Moreschini (on
Phaedrus 250c), 73
p. 226.5–30 Lucarini-Moreschini (on
Phaedrus 259b), 108
p. 279.5–8 Lucarini-Moreschini (on
Phaedrus 279b), 124
p. 279.25–27 Lucarini-Moreschini
(on Phaedrus 279c), 127

# Index of Passages

# Index of Names

Very frequent names ("Greece," "Greeks," "Muses," "Phaedrus," "Plato," and "Socrates") are omitted. Names are usually given in the Latin form, but I have made no attempt at consistency. I have followed common usage and included a number of English and transliterated forms.

## Index of Names

## Index of Names

CPSIA information can be obtained
at www.ICGtesting.com
Printed in the USA
LVHW030721020223
738080LV00001B/5